CISTERCIAN FATHERS SERIES: NUMBER SIXTY-EIGHT

Bernard of Clairvaux

MONASTIC SERMONS

CISTERCIAN FATHERS SERIES: NUMBER SIXTY-EIGHT

Bernard of Clairvaux

Monastic Sermons

Translated by
Daniel Griggs

Introduction by
Michael Casey

α

Cistercian Publications
www.cistercianpublications.org

LITURGICAL PRESS
Collegeville, Minnesota
www.litpress.org

A Cistercian Publications title published by Liturgical Press

Cistercian Publications
Editorial Offices
161 Grosvenor Street
Athens, Ohio 54701
www.cistercianpublications.org

Scripture texts in this work are by the translator of the volume.

© 2016 by Order of Saint Benedict, Collegeville, Minnesota. All rights reserved. No part of this book may be reproduced in any form, by print, microfilm, microfiche, mechanical recording, photocopying, translation, or any other means, known or yet unknown, for any purpose except brief quotations in reviews, without the previous written permission of Liturgical Press, Saint John's Abbey, PO Box 7500, Collegeville, Minnesota 56321-7500. Printed in the United States of America.

Library of Congress Cataloging-in-Publication Data

Names: Bernard, of Clairvaux, Saint, 1090 or 1091-1153, author.
Title: Monastic sermons / Bernard of Clairvaux ; translated by Daniel Griggs ; introduction by Michael Casey.
Description: Collegeville, Minnesota : Cistercian Publications, 2016. | Series: Cistercian Fathers series ; Number sixty-eight | Includes index.
Identifiers: LCCN 2016007880 (print) | LCCN 2016023842 (ebook) | ISBN 9780879074685 (pbk.) | ISBN 9780879071684 (ebook)
Subjects: LCSH: Catholic Church—Sermons. | Sermons, Latin—Translations into English.
Classification: LCC BX891.3 .B4713 2016 (print) | LCC BX891.3 (ebook) | DDC 252/.02—dc23
LC record available at https://lccn.loc.gov/2016007880

Contents

Editor's Note — xi

Introduction — xiii
    Michael Casey, OCSO

List of Abbreviations — xli

The Sermons

S 1: On the Deceptions of This Life — 3

S 2: On Obedience, Patience, and Wisdom — 12

S 3: The Song of Hezekiah — 20

S 4: On Seeking God, and the Triple Bonds by Which We Cling to God — 30

S 5: On the Words of Habakkuk 2:1: *I will stand upon my watch* — 35

S 6: On the Skin, Flesh, and Bones of the Soul — 40

S 7: Concerning the Triple Glory — 44

S 8: On the Various Affections or States by which the Soul Is under God — 49

S 9: Concerning Romans 1:20: *The invisible things of God are clearly seen* Concerning Psalm 84:9: *I will hear what the Lord God will speak in me* — 58

S 10: Discerning the Soul's Life from the Five Senses of the Soul — 62

S 11: Concerning the Double Baptism — 67

S 12: Concerning First Beginnings, Current Days, and One's Last End in Sirach 7:40: *Be mindful of your last end* — 70

S 13: Concerning the Triple Mercy — 75

S 14: Concerning the Seven Gifts of the Holy Spirit against the Seven Faults	78
S 15: On Seeking Wisdom	83
S 16: On the Day of Saint Andrew: Three Types of Good, and Vigilance over Thoughts	87
S 17: Concerning the Triple Custody of the Hand, the Tongue, and the Heart	95
S 18: Concerning Spiritual Joy, or Concerning Romans 14:17: *The Kingdom of God is not food and drink*	103
S 19: Concerning Romans 14:17: *The Kingdom of God is not food and drink*	107
S 20: Concerning Luke 14:11: *Everyone who exalts himself shall be humbled, and one who humbles himself shall be exalted*	113
S 21: Concerning Wisdom 10:10	117
S 22: Concerning the Quadruple Debt	120
S 23: Concerning the Discernment of Spirits; Concerning the Seven Spirits	129
S 24: Concerning the Versatile Usefulness of God's Word	135
S 25: Concerning Four Types of Prayer	139
S 26: How One's Will Ought to Be Subject to God's Will	147
S 27: Against the Most Wicked Vice of Ingratitude	151
S 28: Concerning Job 5:19: *In six tribulations he shall deliver you, and in the seventh evil shall not touch you*	159
S 29: Concerning the Triple Love of God and the Necessity of Loving God	166
S 30: Concerning Wood, Hay, and Stubble	171
S 31: Custody of Thoughts	174
S 32: Concerning Three Types of Judgment	177
S 33: Concerning Psalm 23:3: *Who shall ascend into the mountain of the Lord?*	181
S 34: Concerning a Teaching of Origen on Leviticus 10:9	189
S 35: To the Abbots. *How Noah, Daniel, and Job crossed the sea, each in his own way: on a ship, by a bridge, by the shallows*	196

S 36: On the Occasion of the Preceding Sermon: The Heart's Loftiness and Baseness	197
S 37: On The Time of Harvest: Sermon 3. *This is the generation of those who seek the Lord, of those who seek the face of the God of Jacob*	198
S 38: On The Time of Harvest: Sermon 1. *How a Twofold Evil Works for Good*	199
S 39: On The Time of Harvest: Sermon 2. *Of the Two Harvests*	200
S 40: Concerning Seven Steps of Confession	201
S 41: Concerning the Seven Steps of Obedience	213
S 42: Concerning Five Businesses and Five Regions	226
S 43: The Lord's Ascension: Sermon 5. *Courage, forbearance, and concord*	234
S 44: On the Resurrection of the Lord: Sermon 4. *On the days of the resurrection: How Christ has not yet been born for some*	235
S 45: Concerning the Divine and the Human Trinities	236
S 46: On the Solemnity of the Assumption of the Blessed Virgin Mary: Sermon 6. *To establish "full of grace" in Mary in three ways*	241
S 47: Concerning a Quadruple Pride	242
S 48: Concerning Voluntary Poverty	244
S 49: Concerning the Triple Word	245
S 50: Concerning Rightly Ordered Affections	247
S 51: Concerning the Purification of Mary and Circumcision of Christ	250
S 52 Concerning the Home of Divine Wisdom; Concerning the Virgin Mary	252
S 53: Concerning Names of the Savior	256
S 54: Concerning the Appearance of Christ	258
S 55: Concerning Six Spiritual Water Pots	260
S 56: Concerning the Sacred Water Pots that Are to Be Filled with a Threefold Fear	264
S 57: Concerning Seven Seals	267
S 58: Concerning the Three Women at the Tomb	269
S 59: Concerning Three Loaves	271

S 60: Concerning Christ's Descent and Ascent	273
S 61: Concerning Four Mountains to Be Ascended	277
S 62: Concerning John 12:26	279
S 63: Concerning Matthew 16:24	281
S 64: Concerning Psalm 15:15	282
S 65: Concerning Matthew 13:44: *The kingdom of heaven is like a treasure hidden in a field*	284
S 66: For the Feast of All Saints: The Beatitudes as Remedies for Sins	286
S 67: Concerning the Twofold Precepts of the Law, Moral and Figurative	289
S 68: A Duplicate of Sermo 32	291
S 69: Concerning the Triple Renewal of Triple Oldness	292
S 70: Concerning Reflection	294
S 71: Concerning the Entrance of the Sons of Israel into the Land of Egypt	296
S 72: Concerning Psalm 1	298
S 73: Concerning Psalm 13:1	303
S 74: Concerning Psalm 13:1	304
S 75: Concerning Those Who Sin in the Hope of Confession *in Extremis*	306
S 76: Concerning God's Triple Grace	307
S 77: Concerning Psalm 17:45: *A people that I knew not*	309
S 78: Concerning Three Tabernacles	311
S 79: Concerning a Double Preparation of One's Heart	312
S 80: Concerning the Variety and Utility of Unity	313
S 81: Concerning Praise of Christ	315
S 82: Concerning Custody of One's Heart	316
S 83: Concerning Avoidance of Praise	318
S 84: Concerning Higher and Lower Positions of the Soul	320
S 85: Concerning the Fall of a Tree or Death of a Person	322
S 86: The Difference between Creature and Creator	324

S 87: Concerning Three Kisses	326
S 88: Concerning Four Ways the Holy Spirit Works in Us	331
S 89: Concerning the Holy Spirit's Kiss	333
S 90: Concerning the Lord's Two Figurative Feet and Three Mystical Ointments	335
S 91: Concerning Three Types of Shoots	340
S 92: Concerning Three Introductions	346
S 93: Concerning the Qualities of Teeth	350
S 94: Concerning the Flight of Elijah from Jezebel	353
S 95: Concerning Bitterness in Teaching that Should Be Tempered by Preachers	356
S 96: Concerning Four Fountains of the Savior	359
S 97: Concerning Milk and Honey	367
S 98: Concerning the Triple Peace and the Square Stone	371
S 99: Concerning the Four Types of People who Possess the Kingdom of God	373
S 100: Concerning the Manner of a Shepherd and a Flock	375
S 101: Concerning Four Ways of Love	376
S 102: Concerning the Triple Fall of the Human Being and the Triple Return	378
S 103: Concerning Four Progressions of the Chosen	380
S 104: Concerning Four Impediments to Confession	384
S 105: Concerning Remedies of Souls	387
S 106: Concerning Three States of a Soul	389
S 107: Ways of Praying to God	391
S 108: Concerning Bloodletting	394
S 109: Concerning the Lamps of the Virgins in the Gospel	396
S 110: Concerning a Person's Misfortune	397
S 111: In Paschal Time, Concerning the Lord's Testimonies	399
S 112: Concerning the Fourfold Conscience	405
S 113: Concerning Three Secrets	406

S 114: Concerning Peace	407
S 115: Concerning the Threefold Heart	408
S 116: Concerning the Twofold Death and Resurrection	409
S 117: Concerning Four Spiritual Springs	411
S 118: Concerning the Seven Steps of Ascension	413
S 119: Concerning Three Aspects of the Incarnation that One Must Consider	414
S 120: Concerning a Threefold Ministry	415
S 121: Concerning Doctrines of Fear and of Charity	416
S 122: Concerning Two Vices to Be Avoided during Fasting	418
S 123: Concerning the Vision of Isaiah	419
S 124: Concerning Four Steps of Good Will	422
S 125: On the Necessity of Giving Glory to God's Wisdom	425
Scriptural Index	429
Subject Index	451

Editor's Note

I AM GRATEFUL for assistance in preparing this volume from Emily K. Stuckey, who prepared the indices, and from Brian Patrick McGuire.

The Editor

Introduction

Michael Casey, OCSO

THE TALKS GIVEN in chapter by the twelfth-century Cistercian Fathers are probably the most characteristic expression of their monastic teaching.[1] Each day of the year, including Good Friday, the abbot was expected to give a talk to the community in chapter—nominally by way of commentary on the chapter of the Rule of Saint Benedict that had just been read, but often ranging over any topic that might be useful for the monks to hear. On the greater liturgical feasts (termed "Feasts of Sermon") there was scope for a more formal and more carefully crafted talk.[2] Sometimes these talks were written before delivery, sometimes they were redeveloped in a more literary format (and perhaps expressed in Latin rather than in the vernacular), and sometimes what remains is a collection of more or less full notes probably taken by stenographers and reconstituted afterward.

Bernard's sermon corpus is considerable.[3] Alongside his eighty-six magisterial *Discourses on the Song of Songs* there are over six hundred

---

[1] The reader will notice that, where possible, I try to find an alternative to translating *sermones* as "sermons." This is to avoid giving the impression to a contemporary reader that they were given in the church during the liturgy. They were, at least notionally, addresses or discourses or talks given by an abbot to his community in the chapter room.

[2] On the daily commentaries on the Rule see *Ecclesiastica Officia* 70:27–29 (Danièle Choisselet and Placide Vernet, *Les Ecclesiastica Officia cisterciens du XIIème siècle* [Reiningue: La Documentation Cistercienne, 1989], 204). On the Feasts of Sermon see *Ecclesiastica Officia* 67:3–5, p. 190.

[3] For information on the more technical aspects of Bernard's *sermones*, see Jean Leclercq, "Sur la genèse des sermons de saint Bernard," in *Études sur saint Bernard et*

other *sermones* given on different occasions over a forty-year span and preserved in different forms.⁴ The homilies on the Gospel *Missus est*, the series *Ad clericos de conversione*, and the Lenten series on Psalm 90 (*Qui habitat*) form clear blocks of their own, with a total of forty-three sermons. The 109 liturgical sermons are grouped according to the feasts with which they are associated. In some cases, such as the seven sermons for Advent, it is clear that they were written conjointly but not necessarily at the same time.⁵ Other series of *sermones* are not

---

le texte de ses écrits, = ASOC 9 (1953): 45–83; "Les Sermons sur les Cantiques ont–ils été prononcés?," in *Recueil d'études sur saint Bernard et ses écrits I* (Rome: Edizioni di Storia e Letteratura, 1962), 193–212; "Les sermons de Bernard sur le Psaume 'Qui habitat,'" in *Recueil d'études sur saint Bernard et ses écrits II* (Rome: Edizioni di Storia e Letteratura, 1966), 3–18; "La tradition des sermons liturgiques de S. Bernard," in *Recueil II*, 185–260; "L'art de la composition dans les sermons de S. Bernard," in *Recueil d'études sur saint Bernard et ses écrits III* (Rome: Edizioni di Storia e Letteratura, 1969), 137–62; "Sur le caractère littéraire des sermons de S. Bernard, in *Recueil III*, 163–210; "S. Bernard prêcheur," in *Recueil d'études sur saint Bernard et ses écrits IV* (Rome: Edizioni di Storia e Letteratura, 1987), 81–93; "Introduction," SBOp 4:119–59; "Introduction," SBOp 6a:59–71.

⁴ The *Sermones super Cantica Canticorum* are in volumes 1 and 2 of the critical edition published at Rome by Editiones Cistercienses in 1957–1958. There are 83 *Sermones per annum* in vol. 4 (1966), 69 in vol. 5 (1968), and an additional 8 in volume 6a (1970). Volume 6a also contains *Sermones de diversis* (Div); 10 of the usual collection have been relocated or otherwise rejected. Div 35, *Sermo ad abbates*, is at SBOp 5:288. Div 36, *De altitudine et bassitudine cordis*, is at SBOp 5:214. Div 37–39, *In labore messis*, are at SBOp 5:222, 217, 220. Div 43 = Ascension 5, SBOp 5:149. Div 44 is now Resurrection 4, SBOp 5:110. Div 46 is now Assumption 6, SBOp 5:260. Div 68, which is a duplicate of Div 32, *De iudicio triplici*, is not repeated. Div 114 is a series of sentences from Augustine's *De civitate Dei* 1.19.13 (SCh 48:678). Div 19 is by Nicholas of Clairvaux. English versions of all of these omitted texts are included in John Kelly, trans, "Sermons on Diverse Subjects by Saint Bernard of Clairvaux," *Tjurunga* 85 (2014). Accordingly, there are 114 authentic texts, numbered 1–125. In addition, SBOp 6b (1972) contains three series of *Sententiae*, considered to be free-floating *sermones* or summaries or remembrances of talks given. Of these there are 43 in the first series, 188 in the second series, and 127 in the third. This gives a nominal total of 643 *sermones* or 729 if those on the Song of Songs are included.

⁵ In comparing the different recensions, Jean Leclercq concluded that Adv 4–5 were written first; then followed Adv 1–3, with a final expansion in Adv 6–7. See "La Tradition," *Recueil II*, 269. See also Claudio Stercal, *Il "Medius Adventus": Saggio di lettura degli scritti di Bernardo di Clairvaux* (Rome: Editiones Cistercienses, 1992), 31–33. The text *In celebratione Adventus*, printed in SBOp 6a:9–20, has never been grouped

grouped in these categories: the *sermones de diversis* and three books of *sententiae* or "sayings," two of which Mabillon recognized and the third, comprising some 127 texts, Jean Leclercq compiled. These are miscellaneous pieces gathered together by the editors and judged to be authentic.⁶ They are heterogeneous both in form and content and almost impossible to categorize. The most visible difference between the *Sermones de diversis* and the *Sententiae* is length. Usually, but not always, the former are longer and more developed.

Apart from random exceptions in which small sub-groupings appear, most of these texts stand on their own. Unlike the *Sermones super Cantica canticorum*, they are not part of a sequential commentary on a biblical book, and, unlike the *Sermones per annum*, they are not attached to a liturgical feast. Since, probably, they represent talks given in the chapter room, their content was probably dictated by pastoral considerations and the changing circumstances of community life. In the twelfth century, an abbot's regular teaching of the community was the principal means of what we would term spiritual direction. In a less individualized culture, where monks were many, corporate instruction was the mainstay of monastic formation. The giving and receiving of personal counsel was probably reserved to exceptional situations where no general direction was applicable.⁷

These are not set pieces of oratorical eloquence. They are down-to-earth and practical expositions intended to help the monks live their monastic life more fervently and with less trouble. Even though it was impossible for Bernard to express himself without a certain degree both of elegance and erudition, these talks presuppose a familiarity with the everyday experiences and struggles of the members of the community. Bernard's personality is stamped all over these fa-

---

with Adv 1–7 and is regarded by some as dubiously authentic. See Jean Leclercq, "L'authenticité bernardine du sermon 'In celebratione Adventus,'" *Recueil II*, 271–90.

⁶ On the external and internal criteria used to arrive at a decision regarding the inclusion of a particular text in the critical edition of Bernard's works, see Jean Leclercq, "Introduction," SBOp 6a:59–71. For more detail, see H.-M. Rochais, "Enquête sur les sermons divers de saint Bernard," ASOC 18, nos. 3–4 (1962): 1–183.

⁷ Div 26.3: "If he is thinking of doing something for which there is no definite commandment, he should leave the matter hanging until he asks his superior and seeks the will of God from him." In this case and in all other texts, unless otherwise noted, I am using my own translation.

miliar texts. Far from being lofty discourses of disembodied mysticism, Bernard seasons his talks with references to everyday objects, animals, and plants.[8] Even though he does nothing to disguise the "hard and rough things" to be encountered on the monastic journey, he is never harsh or dictatorial, nor is he impatient with the imperfections he sees around him.[9] His style is simple and expository, sympathetic to the difficulties his monks encounter, and always encouraging, especially to beginners. He follows his own prescription: "There should be moderation in correction, abundance in exhortation, and effectiveness in persuasion" (Div 58.1). What he spoke to his community was a word of upbuilding, *sermo ædificationis* (Div 15.5).

Close examination reveals many connections with Bernard's more literary works, and these may sometimes indicate a degree of synchronicity. Unlike Aelred, however, Bernard is not given to a process of copy and paste.[10] On the one hand, he is prone to using different terms to describe the same realities, and, on the other, he sometimes

---

[8] See the lists compiled by Françoise Callerot, OCSO, in SCh 545: References to animals, 400–401; to parts of the body, 402–4; to objects, 407–9; to plants, 411–12.

[9] Bernard seems reconciled to the fact that humans will never be perfect while they remain on earth. See, for example, Div 13.3, 24.3; see also 124.1: "I call good not only perfect souls but also those who are beginners, because even if they have a vice they do not consent to it but are horrified by it. Such souls, though they fall often through weakness or ignorance (as it is said, the just person falls seven times in a day), yet nevertheless, because their will is good they rise up."

[10] With Bernard there are always exceptions. The poetic outburst in Div 42.1 appears also in Div 22.5: *O quam indebita miseratio, quam gratuita et sic probata dilectio, quam inopinata dignatio, quam stupenda dulcedo, quam invicta mansuetudo.* There is a close parallel in Dil 13 (SBOp 3:129): *Quid namque aliud faciat considerata tanta et tam indebita miseratio, tam gratuita et sic probata dilectio, tam inopinata dignatio, tam invicta mansuetudo, tam stupenda dulcedo?* In Div 22.8, there is a strong reminiscence of Bernard's ode to eternal day in SC 33.6 (SBOp 1:237). Certain phrases in Div 29.1 recall the extended treatment in SC 20 (SBOp 1:114–21): the triple modality of love in Deut 6:5 is understood in terms of loving sweetly, prudently, and strongly: *dulciter, prudenter, fortiter.* In Sent 3.93 (SBOp 6b:149) charity is qualified as *dulcis, sapiens,* and *robusta.* The listing of the steps of the downward trajectory in Div 14.1–7 is paralleled in Sent 3.98 (SBOp 6b:163–68), 3.4 (6:65–66), 3.19 (6b:76), 3.20 (6b:76), 3.89 (6b:136–37); Par 3.4 (SBOp 6b:276), Par 7 (SBOp 6b:299). For further information on other parallels to this passage, see Michael Casey, "Introduction and Translation of the Seventh and Eighth Parables of Bernard of Clairvaux," CSQ 22, no. 1 (1987): 38–45.

employs particular phrases in different senses.[11] Given that these texts are spread out over several decades of abbatial teaching, some repetition, overlap, and nuancing may be expected. In general, however, these shorter pieces are minor masterpieces and may be considered a valuable source for understanding Bernard's monastic doctrine. Though it is clear that they have not received the same degree of authorial attention as his major works, Bernard's practical, literary, spiritual, and mystical gifts are clearly evident. These *sermones* have been ignored for too long.

TITLES

The first things we encounter on reading the *sermones de diversis* are the titles. The titles are not original but were inserted by the editors at the time of redaction. There is some variation in the different manuscript streams. Mostly the assigned titles identify a particular element in the text that makes it distinctive—they do not necessarily provide an indication of what the whole text is about. In eight cases there seems to be an association with a liturgical celebration.[12] Twenty-two texts base themselves on a scriptural passage or an event in the Bible or, in one case, a response to an opinion of Origen, maybe read at Vigils.[13] There are fifty-three numerical sequences in the titles, thirty-one of which offer a tripartite division.[14] These statistics refer only to the titles; there are many more numerical sequences in the sermons

---

[11] Thus Bernard treats the triad *disciplina–natura–gratia* in Div 92.2 differently from the same combination in SCh 23.6 (SBOp 1:142). See also Sent 3.123 (SBOp 6b:233–36).

[12] Div 16, 47, 52, 54, 57, 60, 66, 111.

[13] Div 3, 5, 9, 15, 18, 19 (S 19 is by Nicholas of Clairvaux), 20, 21, 28, 33, 34 (S 34 concerns Origen, *In Levit* 7.2), 61, 62, 63, 65, 72, 73, 74, 77, 94, 109, 123. Five are based on a text from the Psalms and five on the gospels.

[14] Div 2, 4, 6, 7, 10, 11, 12, 13, 14, 16, 17, 22, 23, 25, 26, 28, 30, 31, 32, 42, 45, 49, 55, 56, 59, 64, 69, 76, 78, 79, 87, 88, 90, 91, 92, 96, 98, 99, 101, 102, 103, 104, 106, 112, 113, 115, 116, 117, 118, 119, 120, 122, 124. Twofold divisions occur 5 times, threefold 31 times, fourfold 12 times, fivefold twice, sixfold once, and sevenfold twice. In two cases (Div 13 and Div 90) a title contains two different sequences.

themselves, and, of course, numerical sequences are nearly universal in the *Sententiae*.

The significance of the frequency of the threefold division is that it has a rhetorical function. All the numbered sequences are useful in giving listeners a sense of how the movement of the talk is progressing, but a threefold sequence is especially effective, because three is as many items as most people can easily remember. Beyond three the strict sequence of items is managed in the mind with greater difficulty. Furthermore, because these triads often suggest three sequential stages, beginning-middle-end or past-present-future, they offer a speaker the possibility of outlining a phenomenology of progress or decline that is easy enough to remember. Ongoing reflection enables listeners to engage in a form of self-diagnosis and thence to begin to take whatever steps seem necessary to achieve their goal.

It is a useful exercise to read through the list of titles. That gives an astonishing array of topics covering many aspects of the spiritual and monastic life. As with most of Bernard's work, the *Sermones de diversis* defy systematization. Although occasionally a few of the *sermones* cluster around a common theme, mostly the titles give the impression of a random agglomeration of topics. Reading the *sermones* in sequence, however, leads to a strong impression that their unifying motif is the monastic experience of the listening monks. And it has to be remembered that the titles do not always represent the full content of the individual talks.

These varied talks have a relaxed and familiar tone. They are part of an ongoing conversation between an abbot and his monks, spread over many years. Bernard presents himself as an understanding pastor who is concerned to guide his monks away from self-destructive behavior, not out of a zeal for abstract virtue, but from a fraternal affection that would spare them the suffering consequent upon life-diminishing choices. These are not pontifical discourses from the throne but sympathetic explanations of the way things are in the spiritual life. Often enough, even in the abridged form in which these talks have been preserved, there is a sparkle in the expression that must have endeared them to the listeners, even when he is describing serious realities; for example, "The way is arduous and rough and unwalkable [*sic*: *inambulabilis*]" (Div 111.4). Often we find clever wordplays, subtle reminiscences of biblical themes and language, good humor, and, occasionally, mild witticisms.[15] The personableness and charm of the speaker are evident throughout these talks, but the *sermones* are also notable for the solidity of their doctrine.

CONTENT

It is unrealistic to expect that miscellaneous talks will offer a systematic or comprehensive survey of monastic doctrine. Of necessity, such talks are occasional, tailored to the situation in which they are delivered, emphasizing what is of most relevance to particular situations. With Bernard, however, even the shortest text can be fitted into his whole worldview—almost like a piece of a jigsaw puzzle. He developed his monastic philosophy very early in his career, and it remained operative—with some nuancing—throughout his life. This means that it is possible to take a short text and fit it into a more global synthesis without doing violence to the original. This is what Sister Françoise Callerot has done so well in her notes to the Sources Chrétiennes edition of the *Sermones de diversis*. The monks of Clairvaux were exposed to aspects of Bernard's thinking over the decades of his abbacy, and they knew him well enough to be able to insert everything he said into a more ample context and so more quickly and more faithfully appreciate what he was hoping to communicate. We should attempt the same process. Here, as elsewhere, it becomes evident that the best means to understand anything Bernard has written is to have read closely everything that Bernard wrote.

Underlying Bernard's monastic doctrine is a theological anthropology that permeates all of his writings.[16] In these talks he seems concerned to insist on the essential goodness of the human being. He tells his

---

[15] In Div 93, Bernard reflects on the properties of teeth as indicating the qualities that should be found in those who embrace the monastic profession, a lighthearted yet challenging presentation of the obligations that monks embrace.

[16] For a survey of Bernard's anthropology, see Michael Casey, *Athirst for God: Spiritual Desire in Bernard of Clairvaux's Sermons on the Song of Songs* (Kalamazoo, MI: Cistercian Publications, 1988), 131–89.

monks to be mindful of their basic nobility and beauty (Div 12.2) and describes the human being as "a noble creature" (Div 29.2, 40.3, 42.2) with a special dignity (29.1): "No creature that lives under the sun is of a state closer to God than the human soul" (Div 9.2); "God takes his rest in the higher region [of the soul]" (Div 84.1). And so it may be said that, "God is the life of the soul" (Div 47) and "God is the soul of the soul itself" (Div 10.1). It may also be affirmed that "truth, the sense of charity, is the life of the soul" (Div 10.1). "It cannot be said that a soul is alive that does not have the knowledge of truth. It is still dead in itself" (Div 10.1). The learning of this ultimate truth demands that the monk open himself to God's word: "It is our food and a sword and medicine and confirmation and rest, resurrection and also our consummation" (Div 24.1).[17] Bernard concludes, "Hearing comes first and seeing afterward, as it is written, 'Hear, O daughter, and see.' Therefore it is clearly necessary that whoever desires to see God in the future must first listen to God in the present" (Div 77).

This attention to the revealed Scripture provides the monk with his image of God, and the way he conceives God determines the tone of his spiritual life. If he sees God as just, his spirituality will be marked by a fruitful compunction about the past and a fear-inspired seriousness about the present. If he sees God as truthful he will be led to self-knowledge and confession. God's generosity inspires detachment from material things. The thought of God's omnipotence will support his mortification. If he sees God as the Supreme Good he will more willingly let go of self-will. The eternity of God will motivate him to persevere (see Div 111.5–7 and Sent 3.124). The perceived variety in God is not due to any changeableness in God, however, but to "the changing that takes place in the soul's activity that makes us perceive different flavors [*sapores*] [in God]" (Div 73).

It is important for the monk to be aware of the changing circumstances of his interior life. The whole of Div 70 is devoted to that topic: *De consideratione sui*. It is because of a reluctance to engage in self-reflection that people are led astray: *per incuriam devient* (Div 96.2). Bernard admits that even monks have been neglectful in this regard, *soli*

---

[17] The title given to this talk is *De multiplici efficacia verbi divina*.

nosmetipsos negligimus intueri (Div 70). This necessary self-knowledge recognizes the *miseria* of human existence (Div 110), but it also includes an appreciation of what is good in us, our fundamental dignity, nobility, and beauty. It also understands that where there is light there is shadow and that the lives of even the holiest are not without zones of lesser light. We have to overcome our unwillingness to admit our liabilities instead of denying them, rationalizing them, renaming them, or projecting them onto others. Bernard takes as his own the sentiment attributed to the Delphic oracle, *Nosce teipsum* ("Know thyself"):

> There are many and varied degrees of confession difficult to practise and hard to enumerate. The first path and the first step on the way is self-knowledge. From heaven the maxim came down: "Human, know thyself." See how the bridegroom in the Canticle of love says the same thing to the bride: "If you are ignorant of yourself, O most beautiful among women, go forth" [Song 1:7]. Self-knowledge has three elements: that people know what they did, what they deserved, and what they lost. What is more vile, O noble creature, image of God, likeness of the Creator, than to render your flesh impure with carnal immorality and thus to lose the torrent of pleasure for a brief sensual pleasure? What is so raving mad as to be carried away by anger, exalted by pride, troubled by envy, and tormented by anxiety? Why do you embrace dung, you who were nurtured in saffron [Lam 4:5]? Remember also what you have merited. . . . Turn back your eyes and note what you have lost. . . . If you bind your soul with this triple cord you will know and realize that being convinced of one's sin is the beginning of salvation. (Div 40.3)

The self-knowledge that accompanies this admission provides the necessary foundation for all the elements of monastic *conversatio*. Persons who consider that comfort and happiness are the default state of human beings will never accept the intrinsic pain of being human, will blame others for their condition and be unwilling to accept the monastic remedies that will offer them real relief. "Don't you see how useful it is for persons to know themselves as human [*quam utile sit homini scire se hominem*]? From this [knowledge] they will be prepared to be obedient to the commandments and to tolerate afflictions so that [they will understand] that in this present life they cannot escape from labor or pain and, if they do experience labor and pain, these will become salutary foods for them" (Div 2.5), remedies for the illness of the soul (Div 105). This is why throughout his writing Bernard cites the text of Isaiah 46:8 fifteen times, calling for a return to the heart: *Redite ad cor!* (Div 5.2; Div 115): "We have ceaselessly encouraged you, brothers, so that you will walk the road of the heart; let your soul be always in your hands" (Div 9.2). Conversion begins when God touches the heart and draws the attention away from fleshly and worldly concerns toward spiritual realities. Throughout life conscience will have an important role to play in maintaining the monk in a healthy state of self-awareness (Div 112).

Self-knowledge demands the recognition that growth in monasticity is not a smooth process. There is alternation between moments of light and moments of darkness:[18] "In this present life our faith wobbles [*titubat*]" (Div 111.2). Here below nothing fully satisfies us, and hence as we look for something more gratifying, it is only the prospect of change (*vicissitudo*) that offers some relief (Div 12.3). In glory we will not experience such a yearning for change (Div 1.7). But, for the moment, "there is a manifold variation in our interior feelings [*affectiones*]" (Div 8.1). We do not remain in the same state for long. This essential changeableness is often the source of confusion and difficulty, because as soon as we develop the skills and virtues for responding to one set of circumstances everything changes and we are left bereft. A period rich in spiritual experience is replaced by a time of emptiness and trial. For Bernard the real proof of the stability of a spiritual life was the capacity to negotiate "the many transitions between the visitation of grace and the testing of temptation" (Div 3.1). In these *sermones*, as elsewhere, Bernard is at pains to insist that the default state of spiritual life is neither peace nor warfare, but an unpredictable movement from one to the other: "Perfection does not consist in the visitation [of grace] alone nor in temptation but in both of them simultaneously" (Div 3.3).

---

[18] On alternation, see Casey, *Athirst for God*, 251–80.

Not all monks respond positively to the withdrawal of grace. Without the skills needed to find God in the wilderness they begin to lose focus and to be troubled by a multiplicity of thoughts (Div 32.4). Basing himself on James 3:17, Bernard affirms that where there is no modesty or peaceableness, a person is likely to become alienated from wisdom and thence from God. These troubling thoughts can be expressive of unfulfilled desires (*cogitationes affectuosae*). Otherwise, the mind can be swamped by practical or administrative concerns (*cogitationes onerosae*), or its energies can be dissipated by idle pursuits such as horseracing or falconry (*cogitationes otiosae*) (Div 45.1, 6).[19] In his teaching Bernard continues the age-long monastic tradition of insisting on vigilance regarding thoughts (Div 16.1). Div 31 has the title *De triplici genere cogitationum* and deals with the kinds of thoughts from which monks need to protect themselves. It is written in an inclusive first-person plural as if to underline the fact that the struggle against inappropriate thoughts is a normal and even universal element of monastic experience. Bernard is not preaching at his monks but simply and frankly giving expression to common experience, his own as well as theirs. He summarizes his thought at the end of the talk:

> The first species of thoughts, idle and irrelevant thoughts, are mud, but simple mud since they do not cling or pollute. If it happens that they remain with us for a longer time, then through our unconcern and negligence they are changed into another species—as we daily experience. If we despise idle thoughts as being of minor significance, then we begin to slide into impure and inappropriate thoughts. This second species of thought is not simple mud but, as we have already said, mud that is thick and clinging. Of the third species we must beware, since [such thoughts] are not only dirty and clinging but also extremely impure and foul-smelling. (Div 31.3)

---

[19] See Sent 1.25 (SBOp 6b:16): "The mind [*memoria*] that is in the process of withdrawing from the Father is weakened in three ways: by emotional thoughts, by burdensome thoughts, and by idle thoughts. Emotional thoughts concern our own flesh or our relations. Burdensome thoughts concern the tasks assigned to us. Idle thoughts are those about the king of the English."

Inappropriate thoughts are more than a waste of time. They are the beginning of a process of decline that will take the monk to a level of inconsistency that he had never envisaged. Mental betrayal is the first step in a movement away from God. Bernard, like Aelred, often lists stages of decline in order to make his monks aware of the inherent dynamism of vice. First, there is a mere suggestion of evil, then an increasing delight in it until, finally, consent is given (Div 45.1, 6; 72.1). When the evil action is repeated then an evil habit develops. In a series of complicated images based on the brickmaking of the Israelites under the Pharaoh, Bernard plots the trajectory of decline from first thought to fixed habit:[20]

> Under Pharaoh's yoke they work in the mud, that is, in things that are undisciplined and filthy. They are given straw, that is, thoughts that do not concern serious matters [*leves cogitationes*]. It is a property of straw that it quickly bursts into flame and is consumed in a moment. Thus evil thoughts infused by the devil quickly burst into flames in our minds, a process to which the troublesome flesh gives consent. If we strive manfully to resist, then they are immediately extinguished with God's help. But when the straw is set on fire, the mud is baked and changed into bricks. Evil thoughts are like mud: when set on fire by straw, they give delight. They are baked when they pass into action. When they become habitual they become hard and solid. (Div 71.2)

The stages of decline are mapped most fully in Div 14, where, as in Div 125.3 and elsewhere, Bernard aligns the downward steps with their antithesis—the means of ascent provided by the gifts of the Holy Spirit:

> Pernicious negligence put the wretched soul to sleep, curiosity woke it up for worse things, experience attracted, concupiscence led on, habit bound, contempt cast into a prison, malice strangled. But now fear rouses, piety gently softens, knowledge, which

---

[20] It seems that Bernard was not too knowledgeable about the process of brickmaking in ancient Egypt. The straw was used to bind the clay together, not to bake the bricks; this was done by exposing them to the sun.

indicates what is to be done, brings sorrow,[21] fortitude lifts up the self; counsel unbinds it, understanding leads from prison. Wisdom lays the table, feeds the hungry, and makes good the damage with wholesome foods. (Div 14.7)

Bernard sees evil habit as incapacitating darkness that makes goodness virtually impossible. Before conversion we were resident in the habitual and familiar darkness of a way of life marked by sin (Div 3.6). We were wretchedly bound by the habit of sin (Div 8.5), living in a state that derives not merely from the weakness of nature but, more especially, from the evil habits in whose formation we had been complicit (Div 3.6).

More than a merely defensive vigilance about thoughts is needed. Part of Bernard's pastoral office was constantly to exhort his monks to the active practice of the virtues.[22] The monastery is a *schola dilectionis*, but love is learned not only by the positive experience of being loved and loving but also by the action of teachers who help us to extinguish lust and overcome negligence (Div 121). Thus the monastery is also a *schola virtutum* (Div 3.1). Françoise Callerot has compiled lists of all the virtues mentioned in the *Sermones de diversis*.[23] By my reckoning, using her listings, there are 217 references to the cardinal virtues.[24] The second list has 403 mentions of "monastic virtues."[25]

---

[21] This is a reminiscence of Prov 9:2.

[22] See Michael Casey, "Le spirituel: les grands thèmes bernardines," in *Bernard de Clairvaux: histoire, mentalité, spiritualité*, ed. Dominique Bertrand and Guy Lobrichon, SCh 380 (Paris: Les Éditions du Cerf, 1992), esp. 623–28.

[23] SCh 545:446–48. It seems that some misprints have crept into the listing. Also, it has to be noted that because of Bernard's skill with synonyms, a concordance is of only limited value in attempting to determine his teaching on particular points.

[24] Fortitude (38), justice (129), prudence (39), and temperance (11). To be noted is the ambiguity inherent in Bernard's use of *iustitia*. Sometimes, especially in texts influenced by the Vulgate, it denotes the biblical concept of righteousness. At other times it is used in the more philosophical sense of treating neighbors appropriately. In Div 523–24 Bernard reflects on the role of the cardinal virtues in the life of the Virgin Mary.

[25] Chastity (20), circumspection (10), continence (22), discretion (11), humility (141), obedience (83), perseverance (27), piety (51), shame (*pudor*) (21), and purity (28).

The third list is of 163 "other virtues."[26] The grand total of references to different virtues as compiled by Sister Françoise is 783. One or another of the virtues is mentioned in 99 of the 114 authentic Bernardine pieces in this series. Of course, the vices are also listed.[27] The numbers in every case are approximate and are cited only as an indication; each instance needs to be examined on its own merit. Not every case refers to the behavior of monks; some references are quite general. The evidence is sufficient, however, to demonstrate that Bernard's talks were eminently practical, with a strong emphasis on appropriate monastic attitudes and behavior.

It would be wrong to conclude that Bernard advocated that his monks pursue lives of merely solitary virtue.[28] He insisted that the monk is a social animal (Div 16.3), who leads a social life (Div 92.3) and learns to practice social love (Div 10.2; Sent 3.73). This means that monastic morality has a social form: monastic *conversatio* is built around an objective body of observances. By following and internalizing the values inherent in these observances, the monk is trained to give himself comprehensively to his vocation and so to find happiness and fulfillment in the monastery. Bernard affirms unambiguously the importance of Cistercian *disciplina*, though he recognizes that because it necessarily implies new learning (*disciplina* derives from *discere*), it will be a challenge for many, especially at the beginning: "Whoever strives to attain the summit of perfect monastic life [*conversatio*] must first be a disciple. So he needs to enter the cell of discipline, in which

---

[26] Abstemiousness (*parcitas*) (2), assiduity (4), benignity (13), boldness (14), constancy (3), equanimity (2), equity (2), goodness (10), integrity (*honestas*) (5), patience (48), rectitude (43), and sobriety (17).

[27] Ambition (6), anger (24), apostasy (2), arrogance (6), avarice (4), blindness (8), boastfulness (3), cunning (3), concupiscence (62), confusion (26), contempt (34), contumacy (2), cruelty (7), cupidity (7), curiosity (17), disobedience (7), dissimulation (25), elation (6), envy (16), falsity (33), fatuity (7), foolishness (*insipientia*) (15), fornication (7), fraud (7), hatred (21), hypocrisy (2), impatience (9), impenitence (3), impiety (29), impurity (7), inanity (10), incredulity (3), infidelity (3), inflation (4), ingratitude (18), iniquity (47), injustice (5), levity (6), libido (3), malice (22), malignity (20), mendacity (15), murmuring (3), negligence (16), perversity (9), pleasure-seeking (*voluptas*) (53), pride (46), pusillanimity (13), sexual sins (*luxuria*) (5), uncleanness (16), unconcern (3), unquiet (2), vanity (51), vice (42).

[28] See Michael Casey, "*In communi vita fratrum*: St Bernard's Teaching on Cenobitic Solitude," ASOC 46 (1990): 243–61.

his behavior is shaped by a master by means of different virtues, just as perfume is compounded from different spices" (Div 92.2). Discipline is necessarily hard, but it need not be harsh, since those responsible should temper it to suit the condition of beginners:

> So when some simple men come to conversion, they fear the severity of the Rule. If they are told about contempt of the world, the conflict of vice and virtue, the challenge of vigils, assiduity in prayer, the lean [diet] of fasting, all of which will be demanded of them, they say in complaint, "What is this? Who can fulfil so many and such great requirements?" They do not know how great is the strength of the lifestyle [*ordo*] that they have assumed. The shepherd has to respond in a soothing manner and to be solicitous that they bring flour. (Div 95.2)[29]

The fact that adapting oneself to monastic *conversatio* is difficult means that newcomers must be constantly assured of its value and efficacy: "The rigor of discipline maintains a watch against [the vices of] the flesh" (Div 82.3). By accepting the *dura et aspera* newcomers will gradually come to experience the hidden attractions of Cistercian life, which is "hard on the outside but very sweet inside" (Div 97.2). "Both discipline and the social life are a gift of grace" (Div 92.2).

For Bernard, "bodily observances" (Div 118) were indispensable for progress in the spiritual life. In different places he singles out for mention different aspects of monastic life, but it is clear that he regards the totality of observances as necessary: picking and choosing among them will be ineffectual. "Silence, psalmody, vigils, fasting, manual work, bodily purity" comprise one list that he gives (Div 55.1). Bernard's

---

[29] The last sentence of this passage is difficult. The context is the story in 2 Kgs 4:38-41 about Elisha and the poisoned soup. The prophet ordered flour to be brought, which, when thrown into the pot, neutralized the poison. A miracle will occur, but someone has to provide the flour. So this section of the talk begins, "The wise steward does not himself bring the flour but rather orders that it be brought, since he does not bestow charity but encourages [others] to have it, the addition of which makes sweet what previously seemed bitter." The point is that the Cistercian lifestyle has to be accepted in its integrity even though it is challenging, but, once accepted, it begins to work its magic beyond anything that could be achieved by mere willpower and effort.

"spirituality" cannot be understood without appreciating that its foundation was lifelong perseverance in pursuing a lifestyle that sought to be "ordinary, obscure, and laborious."

Bernard never hides from his monks the doggedness that is necessary if we are to persevere in the practice of prayer. Commenting on the reading of RB 20 about reverence in prayer, he recognizes that often prayer is a matter of mere custom and is characterized by aridity; the mind seems beset by stupidity (*hebetudo*), and the words on the lips do not resonate within (Div 25.7). Yet he also reminds his monks that sometimes the heart is lifted up to the heavenly Jerusalem (Div 19.6), and the monk is taken beyond himself in *excessus mentis* (Div 115). Bernard is interested in the changing patterns of prayer, taking 1 Corinthians 14:28 as his starting point: *obsecratio, oratio, postulatio, gratiarum actio* (Div 25). He returns to this topic in Div 107, relating each form of prayer to an interior disposition and concluding that prayer is sometimes shy, sometimes simple, sometimes large-hearted, and sometimes fervent (Div 107.1).

Granted the reputation for silence that latter-day Cistercians acquired, it may surprise some readers that Bernard often dwells on the dangers associated with undisciplined speech. It is true that he recognizes the "utility of speech" (Div 17.7), and he believes that within fraternal life there is scope for talk that builds up, *sermo ædificationis* (Div 15.5), but he recognizes that there are dangers associated with speaking. In Div 74, talkativeness (*loquacitas*) is associated with *curiositas*, *crudelitas*, and *voluptas* as behaviors that corrupt the body: "This fourfold disease corrupts the four parts of the body: curiosity corrupts the eyes, loquacity corrupts the tongue, cruelty corrupts the hands, and pleasure-seeking corrupts the genitals" (Div 74; Sent 3.9).

He mentions detraction a few times (Div 17.2, 4; 27.5), a topic that he had treated with such vehemence in SC 24, but generally he is more concerned about everyday conversation: "None of you, brothers, should consider of little importance the time that is consumed by idle words" (Div 17.3). The tongue, although it is a small member, is "a most suitable instrument for emptying hearts, as, I believe, the consciences of many among you will attest—unless we are all so perfect that it never happens that after long conversations [*post longas confabulationes*] our mind is found to be empty, as it were, our meditation is less marked by devotion, our inner feeling is drier, and the holocaust of prayer is less rich [*pinguis*]. This happens, as we have said, because of words, whether we have spoken them or even just listened to them" (Div 17.5). He continues: "As for you who, because of many experiences, have skillfully noted to what a great extent words can be harmful, do not be stupid. Sometimes it is necessary to participate in conversation, but be careful not only to be circumspect in what you say but to be cautious about what you hear" (Div 17.6).

Monks are certainly "to abstain from lewd expressions [*impudicis locutionibus*]" (Div 125.2), but there are many other forms of improper speech, including language that is "dissolute, unchaste, boastful [*magniloqua*], or abusive [*maledica*]" (Div 17.2). Such language includes "scurrilities, detraction, boasting, and impatient words" (Div 27.5) and words that are "foolish, empty, lying, idle, deceitful, abusive, and exculpatory" (Div 55.1). Speaking about the influence of the malign spirits, he notes, "The spirit of the flesh always speaks of soft (or pleasurable) things [*mollia*], the spirit of the world always speaks of vain things, the spirit of malice always speaks of bitter things" (Div 23.3, 4; 24.1). From the effect of inappropriate speech on the individual he passes to its impact on the community: "Nothing is to be so avoided as horrible [*tam horrendum et horribile*] as murmuring and dissension" (Div 93).

CASE STUDY: BERNARD ON OBEDIENCE

It has been observed that monks who become abbots quickly develop a wide-ranging appreciation of monastic obedience and a certain eloquence in extolling its benefits. It is to be expected, therefore, that in a series of 125 monastic sermons, the topic of obedience would figure prominently. As so often happens in considering Bernard's writings, however, the expected does not eventuate. Maybe this omission is one reason that Bernard's talks were so well received by his monks and so avidly copied. Before we examine in detail the occurrences of the theme in the *Sermones de diversis*, we need to take a step back to view the broader context of Bernard's teaching.

Bernard followed Benedict in believing that obedience, as an essential element in monastic discipline, was not primarily intended as a means of administrative or organizational control. Its purpose was ascetic rather than merely organizational. He saw it as one means among many, one that was chiefly aimed at neutralizing the harmful effects of self-will: "Let us beware of self-will as if it were a very bad viper, because on its own it can bring our souls to damnation" (Div 11.3). Self-will is the source of the commonest deviations from the monastic ideal—concern with things that do not matter and pleasure-seeking (*vanitas et voluptas*) (Div 21.2). Self-will counteracts the effects of baptism, "putting us back under the power of darkness and subjecting us to the rule of death" (Div 11.2), and sets us on the path to self-destruction:

> The soul is under [the control of] itself when it follows self-will, enjoying a harmful liberty. This is that prodigal son who received that part of his father's property that was to be his, namely talent, memory, bodily strength, and other similar benefits of nature, and used them according to his own will and not according to God's will, so it was as though he were without God in this world. (Div 8.2)

Bernard's rules for discerning between right and wrong choices are simple. Whatever Scripture or conscience declares unambiguously good must be followed. Whatever Scripture or conscience declares unambiguously bad must be avoided. In other cases we should avoid automatically following our own will but, instead, declare a moratorium in the hope that clarity will emerge. If doubt persists, the counsel of a superior should be sought.[30] Bernard discusses this process in Div 26, which has been given the title "How our will should be subject to the divine will in three ways":

---

[30] It seems that Bernard saw his role as abbot more in terms of giving advice than of issuing orders. Probably the most severe of any of the letters addressed to monks was one Bernard wrote to Gamellus, forbidding him to pursue his intention of taking up the eremitic life. He begins by using the verbs *mandare* and *remandare*, but he three times describes his own interventions in terms of counsel: *saniori consilio acquiescens, spreto consilio nostro, hoc est ergo meum, fultum apostolica auctoritate* [1 Cor 7:20], *consilium*.

Therefore, I beg you, brothers, attend carefully. I can think of nothing that would be more useful for you to hear. Where God's will is certain, our will must follow it totally, namely in those matters where we find something certain in Scripture, or the Spirit himself clearly cries to us in our hearts what is correct, for example charity, humility, chastity, and obedience. Let us approve and desire these values without hesitation, which we know for certain are pleasing to God. We ought to hate totally those things which we are certain God hates, for example, apostasy, fornication, evil, and impatience. In those areas where we can find nothing certain let us cling to nothing with certainty. Let us suspend our decision between the two or at least not cling excessively to either choice, being aware that perhaps the other choice is more pleasing to God, and let us be prepared to follow his will in whatever direction we know he is leading us. Let no one hesitate over what is certain. Let no one hold what is doubtful, as certain. In doubt let no one claim the right to judge or hurry a decision. Thus we experience what is written: "Those who love your law have much peace and no scandal" [Ps 119:165]. From where do scandals and tribulations come except that we follow our own will and rashly will what we decide in our own hearts. If someone tries to prevent or stop us, immediately we tend to murmur, be impatient, and be scandalised, not remembering that all things work unto good for those who have been called to be holy. And what seems to us a disaster is the word of God, indicating his will to us. But they who have determined nothing definite in their hearts about such (doubtful) matters will not be scandalised, no matter what happens afterwards. If we wish to do something for which we have no mandate, it is well to suspend our decision until we ask the superior and seek from him the will of God. If we obey him as one holding God's place, we will not be disturbed, for there is much peace and no scandal for those who love your law [Ps 119:165].[31]

This passage demonstrates something of Bernard's highly nuanced approach to monastic obedience. Bernard viewed his own work as

---

[31] This translation is by John Kelly, OCSO, "Bernard of Clairvaux's Sermons on Diverse Subjects," *Tjurunga* 85 (2014): 86.

abbot principally in terms of writing and teaching rather than in issuing orders. He seems to have been content for others to take over much of the temporal administration of his monastery[32] while he concentrated on preaching, prayer, and study—as he notes in his eulogy of his brother Gerard (SC 26.7). This approach corresponds to Saint Benedict's injunction in RB 2.4 that the principal functions of abbatial authority are to teach, to establish policy, and to give commands: *docere, constituere, iubere*. This is quite distinct from the more modern notion that authority is exercised primarily by giving orders.

In a monastery the basic pattern of daily life is set by the Gospel and the Rule: it is the abbot's principal task to communicate moral energy to his monks by his teaching on the beliefs and values underlying monastic practice. Then it is his duty to express these values in legislating for communal practice. Only when these ordinary means are insufficient for the circumstances are administrative orders necessary. Monastic authority is not a military command structure. Furthermore, Saint Benedict insists that the abbot ensure that what he ordains really is the will of God, not only by operating within the parameters set down in the Rule but also by ensuring that he seeks to enforce nothing for which there is no scriptural precedent: *nihil extra præceptum Domini (quod absit)* (RB 2.4).

The question that seems to have preoccupied Bernard was the concordance of abbatial instructions and the objective manifestations of God's will in the Rule and in the Scriptures. He discusses this matter at some length in his treatise *On Precept and Dispensation* (Pre).[33] In the following paragraph Bernard begins his discussion of the subordination of the abbot's will to the Rule; this point he considers most important (*potissimum*):

---

[32] See Michael Casey, "Reading Saint Bernard: The Man, the Medium, the Message," in *A Companion to Bernard of Clairvaux*, ed. Brian Patrick McGuire (Leiden: Brill, 2011), esp. 69–71.

[33] For a detailed commentary on this treatise, see Jean Leclercq, "Saint Bernard dans l'histoire de l'obéissance," *Recueil III*, 267–98.

First of all, whatever pertains to the spiritual elements handed down in the Rule is in no way left in the hand of the abbot. Not even the other part, which comprises bodily observances, is placed in his will so that it is at the service of his will. It serves only charity. The abbot is not above the Rule, since he himself has once and for all freely subjected himself to it by his profession, even if charity, which is God's rule, has precedence over Saint Benedict's Rule. No one should deny this. On occasion, then, let the letter of the Rule yield to charity, when necessity demands it, but let [the Rule] never be made subject to mere human will. He who has been elected abbot is constituted [judge] over the transgressions of the brothers, not over the traditions of the Fathers; he is to cultivate their commandments and punish vices. I consider these holy observances as entrusted to the prudence of superiors rather than made subject to their wills.[34]

Bernard continues by noting that the dispositions of the abbot must flow from his reflection or judgment and not from what is pleasing to his own will (*placitum voluntatis*). In the following paragraph, he reminds the abbot that he also, by virtue of his profession, is subject to the Rule. He concludes that "it is appropriate for the one who is in charge not to unleash the reins of his own will on those subject to him."

The [formula of] profession has "I promise," not "the Rule" but "obedience according to the Rule of Saint Benedict," therefore, not according to the will of a superior. Then if I make profession according to the Rule and if my abbot should try to impose something which is not according to the Rule, for example, something that is according to what Basil or Augustine or Pachomius has established, I ask you, what need is there for me in this case to comply? My judgment is that only that can be demanded of me which I have promised.[35]

---

[34] Translated from Pre 9; SBOp 3:239. Another translation of this text and those following appears in CF 1:111–13.

[35] Pre 10; SBOp 3:260–61.

In the next paragraph he continues his aim of defining the limits of obedience. He excludes from its zone of application anything that is "beside, beyond, or against" the *tenor professionis*. *Tenor* is a legal term signifying the content of a law or judgment. Hence Bernard excludes whatever is outside what has been promised in profession. The prepositions he uses—*citra*, *ultra*, and *contra*—were later incorporated into canonical texts:

> See, therefore, the limits of obedience about which you asked. If obedience is to be defined by the form of the profession, the power of the one commanding cannot go beyond this. It is determined by the vow of the one making profession. Anything that is beside, beyond, or against this I consider to be outside the limits of obedience; its power is circumscribed within these borders. For this reason, anyone who makes profession in any way of life that leads to salvation should not be forced by the law of obedience to go beyond what his profession includes— nor to be compelled to something less. How much less [justification is there to act] against [what has been professed]: *quanto minus contra*.[36]

It is clear from these passages that Bernard's view of religious authority is neither positivist nor authoritarian. He viewed the abbatial office as an everyday task to be done as an expression of the abbot's own obedience to the various manifestations of God's will. This means that at least some of his energies need to be devoted to becoming more familiar with the ways of God through discernment, prayer, meditation, and reading. Bernard understood that the task of those in authority is to mediate the divine will as this has been manifested in the Scriptures and in the particular rule that has been professed, and then to make rulings in situations not directly covered by these sources.

Properly, monastic obedience consists in being open to all the many ways in which the monk is instructed to follow God's ways, including the liturgy, the reading of Scripture, the voice of conscience, the requirements of the Rule and monastic discipline, the needs of the brethren, and the everyday demands of community life. The abbot is

---

[36] Pre 11; SBOp 3:261.

one channel among many, and giving orders is but one of several ways in which he points out the way to eternal life, not the least being his own example, *ut subjectos suos exemplo magis instruat quam verbo* (Div 100).

Leadership came naturally to Bernard, and it seems that throughout his life there were many who were more than glad to follow his direction. He seems to have taken for granted that monks who were serious about their vocation would be generally and substantially obedient; his pastoral concern was less directed to exhorting them to practice obedience than to recommending ways in which the subjective experience of obedience might be improved. He was not apprehensive about potential disobedience; he was more concerned that monks would not gain the full profit from their obedience because of some defect at the level of interior disposition.

According to the CETEDOC concordance to Bernard's works, the noun *obœdientia* and its cognates occur eighty-five times in the *Sermones de diversis* and ninety-two times in the *Sententiae*—compared with 149 and 154 occurrences of *humilitas* and its cognates.[37] It is significant that more than half of the references to obedience occur in Div 41, titled "The Way of Obedience," a *sermo* twinned with Div 40, "The Ways to Life, which are Confession and Obedience." This leaves about forty occurrences in the remaining talks. Sometimes obedience occurs within a list of monastic virtues.[38] Div 2 is titled "On Obedience, Patience, and Wisdom," but there is little about obedience in the talk. In that talk "leprous obedience" is rejected without any indication of what the phrase might mean—perhaps it signifies an outward deference or servility that does not flow from an inward disposition (Div 2.3).[39] He later remarks that "obedience is a good food," but it needs the addition of the condiment of wisdom (Div 2.4), which is compounded of three elements: "justice in intention, cheerfulness in in-

---

[37] *Thesaurus Sancti Bernardi Claraevallensis* (Turnhout: Brepols, 1987).

[38] Div 2.5, 15.5, 26.3, 58.1, 64.2. See also Sent 249 (SBOp 6b:35), 3.26 (83), 3.53 (95), 3.88 (132), 3.121 (228).

[39] It seems likely that the adjective *leprosa* is used (perhaps eccentrically) in the sense of the noun *lepor* (or *lepos*), meaning "pleasantness of behavior," "charm," "blandishment" and has nothing to do with leprosy.

ward feeling, and humility in assessment" (Div 2.6). Clearly, this is a long way from automatic, military compliance with orders.

Obedience is associated with love (Div 10.2; 27.2; 79). Disobedience is the cause of death (Div 2.5), as when Adam obeyed Eve rather than God (Div 11.2; 66.2; 102.1), but, as Saint Benedict had noted, the labor of obedience repairs the damage caused by disobedience (Div 63; 103.2). The practice of virtue gains solidity through obedience (Div 40.2), and by "faithful obedience" (Div 15.5) "continence in the flesh, patience in troubles, and perseverance in working" are acquired (Div 58). Bernard often has in mind Acts 5:29, "It is right to obey God rather than human beings" (Div 29.5; 41.1, 3). Our primary obedience is due to God (Div 26; 77), to God's commandments (Div 45.5), and to the four gospels (27.7). And behind it all lies the example of Christ's obedience (Div 41.1; 42.1).

It seems clear enough, even from this facile summary, that Bernard views obedience as an ordinary element in monastic *conversatio* and holds that it both expresses and reinforces a fervent and dedicated interior life (Div 80.2–3). It is also apparent that he expects those in power to exercise their authority in a manner that promotes the ascetical utility of obedience, not as a mere expression of personal will on the part of the abbot. When discussing obedience Bernard avoids speaking of the abbot but usually refers in general terms either to *prelates* and *priors*, in the plural, or, more functionally, to *the one giving the order* (*præcipiens*); he seems to include himself among those who are bound by obedience. He understands that there is complementarity between ready obedience and discretion in exercising authority (Div 90.3) and that, as Saint Benedict affirms (RB 2.6), the abbot is answerable to God for the obedience of his monks. It is his job not only to command but also to sell what he is commanding, and to be so convincing that the monks want to buy it.

Bernard's insistence on persuasiveness in authority anticipated what the Second Vatican Council required of superiors: "They should govern their subjects . . . fostering in them a spirit of voluntary subjection."[40] This concern for the subjective dispositions of his monks is

---

[40] *Perfectae caritatis* 14. Bernard's acceptance of and respect for different manifestations of the monastic charism even within a single community is lyrically celebrated in his portrayal of the *paradisus claustralis* in Div 42:2.

especially noteworthy in Div 41, the only systematic treatment of monastic obedience included in the *Sermones de diversis*.[41]

This prolonged reflection on obedience as a life-giving way is twinned with Div 40, which discusses the value of confession; both talks are divided into seven degrees or steps and share a common conclusion and doxology (Div 41.11–13). Confession operates mainly in the area of humility and self-knowledge, but it necessarily leads to changes in behavior, *correctio operis* (Div 40.8). Obedience operates externally, but Bernard insists much less on outward conformity than on the inward dispositions that make external compliance life-giving.

Bernard begins by evoking the spirit of wisdom, "who is also a spirit of kindliness [*pietas*], releasing those who are bound, enlightening the blind, and lifting up the wounded. She is also a spirit of truth, who teaches us all truth. She not only teaches but also prompts us. She prompts that we may seek and teaches that we may understand" (Div 40.1). Obedience operates in the sphere of wisdom. This is far from merely external compliance with instructions; it is "a very powerful reality" that demands great purity of heart (Div 41.3). People can do what they are told for a variety of reasons, not all of them adult or honorable. Genuine obedience is opening ourselves to guidance so that we may reach the goal for which we came to the monastery (Div 2.1). To strengthen his case Bernard calls on the example of the apostles and that of Abraham, "who does not murmur or complain or even allow grief to show on his face" (Div 41.2).

To show that monastic obedience is more than mere compliance, Bernard returns to some of the themes he had previously treated in *De præcepto et dispensatione*. Actions that are already good are obligatory even without an explicit command. Actions that are inherently evil do not become good because they are commanded by legitimate

---

[41] There is a long treatment of obedience in Sent 3.121 (SBOp 6b:225–29) in terms of the text of Matt 11:30, "My yoke is pleasant and my burden is light." Here Bernard describes obedience as *virtus virtutum domina*, probably meaning that without a willing conformity to God's will other virtues are bootless. It has to be said, however, that the thought progression in this text is not easy to follow. Bernard uses a wide variety of biblical images to link obedience with different virtues and distinguish it from vices.

authority; on the contrary, they must be resisted and rejected. Mostly obedience concerns actions that are indifferent in themselves but that acquire a moral character by virtue of being commanded. In this case the focus moves away from what is commanded to the fact that it is commanded. Of course, as Bernard insists elsewhere, this imposes a huge burden of responsibility of the one issuing the orders.

Bernard then lists seven qualities that should jointly characterize the monk's act of obedience. His use of adverbs qualifying the verb *obœdire* rather than nouns and adjectives may indicate that he is thinking concretely rather than abstractly. The good monk obeys, willingly, simply, cheerfully, quickly, manfully, humbly, and unceasingly. The bulk of this *sermo* simply expatiates on these qualities. Taken together they indicate an attitude of antecedent willingness to do what is asked, an attitude that presupposes a correspondingly generous trust that superiors will act with deliberation and integrity and not merely seek to dominate or impose their own wills. A monk obeys his abbot only to the extent that he is able to accept that his commands really are life-giving and not just peremptory invasions of personal freedom. This is not something that can be taken for granted; it presupposes considerable progress in the monk, prudent formation, and, probably, an ongoing display of acceptance and affection on the part of the abbot (Aelred's *affectus officialis*). A monk who believes that his abbot does not accept him or that he dislikes him will seek to avoid any occasion in which his obedience will be demanded. A genuinely pastoral abbot will not rely on institutional structures to enforce obedience but will develop a deep and respectful relationship with his monks, one in which they will want to hear what he has to say and do what he recommends.

This reflection on Bernard's teaching on obedience in the *Sermones de diversis* is intended to demonstrate not only the content of one aspect of his monastic doctrine but also the sensitivity with which he addressed himself to his monks. The abbot spoke directly and frankly to his community in words redolent of shared experience. He did not disguise the challenges posed by obedience, but, even while setting a high ideal before them, he somehow managed to make it seem possible. Above all he includes no carping or nagging. If these talks are an example of Bernard's usual method of forming his community, they give a good indication of why his leadership was so readily accepted.

❖   ❖   ❖

An introduction is meant to introduce; to do more than this is to go beyond the remit. Bernard's addresses to his monks are worth reading today because they embody a sound and practical spirituality, expressed in personal and sometimes original terms. They give us a good idea of what sort of man their author was and how he exercised his role as abbot. Each reader will single out individual talks as especially powerful, but the quality of these *sermones* is best assessed by taking their impact as a whole. Together they indicate something of the richness that was provided to the monks of Clairvaux on a regular basis, forming them in the beliefs, values, and practices of Christian, monastic, and Cistercian life. Thanks to this translation the modern reader can now enjoy the privilege of having access to the same solid sources of spiritual nourishment and formation.

Abbreviations

ASOC	*Analecta Sacri Ordinis Cisterciensis / Analecta Cisterciensia*
CCSL	Corpus Christianorum, Series Latina
CF	Cistercian Fathers series (Cistercian Publications)
CS	Cistercian Studies series (Cistercian Publications)
CSQ	*Cistercian Studies Quarterly*
Ep	Epistle
Evang	Gregory the Great, *Homiliae in Euangeliae*, CCSL 141
LXX	The Septuagint Bible
PL	Patrologia Latina, ed. J.-P. Migne
RB	Regula Sancti Benedicti
S	Sermo
SBOp	Sancti Bernardi Opera, ed. Jean Leclercq and H. M. Rochais
SCh	Sources Chrétiennes
Vlg	The Vulgate Bible

Works of Bernard of Clairvaux

Abb	*Sermo ad abbates*
Adv	*Sermo in adventu Domini*
Asc	*Sermo in ascensione Domini*
Asspt	*Sermo in assumptione B. V.M.*
Dil	*De diligendo Deo*
Div	*Sermones de diversis*
In lab mess	*Sermo in labore messis*
Par	*Parabolæ*
Pasc	*Sermo in die paschæ*
6 p Pent	*Sermo in dominica sexta post Pentecosten*
Pre	*Liber de præcepto et dispensatione*
SC	*Sermones super Cantica canticorum*
Sent	*Sententiae*

Bernard of Clairvaux

MONASTIC SERMONS

Sermo 1

On the Deceptions of This Life

1. My brothers, it is absolutely true that *the life of humans on earth is a temptation.** If indeed it is deceptive, then its deceptions are not usually simple. That is, life deceives humans in manifold ways: it changes its face, it changes its voice. At one time it may affirm some point and later deny it without shame; life might say different things about its own span to different people.* In fact, life may suggest contrary and adverse views to the same person at different times. Sometimes life may pretend to be short; at other times it feigns great length. Insofar as this life enjoys sin, all the more does it bemoan its brevity. This brevity is not false, but the lament is false, because the brevity that it recalls with sorrow ought rather to be celebrated.* For surely it is better for those who continue in sin to let the necessity of death put an end to their shameful deeds since their will placed no limit. It is better for one whose soul continually dies to die bodily all the sooner; better rather *if that person had never been born.**

*Job 7:1

*see 1 Cor 12:3-11

*1 Cor 7:40

*Matt 26:24

Finally, the memory of life's brevity should be a remedy for sin rather than a temptation, as it is written: *Remember your final end and you shall never sin.** Because if sin reigns in you unto the end, or rather, if you so enjoy being a slave to sin* that you mourn the short time that you have to serve it, to the point that you so

*Sir 7:40

*see Rom 6:6-12

love the broad way* that you would by any means make it even longer if you could, like it or not, life's end is not far off. But you, I admit, *are far from the Kingdom of God*,* and you seem to have made an unbreakable treaty with death and a pact with hell.*

2. *They have wandered*, says the prophet, *in a lonely place, in a place without water; they have not found the way to a city in which to dwell.** This lonely place is that of the proud, that is, they suppose themselves to be solitaries, and they seek to be regarded as such. If the proud are well educated, then they hate their peers. If they are clever in worldly affairs,* then they hope to find no one like themselves. Though they be wealthy, it tortures them to see others grow rich. They may be strong or handsome, but give them an equal and they wither. They are solitaries* in that they have gone astray. They wander in their solitude, for one cannot dwell alone on the earth.*

Nor is it any wonder that *without water* is added to this lonely place, as it was said, *in a lonely place, in a place without water*. For just as lonely places are usually without water and uninhabited places are usually infertile and arid, so too pride and impenitence go together. Indeed a lofty heart,* hard and devoid of lovingkindness, ignorant of compunction, is dry for lack of any dew of spiritual grace, because *God resists the proud; he gives grace to the humble.** *You send forth springs in the valleys. Amidst the mountains, the waters shall pass through*, says the prophet.* Here is what he says about himself, sadly lamenting: *To you my soul is like a land without water.**

What is more, the lack of water not only makes one dry but also makes one filthy, for there is no way to wash. A human heart ignorant of tears is not only hard but must also be vile. So the prophet says, *I shall wash my bed each night.** That is to say, I shall wash out the stains from my conscience. *I shall sprinkle my blanket* *with my tears* lest it become in me like the scriptural seed that *fell on the rock, and having sprouted, it dried out for lack of moisture.**   *Luke 8:6

3. *They have wandered in a lonely place, in a place without water; they have not found the way to a city in which to dwell.** They wandered in a trackless waste and not on a road.* For the broad road is not really a road.† Indeed straightness pertains to a road; broadness pertains more to a plain than to a road. The lonely place is a way within the broad road, and where there is no road, the whole region is the road. Such a life is exposed to vices because it has the widest limits, or rather it has no limits. Nor should any reasonable person call it life, because those who live alone are dead, as the apostle is our witness, who has said, *if we have lived according to the flesh then we shall die.** Nor is a circle a road, and the way of the wicked is so described where it is written, *The wicked walk in a circle.** This road is spacious† because its space on either side is closed off by no limits: *Where there is no law, there is no transgression.**

*Ps 106:4
*Ps 106:40
†Matt 7:13

*Rom 8:13

*Ps 11:9
†Matt 7:13
*Rom 4:15

So it is for the children of disobedience,* who have wholly given themselves to bodily pleasures and self-will.* This deceitful life confidently presents itself as short so that sinners will suffer carnal grief, because, like their leader, they think that their time is short.* And that is why they lust all the more for every sort of debauchery, just as some such people have been known to say, *Let not the flower of this time pass us by. Let us crown ourselves with roses before they wither. Let no meadow escape our pleasure. Let none of us go without his part in self-indulgence. Let us everywhere leave tokens of joy, for this is our portion and this our lot.** And, more bluntly, *Let us eat and drink, for tomorrow we shall die.** True indeed: *tomorrow their injustice shall answer for them,** and those who did not find the way to a city in which to dwell will not have a lasting city here.* They are truly mad, for they hurry to sin all the more.

*Eph 2:2
*see Rom 1:24-28; Eph 4:19
*Rev 12:12

*Wis 2:7-9
*1 Cor 15:32
*Gen 30:33

*Ps 106:4; Heb 13:14

The deception of this life will at once pretend to belong to these same people if they begin to dread their impending death, and if they tremble at *the terrible expectation of judgment.** Thus those who so recently mourned the shortness of their sinful life suddenly now find the same life so very long that they think they are able to spend most of their life safely in sin. After all, the rest of one's life is long and sufficient for doing penance for sin.*

Nevertheless, just as is true for those who think life is too short, that which they fear shall befall them* unless they come to their senses. No, rather, more horrible things than what they fear shall befall them, for not only shall their time for disgraceful sins pass quickly, but also a time—an eternity really—of punishment shall follow. So too *when they say to these sinners "peace and security," suddenly ruin overcomes them.** Thus they cannot live out half the days that they had hoped to enjoy.* No, they shall not fulfill even half the days that they promise to themselves.

4. For you, brothers, I do not fear that you [are deceived] by an empty sadness over the brevity of life, or by a false consolation of its apparent length, because most certainly you have already begun to enter into the city of our dwelling.* Nor would you *walk in the trackless wasteland, but on the road.** I do however fear for you, but in another way. I fear that life itself wishes to toy with you by feigning great length, not bringing us here consolation, but rather provoking in us greater desolation. Alas, one of the brothers might suppose that he has a very long life ahead of him;* therefore he might think he has an arduous road in store for him; his spirit could be overwhelmed by faintheartedness,* and he would despair of his ability to sustain such long and great toils—as if the divine *consolations do not gladden the souls* of the elect *according to the multitude of the sorrows in their hearts!** Now indeed [joy] is given to [their souls]

*Heb 10:27; Jas 2:19

*Lev 5:5

*Job 3:25

*1 Thess 5:3

*Ps 54:24

*Ps 106:7
*Ps 106:40

*1 Kgs 19:7

*Ps 54:9

*Ps 93:19

more or less according to the measure of their many sorrows.* After this life, they no longer enjoy these consolations; rather, they enjoy the everlasting pleasures at God's right hand.* †*see John 3:34*
†*Ps 15:11*

Brothers, let us desire that right hand that shall embrace the whole of us.* Let us long for those pleasures so that the time may seem so short* and *the days seem so few because of the greatness of our love.** *The sufferings of this time are not worthy to be compared to the future glory that shall be revealed in us.** How delightful is that promise, and how worthy of all our prayers! For we shall not just stand there as idle and empty-handed spectators,* nor shall that glory be revealed to us from beyond, but from within us. For we shall see God *face to face.** That is, not outside us, because the glory shall be within us, so that *God shall be all in all.** Certainly all the earth shall be filled with that glory,* so how much more shall it fill the human soul! *We shall be filled*, the psalmist says, *with the good things of your house.** And why do I say that the glory shall be within us rather than around us? Even now the glory is in us, but then it shall be revealed. For *now we are children of God, but what we shall be has not yet been revealed.**

*Song 8:3
*1 Cor 7:29
*Gen 29:20

*Rom 8:18

*Gen 1:2

*1 Cor 13:12
*1 Cor 15:28
*Isa 6:3

*Ps 64:5

*1 John 3:2

5. My brothers, *if we have not received the spirit of this world, but the spirit which is from God, then we know that what has been given to us is from God.** For, I say, he has given us all things. And if you do not believe me, then believe the apostle* who said, *He who has not spared his own son but has delivered him up for us all, how has he not also, with him, given all things to us?**

*1 Cor 2:12

*see John 10:38

*Rom 8:32

This certainly is the power of God's children that he has given to those who receive him.* This is the glory of each of the faithful: glory as though adopted by the Father, through him whose *glory we have seen, glory like the Only Begotten of the Father.** In short, listen to that power: *All things*, he says, *are possible for one who believes.**

*see John 1:12

*John 1:14

*Mark 9:22

6. "But," you will say, "there are many gravely disturbing problems and many things more obviously in our way. And I am amazed at how you mention all things that are given to us, scarcely any of which serve our wishes. Some things seem to serve us, but only at the cost of our toil or if we have first served them. The beasts of burden do not help us unless first we have nurtured them, tamed them, and sustained them with fodder. Even Mother Earth herself, who ought to be more sincere to us, will not serve us bread without the sweat of our brow. On the contrary, when we till the land, she sprouts forth thorns and spiny plants for us.* Finally, if you carefully consider* all those other gifts, you will see that they take more service from us than they give to us. I shall say nothing about those things that are always ready to harm us: there is fire that burns, water that drowns, wild beasts ready to tear us apart."

*Gen 3:18-19; see Gen 4:12 and Heb 6:8
*Prov 23:1

These things indeed are self-evident. But the apostle does not lie when he asserts more plainly in another place that he knows that *to them who love God, all things work together unto good, to those who are called to be saints according to his purpose.** Still, we must be careful to notice that they do not serve our whims, but he says that they cooperate to the good. For they do not serve our will but what is useful, not for pleasure but for salvation, not for our wishes but for our advantage. In fact, if among all things that cooperate to the good one counts even those things that have no being, such as trouble, disease, death itself, and even sin, all of which are not natural but rather corruptions of nature, then do not sins themselves truly cooperate to the good for one who by sin becomes more humble, more fervent, more watchful, more fearful, and more cautious?

*Rom 8:28

7. These then are *the first fruits of the spirit.** These are the first fruits of the Kingdom, the foretaste of glory. This is the beginning of the reign and a certain pledge of the paternal inheritance.* Moreover, *when that which*

*Rom 8:23

*see Eph 1:14

is perfected shall come, then that which is partial shall pass away.* And in turn, all things shall be put in order as we wish, because the useful and the pleasant will be joined by unbreakable and permanent bonds.* This truly will be that eternal weight of glory about which again the apostle says, *Our light and momentary troubles work in us an eternal weight of glory far above measure.**

*1 Cor 13:10

*see Matt 19:6

*2 Cor 4:17

Go ahead then, go on to complain and say, "The way is long and the burden is heavy. I am not able to carry so grievous a load so very long." Yet the apostle not only bears it but even insists that it is momentary and light. And certainly you have not *five times received forty minus one stripes from the Jews,* nor have you *spent a day and a night in the depths of the sea,** nor have you *toiled more than all others,** and, finally, you have not yet *resisted unto shedding blood.**

*2 Cor 11:24-25
*1 Cor 15:10
*Heb 12:4

See, therefore, that *these sufferings are not worthy to be compared to glory!** See that tribulation is momentary and light, that glory is eternal, and its weight is even far above any measure.

*Rom 8:18

Why do you count your days and years, which are so uncertain? The hour passes, and so also the hardship; neither do they accumulate, but rather they fall and give way. Not so the glory, not so the reward, not so the wages of labor. Glory knows not continual change: there is no end; all remains simultaneously and remains for eternity.* *Since he shall give sleep to those whom he loves,* he says, *behold the inheritance of the Lord.** *For each day has evil enough of its own,** nor is today able to reserve its toil for tomorrow,* but the wages of all toil will be given back on that one day that knows no tomorrow.* *A crown of justice has been set aside for me,* says the apostle, *which the just judge shall return to me on that day.** He does not say "in those days," for *one day in those courts is better than a thousand elsewhere.** Punishment is sipped by the drop, meted out in a solution; it passes through in the smallest bits. On the other hand, the reward is a

*Ps 116:2
*Ps 126:2-3
*Matt 6:34
*see Prov 29:11
*Wis 10:17

*2 Tim 4:8

*Ps 83:11

torrent of pleasure with the force of a river,* a torrent overflowing with happiness, a river of glory, a river of peace.* Clearly it is a river, a river that flows in, not a river that flows past or flows out.* It is called a river—not a river that flows past or flows through, but a river of abundance.

8. He says, *Eternal weight of Glory*,* because neither glorious clothes nor glorious feasting nor a glorious home, but glory itself is promised to us. Truly if any of those things or the like are sometimes mentioned, then it is figuratively. For in truth the expectation of the just is not something joyful, but joy itself.*

People rejoice in food, they rejoice in parades, they rejoice in wealth, they rejoice in vices, but such joys end in grief,* because any joy in a transient good must change with changing circumstances. A lighted candle is not pure light but a lamp. In fact, the fire itself consumes the candle—its own source of nourishment—and it does not endure except by its own consumption. In turn, when the material has failed, even the flame itself shall fail, and when you have seen the candle consumed then you will find the flame completely extinguished as well. So just as that flame is replaced by smoke and darkness in the end, so also the happiness of worldly joy changes into sadness.*

For us, however, God has not reserved a honeycomb, but the purest and clearest honey. Obviously this is joy itself: life, glory, peace, pleasure, pleasantness, happiness, delightfulness, and exultation that our Lord God has treasured up for us.* All these things at once, just as Jerusalem is united.* And this one city is none other than God himself, as we noted above, where the apostle says that *God will be all in all*.*

These are our wages, this is our crown, this is our prize. So *let us run to it so we may seize it*.* Brothers, a prudent farmer never thinks that the time for sowing is too long, because he desires the abundant harvest to

*Pss 35:9; 45:5
*see Isa 66:12
*see Song 4:15-16

*2 Cor 4:17

*Prov 10:28

*Prov 14:13

*see John 16:20

*Sir 15:6
*Ps 121:3

*1 Cor 15:28

*1 Cor 9:24-25; see 1 Cor 9:18 and 1 Thess 2:19-20

come. Your days, moreover, no less than *the hairs on your head, are all numbered.** And just like the hair of the body, so also not a moment of time shall perish.* Having therefore such a promise,* dearest brothers, let us not lose heart or ever grow weary,* nor complain that the burden of Christ is heavy, because, by his witness, it is light, and the yoke is in fact sweet.* Rather, whenever we seem *to carry the weight of the day*,* let us think of *the eternal weight of glory** to which the Lord and king of glory leads us by his compassion,* to whom, meanwhile, we shout with devout humility, *Not to us, Lord, not to us, but to your name give the glory.**

*Matt 10:30
*see Luke 21:18
*2 Cor 7:1
*Heb 12:3

*Matt 11:30
*Matt 20:12
*2 Cor 4:17
*Ps 23:10

*Ps 113:9

Sermo 2

On Obedience, Patience, and Wisdom

1. **B**rothers, by our shared salvation,* I beg you to take up—with eagerness—the opportunity that is given you to work out your salvation. I beg you: act according to your purpose by that mercy for which you have striven to make yourself so lowly,* by that reason for which you have come up from the rivers of Babylon. *By the rivers of Babylon,* says the prophet, *there we sat and wept when we remembered Zion.** Here† you have no worry about children to feed or cares about pleasing a wife.# There is no need to think about business transactions or worldly affairs‡ or even worries about food or clothing.° The greater part of today's evils and the cares of this life are truly far from you.* God has hidden you *in the secret part of his tabernacle.** Therefore, my most beloved brothers, *be still and see that it is God himself.**

In order for you to be truly capable of this, you must first look to yourself in order to see what you are, and, according to the voice of the same prophet, *Let the nations know they are but mortals.** May all your free time be given to this double contemplation, like the saint who prayed, "God, may I know myself, may I know you."† For how can one even seem to know oneself who flees toil and pain?# Or how does one know oneself as a person if unprepared for life's purpose? *A human being,* says Job, *is born to suffer.** For only someone not

*Jude 3

*Rom 12:1

*Ps 136:1
†i.e., in the monastery
#1 Cor 7:33
‡2 Tim 2:4
°1 Tim 6:8
*Matt 6:34; 13:22
*Pss 30:21; 26:5
*Ps 45:11

*Ps 9:21

†Augustine, *Soliloquies* 2.1 (PL 32:885)
#Ps 9:35; see Ps 89:10
*Job 5:7

born in pain would doubt that he was born for pain. But the cry of the mother in labor* and the weeping and whimpering of the newborn both express pain. *For you look upon our toil and pain,** says the prophet. Toil is in actions, pain in suffering. Therefore, those who know their humanity are prepared for both, like the prophet who on his knees prayed, *My heart is ready, O God, my heart is ready.** And he more explicitly expresses this double preparation regarding his action: *I am ready*, he says, *and I am not troubled, so that I may keep your commands.** And about suffering, he says in fact, *I am ready for scourges, and my pain is always before me.**

*see Ps 74:7
*Ps 9:35

*Ps 56:8

*Ps 118:60
*Ps 37:18

2. To be sure, let no one boast of having avoided that double trouble in this wretched life. Certainly no one among the children of Adam lives here without toil, no one without pain.* There may be a few who avoid some sorrow, but they no doubt fall into more serious trouble. *They share not the toils of men*, says the psalmist, *nor shall they be scourged along with other people.** You see, they are not always free from toil and scourges. *Therefore, he goes on, pride holds them,** and pride is heavy toil indeed. *They are covered by their injustice and their wickedness.** Clearly, these are heavy scourges, since *there is no joy for the wicked, says the Lord.**

*see Sir 40:1

*Ps 72:5

*Ps 72:6

*Ps 72:6
*Isa 57:21

Although they do not feel the anxiety of toil or the wounds of scourging, yet their insensibility itself reveals the depth of their suffering. The poor person sweats while working outdoors, but indoors, does the rich person toil any less with anxious thoughts? The poor man yawns, weary with toil, while the rich man opens his mouth to belch. Sometimes the rich are more gravely tormented by disgust than the poor by hunger. Finally, whether they wish it or not, both human beings and demons* work and suffer as the Most High Providence ordains.

*see Jas 2:19

3. Moreover, neither an obedient leper nor a patient dog is to be commended. Therefore, we do not merely

pray that the Lord's will be done, for certainly everything that happens depends on God's will—for *who can resist his will?**—but we pray his will be done *on earth as it is in heaven.** This of course, I believe, is aptly applied to the two previous petitions as well: as we beseech our Father in heaven, we pray that his name be hallowed and that both his Kingdom come and his will be done.* We pray that just as his will and Kingdom are in heaven, so also may they be on earth. In any case, where would his name not be hallowed? Where now does his Kingdom not come, seeing how in the name of Jesus every knee bends, that is, every knee in heaven, on earth, and under the earth?* Indeed, the Evil One himself says, *I know who you are, the Holy One of God.**

*Rom 9:19
*Matt 6:10

*Matt 6:9-10

*Phil 2:10
*Luke 4:34

On the other hand, with a very different sentiment is God's name hallowed in heaven, where with most ineffable pleasure angels shout, *Holy, holy, holy Lord God Sabaoth.** So also God reigns not on earth alone; in fact he reigns even in hell, having the power of life and death.* But how very differently does he reign over these demons who obey him unwillingly, as opposed to those who serve voluntarily.

*Isa 6:3

*see Wis 16:13

4. Obedience is the good food about which the Lord himself says, *My food is to do the will of my father.** And the prophet says, *For you shall eat the labors of your hands; you are blessed, and it shall be well with you.** The good food is *the patience of the poor*, which *shall not perish in the end: a bread of tears, a bread of sorrow.** Nevertheless, a seasoning is necessary for both, without which bread is neither tasty nor sustaining and may even cause death. Of course, both of these foods* are hard to swallow, brothers, and unless some third flavoring is added, then for each *death is in the pot.**

*John 4:34

*Ps 127:2

*Pss 9:12; 79:6; 126:2

*tears and sorrow
*2 Kgs 4:40

Truly, what is more flavorful than wisdom? Wisdom indeed is the tree of life that, through Moses, sweetened the waters of Mara.‡ It is the fine flour that through Elisha made the prophets' stew edible.* It is the fire

‡Gen 2:9; Exod 15:23, 25
*see 2 Kgs 4:38-41

that God commands to be burned on the altar at all times.* It is the oil for lack of which the door to the wedding was closed to the foolish virgins.* Wisdom is the salt that, by divine command, no sacrifice should be without.* That is why we sometimes say that dull people are tasteless,¹ and the Lord bids us to have salt among us.* And the apostle also advises us to season all our speech with salt.*

*Lev 6:12
*Matt 25:8-12
*Lev 2:13; Mark 9:48
*Mark 9:49
*Col 4:6

5. I believe, however, that our third ingredient—wisdom—which we want to add to obedience and patience, likewise has a threefold nature. Our seasoning consists of three particular herbs, for there need to be justice in our purpose, joy in our disposition, and humility in our consideration. Insipid to God, and unsalted (so to speak) is all our obedience, and even our patience, unless God himself is the final cause of everything that we do and suffer. For whatever we do, we are commanded *to do for the glory of God,** and we are blessed not just because we suffer but only when we suffer for the sake of justice.* It is also necessary, moreover, to guard against faint-heartedness and sadness in everything that we do and everything that we endure, because *God loves a cheerful giver.** Furthermore, we know that cheerfulness itself and a conscious devotion to cheerfulness pertain specially to the preparation† of which we spoke above.*

*1 Cor 10:31
*1 Pet 3:14
*2 Cor 9:7
†for pain and suffering
*see §1

Finally, one must avoid haughtiness above all. For if anyone be high-minded,* then both that person's works and his patience will taste of emptiness, an emptiness that is most serious and most contrary to the truth. Do you see how useful it is to recognize one's humanity* in order to be prepared to keep the commandments and endure scourgings? May we therefore always press on! Since we cannot avoid toil or sorrow, then let us

*Rom 11:20
*Ps 9:21

---

¹ *Inde est quod insulsos homines dicimus, quos intelligi volumus minime sapientes*, a play on the terms *sapor* (flavor) and *sapiens* (wise).

at least work and suffer in such a way that our toil is transformed into spiritual nourishment! *Obedience, indeed, is better than sacrifice,** and *a patient man is better than a strong man.** Disobedience can cause death; we are all tested, and we die on account of disobedience.* Impatience is the ruin of the soul, for the Lord says, *By your patience you shall possess your souls.** Wisdom is likewise necessary, as we said, for salvation. Similarly, not only do we lack obedience because of our disobedience, and we might lack patience because of impatience, but if *we also lack wisdom, then we perish in our folly.**

*1 Sam 15:22
*Prov 16:32
*see Rom 5:19; 1 Cor 15:22
*Luke 21:19

*Bar 3:28
*Ps 9:21

6. By this we know that we are only human,* assigned to lives of work and suffering. There was a time when humans were created for work and meditation, enjoying action without suffering, and even without toil. I mean, of course, when humans were put in Paradise to work and to watch over God's garden.* In fact, even in this Paradise, if not for the Fall, humans would have advanced to a state where they could have enjoyed contemplation alone. So also we are in danger of falling from our present, lower, condition, for unless we busy ourselves with rising higher, then we all fall into hell. We most certainly risk exchanging our present condition for one of pure suffering, because in hell there is neither work nor reason, but only great suffering.

*see Gen 2:15

Happy indeed was that first man, whose body was not corrupted; nor did it weigh down his soul.* But how much more happy would Adam have been if he had arrived at that less active state, where he would have perceived Wisdom more fully, more perfectly,* loving the body freely, as though having no bodily needs. For this would have been a most beautiful arrangement, and so will it be when it shall be. Nor should we despair when in the end the flesh seems to say to the soul (just as the soul now says to God), *You have no need of my goods*; it says, *You shall fill me with the*

*Wis 9:15

*Sir 38:25

joy of your countenance.* Thence the fullness and satisfaction *when your glory shall appear.**

As for our expectations about the reformation of our bodies and our conformity to the Lord's glorious body,* it shall be from an abundant and overflowing measure.* Happily indeed shall we rejoice in the body's glorification, but not as our primary joy. *Your wife*, it is written, *like a fruitful vine on the sides of your house.** Thus shall the flesh be honored, but according to its own measure, not dwelling in the middle of the divine home* but rather separately, not before the soul but on the side. *Your children like olive shoots around your table.** Certainly our good works shall not be lacking, but we must do our good deeds now, not then,* as it is written: *For their works follow them.** Certainly then, let us rejoice and give thanks to God for these works that we accomplish by God's grace. However, we shall not give works first place but seat them *around the table*, so to speak.

7. As we now dwell in the corporeal world, we are dependent on our bodies, by which our first parents violated the law of the Lord.* So this is not only a time for action but also a time for suffering and even more toil and sorrow for us all.† This is unappetizing food indeed, like barley bread.* It is as if a knight, one accustomed to luxury, offended the king and were forced from the palace.* He must then resort to the hospitality of one lowly servant. The knight will have to keep a servant's hovel as a hiding place and take strange food with his servant, exchange royal delicacies for rustic porridge and a nobleman's bed for a servant's dung heap, like that of the prophetic lamentation, *Those who were brought up in scarlet have embraced dung**—unless, of course, the prophet is actually deploring those noble creatures who forget their own* condition and deny their extreme wretchedness. They not only lower their standards on what they can tolerate but even embrace

*Ps 15:2, 11
*Ps 16:15

*Phil 3:21
*Luke 6:38

*Ps 127:3

*Ps 100:7
*Ps 127:3

*see John 14:12
*Rev 14:13

*Ps 118:126
†Eccl 3:1-8; Ps 89:10
*see John 6:9, 61

*2 Sam 3:39

*Lam 4:5

*natural

as a great good that which they recently considered beyond the pale. So the prophet says about himself, *I am a man seeing my poverty as being from the rod of God's indignation.**

*Lam 3:1

8. Let us cry out under this burden, brothers, and let us deplore our present affliction. Let each one of us continually give voice to our sincere complaint, shouting, *Unhappy man that I am, who shall deliver me from the body of this death?** Now and then, let us be eager to withdraw ourselves and to steal away from the worst preoccupations for an hour: to thrust our souls, to stir our hearts unto what is their own right and to what is much more natural, to what is so much more pleasant for the human heart. For this is what is meant by the exhortation, *Be still and see that I am God.** For the vision is not for the eyes but for the heart, when the Lord says, *Blessed are the pure of heart, for they shall see God.** This essential good of the heart has no need for the body's services. There is a more appropriate food for the soul, concerning which the prophet says, *My heart has withered because I forgot to eat my bread.**

*Rom 7:24

*Ps 45:11

*Matt 5:8

*Ps 101:5

Most sensibly do we say, "Talk is cheap," especially compared to deeds. For the tongue is far more nimble than the hand, and the tongue is quicker to speak than the hand is moved to strike. Besides both talking and acting, thinking is easier still because in thought the soul speaks with its own mouth, sees with its own eyes, and works with its own hands. Yet even then the soul is wearied by its groans and cries of compunction upon its bed.‡ If indeed our lives have come so close to hell,* then this life is only a place of suffering for each and every one of us.

‡Ps 6:7; see Ps 4:5
*Ps 87:4

So it seems that suffering occupies all our actions, and what is more, action and suffering equally burden our thoughts. For is it not true that we have passive actions and both toil and sorrow in our thoughts?* How sad for the calf of Ephraim who has learned to

*Ps 89:10

love the threshing floor, having grown accustomed to
the yoke, having become a stranger to serenity!* *When
shall I come and appear before the face of God?** When will
all these troubles cease?* When will there be no longer
any mourning or wailing, or any sorrow, or any
toil?* When will the abundance of God's home and
the unfailing torrent of divine pleasure inebriate my
soul?* When will the contemplation of that most tranquil light set free my entire soul?

    *Hos 10:11
    *Ps 41:3
    *see 1 Cor 13:8

    *Rev 21:4

    *see Ps 35:9

Little children, let us long for the courts of the Lord.*
Let us often sigh with yearning for those halls. It is
indeed our homeland. Let us at least breathe its fragrance and hail it from afar.*

    *Ps 83:3

    *see Heb 11:13-14

Sermo 3

The Song of Hezekiah*

*commentary on Isa 38:10-20

1. **M**en of blood and deceit shall not live out half their days,* persevering in their old age¹ until death, because they do not fear God.* However, those who are initiated into wisdom by the fear of God* have already attained half of their days when they cry out in fear, *I shall approach the gates of hell.** When for fear of hell they begin to withdraw from bad behavior, they begin to seek consolation from good behavior, because it is necessary to be consoled in living either well or badly. There is moreover good consolation from the hope of eternal salvation. For once sins have been removed, sins that *separated you from your God,** God's grace gives renewed life and joy.

When one begins to make progress in this new life, that is, *to live divinely** in Christ, Scripture testifies that one must also s*uffer persecution.** One's newfound joy is changed into grief,* and the sweetness of a good life has scarcely touched the lips, so to speak, when it is changed into bitterness. So one may well say, *My harp is turned to mourning and my singing into the voice of those who weep.** Therefore we weep more bitterly for losing the sweetness than when weeping previously for allowing the bitterness of sin. We weep for so long until, after God takes pity, consolation returns.

*Ps 54:24

*Ps 54:20
*see Sir 1:16

*Isa 38:10

*Isa 59:2

*pie
*2 Tim 3:12
*see John 16:20

*Job 30:31

---

¹ *perseverantes in sua vetustate*: perhaps an allusion to Rom 6:6; see also Eph 4:22; Col 3:9.

When consolation returns anew, we recognize that we have suffered a temptation, that it was a test and not abandonment. What is more, it was a test for our edification,* not for destruction, as it is written: *You visit him early in the morning, and you test him suddenly.** When we realize that progress is made in temptation, then we will not only cease to flee temptation but even strive to be tested: *Test me, O Lord,* he says, *and try me.** *Taste and see,* for a time, *that the Lord is sweet.** We make progress by the frequent alternation between the visit of grace and the test of temptation in the school of virtue, so that the visits of grace keep us from failing and the temptations keep us from becoming proud. Finally, by such exercise, the interior eye becomes cleansed; at once the light is present, light to which we desire to cling firmly. But then, pressed by the body, we do not prevail; unwilling and grieving, we bounce back to ourselves.

*see Rom 5:3-4
*Job 7:18

*Ps 25:2

*1 Pet 2:3; Ps 34:8

Having tasted, to some extent, *that the Lord is sweet,** when we have returned to ourselves we will retain the taste of the Lord in the palate of our heart. We will then desire God himself rather than some goods from God. And this is the charity that *does not seek its own,** charity that makes the Son seek not his own will but to love the Father.* Fear would certainly make slaves seek their own interest, but hope makes employees pursue their own profit.

*1 Pet 2:3; Ps 34:8

*1 Cor 13:4-5

*see John 14:31

2. No doubt Hezekiah has passed through these steps; he made it known to those who were about to pass through when he said, *In the midst of my days I shall go to the gates of hell,** as if he were to say, "When, having laid aside the image of the earthly man, I began wishing to bear the image of the heavenly man,** which I conceived by a fear of God,** as Scripture teaches, I exclaimed, *I shall go to the gates of hell.*"*

*Isa 38:10

*1 Cor 15:47-49
*see Isa 26:17-18
*Isa 38:10

By this fear, however, I never despaired; rather, *I sought the remainder of my years.** Thus I could begin to

*Isa 38:10

live for myself, though I had lived contrary to my own good up until then. Moreover, I sought him who has said, *Without me you can do nothing.** For I say that I could not return to him without him; rather, I could not even turn toward him, insofar as I was *a wind going and not returning.*‡ *I sought*, therefore, *the remainder of my years.** Having received it—for God does not refuse those whom he inspires to seek him—at once I experienced the true meaning of Wisdom, who says, *Son, when you come to the service of God, stand in fear, and prepare your soul for temptation.**

*John 15:5

‡Ps 77:39; *wind = spiritus*

*Isa 38:10

*Sir 2:1

And so when I was hard pressed by temptations and the newfound hope of salvation seemed already to be cut off, I said, *I shall not see my Lord in the land of the living*,* because in my abundance I had been presumptuous. For *I have said in my abundance: I shall never be moved*,* on which account, *You turned away your face from me, and I became troubled*;* never now *shall I see the Lord God*, that is the Father, *in the land of the living. I shall behold humans no more.** Clearly the latter refers to the Son, who is said to be human, yet Scripture also asks, *who has known him?*# Even less shall I see *the one who dwells in repose*,* that is, the Holy Spirit, about whom it is written, *Over whom shall my Spirit rest if not over the one who is humble and peaceful?**

*Isa 38:11

*Ps 29:7
*Ps 29:8

*Isa 38:11

#see John 10:33; 14:9; Rom 11:34

*Isa 38:11

*Isa 66:2

3. Hezekiah also adds, *My generation has been swept away, and it has been rolled away from me.** This *generation* means the offspring of good works, which I had started to bring forth out of fear.* Therefore it could be said about our soul, *She that had many children is weakened.** This godly° progeny, moreover, *has been swept away, and it has been rolled away from me like a shepherd's tent.** It was entrusted to me for a time, though not handed over forever. In the same vein Hezekiah continues, *My life has been cut off as by a weaver*,* so that I would learn that the progress of my life is not in my hand but in the hand of the Creator, just like threads

*Isa 38:12

*see Isa 26:17-18

*1 Sam 2:5
°*pia*

*Isa 38:12

*Isa 38:12

in the hand of a weaver. For *while I was only just beginning*, that is, right at the start, *he cut me off.** Nearly at the same moment that God gives, he also takes what he gives.* But if my strength has failed, he does not abandon me, lest he who had begun a work seem unable to finish.* So then what?

In truth, I soon discovered that *power is made perfect in weakness.** I say, *It is good for me that you have humbled me.** I have learned that *from morning until evening you will finish me,** that is, you shall bring me to perfection. Not only in the morning of your visit or just in the evening of temptation,* but in both together will be my perfection. I was the stupid one who only *hoped until morning,** when David would say, *From the morning watch even until night; let Israel hope in the Lord.** *As a lion so has he broken all my bones** because of my puny hope. That is, he broke all my strength, on which I had naïvely relied for the future when I was still under the protection of grace. Who, however, has broken my strength if not *our adversary the devil*, who, *as a roaring lion, goes about seeking whom he may devour?** So you, Lord, having brought me humbled and tested out of this grief, *from morning until evening you finish me,** because *morning and evening was made, one day.**

4. For that reason have I learned: *I will bless the Lord at all times,*† that is, *morning and evening,*# not like the one who *will praise you when you do well for him,** not like those *who believe for a while, and in time of temptation, they fall away.** Rather, I shall say with the saints, *If we have received good things from the hand of the Lord, then why should we not bear bad things?**

In the morning indeed, *I will cry like a young swallow.* In the evening, however, *I will meditate like a dove.** For when the morning of grace shall smile, like a swallow exulting and calling, I will give thanks for the visit. And when the evening shall approach, an *evening sacrifice** will not be lacking. Moaning like a dove,* I will shed

*Isa 38:12

*see Job 1:21

*see Ps 70:9; Phil 1:6

*2 Cor 12:9
*Ps 118:71
*Isa 38:12-13

*see Matt 4:1-4

*Isa 38:13
*Ps 129:6
*Isa 38:13

*1 Pet 5:8

*Isa 38:13
*Gen 1:5
†Ps 33:2
#Gen 1:5
*Ps 48:19

*Luke 8:13

*Job 2:10

*Isa 38:14

*Ps 140:2
*see Isa 59:11; Nah 2:7

tears in distress. For thus each time serves God, when both *in the evening weeping shall linger and in the morning gladness.** I will grieve mournfully in the evening, and so all the more happily I will enjoy the morning. Each is pleasing to God, both the sinner who is remorseful and the just one who is faithful. On the other hand, an ungrateful righteous person displeases God as much as a self-satisfied sinner.

*Ps 29:6

Or certainly *like a young swallow* rushing about here and there, I will surrender myself to the duties of Martha,* offering myself as a cheerful giver‡ to everyone who suffers need.# Likewise, *I will meditate like a dove* by lamenting whatever stands in my way while considering what remains to be done. I will do this morning and evening, that is, before and after,* according to both the active and the contemplative life, about which Laban spoke: *It is not our custom to give the younger daughter in marriage first.** Nevertheless, one alternates from one life to the other indifferently.* I think that Job also signified this when he said, *If I lie down to sleep, I will say, When shall I arise? And then in turn I will look for the evening.** I rest, of course, in the evening of contemplation, desiring the morning when I will arise and act. Then again I wearily await the evening, gladly returning to the leisure of contemplation.

*see Luke 10:40
‡see 2 Cor 9:7
#see Eph 4:28

*my work

*Gen 29:26
*see Gen 29:16-30

*Job 7:4

5. One could interpret the chattering little swallow as the singing in church and the moaning dove as the private sighs of prayer. But the following verse offers a better interpretation of the two: *My eyes are strained looking upward.** Does Hezekiah mean by *strained* that his eyes see more subtlety because he attentively looks to heaven, that is, he contemplates sublime and lofty matters? Or should we understand *strained* to mean dazzled, that the sharpness of his eyes is somehow diminished, according to the psalm: *My eyes have failed for your word.** And again: *I remembered God and was delighted, and I was exercised, and my spirit swooned away.** Whether we accept the former or the latter in-

*Isa 38:14

*Ps 118:82
*Ps 76:4

terpretation, Hezekiah must mean nothing other than contemplation.

This latter explanation seems to harmonize better with the following verse, for Hezekiah says, *Lord, I suffer violence,** as if he were to say, "Lord, not voluntarily, but reluctantly am I brought back and prevented from contemplation of you." *For the corruptible body weighs down upon the soul, and the earthly habitation presses down the mind that muses upon many things.** Therefore, *Answer for me,** my Creator, you who have known firsthand the condition of my nature. Or if my sins weigh me down, then it is not the fault of nature, but of my worst habit. Just the same, *answer for me, fastening* my sins *to the cross and blotting them out with your blood** so that nothing may hinder me from contemplation. For *what shall I say, or what shall he answer for me, when he himself has done it?** To whom else shall I turn, or who else will answer for me, since he himself, not another, has imposed this difficulty, impossibility rather, upon me, by uttering the sentence upon me, *In the sweat of your face you shall eat your bread.**

*Isa 38:14

*Wis 9:15
*Isa 38:14

*Col 1:20; 2:14

*Isa 38:15

*Gen 3:19

6. But if Hezekiah had said, "I have done it" rather than "he has done it," then he would have blamed himself. In this matter, when he offered the excuse of nature, he as it were threw the blame back on his Creator, and he ascribes the whole matter to himself and to his sins, saying, *What shall I say or what shall he answer for me, when* I myself *have done it?** In other words, I have deserved that which I suffer for my sin.

*Isa 38:15

On that account I am able to do one thing: *I will recount to you all my years in the bitterness of my soul.** Truly I am not worthy to ponder you with sweetness. I will do what I am able: I will consider myself *in the bitterness of my soul. You dwell in inaccessible light,** so I cannot fix the weak glance of my mind on the ray of your splendor for long. For that reason I return confused to the usual and familiar darkness of my former life.* I certainly do not return so to be thrown into darkness again

*Isa 38:15

*1 Tim 6:16

*see Eph 4:22

with fatal pleasure, but by punishing and recalling it *in the bitterness of my soul.*

Indeed it was necessary, if it had been possible, to revive myself anew, as I speak, because I have lived badly. Because I cannot do this, then at least *I will recount to you all my years in the bitterness of my soul.** I will revive myself by remembering because I am not able to redo my life. Moreover, *I shall recount to you,* because *against you alone have I sinned.* That way, in whatever I condemn myself, *you,* Mercy, *shall be justified and you shall prevail when you judge me.** Indeed, I had already considered my sins before, but because they were not punished enough, they can still hold me back. So again I return to recounting my former life *in the bitterness of my soul* until the time that my sins may be so deeply rooted out that they are no longer able to impede me.

7. I do not believe that this devotion will be fruitless. It is certainly not fruitless *if one's life is thus,** or rather, because one's life is in the spirit‡ and certainly not in the flesh, *and the life of my spirit is in such things as these.*# In other words, by so considering myself and so contemplating you, more and more *you shall correct me and make me to live.** If indeed I am corrected when I feel remorse by examining my life, then I have been raised up with you, and I am revived insofar as I gaze upon you. And so by my showing myself to myself, you shall correct me; by you showing yourself, you make me live.

It is necessary, in turn, that you make me live, because *behold, in peace is my bitterness most bitter.** I have suffered a bitter bitterness for my sins in the beginning of my conversion, whence I have *exclaimed: I shall go to the gates of hell.** It was more bitter still in the face of my fears when I set out on my conversion, and so I said, *I shall not see the Lord God in the land of the living.** But behold now, my sins have been punished by repentance, and my fears have been put to rest, fears that routinely assailed me. In this peace, however, I suffer a most bitter bitterness for lack of contemplation.

*Isa 38:15

*Ps 50:6

*Isa 38:16
‡see Rom 2:28-29
#Isa 38:16

*Isa 38:16

*Isa 38:17

*Isa 38:10

*Isa 38:11

Truly you have also forgiven my sins by your compassion, and you have conquered my temptations by helping me, so even now, O Lord, *restore to me the joy of your salvation.** This indeed is what Hezekiah says: *You have delivered my soul so that it should not perish.** In the combat of sins or in the attack of temptations, *You have cast all my sins behind your back,** *according to the multitude of your mercies.**

*Ps 50:14
*Isa 38:17
*Isa 38:17
*Ps 50:3

8. Not without reason: *for hell shall not confess to you.** I myself had nearly descended to hell when I was struck by an onslaught of temptations. Indeed, *Unless the Lord had been my helper, my soul had almost dwelt in hell.** But *death shall not praise you,** death that evidently detained me for some time, so long as I lay dead in my sins. *Nor shall they who go down into the pit look for your truth.** This of course refers to those who, after tasting the sweetness of contemplation, descend into the pit of despair. *Death* is for those who lie in their sins before their conversion; *hell* is for those who succumb to temptations after receiving forgiveness; the *pit* must be for those who despair after losing contemplation. For the more one achieves the heights, the more heavily one is crushed and ruined if one falls.

*Isa 38:18
*Ps 93:17
*Isa 38:18
*Isa 38:18

And *so hell shall not confess to you*, that is, those who have already been converted but are overcome by temptations. *Nor shall death praise you,** which refers to those who, not yet converted or confessing, *are* more *glad when they have done evil, and they rejoice in the most wicked affairs.** Indeed, *praise*† *perishes from the dead as though it were nothing.*# *Nor shall they who go down into the pit look for your truth*, which perhaps refers to those who have fallen down from the summit of divine contemplation into the pit of deep faithlessness. This without doubt would be anyone who after having received so much joy is overwhelmed by excess sadness.

*Isa 38:18
*Prov 2:14
†*confessio*, alternatively "confession"
#Sir 17:26

But in fact, *Living, the living shall give praise to you.** One who lives in the flesh is dead in the spirit, and likewise one might be as dead in the flesh as such a one

*Isa 38:19

is in the spirit,* but neither of these shall praise you or confess to you. On the other hand, *Living, the living shall give praise to you*, namely, those who live not just in the flesh but in the spirit: *He shall give praise to you as I do this day.** I trust that I live this twofold life by your gift.

9. It follows, *The father shall make known your truth to the children.** Truth is not revealed to the slave, *for the slave knows not what his lord does.** But neither is the employee snatched up in contemplating truth, the employee who seeks his own advantage.* To the son, however, *the Father will make known his truth*, the son whom he hears saying, *Nevertheless, not what I will, but what you will, Father.**

And so the *power* of God is revealed to the slave,* *happiness* is revealed to the employee, *truth* to the son. Not that these things are separate in God, to whom they are all one power, for what is happy is also truthful. But of course the Creator is perceived by the creature from various aspects and according to various affections of the same creature, for *With the holy, I shall be holy, and with the perverse I shall be perverse.**

Hear at last the voice of the son: *O Lord, save me.** Why? Perhaps he fears to burn in hell, or perhaps he may be cheated of his reward? No, he says, *But we will sing our psalms all the days of our life in the house of the Lord.** I do not, he says, seek salvation so to avoid punishment or to reign in heaven, but to praise you for eternity with those of whom it is written, *Blessed are they who dwell in your house, O Lord. They shall praise you for ever and ever.**

The slave says, *I shall go to the gates of hell*. The employee says, *I shall not see the Lord God in the land of the living*. The son says, *We will sing our psalms all the days of our life in the house of the Lord.** The last verse is similar to the following: *Open to me the gates of justice. I will go into them and give praise to the Lord.**

*Rom 8:9, 13

*Isa 38:19

*Isa 38:19
*John 15:15

*see John 10:12

*Matt 26:39; Mark 14:36

*see Rom 1:18

*Ps 17:26-27
*Isa 38:20

*Isa 38:20

*Ps 83:5

*Isa 38:10-11, 20

*Ps 117:19

Surely both the one who fears to go to the gates of hell and the one who wants to see God for his own repose *seek things that are their own.** In turn, those who desire to sing psalms in the house of the Lord flee not even their own dangers or even strive after profit, but without doubt they love the Lord, whom they are eager to praise all the days of their life. He is praised for eternity, and not without cause, he who lives and reigns through all ages forever. Amen.

*1 Cor 13:5; Phil 2:21

Sermo 4

On Seeking God, and the Triple Bonds by Which We Cling to God

1. We do not *stand here the whole day idle*, for we know both what we seek and who is the one who *hired us*.* We seek God; *we wait for God*.* This is no small matter, and not for a petty soul, since she who boasts the singular name of Piety very often complains that her quest is in vain, saying, *I sought him, and I found him not*.* For just as he is to be loved, so he is also to be admired, because when *he is not sought, then he is found, and when he is sought, then he is not found*.* If we had been born when the first man on earth was created, and our life were extended for one hundred thousand years, the quest *of this time* would not be *worthy of comparison to the future glory that shall be revealed in us*.*

Behold now the time of seeking, *behold now the day* of finding are at hand.‡ *Seek*, he says, *the Lord while he can be found; call upon him while he is near!*# There will come a time when there shall be no opportunity, when that spring of mercy shall dry up with an endless dryness. *You will seek me*, he says, *and you shall not find me*.*

You are good, Lord, to the soul who seeks you.* If you are good to one who seeks, how much more to one who finds? If the memory is so sweet, how excellent will be

*Matt 20:6-7
*Mic 7:7

*Song 3:2

*Isa 65:1

*Rom 8:18
‡2 Cor 6:2; see Eccl 3:6
#Isa 55:6

*John 7:34
*Lam 3:25

your presence? If *honey and milk* is sweet *under the tongue,** then how will it taste over the tongue?

2. Henceforth test yourselves, brothers, so you will know whether you are on the right path or if you have gone astray. *Let the heart of them rejoice that seek the Lord*, says the psalmist.* If you rejoice in your toil, if *you run the way of God's commands** with an uninterrupted and tireless stride, if every day the condition of both your inner man and outer man is more ready for progress and perfection than it was in the beginning,† then indeed *you always seek his face.**

Then *to where has your beloved departed from his loved one? We also shall seek him.** In other words, where is God? What have I said? Wretched me! For where is he not? He is higher than heaven, deeper than hell, wider than the earth, more vast than the sea. He is nowhere and he is everywhere, because no place is without him, nor does any place contain him. He himself is here,* but I myself am not here. It should seem more plausible, Lord, that I would be here and you would not! But I myself am not here, nor am I elsewhere, because *I am brought to nothing and I knew not.** Truly *to nothing*, that is, to sin, *and I knew not* because I was not there when my first parent *devoured* me *with a most bitter bite.** This is why, broken in heart and body, I waste away in carnal pleasures, wholly feeble and limp, in bitter feelings, having an inborn guilt and its associated punishment. God, however, *is always the same.*† He has said, *I am who I am;** he is in truth the one for whom *being* is what he is.

3. Therefore, *what participation, what fellowship** can there be between one who is not and him who is? How can two such diverse natures be joined? *For me*, says the saint, *it is good to adhere to my God.** It is not possible to be joined to him directly, but perhaps this union can be made through some medium.

Let me come right to the point: there are three bonds by which we are bound to him, only three. With these

*Song 4:11

*Ps 104:3
*Ps 118:32

†see Luke 14:28, 30
*Ps 104:4

*Song 5:9, 17

*see Matt 24:23

*Ps 72:22

*Deut 32:24

†Ps 101:28
*Exod 3:14

*2 Cor 6:14-15

*Ps 72:28

alone, or bonds similar to them, everything that is fastened may be fastened. First, know that there is rope, second is wooden pegs or iron nails, and third is glue. The first one binds strongly and durably, the second more strongly and more durably, the third gently and securely.

In a way, one is tied to the Redeemer with a rope if perhaps while troubled by a violent temptation one keeps in mind a vision of integrity and a memory of God's promise. And all the while one restrains oneself by this rope lest one's commitment be completely severed. This bond certainly is harsh and troublesome, but it is also exceedingly dangerous, because it cannot hold for a long time. The ropes rot, you see, and we either forget or quickly break the bond of shame.* *Jer 13:6-9

One is also fastened to the Lord of Majesty by nails. That is, one who is bound by fear of God,* one who is not frightened in the face of human beings but rather at the memory of Gehenna's torments. Such a person does not so much dread to sin as to burn in hell. Nevertheless, this bond has a stronger and more durable impact than the first. For while the first wavers in its commitment, this fear of God does not lose its commitment. *see Ps 118:120; 1 Cor 2:8

Third, one sticks to God with glue, that is by divine love, which binds as gently as it does securely: *one who is joined to the Lord is one spirit* with him.* This is one who in every way and in every circumstance, whether in what he does or in what happens to him, recovers it and turns it to his advantage. Such people are blessed, and their spirits flow with abundant majesty. Gentle and anointed, they bear all and are carried by all, yet they burden no one. In fact, they consciously consider that offending the face of the All Powerful, even in a small matter, is more frightful and horrible than Gehenna. *This is a lover of his brothers and of the people of Israel. This is he who prays much for the people and for the* *1 Cor 6:17

holy city Jerusalem.* *The soldering is good,* says Isaiah.† This third bond—divine love—is good and pleasant indeed# because, though I would not say the first two fasteners are bad, they are by comparison *heavy and hard to bear.*‡

4. But that merciful eye that *knows how we are made** leaves none of those who are to be saved stuck in the first bond (shame), but he carries them forth to the second bond (fear), and, not abandoning them there, he leads them through from the second to the third (divine love). With the first bond, since we are ashamed to give up, we become so agitated that we can scarcely hold back for an hour. With the second bond, we already make progress with hope and fear. With the third bond, we are perfected by loving. So therefore, having removed the two preceding bonds (both fear and shame equally), we abide on the seat of love alone.*

So even Christ was first tied up with ropes, second nailed to a cross, and third rubbed with a sticky ointment of spices. Not that his body needed to be preserved whole with such spices, because it could not in any way be dissolved,* nor could it *see corruption,*† but he suffered spit from the Jews for us,# and so also for us he did not spurn the ointments of the faithful.‡ Notice that he remained tied by ropes and nails for scarcely one day; then, anointed and triumphant, he was resurrected to eternal life.

So also God does not suffer the elect to remain in the two aforementioned bonds. Rather, he anoints them with the ointment of his mercy as they are *crucified to the world and the world to them,** now rising up in a *newness of spirit,** so they may well ask, *Who will separate us from the love of God?**

5. With this glue, the divine vision has glued us to itself *from the foundation of the world so that we should be holy and unspotted in his sight, in divine love.**

We know that whosoever is born of God does not sin, because the generation of heaven preserves him.* The *generation*

*2 Macc 15:14
†Isa 41:7
#see Ps 132:1

‡Matt 23:4
*Ps 102:14

*see Song 3:10; 1:12

*see John 19:40; Phil 1:23
†Acts 2:27
#see Matt 26:67
‡see John 12:7-8; 19:40

*Gal 6:14
*Rom 7:6
*Rom 8:35

*Eph 1:4

*1 John 5:18

of heaven is eternal predestination, by which God has foreseen that we are *to be made conformable to the image of his Son.** None among those who are predestined shall sin;* that is, none persevere in sin, because *the Lord knows who are his own,** and God's commitment remains steadfast.*

Even if David was burned and branded by the mark of horrible crimes,* even if Mary Magdalene was possessed by seven demons,† and even if the prince of the apostles sank into a profound denial,# *there is* nevertheless *no one who can rescue anyone from God's hand.*‡ For those *whom he predestined, he also called. And those whom he called, he also justified.** Is it not *good for me to adhere to my God?**

Seek, brothers, *seek the Lord and be strengthened! Seek his face evermore!** *Seek the Lord and your soul shall live.*† *And my soul*, he says, *shall live for him*,# my soul that is dead to the world. For the soul that lives for the world does not live for God. So therefore let us seek him; let us always seek him so that when he comes to seek us, he will say about us, *This is the generation of them that seek him, of them that seek the face of the God of Jacob.** And so *be lifted up, O eternal gates, and let him enter, the King of Glory,** and we with him *who is God, blessed forever.** Amen.

*Rom 8:29
*see 1 John 3:6
*2 Tim 2:19
*see Rom 9:11; Heb 6:18
*see 2 Sam 11:1-12
†see Luke 8:2
#see Matt 26:69-75
‡Deut 32:39
*Rom 8:30
*Ps 72:28
*Ps 104:4
†Ps 68:33
#Ps 21:31
*Ps 23:6
*Ps 23:7
*Rom 9:5

Sermo 5

On the Words of Habakkuk 2:1:
I will stand upon my watch

1. **W**e read in the gospel that, while the Lord was preaching, he admonished his disciples *to share in his sufferings** under the mystery of eating his body.* At this, certain disciples said, *This saying is hard.** And *from then on* they were *no longer with him.** When Jesus asked the other disciples if they *also wish to go away,* they answered, *Lord, to whom shall we go? You have the words of eternal life.** So I say to you, brothers, even to this day it is obvious to certain people that *the words that* Jesus *speaks are spirit and life,** and so they follow him. To others Jesus' words seem hard, and they seek wretched consolation elsewhere.

Wisdom shouts in the streets,* that is, in *the wide and broad way that leads to death** in order to call back those who stray down the deadly way. *For forty years,* God says in fact, *was I close to this generation, and I said, They always err in heart.** You find in another psalm, *God has spoken one time;** certainly only one time, because always. For his speech is one and constant, continuous and perpetual.

2. *He calls back,* moreover, *sinners to their heart,** and he refutes the heart's error, because God himself dwells there. And he speaks in the heart as well, doing what he teaches, of course, through the prophet who says, *Speak to the heart of Jerusalem!**

*1 Pet 4:13
*see John 6:52
*John 6:61
*John 6:67

*John 6:68-69

*John 6:64

*Prov 1:20-21
*Matt 7:13

*Ps 94:10
*Ps 61:12

*Isa 46:8

*Isa 40:2

For Babylon, because she is *the land, is not able to bear all his words.** She is withdrawn from the heart, and *she walks* more *in the flesh,*† *as though dead from the heart,*# rather *like a dove that is led astray, not having a heart.*‡ Indeed Babylon wants *to rejoice when she has done evil and to exult in the most wicked deeds.** When Babylon hears the voice of the Lord, which in no way approves such joy but instead detests, but instead accuses, but instead condemns, then she flees and hides herself in imitation of Adam.* But woe is me! How worthless is the covering you seek, my wretched soul! How useless to seek a covering! For leaves are what you weave,* leaves, I say, that provide no warmth for you and are too flimsy to last. So in the end *when the sun rises they shall be scorched;** *as a burning wind will I scatter them.*† *You* shall in fact remain *naked and wretched.*#

And so *there is nothing covered that shall not be revealed,*‡ because *the Lord will come who will bring to light the hidden things of darkness and will make manifest the counsels of hearts.** Then there will be nothing with which to hide, wretched Babylon. In vain *you will say to the mountains: Fall upon us! And to the hills: Cover us!*† For *naked* and *exposed*# *you* must stand *before the judgment seat of Christ,*‡ so that you hear the voice of Judgment, you who scorned the voice of counsel. For behold what the Lord says: *Do penance!** And many ignore him and *stop their ears,*† and they say, *This saying is hard.*# *Not so the wicked, not so*‡ will you be able to ignore him when that *sharp word*° and *the evil report* shall sound:∞ *Depart, you cursed ones, into everlasting fire.*◊

3. You see, brothers, how beneficially the prophet admonishes us: *If today we hear his voice, harden not our hearts.** You read nearly the same words in the gospel as in the prophet, for the Lord says in the gospel, *My sheep hear my voice.** And Saint David says in a psalm, *we are his people* (no doubt the Lord's people) *and the sheep of his pasture. If today you shall hear his voice, harden not your hearts.**

*Amos 7:10
†2 Cor 10:3
#Ps 30:13
‡Hos 7:11

*Prov 2:14

*see Gen 3:8

*see Gen 3:7

*Matt 13:6
†Jer 18:17
#Rev 3:17
‡Luke 12:2

*1 Cor 4:5

†Luke 23:30; Hos 10:8
#Heb 4:13
‡2 Cor 5:10

*Ezek 18:30; Matt 3:2
†Acts 7:56
#John 6:61
‡Ps 1:4
°Ps 90:3
∞Ps 111:7
◊Matt 25:41

*Ps 94:8

*John 10:27

*Ps 94:7-8

It is in fact much more useful and beneficial to hear the Lord's voice today counseling, consoling, admonishing, teaching, and, just as likely, accusing us, than later to hear God's angry voice punishing and condemning us. I say *it is good for me that he humbles me;** it is good that *the just shall correct me in mercy and they shall reprove me* rather than let *the oil of the sinner anoint my head,** lest perhaps I am found to be a *land which he strikes with the rod of his mouth,** when *vessels of a potter are shattered with a rod of iron.** It is good for me, along with the prophet, *for the sake of the words of his lips to keep hard ways,** rather than together with *the wicked to be slain by the breath of his lips.**

*Ps 118:71

*Ps 140:5

*Isa 11:4
*Ps 2:9

*Ps 16:4
*Isa 11:4

4. Now if I sense any bitterness in his voice, it is not without sweetness, because *when he is angry, he will remember mercy.** What is more, even his indignation itself comes from nowhere else than his mercy. For *those whom he loves, he accuses and chastises,** and he *scourges every son whom he receives,** visiting his iniquities with a rod and his sins with flogging, but he will not take away his mercy from him.*

*Hab 3:2

*Rev 3:19
*Heb 12:6

*Ps 88:33-34

Therefore, those who are sensible do not cover their wounds but reveal them, and *they give praise to the Lord, for he is good, for his mercy endures for ever.** That way God pours in the wine of correction, and the oil of consolation will not be lacking.* Therefore, I say, the wise person *embraces discipline lest at any time the Lord be angry.** Even then, *God will not seek him according to the multitude of his wrath,** and *his jealousy shall depart from him.** For thence *the heart of the wise is where there is mourning, and the heart of fools where there is mirth,** but *the wise person's sorrow shall be turned into joy,** and *in the end, mourning shall replace the joy* of fools.*

*Ps 117:1

*Luke 10:34

*Ps 2:12

*Ps 2:12
*Ps 9:25
*Ezek 16:42
*Eccl 7:5
*John 16:20
*Prov 14:13

Hear again the prophet Habakkuk, how he does not ignore the Lord's rebuke; rather, he is turned around with attentive and anxious thoughts about the rebuke. For he says, *I will stand upon my watch and fix my position* upon the fortification so that I may see what is said to me and what I may answer to the one who accuses me.*

And I beseech you, brothers, let us stand upon our watch, because now is the time of soldiery. Let not our conversion be on the dunghill of this wretched body, but *in the heart* where *Christ dwells*.* Let our conversion be on the judgment and counsel of reason, so that we do not rely so much on our conversion or lean on the fragile *watch,* but *let us fix our position on the fortification,* leaning with all our might on the most solid *rock that is Christ,* as it is written: *He set my feet upon a rock and directed my steps.* And so thus established and made firm, *let us now contemplate in order to see what he might say to us and what we might answer to the one who accuses us.*

5. The first step of contemplation is this, beloved brothers, constantly to consider what the Lord wills and what pleases him, *what is acceptable before him.* Because *in many things we all offend,* and our crookedness offends against the rectitude of his will; our crooked wills cannot be joined or conformed to his will. So *let us be humbled under the mighty hand of God* most high,* and may we be in every way anxious not to present ourselves as wretched in his merciful eyes, saying, *Heal me, O Lord, and I shall be healed. Save me, and I shall be saved.* And again, *O Lord, be merciful to me. Heal my soul, for I have sinned against you.*

For after the eye of the heart has been cleansed by thoughts of this kind, we no longer dwell in our spirit with bitterness, but more in the divine spirit with much pleasure. And we no longer consider what is the will of God in us, but what is God's will in itself. Since *life is in his will,* we do not doubt that everything that corresponds to his will is more useful and therefore more advantageous for us. And therefore, just as we anxiously wish to preserve the life of our souls, let us be equally anxious not to deviate from God's will for as long as we can.

*Hab 2:1

*Eph 3:17

*Hab 2:1

*1 Cor 10:4
*Ps 39:3

*Hab 2:1

*Wis 9:10
*Jas 3:2

*1 Pet 5:6

*Jer 17:14
*Ps 40:5

*Ps 29:6

When we have made some progress in spiritual exercise, following the leader, the *Spirit, who searches even the deep things of God,** let us then ponder *how sweet is the Lord,** how good he is in himself, praying with the prophet *that we may see the will of the Lord, and we may visit* no longer our own heart but *his temple.** And we will likewise say with the same prophet, *My soul is troubled within myself; therefore will I remember you.** That is to say, the whole summit of spiritual conversion dwells in these two:* that when we consider ourselves we are troubled and saddened in a salutary way,[1] and that in the divine, we enjoy rest and consolation from joy of the Holy Spirit.* From considering ourselves comes fear and humility; from divine consolation we take up true hope and charity.

*1 Cor 2:10
*Ps 33:9

*Ps 26:4

*Ps 41:7

*Matt 22:40

*1 Thess 1:6

---

[1] *ad salutem*: with remorse and humility, which bring healing and edification, not unlike tears of repentance.

SERMO 6

On the Skin, Flesh, and Bones of the Soul

*Ps 33:20-21

1. In Psalm 33, blessed David speaks about the just, saying, *Many are the afflictions of the just, but out of them all will the Lord deliver them. The Lord protects all their bones; not one of them shall be broken.** Let no one suppose that David was speaking about bodily bones, especially when the bones of so many blessed martyrs were broken at the hands of wicked people and were crushed by the teeth of beasts.

Still, the condition of human souls ought to inspire both wonder and pity. Although souls keenly perceive so much of exterior nature, they nevertheless have no insight by which they can consider or know themselves just as they are. Rather, souls are utterly dependent on certain *riddles and figures** from corporeal images, so that, to some extent anyway, they are able to imagine the invisible and internal by means of visible and exterior images. And so, for instance, let us suppose that a soul's thought is its skin and the affection[1] is its flesh; consequently we can accept bone as the soul's intention. So the life of the soul will be in the integrity of the bone,

*Num 12:8

---

[1] *affectionem* "feeling," "disposition," or "emotion" may also be implied. *Affectio* and *affectus* are sometimes used interchangeably. In this sermon, the translator always translates *affectus* as *affection*, but he begs more flexibility for *affectio*.

health in the purity of the flesh, and beauty in the appearance of the skin.

What, therefore, are *afflictions of the just** if not the occasions when the skin is stained by a useless thought turning in the heart? In fact, sometimes even the flesh is wounded when a truly destructive thought proceeds beneath the skin to corrupt the affection with a perverse pleasure. For at least the bones of the just are protected completely whole and uninjured by the Lord,* so that the commitment of their heart is never broken, the intention of their salvation is never crushed, lest their approval should be given even to titillating concupiscence. For just as thinking about sin stains the skin and affection for sin wounds the flesh, so also consent surely kills the soul.

2. Therefore, my most beloved brothers, let us beware useless thoughts so that the face of our soul will remain handsome, as we *forget the things that are behind*,* that is, *our people and our father's house, so the king may desire our beauty.** *Let us go forth from our country*† so that thoughts that look to the pleasure of the flesh do not overtake us. *Let us go forth from our kinfolk*,* that is, from thoughts of curiosity, which undoubtedly, when it dwells in bodily senses, is at least akin to carnal pleasure. *Let us even go forth from our father's house*,* so that we may flee thoughts of pride and vanity. *We were at one time children of wrath even as the rest.** We were also *from our father the devil*,* who undoubtedly *is king over all the children of pride*,* and on the mountains of exaltation he has prepared for himself a throne and a most wretched dwelling place. If, at perhaps any time, some such thought sneaks up to the mind, let us quickly labor with all care to wash away and cleanse the filth by which we appear tainted, shouting with the prophet and saying, *sprinkle me with hyssop, and I shall be cleansed. You shall wash me, and I shall be made whiter than snow.**

*Ps 33:20

*see Ps 33:21

*Phil 3:13

*Ps 44:11-12
†Gen 12:1
*Gen 12:1

*Gen 12:1

*Eph 2:3
*John 8:44
*Job 41:25

*Ps 50:9

Now even if ever, through our carelessness and neglect, a useless thought shall *pass even into the affection of the heart*,* knowing that it is not now a stain but a wound, with all haste let us have recourse to the help of *the Spirit* who *helps in our weakness*,* shouting the word of the psalm and saying, *O Lord, be merciful to me. Heal my soul, for I have sinned against you*.* For these *temptations* are *human*,* and they cannot be completely avoided *as long as we sojourn from the Lord in* this *body of death*.* Let no one, however, make light of or ignore temptations, for if they are not deadly, they are certainly dangerous.

*Ps 72:7
*Rom 8:26
*Ps 40:5
*1 Cor 10:13
*2 Cor 5:6; see Rom 7:24

3. Let us be sure to guard carefully the intention and commitment of the mind, brothers, by which we wish to guard the life of our souls. For when *we commit offense, condemned by our own judgment** with consent and deliberation, then certainly it *is sin unto death*.* However, I should not have said that to cause anyone despair if perhaps one among you is conscious of this sin. Rather, I say it so he will fear that dangerous abyss, and *let one who has fallen* quickly turn his attention *to rising again*.*[2] Anyone who has deliberately sinned knows that he has fallen out of justice. His bone is broken and crushed. He knows that he is cut off from the body of Christ, concerning whom, no doubt, it is written, *You shall not break one of his bones*.*

*Titus 3:11
*1 John 5:16
*Jer 8:4; Ps 40:9
*Exod 12:46; John 19:36

Whence also in Christ's passion, granted that his skin was discolored by bruises from the blows of sticks, so that *by his bruises we were healed*,* granted that his flesh was wounded by clubs and [a soldier] *opened his side with a spear*,* so that we were redeemed by his blood, his bone, however, was not crushed. On that account, Saint David says, *My bone which you have made in secret is not hidden from you*.* And in another psalm he says,

*Isa 53:5
*John 19:34
*Ps 138:15

---

[2] Here Bernard is not so much quoting the Bible as using biblical language. He inserts *adjiciat citius*, paraphrased here.

My bones are grown dry like fuel for the fire,* because that is the point where the soul seems to have lost all enjoyment in good and reserves for itself only the strength of a dry intention.

And see, brother,[3] perhaps even blessed Job suffered such dryness, for he says, *my flesh has been consumed and my bone cleaves to my skin.** That is, with his affection corrupted, only spiritual intention (with difficulty) protects his thought.

*Ps 101:4

*Job 19:20

---

[3] The imperative *vide* is in the singular, suggesting that Bernard is speaking to only one of the monks.

Sermo 7

Concerning the Triple Glory

1. *Let the one who glories, glory in the Lord.** The apostle knew that glory properly belongs to the Creator, not the creature, according to the saying, *I will not give my glory to another.** And, *Glory to God in the highest and peace to human beings on earth.** And likewise, *Not to us, O Lord, not to us, but to your name give glory.** But the apostle considered this: rational creatures aspire to glory so much that they can almost never restrain this desire. The rational creature, of course, *was made to the image* of the Creator.* For that reason, *according to the wisdom given him* by God,* the apostle found this advice most edifying: Seeing that you cannot be persuaded to stop boasting entirely, at least *let one who glories, glory in the Lord.**

*1 Cor 1:31

*Isa 42:8
*Luke 2:14

*Ps 113:9

*Gen 9:6
*2 Pet 3:15

*1 Cor 1:31

Consider also how much the philosophy of Paul surpasses the philosophy *of the wise of this world,** which undoubtedly *is foolishness before God.** For when philosophers saw that some people enjoy the praise of others and that *they seek glory from one another,** the more distinguished among them wisely pointed out that such glory is empty and wholly to be condemned.

*1 Cor 1:20
*1 Cor 3:19

*John 5:44

But thence by considering and eagerly seeking what glory the wise person should desire, *they* obviously *became foolish in their thoughts,** for they supposed that one's own glory suffices for oneself, as if the soul, which cannot even exist by itself, could be blessed by itself. Therefore, just as those who desire praise from others

*Rom 1:21

dedicate, with all care, their effort to perform deeds that human beings admire and praise, so also these sages decided that this alone should be pursued: whatever the interior judge—the soul—approves.

2. And this notion is indeed the highest philosophy *of the wise of this world*,* yet it also falls short, even though it is nearer to truth. That is why the apostle who transcended both types of glory in contemplation of sublime truth says, *Let the one who glories* glory not in another person, glory not in oneself, but *let that one glory in the Lord*.* And the apostle refutes more carefully that glory that seemed to be nearer to truth; he condemns it with the sure judgment of truth when he says, *For the one who commends himself is not approved, but he whom God commends*.* Why then would I care about being judged by myself or by other human beings when their reproaches would not condemn me, nor would their praise make me worthy?

    Brothers, if I *must stand before* your *judgment seat*,* then rightly would I glory in your praise. On the other hand, if I were to be judged by my own standards, by rights I would be content with my own testimony and I would take pleasure in my own praise. But now since I must be presented for judgment neither by you nor by myself, but by the judgment of God, how great a foolishness, or rather, how great a madness is it to glorify myself either by your testimony or by my own? Especially because, for God my judge, *all things are naked and open to his eyes*,* and *he needs not for anyone to give him testimony concerning a human being*.*

    So then, rightly the apostle himself condemns empty and false glory: *For me*, he says, *it is a very small thing to be judged by you or by a human court, but neither do I judge my own self. For I am not conscious to myself of any thing; yet I am not justified in this, but he who judges me is the Lord*.* In these words one must also diligently consider that the judgment of another counts for almost nothing

*1 Cor 1:20

*1 Cor 1:31

*2 Cor 10:18

*2 Cor 5:10

*Heb 4:13
*John 2:25

*1 Cor 4:3-4

indeed. Also, he would by no means follow his own judgment. Still, the apostle judges that one's own judgment should not be dismissed completely: *For no one knows what is within a person except the spirit of the person that is in him,** so that in comparison to testimony from within, testimony from the outside should be held as absolutely nothing. For what is it to me if I should receive praise from people who do not really know me? Because if even the spirit itself within a person could know everything about the person, surely its testimony would suffice. Now, however, *the heart of a human being is perverse and inscrutable** even to the self. For you see, we are ignorant of the present for the most part, and we cannot know our own future at all. Nevertheless, because we know the present to some extent, *if our heart does not blame us*, we certainly do not have glory, but *we have confidence before God*,* just as blessed John says. When however we merit to possess knowledge of Truth itself, for which nothing about us lies hidden, clearly then we shall be able to glory in that knowledge more securely.

*1 Cor 2:11

*Jer 17:9

*1 John 3:21

3. In the meantime, *do not judge before the time*, says the apostle, *until the Lord comes who will bring to light the hidden things of darkness.** For that will be utterly perfect and safe glorification, when *every man shall have praise from God.**

*1 Cor 4:5

*1 Cor 4:5

Now also, though not fully, though not without fear and much concern, yet to some extent, let us glory in the Lord, for *the Holy Spirit himself has given testimony to our spirit that we are the children of God.** For in this we can truly glory, because we have so great a Father that, by his inexpressible majesty, *he has care of you.** Whence also the prophet says, Lord, *what is a man that you should magnify him? Or why do you set your heart upon him?**

*Rom 8:16

*1 Pet 5:7

*Job 7:17

And so let those who glory glory no longer in their own merits. For *what have you that you have not received? And if you have received, why do you glory as if you had not received it?** Therefore, let us glory in him from whom

*1 Cor 4:7

we have received, not as if we were great ourselves, but because God magnifies us.* In other words, let us glory in that which we have received, not as if we had not received from God, but as those who have received. For neither does the apostle say, "If you have received, why do you glory?" But rather, he says, *why do you glory as if you had not received?* So he does not prohibit glorying, but he means to teach us how to glory.

4. But what does the apostle mean when he says, *For no one who commends himself is approved, but only the one whom God commends?* Indeed, who is it whom God commends in this world? How will Truth commend one who is found thus far reprehensible? God says, in short, *Those whom I love, I rebuke and chastise.* Is this the whole commendation? By all means—it seems as much to me. For what could be a better and more effective commendation than witness of divine charity against us? Truly no testimony of his love is more credible, none more certain in this life, than what the prophet desired when he said, *The just one shall correct me in mercy, and he shall reprove me.*

In fact, by this rebuke, the Spirit of truth, in secret, will continually furnish to us what is lacking in us.* And so this rebuke will drive back pride, negligence, and ingratitude. All types of religious people labor more or less dangerously under this triple vice. That is why they have a less attentive heart's ear, and so they perceive less of what the Spirit says interiorly, the Spirit of truth, who flatters no one. For that reason, if I am not mistaken, it sometimes happens that those who desire self-glorification cannot rest on any account, for deep within themselves they find nothing about which they can boast at all. On the other hand, glorification is perfect and secure when *we fear all our works,* just as blessed Job testifies about himself,* and when we recognize with the prophet Isaiah that *all our righteousness is to be considered as the rag of a menstruating woman.**

*Job 7:17

*1 Cor 4:7

*2 Cor 10:18

*Rev 3:19

*Ps 140:5

*see John 14:26 and Ps 38:5

*Job 9:28

*Isa 64:6

Nevertheless, we trust in and even glory in the Lord, whose mercy upon us is so great that he even protects us from more serious sins, which *are unto death*.* And he so kindly deigns to show to us and to forgive the misdeeds of our imperfections and the impurity of our way of life insofar as we acknowledge them. To that extent, to which we are firmly rooted in humility, solicitude, and giving thanks, now *not in ourselves, but in the Lord let us glory*.*

*1 John 5:16

*Ps 113:9; 1 Cor 1:31

Sermo 8

On the Various Affections or States by which the Soul Is under God

1. We call God by various names: sometimes Father, sometimes Master or Lord. This is not because of any diversity in God's most simple and utterly invariable nature, but rather because of the multiple variations of our affections, according to varied progress or failure of the soul. For it seems that certain souls operate under the Head of the Household, others under the Lord, others under the Master, some others also under the Father, and a few with the Bridegroom. So God seems to progress with those who progress, to change with those who change.* Although, according to the prophet, God indeed *changes creatures and they shall be changed*, God himself is *always the same, and his years shall not fail.**

*see Ps 17:26-27

*Ps 101:27-28

What is more, listen to what the same prophet says to God in another psalm: *With the holy you will be holy. And with the innocent man you will be innocent. And with the elect you will be elect.* To our even greater astonishment, he says, *And with the perverse you will be perverted.** As to how he so changes, no, rather, how the immutable one himself makes change, the psalmist adds, *For you will save the humble people, and you will bring down the eyes of the proud.**

*Ps 17:26-27

*Ps 17:28

2. But seeing that *what is spiritual is not first, but that which is natural comes first and afterward that which is spiritual,*[*1 Cor 15:46*] there seem to me four states that sometimes precede our conversion: one under ourselves and three under *the prince of this world.*[*John 12:31*] I mean that the soul is under her own authority when she follows her own will, rejoicing in destructive liberty. This is that prodigal son who received *the portion of inheritance that falls to himself.*[*Luke 15:11-12*] That inheritance is of course his natural memory, his powers of the body, and other similar goods of nature, which he uses not according to the divine will but according to his own will. Therefore he was as though *without God in this world.*[*Eph 2:12*]

He*[*the prodigal*] is still at this time under his own power when he satisfies his will, though he is not yet possessed by vices and sins. For you see, *whosoever commits sin* serves not himself but *is the servant of sin.*[*John 8:34*] Now from here on, in fact, *he sets out into a far country,*[*Luke 15:13*] the prodigal who had earlier been separated from his father but had not yet departed. For indeed once he received his portion of the inheritance, he became independent.[1] Although he withdrew from his Creator,[2] he was nearby so long as he did not leave his work. His situation remained like this so long as he followed his own will within God's law, though not following what was truly expedient.

But afterward, he withdrew even from himself, turning aside even into sin. Truly then *he sets out into a far country*[*Luke 15:13*] because nothing is farther from God—who exists most singularly and superlatively*[*qui summe et singulariter est*]—than that which is nothing at all, i.e., sin. And nothing is more remote from God, *by whom and through whom and in whom* are *all things*[*Rom 11:36*] than sin, which, among all things, is nothing at all.

---

[1] *sui juris,* competent to manage his own affairs
[2] *auctore,* i.e., both parent and authority

3. In turn, the judgment of divine retribution is just, as when a foreigner took the father's runaway son as his slave. So we also read, *Having gone abroad into a far country,** *the son cleaved to one of the citizens.*† I think that we should understand this citizen to be none other than one of the malicious spirits who sin on account of their unreformed obstinacy. Such spirits have passed into an affection for malice and wickedness.* *Now they are strangers and foreigners,*# citizens and inhabitants of sin.

*Luke 15:13
†Luke 15:15

*see Ps 72:7; 1 Cor 5:8
#Eph 2:19

Why does it say that the poor young immigrant cleaved to a citizen if not because he was made subject to him? How he cleaved to the citizen is revealed further by what follows, for thus we read, *He cleaved to one of the citizens of that country, who sent him into his farm to feed swine.** And note how it says that he cleaved to the malicious citizen by the necessity of famine, just as we read that Israel descended into Egypt at the time of famine.* Hunger that enslaves free people into wretched servitude is clearly dangerous and destructive. It subjects them *to work in clay and bricks;** it associates them with pigs; no, rather, hunger even makes them slaves of pigs.

*Luke 15:15

*see Gen 46:6

*Exod 1:14

After having collected all his property, after receiving his own portion of the paternal inheritance, how has this young man, who had arrived wealthy, come to so great a poverty? No doubt this happened because he squandered his goods by living wantonly with harlots.* Therefore it says, *he began to suffer want.**

*Luke 15:13, 30
*Luke 15:14

4. Now understand these harlots to be carnal desires, with which the prodigal squandered nature's goods by living wantonly,* all the while misusing those goods for illicit pleasure. Hence, as we have said, a destructive poverty follows, as Scripture testifies: *The eye is not filled with seeing, neither is the ear filled with hearing.**

*Luke 15:13, 30

*Eccl 1:8

Therefore the prodigal is sent to feed pigs,* meaning, of course, bodily senses, which delight in wallowing in mud and filth.* And look, are these not perhaps the pigs that the evil spirits entered after being cast out

*Luke 15:15

*see 2 Pet 2:22

from a human being?* When sin has been cast out from our reason, that is, from the mind, it clings to bodily senses. The apostle so testifies that the mind consents to the law of God, but the flesh consents to the law of sin that is in our members.* So naturally the apostle says in another place, *I know that good dwells not in me, that is, in my flesh.** Then what should be done when the vile spirits have been cast out from a human being and they possess these proverbial pigs? We can only seek the remedy of tears; we run to these waters whose abundance drowns the wickedly vigorous root of sin,* although such an absolute extinction of sin seems reserved more for the end of time.

5. This digression was offered so that I might now more clearly explain how the Evil One subjugates anyone whom he gets under his power. He does so like an armed strongman entering and taking possession of a house* in which he finds the occupant poor and weak.‡ Still, there seems to me a triple manner in which human beings become subject to the Prince of Darkness.*

First, some victims are neither willing nor unwilling, in that the evil spirit unites with victims who do not yet have the use of their own will. They are no less *vessels of wrath** on account of original sin, until the strong spirit is tied up and he who is stronger arrives through the sacrament and plunders his vessels.* The stronger one is of course the true Moses, *who comes by water; not by water only, but by water and blood.**

The second way in which humans come under the devil's power is willingly, when they now sin voluntarily. In the third way, as in the first, the victims are unwilling, since they wish indeed to be sensible, except that, wretchedly bound by the habit of sin *by the just judgment of God,** those who are filthy remain filthy still.°

The prodigal son seems to have toiled in this third state. He was a truly and exceedingly wasteful son who not only squandered his goods but even subjected himself to wretched servitude.* This *unhappy one, sold under sin*,* after coming to his senses, says, *How many hired servants in my father's house abound with bread! And I here perish with hunger.** Anyone who has been tested in his own life would easily, I believe, recognize a wretched soul by these words. For what people who are bound by a habit of sin would not suppose themselves fortunate if they could be like one of these tepid people whom they see in the world? They live without committing crime, but they scarcely *seek the things that are above* and instead seek *the things that are upon the earth.** *How many*, he says, *hired servants in my father's house abound with bread*; that is, they take comfort in their innocence, and they enjoy their own good conscience. *And I here perish with hunger;** that is, I am tormented[†] by the insatiable desires of my sins and the emotions of my vices.

*see Luke 15:15
*Rom 7:24, 14

*Luke 15:17

*Col 3:1-2

*Luke 15:17
†see Luke 16:24

This torment could be understood to mean that the prodigal considered himself to be suffering *not hunger for bread or thirst for water, but* a hunger and thirst *for the divine word*,* that is, the same famine with which the prophet threatened Judea. I don't mean to say this is necessarily so; rather, this is how the wretched son feels when humiliated under the burden of sin. Nor can worldly people boast in the testimony of their conscience,* because their goal is secular gain. Nevertheless, remorseful sinners consider someone to be most holy whenever they see another's innocence, no matter what the other's motive. *Make me*, he says, *as one of your hired servants.**

*Amos 8:11

*2 Cor 1:12

*Luke 15:19

6. See here, this is the first stage by which they start to come under God, I mean those who live under a head of household like hired servants. These are people whom we see in the world, those who have little or no desire for eternal goods. Worldly people serve God as though for wages and ask from God worldly things that they desire.

However, now at the second stage, one begins to come under the Lord. At the second stage one is like a slave who fears prison and dreads being subject to punishment. In this stage, of course, is conversion, leaving the world and entering the religious life. So also you read, *Fear of the Lord is the beginning of wisdom.** And a certain other prophet says that by fear of you, Lord, we have conceived and have given birth to a spirit of salvation.*

*Prov 9:10

*see Isa 26:17-18

The third stage is very near to this second and, in a way, mixed with it. I speak of those who are like *little ones in Christ* who still long for milk,* as though living under a teacher and a pedagogue.* This, in fact, is especially appropriate for novices who may have begun to enjoy the consolations of holy meditation, of tears, of psalmody, and other religious practices. They fear, rather like a child, to offend the teacher, lest they get a beating, lest they be cheated of some little gift by which that kindly educator entices them.

*1 Cor 3:1-2; 1 Pet 2:2
*Gal 3:25

These are people who *set the Lord always in their sight** and are deeply moved if he should be absent even for an hour. They no longer have a servile fear of punishment, but like little children they still dread blows from the rod, *embracing discipline* of the teacher, *lest at any time the Lord be angry and they perish from the just way.** They fear that the grace of devotion might be taken away and everything should become tiresome. They might then toil under a certain loathing, like being beaten interiorly in the soul with bitterness of thoughts. These are in fact the spankings by which God corrects his little ones, which we learn to recognize better by experience than by lectures. Whence the Lord himself says through the prophet, *And if his children forsake my law, I will visit their iniquities with a rod and their sins with blows.**

*Ps 15:8

*Ps 2:12

*Ps 88:31-33

7. Accordingly, in these beginnings and during a sort of infantile stage, fear of the Lord and instruction from

the teacher thus follow one another in turns, so that the soul finds itself now in this stage, then in the other, if anyone would be careful to observe this diligently. That is why, speaking to the still young church, Jesus recalls both names at the same time, saying, *You call me Teacher and Lord, and you say well, for so I am.** *John 13:13

So as disciples of Jesus, let our novices recognize their own place so they will be diligent and attentive in staying more [in fear of the Lord and in the Teacher's instruction] than elsewhere. Indeed, before all else, fear is more necessary to them. By fear they are able to wipe out past sins and to beware of future sins. For *fear of the Lord*, as Scripture says, *drives out sin*,* whether it has already been let in or is still trying to enter. To be sure, in the first case, fear drives out sin by repentance, and in the second case by resistance. *Sir 1:27

But seeing how *narrow* and arduous *is the way that leads to life*,* as for *little ones in Christ*,† a pedagogue is necessary for you, O little ones, as well as someone to nurture you, one who teaches, who escorts, who keeps you warm, who plays with the little ones, so to speak, and who consoles with certain caresses, lest one's tender age go to waste. Besides, not I, but even more the Prince and Pastor of the church admonishes you, *As newborn babes, desire the rational milk without guile*, clearly not so that you have permanent need of it, but *thereby you may grow into salvation.** Another passage in Scripture, expressing it more explicitly, says, *Rejoice for joy, all you that mourn for her* (for Jerusalem no doubt, concerning whom he was speaking) *so that you may drink her milk*, he says, *and be satisfied by the breasts of her consolations. And when you have been taken away from the milk, you may feast when she enters her glory.**

*Matt 7:14
†1 Cor 3:1

*1 Pet 2:2

*Isa 66:10-11

8. This is in fact the status of a son already grown up, one who lives under the Father's authority, who no longer drinks milk but eats solid food,‡ *having forgotten things that are behind*,* in which a servile eye dwelt in

‡Heb 5:12; see Isa 66:11
*Phil 3:13

bitterness.* But on the other hand, neither does he consider the present nor does he aim for the little consolations for children; rather, he *stretches himself to things that are ahead, to the prize of the heavenly calling** and the entrance into future beatitude, *looking for the blessed hope and coming of the glory of the great God.** For *he put away the things of a child*,* and he is no longer occupied by such pleasant but ephemeral consolations for children.

But now that he has attained the perfection of adulthood,* *he must be about the father's business.*‡ He must sigh in longing for his inheritance and turn it over in attentive meditation. For is it possible that anyone would consider him a hired servant when he covets his paternal inheritance, and he both expects it and seeks it with all his affection, that inheritance that the prophet testifies to be the reward of the son rather than a hired servant's pay? *When he shall give sleep to his beloved*, it says, *behold the inheritance of the Lord is children, the reward, the fruit of the womb.**

9. There exists however another step more sublime and an affection more worthy than that just mentioned—when a soul having a deeply chastened heart desires nothing else, seeks nothing else from God than God himself, since indeed the soul has learned by repeated experience that *the Lord is good to those who hope in him, to the soul that seeks him.** So now with the conviction and affection of her heart, the soul can shout with the psalm, *For what have I in heaven? And besides you, what do I desire upon earth? For you my flesh and my heart have fainted away. You are the God of my heart and the God who is my portion for ever.**

Nor does the soul desire anything for herself: not happiness, not glory, nothing else whatever of the sort that comes from a private love of self. Rather, the whole soul proceeds into God, who is for her the perfect and singular desire, so that *the king brings her into his bedroom* so that he can cleave to her and enjoy himself.* It also

*Job 17:2

*Phil 3:13-14

*Titus 2:13
*1 Cor 13:11

*Eph 4:13
‡Luke 2:49

*Ps 126:2-3

*Lam 3:25

*Ps 72:25-26

*Song 1:3; see 1 Cor 6:17

follows that with *the face revealed* continually, as long as possible, *beholding the glory* of the heavenly spouse, the soul is *transformed into the same image from glory to glory as by the Spirit of the Lord.** From this transformation, clearly, she merits to hear, *You are beautiful, my love.** And she dares to say, *My beloved for me, and I for him.** Now the glorious soul will enjoy these most happy and delightful exchanges with her spouse.

*2 Cor 3:18
*Song 4:7
*Song 2:16

Sermo 9

Concerning Romans 1:20: *The invisible things of God are clearly seen*

Concerning Psalm 84:9: *I will hear what the Lord God will speak in me*

1. *The invisible things of God are clearly seen*, as the apostle bears witness, *from the creation of the world, being understood through the things that God made.** And the perceptible world is even like some communal book tied to creation by a chain so that anyone who wishes may read in it the wisdom of God. There will be a time when the heavens are folded up like a book,* and thereafter no one will need to read in it anymore, because *they shall all be taught of God.** Like the heavenly creatures, so also the creatures of the world shall no longer *see through a glass in a dark manner, but face to face.** And they shall contemplate God's wisdom itself clearly and directly.

In the meantime, of course, the human soul needs some vehicle of creation in order to rise to knowledge of the Creator. It is quite the contrary for angelic nature; angels have a far more blessed and perfect acquaintance with creation in the Creator. Apparently one blessed soul actually beheld this excellent vision, although for just a moment; while enraptured he watched the whole world gathered under a single ray of the sun. Writing

*Rom 1:20

*Rev 6:14
*John 6:45

*1 Cor 13:12

about this miracle in his book of dialogues, the blessed Pope Gregory says, "To one who sees the Creator, every creature seems small.‡ In the same way, happy are those who are nourished *with the fat of wheat** and have no need to *suck honey out of the rock and oil out of the hardest stone.** They certainly do not search everywhere for the invisible things of God by probing visible things. Rather, they see and understand them clearly and directly.* However, as I already said, that is proper to the blessedness of angelic nature, not fragile human nature.

‡*Dialogorum libri* 2.35.3; SCh 260:339
*Ps 80:17

*Deut 32:13

*Rom 1:20

2. Therefore let us seek the meaning *of invisible things of God* at least *through what God has made.** If the understanding soul already sees aspects of the divine in other creatures, it is essential for the soul to see far more fully and understand much more subtly in that creature that was made in God's image,* that is, in herself. For no creature that dwells under the sun has a position closer to God than the human soul. So rightly does the prophet say to God, *Blessed is the man whose help is from you! In his heart he has arranged his ascents;** and a little afterward he says, *They shall go from virtue to virtue. The God of gods shall be seen in Sion.** On that account, we incessantly exhort you, brothers, *to walk in the ways of your heart,** and may your soul be always in your hands† so that *you will hear what the Lord God will speak among you, for he will speak peace.** For to whom will he speak of peace? Certainly *to his people and to his saints.** What are his people, and who are his saints? Undoubtedly those who are converted to the heart, and so it follows: *And to those who are converted to the heart.**

*Rom 1:20

*Gen 1:27; 9:6

*Ps 83:6

*Ps 83:8

*Eccl 11:9
†Ps 118:109
*Ps 84:9
*Ps 84:9

*Ps 84:9

3. We, however, are accustomed to understand three types of people in these words to whom alone *God speaks peace,**[1] just as another prophet foresaw only three

*Ps 84:9

---

[1] It is useful to have the whole verse at hand in order to understand Bernard's argument: *I will hear what the Lord God will speak in*

bound to be saved: Noah, Daniel, and Job.* In fact, the psalm expresses the same categories, though naming Daniel's type first: celibates, of course, prelates, and married people. God speaks peace to them on the condition that celibates refrain from carnal enticements and prefer things of the heart. That is, they are converted to spiritual desires, whence Daniel is called a *man of desires* by the angel.* Likewise prelates must strive more to benefit others than to rule over them,* seeing that holiness especially becomes them,* whence also in the psalm they are especially called *saints*. Likewise married people must not transgress God's commandments, so that they should deservedly be named people of God and *the sheep of his pasture*.*

4. As a matter of fact, we are accustomed to designate these three categories even within our own community, wherein lies our main concern. Indeed we understand the *people* to be the office brothers,* who are occupied with exterior and mundane business, as it were, whereas *those who are converted to the heart** are the choir monks, whom no employment hinders. Rather, since they are unoccupied, they *see that the Lord is sweet*.* God speaks peace‡ over both these walls because they tend to the same end, although not by the same path. *The psaltery is pleasant with the harp*.* The sound of the harp is not less pleasant than the sound of the psaltery, but the harp renders a sound from a lower range, and the psalms from higher range. Nevertheless, *Mary has chosen the best part*,* though perhaps, before God, the humble way of Martha might not be of less merit. So on the one hand, Mary is praised for her choice to show that we must choose as she did whenever we can. On the other hand,

*see Ezek 14:14

*Dan 10:11
*RB 64.17
*Ps 92:5

*Ps 99:3; see also Ps 84:9

*officiales fratres

*Ps 84:9

*Ps 45:11; see also Ps 33:9
‡Ps 84:9; see also Eph 2:14
*Ps 80:3

*Luke 10:42

---

me, for he will speak peace to his people, and to his saints, and to those who are converted to the heart. That is, his people are married people like Job, his saints are prelates like Noah, and those converted to the heart are celibates like Daniel.

Martha's labors, if they are imposed upon us, must be patiently tolerated.

5. Now the category placed between, I mean *his saints*,* pertains to religious leaders, for whom both Mary's and Martha's lifestyles are necessary. It is the prelates' role to provide for and to join in themselves these two walls, which meet at different angles, because prelates are set up as vicars of the cornerstone, who is Jesus Christ.* No doubt their duty is far more dangerous than that of the other two. However, if *they have ministered well, then they shall purchase for themselves a good standing*,* and they shall receive a more abundant and overflowing measure of peace.* For good reason the psalm says of them, *God speaks peace to his saints*.* Can it be that anyone still has doubts about who the saints are? Listen to Isaiah: *You*, he says, *shall be called saints of the Lord, ministers of our God*.*

I had set out to give an example of how the human soul ought to rise to spiritual intelligence by contemplating itself, but it is necessary to save it for another day and another sermon.

*Ps 84:9

*Eph 2:14, 20

*1 Tim 3:13
*Luke 6:38
*Ps 84:9

*Isa 61:6, from the Cistercian liturgy

Sermo 10

Discerning the Soul's Life from the Five Senses of the Soul

1. I tell you, my dearest, our negligence is great and inexcusable beyond measure when we lose time idling in empty thoughts. We certainly do not need *to pierce the clouds** or *cross the sea*‡ in order to find wholesome thoughts. Rather, as Moses says, it is near: *The word is even in our mouth and in our heart.** So we can find within ourselves infinite occasions and seed plots of useful thoughts. What is more, if a soul were so uneducated and negligent that she was not capable of searching her own interior, she could at least turn to that which is exterior and obvious,* and in these things also, if she seeks diligently, the soul shall find wisdom.

*Sir 35:21
‡Deut 30:13
*Rom 10:8

*see John 7:4

Behold—for it is written, *Give an occasion to a wise man and he shall be wiser**—consider, O soul, what you expend for your body and you shall find, without doubt, that you provide life and senses[1] to it. And indeed, you shall find that life is uniform throughout the whole body. For example, the life in the eye is not different from the life in a finger's joint. Not so for the senses. Demand therefore that your soul, which is with-

*Prov 9:9

---

[1] *Senses* = *sensum*. This word is singular in the first section of Sermon 10 but translated as plural in anticipation of the argument that follows.

out doubt your God himself,[2] generously give similar goods to you also. For the soul that does not have knowledge of truth must not be considered alive, but as yet she is dead in herself.* Likewise, the soul that is without senses lacks love. Therefore truth is the life of the soul, divine love the senses.

*see Jas 2:17

Do not be amazed that sometimes the souls of wicked people have knowledge of truth even though they are lacking in divine love. You will find that these wicked souls may be compared to certain bodies in nature that have life without senses, such as trees and the like. Indeed, they are animated, but by a sort of life, not by a soul.* In a similar way, souls of the unjust also have knowledge of truth by natural reason. Although they are still sometimes helped by grace, they are by no means truly animated by truth.

*animata quidem, sed animatione, et non anima

On the other hand, souls for whom the spiritual Soul pours in knowledge of truth and love, not from the exterior by any means but animating from within as the Soul of the soul, join to the Lord and become one spirit with the spiritual Soul.* In these souls, I say, knowledge of truth is indivisible in the same way as we explained about the uniform life of the body. For by the same knowledge you comprehend both the smallest and the greatest.

*1 Cor 6:17

2. What is more, even love is multiple. If you look carefully, perhaps you will be able to discover that love is fivefold according to the five senses of the body. For there is family love, by which we love our parents. There is congenial love, by which we love our companions. There is also a just love toward all human beings. There is violent love toward enemies. There is holy

---

[2] God is, in a way, "the soul of the soul," because he gives life to the soul. Bernard here asks God to give knowledge of truth (spiritual life) and love (spiritual senses) to the soul in the same way that the soul gives life and senses to the body.

or devout love toward God. In each of these types of love, if you pay careful attention, you shall find a characteristic unique to itself and completely different from the others.

Again, if it pleases you to consider this in more detail, perhaps the first love, that is love of parents, will seem to correspond not unworthily to the sense of touch. For you see, this sense perceives only that which is nearest and in contact with the body, in the same way that family love is expressed to none except those who are nearest to us by ties of the flesh. This comparison is no less reasonable if one notes that touch alone among all the senses is diffused throughout the whole body, for you see, family love is also natural to every flesh, to the point that even brute animals love their offspring and are loved by them.

Likewise, social love for companions most properly corresponds to the sense of taste on account of the fact that it is certainly very agreeable, and since human life has greater need for this sense alone. Nor do I see by what reason someone should be considered alive, at least in this community life, if he does not love those among whom he lives.

On the other hand, a general love, clearly that by which all human beings are loved, has a likeness to the sense of smell, at least in that this sense perceives more remote things, and because, though not entirely lacking in bodily pleasure, the enjoyment is still less intense because the object is more diffuse.

Hearing, however, takes in much more remote sensations. Among human beings, no one is more remote from the one who loves than one who is unloving. Again, in the senses of touch, taste, and smell there is some enjoyment of the flesh, and they seem to pertain more to the flesh, but hearing scarcely comes from the flesh at all. So, not unworthily, hearing seems to correspond to the love whose whole motive is obedience.*

*Lat *obedientia*, from *obaudeo*

It is evident enough that obedience to God pertains to hearing, since, as we said, the other loves depend at least in part on the flesh.

3. Finally, sight claims for itself a likeness to divine love. It has a certain unique nature that is more excellent and more penetrating than all the other senses. Sight also discerns much more remote realities. Again, smell certainly, and hearing as well, seem to sense things at a distance, but they are believed to draw to themselves and to sense the air more than distant realities themselves. Not so the sense of sight; vision itself seems rather to go out and proceed to distant realities.[3] Likewise also in those who love. For by a certain means we attract neighbors whom we love like ourselves. We attract also enemies, whom to this purpose we love so that they may also be like us, that is, so they may be friends.* If in fact, as is proper, *we love God, with the whole heart, and with the whole soul, and with the whole strength*,* then we must ourselves proceed into him even more and with all haste hurry into him who is ineffably over us.

*see John 17:11, 21, 24

*Mark 12:30; see Deut 6:5

4. It should now be obvious that eyesight certainly has more worth than all the rest of the other senses, and hearing is more worthy than the remaining three. Smell also seems to surpass taste and touch, if not in usefulness at least in worthiness, and taste excels touch. Even the physical arrangement of the members reveals this hierarchy. Who does not know that the ears are below the eyes, which are indeed situated in the highest place? So also it is obvious that the nose is below the ears, and the mouth below the nose. Obviously the hand is also below the mouth, as are the remaining parts of the body that share the sense of touch. Therefore, according to this hierarchy, one may consider the senses

---

[3] Medieval ocular theory explained sight as the result of the eye's emitting a beam of light.

of the soul as each being more worthy than the other. Because you can now easily see that yourselves, and for the sake of brevity, I move on.

I also leave this as well to your diligent consideration: in the same way that the members of the body must decay as soon as the soul stops giving life to them, so also those affections, as we said, which are like certain members of the soul, must by all means decay without the soul of the soul (which is God). The soul decays, you see, to the extent that one does not entirely love what one should love, or does not love to the extent that one should love, or in the way one ought. For there are those who love parents only in a carnal sense, and they likewise *praise the Lord when he does well for them*.* But this sort of love either should not be called love at all, or it is a wavering love *and falling to the ground*.*

*Ps 48:19

*Acts 22:7

Sermo 11

Concerning the Double Baptism

1. You know, brothers (for you keep catholic truth most firmly), that in baptism the Father of Heaven adopts those who renounce the devil, and he transfers them from the power of darkness into the kingdom of his Son, of his glory.* *Col 1:11, 13
Of course this is the first robe that paternal affection truly orders the servants to bring forth at once,* not *see Luke 15:22
waiting for a verbal request or the heart's desire,* but *Ps 20:3
even *anticipating* the intellect *with blessings of sweetness.** *Ps 20:4
*For as many of us that have been baptized in Christ have put on Christ.** Concerning this, another apostle—him- *Rom 6:3; Gal 3:27
self a faithful witness*—proclaims, *As many as received* *see Rev 1:5
*him, he gave them power to be made the sons of God.** It is *John 1:12
truly no empty or ineffective power, because no doubt we are always certain that *neither death, nor life, nor angels, nor powers, nor height, nor depth shall be able to separate us from the love of God which is in Christ Jesus.** *Rom 8:38-39

But note how many powers the apostle has listed (for they are his words) without adding in any sense "nor we ourselves." Certainly this is *the freedom by which Christ has made us free,** so that absolutely no other *Gal 4:31
creature can tear us away from him or divert us from him by force. Only by our own will can we forsake God's love, voluntarily *drawn away and allured by* our *own concupiscence.** Besides this, there is nothing that we *Jas 1:14
need fear. What is more, until anyone who is reborn receives the use of the will and the faculty of reasoning,

he cannot be separated from the love of God by any means.* Until then, one carries on secure under the protection and advocacy of one's Lord God; there is nothing that one should fear in all the world.

But when someone passes well beyond the limits of childish ignorance and is returned to one's self, it is certainly no longer necessary to dread the violence of all the rest of the world. But of course, beware your own will, beware *her that sleeps in your bosom.** *There shall be*, perhaps, *sin present at the door, but the desire for sin is beneath you.** You need only refuse to open; you need only reject consent.

2. Again, a lion or a bear did not trip up our first parents,* but rather a serpent more cunning—not stronger—than the other animals.* Nor did the man trip up the woman, but rather the woman the man.* The serpent, O Eve, deceived you.* He surely deceived, but he did not impel or force. O Adam, *the woman gave to you from the tree** by merely offering, not compelling you with violence. It happened by your own will rather than by Eve's power: *You have obeyed more the voice of your wife than of God.**

If Adam, out of ignorance, failed to beware, then let us in all events be on our guard, since we have been forewarned by so many examples. Certainly, in fact, since we have miserably put ourselves at risk in this duty, from now on let us strive with anxious care to provide some remedy for so great an evil. For when does that strong, armed man, whom a stronger man overpowered and tied up, occupy his house by some violence?* Rather, he finds his home empty and stupidly exposed, and with seven others more wicked, not stronger, he enters; without forcing his way in, he dwells there freely.* For who really admitted him, if not his own will? It is the will itself that drives us once more into the power of darkness,* that subjugates us again to the empire of death.*

*see Rom 8:39

*Mic 7:5

*Gen 4:7

*see 1 Sam 17:36-37
*Gen 3:1
*see 1 Tim 2:14
*Gen 3:13

*Gen 3:12

*Gen 3:17

*Luke 11:21-22; Matt 12:29

*Matt 12:44-45

*Luke 22:53
*Heb 2:14

3. *Come, Lord Jesus*,* come even now, good Jesus, boldly cast out once more the one whom we have so stupidly admitted. For then, *Even now we shall be free indeed if you will make us free.** We have made void the first covenant.* We have sinned against you,† Lord, binding ourselves once more to Satan and his works, deliberately submitting our necks to the yoke* and subjecting ourselves to miserable servitude.

*Rev 22:20

*John 8:36
*Deut 31:16
†Ps 50:6
*Lam 1:14

Therefore, my brothers, it is fitting for us to be rebaptized; it is necessary to enter a second covenant; a second profession is needed: it no longer suffices to renounce the devil and his works. The world equally must be renounced, and our will. For the world seduces* us, and our will gives in to it.

*2 Cor 11:3

Certainly in the first baptism, when our will had not yet harmed us, it was enough to renounce the devil, by whose envy both sin and death entered through one man and passed into all human beings.* Moreover, after we have plainly experienced the enticements of this deceiving world and the infidelity of our will, from now on, in the second baptism of our conversion—as we have rightly said *and it shall not be reputed as folly in us**—let us be careful not merely to repair the first covenant but even to strengthen it, and let us equally renounce our will.

*Wis 2:24;
Rom 5:12

*Ps 21:3

From now on let us strive, most beloved, *to keep ourselves unspotted from this world*, knowing that *this is religion clean and undefiled before God.** Moreover, let us beware will as if it were the worst sort of wicked viper, which alone can harm our souls.

*Jas 1:27

Sermo 12

Concerning First Beginnings, Current Days, and One's Last End in Sirach 7:40: *Be mindful of your last end*

1. *C*hildren, be mindful of your last end and you shall never sin.* Consider your first beginning, pay close attention to your current days, and be mindful of your last end. The first induces shame, the second heap up sorrow, and the last instills fear. Consider where you came from and blush, where you are and groan, where you are going and tremble! See that you do not continually increase your ignorance of yourself lest perhaps that terrible threat come upon you in which the Spouse thunders, saying, *If you know not yourself, O fairest among women, go forth and follow after the flocks of your companions.**

At first, indeed, *when you were in honor, O human, you did not understand.* So also *you were compared to senseless beasts and you have become like them.** Now if *trouble will not make you understand what you hear,** then you shall indeed follow after the flocks; you shall be exposed to those beasts who understand nothing of evil, exposed to all evil creatures. Recognize therefore your first beginning and blush to be compared to beasts. *Be mindful of your last end* and fear lest you follow even after beasts.

Blush, I say, because you have obtained the fellowship of cattle instead of the fellowship of angels, not only in

*Sir 7:40

*Song 1:7

*Ps 48:13
*Isa 28:19

the necessities of the body but even in the affections of the heart.* You share the food of the earth with beasts because you have disdained the angelic bread, the heavenly bread.* Not only that, but what is even worse, your soul has been bowed down in an upright body,* though the likeness of a human soul remains in your body. In your soul the likeness of God has been truly changed to the likeness of a beast.*

*see Ps 72:7

*Ps 77:25

*Bar 2:18

*see Ps 48:13

2. Are you not ashamed to hold up your head, you who do not hold up your heart? Are you not ashamed to stand with an upright body, you who crawl on the earth? Does not crawling on the earth really mean *to mind the things of the flesh*,* to desire and to seek things of the flesh? Although *you have been created according to the image and likeness of God*,* if you have lost the likeness, then you have been made like the beasts.* Nevertheless, you have still retained the image.* Therefore, after having been placed on high, if you still have not understood* because you were slime,† *stuck fast in the slime of the deep*,# then do not ignore the fact that you are the image of God, and you should blush because you have covered it with an alien likeness.

*Rom 8:5

*Gen 1:26
*Ps 48:13
*Ps 38:7

*Prov 30:32;
Eccl 10:6
†see Gen 2:7
#Ps 68:3

Be mindful of your nobility, and let it make you ashamed of your great degradation. May you not ignore your beauty;* let it make you even more dismayed by your beastliness. This is, according to Salomon, the *shame that brings glory*ature* when you are dismayed at the fall of so great a glory.

*see Song 1:7

*Sir 4:25

You had been at one time *crowned with glory and honor, set over the works of the Lord's hands*,* a resident of Paradise, a fellow citizen of angels, and a member of the household of the Lord Sabaoth.* But now you have tossed yourself into this interior darkness;* so also, at some time, you shall be ejected to the exterior and palpable darkness if you do not beware. You have removed yourself, I say, from that *glory of the children of God*.* You have made yourself an exile from that blessed

*Ps 8:6-7

*see Eph 2:19
*Matt 25:30;
Deut 28:29

*Rom 8:21

and most pleasant homeland, from that garden of delight.*

3. Behold from where you have come. Do you wish to know where you have arrived? Certainly *into a place of affliction;** indeed *your life has approached hell.*‡ For what is here except hardship and sorrow* and affliction of spirit?* Your condition is indeed like that of a child who had been born in prison and raised in prison. He was bewildered by the sadness and anxiety of his mother because he had never seen the light. She of course knew why she grieved. Because she knew about good things, the evil things were more grave to her, and when reminded of peace, *her bitterness is most bitter.** Good things seem like lesser evils to you, and because of the larger shackles to which you have been accustomed, you reckon smaller chains a respite. You devour your food because hunger torments you. Both are hardships, but because hunger is heavier to bear, you do not know that gorging food is a hardship. Finally, after hunger has been driven out, see if you do not consider eating to be a greater burden than hungering.

So it is for everything under the sun: people find nothing among themselves truly pleasing.* A human being always wants to move on from one thing to another. Only by change does one find any relief, and indeed, it is as if one jumped from water into fire and then jumped again back into the water, like one who cannot bear either. So every remedy for hardship is the beginning of another hardship. No one in this wicked world* can have what he wants, for the just person never has a fill of justice, the sensuous person never gets enough pleasure, the curious person's inquisitiveness is only spurred by more knowledge, and the ambitious person is not satisfied by empty glory.*

Behold the cause of your suffering if you have not yet become insensible. Behold why you suffer: because you have been placed in exile. You abide in a desert,

*see Gen 3:23

*Ps 43:20
‡Ps 87:4
*Ps 89:10
*Eccl 1:14

*Isa 38:17

*see Eccl 2:17

*see Gal 1:4

*see Gal 5:26

you walk in darkness and on the slippery way,* and *by the sweat of your face shall you eat your bread.** Does not your *eye abide in bitterness** as often as it considers these things, and does it not equally lament with the prophet, *Woe is me, that my sojourning is prolonged!**

*see Ps 34:6
*Gen 3:19
*Job 17:2

*Ps 119:5

4. You realize now your beginning; you realize your current days as well, but what about your last end? For concerning the end, Scripture says, *Be mindful of your last end, and you shall never sin.** One's last end is death, judgment, Gehenna. What is more horrible than death? What is more terrible than judgment? Nothing can be considered more intolerable than Gehenna. What would someone fear who does not tremble at these horrors, does not become frightened or terror stricken?

*Sir 7:40

O human being, even if you have lost the shame that is proper for a noble creature, if you were not feeling the pain of affliction, which is actually carnal, then at least you do not lack fear, because even beasts know fear. Let us burden a donkey, and let us tire him with many labors;* he will not care, because he is a donkey. But if we want to push him into fire or cast him headlong into a pit, then he will defend himself as much as he can, because he loves life and fears death. Does it not therefore seem just to you that one who has been in a way more senseless than beasts is also compelled to follow after the beasts themselves, and once put in torments, he holds a lower place?

*see 2 Thess 3:8;
2 Cor 11:32

Fear therefore, O human being, because in death you must be separated from all good things of this body, and so sweet a bond of flesh and soul must be severed with a most bitter separation. Fear because in the terrible Judgment you must be presented to him into whose hands *it is a fearful thing to fall** and to whose examination nothing is hidden.* If indeed *iniquity has been found* in you,* then you must be deprived of all rest and glory and be segregated from the number of the blessed. Fear, because in Gehenna you must be

*Heb 10:31

*see Job 42:2
*Ps 16:3

exposed to eternal and innumerable tortures, into the same *everlasting fire which was prepared for the devil and his angels!** *Matt 25:41

So here it says *fear is the beginning of wisdom*:* not shame, not pain, because neither of them so initiates wisdom, neither has so much effectiveness. So it does not say to remember your first beginnings or your current days, but rather, *Be mindful of your last end and you shall never sin.** For the spirit of fear is stronger and more vigorous* in resisting sin than is shame or pain. For shame takes solace in many worldly pleasures, and pain takes solace from certain consolations of this world. Fear in fact does not find consolation in this world, and in death you do not bring with you any goods of this world, large or small. In Judgment it shall not be possible to deceive or to resist. In Gehenna there is no deep consolation, but perpetual woe: *wailing, and weeping, and gnashing of teeth.**

*Ps 110:10

*Sir 7:40
*Isa 11:3

*Esth 4:3;
Matt 8:12

Sermo 13

Concerning the Triple Mercy

1. *Have mercy on me, O God, according to your great mercy.** Just as there are very small sins, there are also moderate sins, and there are great sins. So likewise there are small mercies, moderate, and great. A great sinner therefore has need of great mercy so that *where sin abounded, grace may abound the more.**

*Ps 50:3

*Rom 5:20

I mean by a small mercy the patient anticipation by which God does not punish the sinner right away; rather, he waits for him to repent. However, I do not mean that such mercy is small in itself, but it is small compared to the others. In itself, God's patience is obviously great; the Lord's patient anticipation is certainly a great mercy. For God did not give the sinning angel any time at all to repent; rather, he cast him out of heaven. God also did not keep waiting the first human being who sinned but immediately expelled him from Paradise.*

*see Gen 3:24

Yet now the Lord waits; he looks the other way;* he holds back for ten or twenty years *unto old age and gray hairs.** And if we were to consider how many and serious sins are committed daily, wouldn't we then reckon those sins as venial that nevertheless received an immediate sentence of condemnation? Hence it is no wonder if the prophet himself has also said, *My feet were almost moved; my steps had nearly slipped because I was jealous on account of the wicked, seeing the peace enjoyed by*

*see Wis 11:24

*Ps 70:18

sinners.* [Likewise, no wonder] if sinners themselves say, *How does God know, and is there knowledge in the most High?**

But this is the grace of Christ's cross and its power. *As I live, says the Lord God, I desire not the death of the wicked, but that the wicked turn from his way and live.** How much it seems to me that this is the voice of the resurrected Christ, and indeed as if he were to say, "If the Jew wishes it or not, *I myself live. I do not wish the death of the sinner*, I who was willing to die for sinners. I will that my death be fruitful and through it a bountiful redemption."*

2. Therefore, this mercy of the Lord, by which he delays the blow while he is prepared to pardon, I call small, indeed not small in itself, but in comparison with others. This patience, if it were the only mercy, would by no means suffice for salvation. Nay rather, it adds to the verdict of condemnation, as God says, *These things you have done and I said nothing.**

Therefore let us hear the apostle thundering, as is his custom: *Or do you despise the riches of his goodness*—no doubt God's goodness—*and longsuffering? Do you know not that the patience of God leads you to repentance? But according to your hardness and impenitent heart, you treasure up for yourself wrath in the day of wrath.** You treasure up for yourself, he says, treasures of wrath instead of the prepaid treasures of mercy that you spurn, and you empty the mercy of God out of yourself. But according to what? According to your hardness, he says, and your impenitent heart. Who, however, will break that hardness, except him who broke the rocks by his suffering?* Who will give a repenting heart, except him who is *every best gift?**

3. This [repentance] is the second mercy, much greater than the first, which acts lest the first mercy be fruitless and converted into a condemnation of death.* Indeed, without repentance, God's patient anticipation

not only does not bring benefit but even does more harm. And this repentance indeed can suffice for venial sins. Daily repentance can suffice unto salvation for these sins from which we cannot entirely abstain while we bear the body of sin.* *Rom 6:6

But certainly for more grave sins and for those that *are sins unto death*,* there is need not only for repentance but also for self-control. By all means this is a difficult matter and possible for divine power alone, after taking up the yoke of sin, *to shake off the yoke* of sin *from their necks*.* For *whosoever commits sin is the servant of sin*,* nor can such a one be freed any longer except by a strong hand. *1 John 5:16 *Gen 27:40 *John 8:34

4. This is the great mercy, necessary for great sinners, concerning which Scripture says, *Have mercy on me, O God, according to your great mercy, and according to the multitude of your tender mercies, blot out my iniquity*.* It has been said that there are four daughters of this great mercy: allowing bitterness to enter, removing the opportunity for sin, giving strength in resisting sin, and creating healthy affection. For whenever someone is held bound by one sin or another, the Lord faithfully sends in certain bitter feelings that occupy the mind of the person and expel the destructive enjoyment of sin. Whenever God removes an opportunity for sin, he does not allow weakness to be tempted.* *Ps 50:3 *see 1 Cor 10:13

Another, even greater mercy, is whenever God gives strength to resist sin, so that when one senses a temptation, one may indeed *act manfully** and not consent. Finally, the most perfect mercy is whenever God heals one's affection so that every temptation is entirely rooted out, so that not only does one not consent to temptation, but one does not even sense it. *Ps 26:14

Sermo 14

Concerning the Seven Gifts of the Holy Spirit against the Seven Faults

[*]see Wis 7:30
[*]1 Cor 1:24
[*]Rom 16:20
[*]Wis 8:1

[*]Wis 8:1

[*]Song 6:9
[*]see Isa 11:3

[*]Eccl 7:19
[*]Job 9:28

[*]Job 41:6-7

[*]Prov 19:13; 27:15

Wisdom overcomes evil* while *Christ the power of God and the wisdom of God** crushes Satan.* Wisdom *reaches therefore from end to end mightily*,* even in heaven by casting out pride, in the world by overcoming evil, and in hell by plundering the covetous one. And Wisdom *orders all things pleasantly** by securing the angels who stand in heaven, by redeeming those in the world who are sold into sin, and by liberating the captives in hell.

Or, if it is more pleasing, let us admit the following interpretation. The Spirit with the seven gifts goes forth as *an army set in array** against the seven steps of sin. At first, fear rises up against negligence.* Undoubtedly fear itself shakes the soul: the conscience is shaken up by fear, a lethal stupor is shaken out, and concern is shaken in. Finally, *he who fears God, neglects nothing*;* rather, *he fears all his own works*.*

2. Moreover, to make the conflict more serious, *scales press upon scales*.* In the human heart, neglect of self goes along with curiosity about others. For as Wisdom says, there are three annoyances that can force a resident from his home: smoke, a leaky roof, and a bad wife.* When, however, are these things lacking for a negligent person? That is, one who neglects his own affairs: who

fails to expel the smoke, who does not correct his wife, who does not repair the roof. Smoldering sins continue to smoke when there is no zeal for mercy, when not extinguished by waves of tears—and that smoke is most offensive and intolerable. The will (i.e., the bad wife) acts wickedly; by neglecting herself, she becomes more degenerate every day. The indignation of the Heavenly Judge drips through the gaps in one's charity, i.e., the only roof that *covers a multitude of sins.** *1 Pet 4:8

Consequently it is necessary for the negligent person to go prying into outside affairs, that is, one who disdains internal concerns, does not look back to the past, does not look into the present, or look out for the future. So then, it is obvious that loving-kindness opposes curiosity; loving-kindness calls back to the heart the one whom curiosity calls away. Undoubtedly that loving-kindness is the worship of God, and God is worshiped in the heart, for he is known to dwell in the heart.* *see Eph 3:17

Curiosity, however, begets the experience of evil, so that one who wanders about many places easily offends, easily falls into a trap, easily finds what is dangerous to enjoy. The spirit of knowledge is at war against this experience of evil: teaching *to refuse evil and to choose good,** teaching what is dangerous and what is useful to experience. *Isa 7:15

3. Nevertheless, within many people these days, experience seems to cross over into concupiscence. You have these steps in Dinah, the daughter of Jacob, of course, who *went out to see the foreign women* when *Sichem the son of Hemor took her away and ravished the virgin.* And then it says that *whereas she was sad, he comforted her with sweet words* so that *his soul was fast knit to her soul.** I say, moreover, that his experience crossed into concupiscence, and as the prophet reminds us, one who has spurned the Law *has passed into the affection of the heart,** has cast aside integrity, bade farewell to shame, and *Gen 34:1-3, 8

*Ps 72:7

completely passed over fear of the Lord, and is carried by appetite alone. Such a one follows only concupiscence and is dragged by physical pleasure, and in him the will holds the place of reason.

Accordingly, fortitude does battle against this concupiscence of evil, for there is now no liberation except by a strong hand. Let the human being commit to fasting, let him *chastise the body and bring it into subjection lest perhaps** even now *out of the root of the serpent shall come forth a basilisk,** that is, bad habit from concupiscence.

*1 Cor 9:27
*Isa 14:29

How extremely wretched and pitiable indeed is human frailty! Even without the itching of concupiscence or the violent urging of desire, one is dragged into unlawful behavior by habit alone—if only it were all right for us to ignore! Certainly *whosoever commits sin is the servant of sin.** Clearly such people are servants of the devil, *by whom they are held captive at his will,** following through with any depravity to which they are dragged.

*John 8:34
*2 Tim 2:26

4. This habit is a type of heavy and dangerous chain, more easily unfastened than broken. So especially here is it proper to employ that common proverb: skill is more powerful than violence. Just as force is repelled by force, and the fervor of desires is extinguished by fervor of spirit, so you must outsmart the Evil One's trick and oppose bad habit with counsel. Otherwise, if perhaps you seek violence and you hope to prevail over bad habit by castigating your body, then there is great reason to fear that your toil might be dangerous and your bodily nature itself might fail before ingrown concupiscence fails, especially because the bad habit might have become second nature. And so counsel is necessary, supplied either by the angel of great counsel himself* or by some spiritual person who is ignorant neither of Satan's devices nor of spiritual remedies.* We must take away occasions for sin, and we must flee opportunities for sin.

*Isa 9:6

*2 Cor 2:11

We read, brothers, that some monk in the desert was gravely attacked by the spirit of fornication and was cured by the praiseworthy and resolute skill of his spiritual father. For the elder secretly called upon another brother and ordered him to assail the troubled brother with insults. The first brother himself, just as if he had received real insults from the second, complained. The brother was troubled, and deeply perplexed, so in a short time he forgot the first temptation to fornication. In fact, when the elder asked him about it, not without great surprise he answered: "Father! I should not be allowed to live; should I then be given to fornication?"* *Jerome, *Epistulae* 125:13

5. But perhaps one has not yet come to the point where victory is restored, as one whom triumph awaits, to whom the crown is owed, and bad habit brings forth contempt so that the more the sinner despairs, the more freely he sins. At this point, the sinner relaxes all the reins of concupiscence and is brought headlong over a cliff,* just as Scripture says: *The wicked man, when he comes into the depth of sins, pays no heed.** *Matt 8:32 *Prov 18:3

Therefore it is necessary for the spirit of understanding* to attack the sinner's contempt, illuminating the darkness of the heart* and pouring in the light of divine mercy and of copious compassion. Certainly understanding should give itself to divine and lofty matters that human reason cannot understand at all and that even faith itself can grasp only with difficulty, as it is written, *Where sin abounded, grace did more abound.** *Isa 11:2 *1 Cor 4:5 *Rom 5:20

6. Now if contempt should persist, then vice* necessarily follows; the despairing wretch permits whatever consolation he can. One who has no part in good things rejoices even in wickedness. The sinner is *glad when he has done evil and rejoices in most wicked affairs.** There is only one remedy therefore from these circumstances: Wisdom herself must join battle against vice and fight with her own right hand, which has never known defeat. For when has anyone who had descended into *malitiam *Prov 2:14

Babylon ever been set free unless heavenly blessings came first,* as a nail pushes out a nail and the joy of spiritual anointing drives out the destructive sweetness of sins?

*Ps 20:4

7. The conqueror Wisdom* *reaches therefore from end to end mightily** by rooting out every vice and planting a virtue in place of each fault. Indeed negligence is shaken out so that the spirit of fear fills the mind, curiosity is cast away so that loving-kindness may succeed, and experience of evil is put to flight and knowledge is put in its place. So also fortitude prevails over concupiscence, counsel cuts out bad habit, vigorous understanding banishes contempt, and as vice disappears completely, Wisdom reigns.*

*see Wis 7:30
*Wis 8:1

*see Isa 11:2-3

Destructive negligence had put the wretched soul to sleep: more wickedly, curiosity had excited her, sinful experience had attracted her, concupiscence had held her, bad habit had tied her up, contempt had pushed her into jail, and vice had murdered her. Hereafter, once Wisdom triumphs, fear rouses the soul, loving-kindness soothes with its charm, knowledge, revealing suffering, shows what to do,* fortitude, according to its nature, rouses the soul, counsel unties the bonds, understanding leads the soul out of the prison, and Wisdom lays a table, revives the starving, and renews the soul with wholesome foods.*

*see Eccl 1:18

*see Prov 9:2

Sermo 15

On Seeking Wisdom

1. What are we doing in this world, brothers? Or what do we make of this world? If we strive to be saved *from this present wicked world*,* then why do we still worry ourselves about this world? If we wish to escape, then why do we take pains to drag our shackles with us? Let us suppose that the shackles were made of gold: even then it would be much better to be free of them than to be held back on account of them. Let us not esteem their value, but let us consider how they hinder us. In addition to the inherent privation of our human condition (which is generally considered harsh enough), we even start clinging to these shackles with the glue of cupidity, and we start to be entangled in the obligations of foolish worries.   *Gal 1:4

Let us assume that it is perhaps less conclusive to explore what anyone in shackles may do, because human beings are put in shackles more to make them suffer than to make them do anything; shackles are meant to prevent action, being instruments of passivity. Nevertheless, there is something that we must do in this world: we must at least do penance. Although this will seem to pertain more to suffering than to action, nevertheless, we must do something here indeed: *in this world, but not of this world.*   *John 17:11, 14

For when we read that in the beginning Adam was put in a *paradise of pleasure in order to work,** what wise   *Gen 2:15

and sane person would suppose that Adam's children were put *in the place of affliction** to take a break from toil? Therefore, let us *labor not for the food which perishes.** Rather, let us perform the work of our salvation. Let us work in the Lord's vineyard so that we deserve to receive our daily wage.* Let us work in Wisdom, who says, *they who work by me shall not sin.**

Truth says, *The field is the world.** Let us dig in it! A hidden treasure lies buried within.* Let us dig it out! For *wisdom itself is drawn out of secret places.** We all seek her; we all long for her.

2. But one who *seeks on his little bed** seeks wisdom in vain. *Neither is wisdom found in the land of those who live in delights.** The bed is small, and yet in it you seek a giant? It is your bed, and yet you hope to find him there, him who never knew a bed at the inn?*

If you seek, says Isaiah, *then seek; be converted and come.** Come where, you ask? Away from your little bed. Do you ask from what you are converted? *Turn away from your own will*, says Scripture.* And if I do not find wisdom in my own will, where, you say, shall I find it? For my will vehemently desires wisdom. Nor shall it suffice to find wisdom unless I put it *into my bosom, in good measure and pressed down, shaken together and running over.** Rightly indeed, for *Blessed is the person who finds wisdom and is rich in prudence.**

Seek, therefore, Wisdom *while he may be found; call upon* him *while* he *is near.** Do you wish to hear how near Wisdom is? *The word is near, even in your mouth and in your heart,** if only you seek with an upright heart. Lift up your heart! Get up from your little bed* so that you do not hear in vain him who urges us from on high to have a heart. For thus shall you find wisdom with your heart. You shall pour prudence from your mouth. That is, wisdom shall overflow from abundance. See that it does not just escape or be expelled.

3. Certainly you have found honey if you have found wisdom. Only do not eat too much, *lest being glutted*

---

*Ps 43:20
*John 6:27

*see Matt 20:1-15
*Sir 24:30

*Matt 13:38
*Matt 13:44
*Job 28:18

*Song 3:1

*Job 28:13

*see Luke 2:7
*Isa 21:12

*Sir 18:30

*Luke 6:38
*Prov 3:13

*Isa 55:6

*Rom 10:8
*see Song 3:2

you vomit it up.* Eat in such a way that you always hunger for more. For Wisdom says, *They who eat me shall yet hunger.** Do not suppose that you have a great deal of wisdom. Do not be gorged lest you vomit, and even that which you seem to have acquired will be taken away from you,* especially if you have given up seeking too soon. For not *while the Lord may be found* nor *while he is near** should you end the search or discontinue the invocation.

    Likewise, *just as it is not good for one to eat much honey,* as Solomon similarly says, *so one who is a searcher of majesty shall be overwhelmed by glory.** You, Pilate, why did you ask the Lord privately what truth is,* as if he might whisper into your ear? Truth is too much for you, for the Lord *does not give what is holy to dogs; neither does he cast pearls before swine.** Seek rather the taste of faith! Do not seek for now to satisfy your intellect! Rightly, brothers, was Pilate's disputation put down, and so he promptly withdrew. What is more, not bothering to wait for an answer, *he went out again to the Jews.** Such a one was Pilate, who had begun *to walk in great matters* and *in wonderful things above* him* when he asked, *What is truth?*

    4. That is why we seek wisdom in our hearts and the wisdom that is from faith,* just as the apostle says: *Not to be more wise than is necessary to be wise, but to be wise unto sobriety.** Indeed, sober wisdom is in repentance for past sins, in contempt for present comforts, and in desire for future rewards. Clearly, brother, you have found Wisdom if you have lamented the sins of your earlier life, if you consider the desires of this world trivial, if you long for eternal blessedness with the whole of your desire.

    Brother, you have found wisdom if you understand each of these for what they are: if you judge and discern with your soul's interior taste that your sins are bitter and must be avoided in every way, that present comforts are futile and transitory and should be spurned, and

*Prov 25:16

*Sir 24:29

*Matt 13:12;
see Luke 8:18
*Isa 55:6

*Prov 25:27
*see John 18:38

*Matt 7:6

*John 18:38

*Ps 130:1

*see Rom 9:30

*Rom 12:3

that eternal blessedness must be sought with all your desire as the perfect good.

Truly this is the sober wisdom that knows not regurgitation, removing the tepidity* of the lowest preoccupations with present circumstances and giving the cold recollection of sins and the warmth of divine love that stem from a hunger for divine promises. That way you do not throw up wisdom, nor are you thrown up by wisdom. For just as *blessed is the person who finds wisdom,** so also *blessed is the person*, or even more blessed, *who remains in wisdom.** For perhaps this is the overflowing abundance that the wise person observes.*

*Rev 3:16

*Prov 3:13
*Sir 14:22
*see §2 above
*Prov 3:13

5. To be sure, wisdom, or prudence,* overflows from your mouth in three ways: if you confess your own iniquity with the mouth,* if you offer *thanksgiving and the voice of praise,** and if you speak words of edification. Of course *we believe with the heart for justice, but, with the mouth, confession is made for salvation.** And indeed, in speech, *the just person is the first accuser of himself.** For in the middle of his speech he magnifies the Lord. In the third part of speech as well, if wisdom continues to overflow,* the just person must edify the neighbor.

*Rom 10:10
*Isa 51:3

*Rom 10:10
*Prov 18:17

*see Prov 3:13

And should wisdom even overflow in our work? Most certainly! Therefore we seek in our work the triple overflow, for a certain wise man of old has described wisdom in a threefold way.* So if you do not have a better idea, I myself think that wisdom pertains to work when it overflows with sufficient abundance. That is, in whoever among you conducts himself with self-control, patience, and obedience to the point that faithful obedience subdues self-will, humble self-control also cuts off carnal and worldly lust; likewise, patience cheerfully and manfully puts up with adversity from both the body and of course from the world.

*see Prov 22:20

Sermo 16

On the Day of Saint Andrew: Three Types of Good, and Vigilance over Thoughts

1. Would that we had both more eager zeal and more vigilant care for our thoughts, my brothers. For by our thoughts, I say, we regularly attend to the material of such holy meditation. You see, night and day, we read and sing for our edification the words of the prophets, the evangelists, and the apostles. They warn about the punishment of hell, and they promise the glory of the Kingdom. So how do such vain, such harmful, such obscene thoughts come to us? Sometimes dirty and vainglorious thoughts, sometimes pride, ambition, and the rest of the passions agitate us so that we can scarcely ever take a rest in the serenity of holy thoughts. For good reason it is said that the souls who suffer in places of purification[1] run through foul and muddy places because in this life they did not fear to inhabit such places by their thoughts.

Is it not tragic for us, for our numb and lukewarm hearts, for us who permit ourselves to be occupied by these vanities? We fail to cross from the present into *the good things of the Lord*,* into either natural goods or spiritual goods or even eternal goods. And indeed

*Ps 26:13

---

[1] *in locis purgatoriis*. The term *purgatory* came to be used only as a proper noun after Bernard's time, in the thirteenth century; see SCh 496:29n3.

natural goods are great, spiritual goods are greater, and eternal goods are greatest. In the first we are renewed, in the second we are exercised, and in the third we are increased and blessed.

If you cannot fix your eye of meditation on that height of eternal goods because they are distant and *surpass all understanding,** then turn your vision to the good things of grace that are in the exercise of virtue. That way you may see how a pure conscience and an unburdened brow may be turned and converted in chastity and charity, in patience and humility and the rest of the virtues* that render a person lovable to God. And thus to other human beings one becomes conciliatory and worthy of imitation. But if these things are exceedingly sublime and pass beyond your weakness, then direct your eyes to the goods of nature, which ought to be as familiar to you as you are familiar to yourself.

*Phil 4:7

*see 2 Cor 6:4-6

Let us not speak of nature's goods as if they were not a grace. But you see, natural goods were instilled and planted together in a certain way for nature itself, before the sin that corrupted not only character but even nature. Since then, the good things at hand do not seem to come to us as graces because of the inflicted wound, even though we sense nature's goods in and around ourselves, as much by our reason as by feelings generally. And because we consist of both soul and body, according to the voice of the apostle, from the animal part, that is from goods of the body, we begin *not first that which is spiritual but that which is natural.**

*1 Cor 15:46

2. All goods of the body are a matter of health, and that is the one and only thing that we owe to the body. Moreover, nothing beyond health should be given or sought for the body. Rather, by this limit, the body should be tied and restrained, seeing how the fruit of the body is nothing and its end is death.

Yet even the service of bodily health has a pitfall that I would not let escape your notice. For pleasure might lay traps for health, and it follows with such subtle malice that one is scarcely able to avoid or even recognize it, because, if pleasure serves pleasure, not health, then it is no longer about nature, but actually beneath nature, which gives hands to death when it sets up pleasure as master. Furthermore, that is how many people have descended to such a bestial urge, or, as I might say, more to the point, they have fallen so that they prefer pleasure to health. They frequently roll in those things when they know that difficult and severe sufferings shall follow.

Moreover, just as health is natural to the body, so purity is natural to the heart. For God shall not be seen with a troubled eye,* and the human heart was made for the very purpose of seeing its Creator. If, however, one must provide careful protection for the health of the body, so much more imperatively must one be concerned about purity of heart, insofar as that duty is proved to be more worthy. Yet here we simply receive purity, so that, plainly, all that we do we may confess to the Lord purely and humbly in prayer, in confession to a human being, and let us say, *I said: I will confess against myself my injustice to the Lord, and you have forgiven the wickedness of my sin.**

3. And because we are social animals, let us cross over from what is within us to those who are around us, so that *if it be possible, as much as is in us, we may have peace with all persons.** For this is the law of natural society, since *all things whatsoever that we wish not done to us, let us not do to another;* and *that which we wish to be done for us,* let us strive to do for others.* Therefore just as we owe health to the body and purity to the heart, so also we owe peace to a brother.

Now from here, it is necessary to continue on to the souls of the saints who have flown from this mortal prison to the joys of heaven. To these certainly we owe imitation because they were *capable of suffering like us,** and they *made known to us the ways of life** that they kept

*Ps 6:8; see Matt 5:8

*Ps 31:5

*Rom 12:18

*Tob 4:16; Matt 7:12

*Jas 5:17
*Ps 15:11

so tirelessly as well as unceasingly. But we also owe compassion and prayer to those souls who have not departed in such great holiness or such thorough repentance, for we share a similar nature. Let us pray that the devoted Father take away their ashes and transform their floggings into benefits and so finally consign them to the joys of the blessed citizenry. For if bulls when they find a dead bull will weep, bellow, and follow fraternal funeral rites as though with certain ceremonies that humanity requires, then what does a human being—whom both reason teaches and affection draws—owe to a deceased human being?

Therefore, just as we owe imitation to holy souls, so we also owe compassion to those with little holiness, the former for their example, the latter for their exhausting groans.

4. From the holy angels, however, help is to be sought with both secret sighs and frequent tears so that they may offer our prayers to that super-eminent majesty, so they may bring back our thanks, the angels who are *ministering spirits sent to minister on our account,* and so we *shall receive the inheritance of salvation.**

*Heb 1:14

Loving-kindness must be sought from the Lord of all things so that he whose nature is goodness, who naturally saves and shows compassion, will not look upon the multitude of our iniquities* but *according to the multitude of* his *tender mercies* will *have mercy on us.** For we owe to him love and submission with all reverence and humility: love, because he made us and benefits us, submission, because he is over us and because he teaches us that he is *terrible in his counsels over the children of men.**

*see Ps 5:11
*Ps 50:3; see Ps 66:2

*Ps 65:5

So also, therefore, we owe health to the body, purity to the heart, peace to a brother, imitation to the saints, compassion to the dead. Likewise from the treasure chest of natural goods we ought to seek and to keep help from an angel and loving-kindness from God. So then, when we have done that which has been commanded and given to our nature, *We are unprofitable servants; we have done only that which we ought to do.** For scarcely ever, or even never, does one find some command given to human beings* that passes beyond the limits and possibilities of nature.

*Luke 17:10

*Acts 4:12

In these goods, however, just as we have said, we are renewed, and in a certain way we are restored to the ancient condition. We revert to the innate sweetness of nature, while indeed to us, and to those who are around us, and to those who are above us, we produce the appropriate order of things. So much then for the natural goods.

5. Spiritual goods, in which we are trained so to strive for eternal goods, are the same as natural goods, but they seem different because they are considered from different points of view. Nevertheless, there are also many other goods that would be too long to enumerate. Natural goods are consistent with nature; spiritual goods, we know, are above nature. For in spiritual training we do not owe health to the body, but rather servitude, affliction, and toil according to the voice of that spiritual and supremely spiritual person who said, *I chastise my body and bring it into subjection.**

*1 Cor 9:27

As for that purity of heart that we just spoke about, we do not owe so much purity of heart as pure and humble confession of our sins. Thus we demonstrate this careful attention in our intention, in our thought, and in our work. Thus our life is made more fruitful and our reputation glorious, not to bear fruit for ourselves, but for God,* not what glorifies us, but what *glorifies the Father who is in heaven.**

*Rom 7:4
*Matt 5:16

We say also not only that we should show peace to brothers in this life but that we should even be peaceable with those who hate peace,* to carry all and to be carried by no one. Furthermore, we not only admit compassion and prayer for the dead but should even

*Ps 119:7

offer them congratulations in hope. For, though one may be saddened because the dead suffer in places of purification, so much the more should one rejoice with them because they are near to the time when *God shall wipe away all tears from their eyes, and neither mourning, nor crying, nor sorrow shall be any more, because the former things have passed away.** *Rev 21:4

In fact, we owe to the holy souls no longer imitation, nor should we seek from the holy angels mere help, but ardently to desire their vision and to be with them and to see what are those *columns of heaven** that support the sphere of the world, that reflect and glow with so great and so preeminent a sign of divinity. *Job 26:11

We must not only seek from the Lord lovingkindness, but also the whole of our affection must be directed into him so that we love ourselves for the sake of God. Thus we may adore the majesty that makes all things and contains all things and on whom rational creatures desire to fix their gaze.* *1 Pet 1:12

6. These are the ways of spiritual training in which the religious mind is expanded and enticed, *forgetting the things that are behind and stretching forth to those that are ahead*, that is, eternal goods, *pressing toward the mark, to the prize of the heavenly vocation.** Is it possible that the blessed apostle Andrew, whose feast day is at hand, had not passed beyond nature when he said, "O good cross, for a long time desired, and already prepared for the soul who longs for you! I come to you confident and rejoicing"?[2] This is the voice of a person who has been transformed and who has risen from the goods of nature to the goods of grace, so to *glory not only in the hope but glory also in tribulations*,* and he goes from the presence of the council, *rejoicing that he was worthy to suffer reproach for the name of Jesus.** Not only patiently, but even *Phil 3:13-14 *Rom 5:2-3 *Acts 5:41

---

[2] Antiphon from Magnificat of Second Vespers for the feast of Saint Andrew.

happily he truly and ardently hurried to torture as to a crowning, to punishments as to pleasures.

7. In the future, those eternal goods are the goods that *eye has not seen nor ear heard** and that never go out from the homeland that knows nothing except joy and jubilation. In that place nothing is lacking; behold the abundance by which human desire is filled! What is that copiousness where there is nothing that you would not wish, but rather everything is what you want? *Let peace be in your strength*, says the prophet to Jerusalem, *and abundance in your towers.** In those towers, I say, which according to another prophet shall be built with precious stones,* where God shall satisfy us with the fat of grain and no longer with the husk of a sacrament.*

If nothing is lacking for us,* but something might be hidden from us, would that be the perfection of glory? It follows that nothing shall escape our notice. Behold Wisdom, by which human curiosity shall be satisfied! O Wisdom, by which we shall then know perfectly all things that are in heaven and on earth, drinking in knowledge of all things from the very spring of Wisdom! I shall not dread suspicions; I shall not fear debates, because that community, according to John, shall be like very pure glass,* so that, just as we discern details through the most transparent glass,* we may see the consciences of others most clearly.

If both nothing is lacking and nothing is hidden, then would anxiety and fear of loss remain? There is nothing to fear on that account. Behold the power by which human infirmity is strengthened! *He who has placed peace on your borders has strengthened the bolts of your gates** so that no enemy may enter,* no friend may go out.

There is the place of highest abundance, the highest Wisdom, the highest power. I think that nothing is lacking for the plenitude of blessedness and for the highest human happiness. These are the goods of nature, of grace, of glory, goods of humanity, goods of virtue,

*1 Cor 2:9

*Ps 121:7

*Tob 13:21
*Ps 147:14
*Ps 22:1

*Rev 21:19
*Rev 21:21

*Ps 147:13, 14
*Rev 21:27

goods of eternity. Let us think about these things, let us ruminate on these things, brothers, and, according to the precept of the law, let us recall the rumination* *so life be such and the life of* our *spirit be in such things.* For thus holy thought shall protect us* so that we may say with the saint, *the meditation of my heart always in your sight, O Lord, my helper and my redeemer.*

*see Lev 11:3
*Isa 38:16
*Prov 2:11

*Ps 18:15

Sermo 17

Concerning the Triple Custody of the Hand, the Tongue, and the Heart

1. All of us make the excuse that we suffer a lack of grace, but perhaps it is more proper for grace itself to complain that some have forsaken it. To be sure, the grace of devotion that we seek is a matter of the heart, and the heart that neglects to furnish an internal receptacle cheats itself of this gift. On the other hand, how can we be concerned about our heart if we are not yet cautious about our mouth or do not yet keep ready custody of our hand? It is no wonder that someone who has not even taken the first steps to grace should lack its consummation, not to mention that one who has yet to grasp the beginners' level also has not attained the intermediate.

It is a great thing for a worldly person to have clean hands. For a monk it is not great, but obviously it is a great evil for monks if they do not avoid defiling their hands. On the contrary, the purity of monks' hands is considered more important, and our justice is expected to be more ample, than that of worldly people. Undoubtedly Scripture says to those people, *Flee fornication*,* and, *He who stole, let him now steal no more*,‡ and another similar saying: *They who do such things shall not obtain the kingdom of God.**

Should we not also fear such defilement of our works and such serious contamination of our hands? But the

*1 Cor 6:18
‡Eph 4:28
*Gal 5:21

brighter the hands, so also the more seriously offensive a small stain on them looks. Likewise, an ever-so-small spot discolors a precious garment in a more ugly manner. For us the least disobedience that we can imagine counts as dirtiness. If neglect of even the least of the commandments persists in our actions, then it is no longer a stain but a serious blemish.

Therefore, diligently guarding works nurtures the beginning of our monastic conversion, while indeed still little light—but nevertheless now light—is among us.* Truth says to those who perhaps do not think that they have a great light, *When you have done all these things that are commanded you, say: We are unprofitable servants; we have done only that which we ought to do.** "But," you will say, "he advises us to say that for the sake of humility." Obviously on account of humility, but could it be contrary to truth? Moreover, if we are still found to be very negligent about custody of deeds, no wise person would advise us to strain out the gnat of proud thoughts if we are at risk of swallowing the camel of sinful deeds.*

2. But even if our hands have already been washed, we do not so quickly move on to the heart. The sensible person owes the next pursuit, the intermediate concern, to cleansing the lips. If you will say, "Rare is the one who seems to control his speech with judgment," then from this indeed you shall learn how rare is perfection, and you shall find that success is not common to all.

To be sure, who would reckon how much filth that little member,* the tongue, can gather, how thick the dirtiness can be piled up with uncircumcised lips,* how serious the mischief of a careless mouth? For there is a loose tongue in idle speech. It is a shameless tongue; it is also boastful:* the shamelessness serves lust, the boasting serves arrogance. It is likewise a deceitful tongue* as well as an abusive tongue. The deceitfulness is subdivided into lies and flattery. The abusive tongue, how-

*John 12:35

*Luke 17:10

*Matt 23:24

*Jas 3:5
*Exod 6:30

*Ps 11:4
*Ps 108:3

ever, first inflicts insults on one's face and then disparages in secret.* If *for every idle word that people speak they shall render an account* to God *in the day of judgment,** then how much more severely shall they be judged for words that are deceitful, mean and insulting, proud or wanton, flattering or slanderous?

*see Eccl 10:11
*Matt 12:36

3. How true is that proverb, brothers: *In a multitude of words you shall not avoid sin!** So then, if I may pass over profanity and cursing, if a word is idle because it has no reasonable cause, then what reason can we offer for a word that is contrary to reason? Brothers, let none of you consider it a small matter when time is wasted in idle words, for indeed, now is the *acceptable time* and *a day of salvation.** The irrevocable word flies, the time of no return flies, and foolish people do not notice what they lose. "It is pleasing to make conversation," they say, "until the hour passes." Oh, until the hour goes by! Oh, until the time passes away! Until the hour passes that the compassion of the Creator bestows upon you for doing penance, for acquiring a pardon, for acquiring grace, for meriting glory. "Until the time passes by" in which you ought to have won back God's loving-kindness, to have hastened to fellowship with the angels, to sigh with longing for your lost inheritance, to aspire to the promised happiness, to arouse your lackadaisical will, to weep over injustice that you have committed!

*Prov 10:19

*2 Cor 6:2

So the farmers when the long-desired opportunity for planting is at hand, or vineyard workers when the expected *time of pruning has come,** do they rejoice to find other business and to have finished the day without their work? So when market day arrives, do the merchants usually seek excuses for delays, lest they make a profitable transaction with someone? Finally, is this how poor beggars, when their cries have finally drawn the one who distributes alms, wish to take a detour away from that person? And when their fellows flock to the

*Song 2:12

philanthropist, would they hide in the corners, take refuge out of sight *in the corners of the streets?**

4. If only the time of life were all that is lost in words! But there are many who are proved to have lost even their lives in words. They not only lose their own lives, but they also take life away from their own brothers. Could it be that *detractors, hateful to God,** hateful to life, do not lose life? Life flees from those whom it hates, and those whom life flees must die. Is it possible that one does not die after drinking the poison given by the malicious tongue of a detractor? Indeed the life of love is secretly taken away from such a person, and, without his knowing it, fraternal charity gradually grows cold in him.*

Perhaps the one who was disparaged is going to hear [the poisoned words], for the words fly in all directions. The rumor first passes through the mouths of many, and it cannot help increasing on the tongue of each gossiper; as rumors do, after they have been passed around, it is then brought back to the one whose offense it reflects. And so the one who hears shall be scandalized and shall wither away. Because of this, charity shall be extinguished more easily in such people, charity for which they previously lived more fully. *For if my enemy had reviled me*, he says, *I would at least have borne with it.**

And indeed prudent listeners look out for themselves. If people are wise, they also take precautions when they know that they themselves have been slandered. The prudent listener avoids being corrupted by the poison; the wise will not let themselves be perturbed by scandal. The tongue equally kills both the listener and the wise, because it is in itself evil-speaking; it strikes the conscience of the prudent listener and wounds the charity of the wise.

Is not the tongue a snake? It is clearly most ferocious, because it so lethally poisons three with one breath. Is not that tongue a lance? It is very sharp as it penetrates

*Matt 6:5

*Rom 1:30

*Matt 24:12

*Ps 54:13

three with one stab! *Their tongue,* Scripture says, *is a sharp sword.** The sword indeed is two-edged,‡ but more correctly the tongue of the detractor is three-edged.

*Ps 56:5
‡see Ps 149:6

5. You need not fear to say that the tongue is even more cruel than the spear point that pierced the Lord's side.* For the tongue stabs even *the body of Christ and members of the body.** It does not pierce an already lifeless body but by stabbing makes the body lifeless. The tongue is also more harmful than the thorns that the soldiers' madness placed on that so exalted head,* or even more cruel than the iron nails that the ultimate iniquity of the Jewish nation pounded into those most holy hands and feet.* If Jesus had not preferred the life of the Body that is now poked and stabbed to his own life in the body, then he would never have surrendered that body to an unjust death on the disgraceful cross.

*see John 19:34
*1 Cor 12:27

*see Matt 27:29

*see John 20:25

And we say: A rumor is a light matter; the tongue of a human being is tender, soft, and meager flesh. What wise person would give it great weight? A light matter indeed is a rumor because it flies lightly,[1] but it wounds heavily. Lightly the rumor crosses over, but it burns heavily. Lightly it penetrates the mind, but it does not exit lightly. It is brought forth lightly but is not recalled lightly. Easily it flies, and therefore it easily violates charity.

A *dying fly* is a trivial matter, but it *spoils the sweetness of the ointment.** A tender member is the tongue, but yet it can scarcely be mastered.[2] The substance is indeed weak and meager but big and strong in its use. It is a small member,* but it is a big evil if you do not beware. The tongue is thin but wide. The tongue is a most

*Eccl 10:1

*Jas 3:5

---

[1] Bernard employs some wordplay here. *Levis* means "light weight"; *leviter* can mean both "lightly" and "thoughtlessly," yet rumors can wound *graviter,* "heavily."

[2] This is another play on words; the adjective *tenerum* means "soft" or "tender"; the verb *teneri* means "to be held" or "mastered."

suitable instrument for emptying hearts, as I suppose the consciences of many among you would bear witness for me—unless perhaps we are all so perfect that our minds may never be found somewhat empty after a long conversation: meditation less devout, affection less dry, and the whole offering of prayer less fat* because of the words, either what we have said or even what we have heard, words either way.

*Ps 19:4

6. For if the tongue easily slips, then no less easily does the tongue slip into the heart. So for many people there is less benefit in restraining one's own tongue during conversation if one does not also beware the tongue of another. Practical is the brother who now speaks to you; he is wise, *religious and fearing God.** What is more, I say, he is an angel and an angel of light.* Even so, take care lest you hear something harmful. I would not have you be suspicious of his character, but beware his tongue, especially in community discussion.

*Acts 10:2
*see 2 Cor 11:14

Good indeed is the simplicity of the dove, but in this role may you not omit the cunning of the serpent.* Mary did not pass over the angel's word without discussion: *She thought within herself what manner of greeting this might be.** You also, you who have at least noticed in your wisdom and frequent experience how much words harm, you will not act foolishly if you are careful—since it is necessary to take part in conversation—both to employ wariness about the mouth and likewise take precautions for the ear. It is no wonder that we delay longer at this stage in our progress, for indeed most of us, we may suppose, are still making progress and not yet perfected.

*Matt 10:16;
2 Cor 2:11

*Luke 1:29

7. For all that, perhaps we seem excessive in our scoffing at words. Nevertheless, keep in mind that it is the tongue that speaks against the tongue's vices. So the tongue actually should be excused since it did not spare itself and even protected its listeners against the tongue's dangers that are specific to itself. A word is a

wind, but it is not always a burning wind.* *Arise, O north wind*, Scripture says, *and come, O south wind, blow through my garden and let the aromatic spices flow.*

There is also great utility in words. Often a most precious benefit is found in the tongue. Truly *the just man lives by faith,* and *faith then comes by hearing, and hearing by the word* of God.* For how shall anyone live unless one believes? How shall one believe unless one has heard? And how shall one hear if no one preaches the faith to him?* To be sure, that is why we must give words greater attention and more careful vigilance. It might be that, as Scripture says, *Death and life are in the power of the tongue.* Otherwise, if it were only involved in life, then the tongue would not need circumcision. Likewise, if it pertained only to death, it should even be cut out.* Now then, *a watch must be set before our mouths, and a door round our lips,* lest if our mouths were closed forever that would doom life-giving edification, or give free passage to a deadly destruction. Therefore brothers, let us keep watch over our actions lest we omit what has been commanded or commit what is forbidden. To this double vigilance the prophet exhorts us, saying, *Decline from evil and do good.**

Likewise, let us also keep vigil over our words lest by our words we offend God or harm our neighbor. Fortunate is the one who is truly worried by that double fear in every conversation and who is urged by the consideration of the two types of listeners. First, consideration of the divine majesty, for *it is a fearful thing to fall into the hands of the living God.** Second, consideration of fraternal weakness, for which it is likewise very easy to cause offense.

8. I do not think, however, that we ought to call someone perfect who never offends with words,* except perhaps by comparison to one who only keeps watch over his actions. For Truth himself in the gospel says this about vigilant servants who stand ready for the

*Job 27:21

*Song 4:16

*Rom 1:17
*Rom 10:17

*Rom 10:14; see Isa 52:7

*Prov 18:21

*see Gal 5:11-12
*Ps 140:3

*Ps 36:27

*Heb 10:31

*Jas 3:2

coming of the Lord: *If the Lord shall come in the third watch and find them so, blessed are those servants.** You will notice that by no means does he say this about the first watch or even about the second.

 This third watch, you see, is over the heart. Wisdom now rightly advises us to employ *all watchfulness* over the heart, no doubt *because life issues out from the heart.** For my part, I even think that this especially consists of two [types of] vigilance: the concerned mind watchfully turns its attention equally to its two flocks: the flock of the affections and the flock of the thoughts. And the heart is rightly given every vigilance because the hands and tongue also depend on it, unless perhaps, God forbid, some bear a zeal for pretense, and *they have an appearance of godliness* but *not the virtue.**

 For just as the bubbling flow of a spring, before it fills the ditches around it, cannot flow back or settle or be able to rise up to a higher basin because it flows elsewhere, so is the human spirit until one realizes exactly the double vigilance about which I spoke above—of the hand and of the tongue. Nor will one be able to turn back to this perfect care of oneself, or to enjoy the pleasant tranquility of devotion, or progress to the sublime step of divine contemplation.

 See, brothers, if we seek the grace of a heavenly visit, then thus should we seek. If we desire to experience spiritual consolation, then thus should we beg. If we want to see the heavens open for us, then thus should we knock.* Finally, in this triple manner let us keep vigil if we wish *to enter into the wedding with the Bridegroom,** Jesus Christ our Lord, *who is blessed for ever. Amen.**

*Luke 12:38

*Prov 4:23

*2 Tim 3:5

*see Matt 7:7

*Matt 25:10, 13
*Rom 1:25

Sermo 18

Concerning Spiritual Joy, or Concerning Romans 14:17: *The Kingdom of God is not food and drink*

1. Why do we turn aside from the way,* we who hasten to joy? It is indeed joy of God's Kingdom, though it does not come first. It is joy of God's Kingdom, but not a carnal joy, not a worldly joy, not the joy whose end is overcome by mourning.* Rather it is the joy born of great sadness.* Again, not the joy of those *who are glad when they have done evil, nor rejoicing in the most wicked things*,* but *joy in the holy Spirit*.* During this meantime, however, where does this joy come from if it does not proceed from justice and peace? Justice, peace, and joy continue then like cells of honeycomb in that a more solid material can easily contain the runny liquid.

*see Ps 79:13

*Prov 14:13
*see John 16:20
*Prov 2:14
*Rom 14:17

There will be a time now when we will enjoy simple honey itself and *our joy shall be full** and pure, so that we will rejoice not only *in* the Spirit, but also *by* the Spirit himself. There will be a time when our joy shall be in every way spiritual. That is, our joy shall no longer be excited by any bodily experience, not by works of compassion, not by tears of contrition, not by practice of justice, not by proof of patience, but by the great presence of the Spirit himself, *on whom even the angels themselves desire to look.**

*1 John 1:4

*1 Pet 1:12

In this meantime, Wisdom seasons all the rest for me in place of salt, as if Wisdom itself were not food.* In this meantime, *I sigh before I eat.** And even then *I am not allowed to swallow down my saliva.** For the wise person is one for whom all things taste just as they are. The one for whom Wisdom already tastes of itself, exactly as it truly is, is not only wise but even blessed. Certainly this is *to see God just as he is.** Indeed this *flow of the river makes the city of God joyful*;* this is the torrent of pleasure. Finally, this is the intoxicating abundance.*

*see Mark 9:48
*Job 3:24
*Job 7:19

*1 John 3:2
*Ps 45:5
*Ps 35:9

2. Now truly, Lord, *they have no wine*: for *the wine has failed* in this wedding during the meantime,* at least the wine of carnal enticement and of worldly concupiscence. *Their wine*, Scripture says, *is the gall of dragons and the venom of asps, which is incurable.** May this wine always fail for us, my brothers, because it is not good wine. Good wine is not from the vine of impurity but is drawn from the water pot of purification.* Good wine is not made from the grapes of Gomorrah,* but from the water of Judea.

*John 2:3

*Deut 32:33

*see John 2:6-10
*Deut 32:32
*John 2:10

You have kept, it says, *the good wine until now*,* for indeed he saves the best wine even until now. Clearly that wine must not be made from water but must be experienced rather from the large grape of the Promised Land. That grape, during this meantime, is *suspended on a pole** while *we know Christ according to the flesh*‡ *and him crucified.**

*Num 13:24-25
‡2 Cor 5:16
*1 Cor 2:2

Surely the wine had not failed for the one who said, *My soul refused to be comforted.** But he also seems to have tasted water made into wine when he adds, *I remembered God and was delighted.** For what else will the one who enjoys only God's memory do in the present time? So also, clearly, the apostles *tasted water made into wine** when *they went from the presence of the council, rejoicing that they were accounted worthy to suffer reproach for the name of Jesus.**

*Ps 76:3

*Ps 76:4

*John 2:9

*Acts 5:41

How could the joy from reproaches not be the wine made from water? No doubt the promise of Truth was already fulfilled, which had been made to them in these words: *Your sorrow shall be turned into joy.** That is, your water shall be turned into wine. Are you amazed that water is changed into wine? It even changes into bread, unless perhaps *you forgot to eat your bread,** the bread about which you have read, *You will feed us with the bread of tears and give us for our drink tears in measure.**

Finally, hear the measure: *Now there were set there six water pots of stone*, Scripture says, *according to the Jews' manner of purifying.** If truly *you are a Jew not in the flesh but in the spirit,** then *you shall serve for six years; in the seventh year you shall go free.** By six water pots you shall be purified; *within six days you shall labor.** *In six tribulations you shall be set free, and in the seventh, evil shall not touch you.** Moreover, not only will you be liberated by tribulations, but also you will drink wine from them, when, according to the apostle, you will have begun to glory not only in hope but even in tribulations.*

3. During the meantime, this is the double joy that you have in the holy Spirit:* joy for memory of future goods and tolerance of present evils. Of course one tastes nothing carnal in these, nothing worldly, nothing of vanity, but it is the Spirit of Truth* and the Wisdom of heaven. And in both one gets a foretaste of sweetness.

Rejoice in the Lord always, says the apostle, *again, I say rejoice.** And he follows up by adding the material of this double joy: *Let your modesty be known to all men. The Lord is near.** What is our modesty if it is not gentleness and patience? Let us rejoice therefore over that which we expect, seeing how *the Lord is near*. Again let us rejoice over that which we endure so that our modesty may be known to all. No doubt *tribulation works patience, patience trial, and trial hope. Hope however does not confound.**

4. Then let the soul be made suitable for taking on this twin spiritual happiness. Two conditions are equally

*John 16:20

*Ps 101:5

*Ps 79:6

*John 2:6
*Rom 2:28-29
*Exod 21:2
*Exod 20:9

*Job 5:19

*Rom 5:2-3

*Rom 14:17

*John 16:13

*Phil 4:4

*Phil 4:5

*Rom 5:4-5

necessary for the exercise of justice. Likewise two are necessary for the preserving of peace, both of which, of course, sacred Scripture often recommends to us.* Indeed, the exercise of justice seems *to depend entirely on these two commandments*:* that *one never do to another what one would not have done to oneself*,* just as the apostles' letter to the nations maintains* and just as the Lord says to the same apostles: *Whatsoever you would want others to do to us, let us do also to them.**

On the other hand, seeing how *in many things we all offend*,* peace is impossible in this place and time of scandals, for not yet have *the angels* come *who would remove all scandals from the Kingdom of God*,* for we are not in that blessed city on whose *borders God has placed peace*.* Therefore it is impossible here to preserve peace entirely among us. It is impossible, unless both those people who somehow offend their neighbor shun bold self-exaltation and the neighbor who is offended likewise shuns unappeasable stubbornness.

5. And so let us strive, my brothers, to be found humble enough both to make amends with those who have something against us* and good natured enough to forgive those who have offended us. Not just because preservation of mutual peace among us consists *in these two commandments*,* but also because we cannot obtain divine atonement without them. Nor does God receive an offering from one who does not *go first to be reconciled to his brother.** Finally, God demanded a more strict account from the servant who had not forgiven the debt of his fellow servant.*

Now if these three, *justice and peace and joy in the Holy Spirit*, remain in us,* then it is not as if we are secure before him that *the Kingdom of God is within us*,† but rather *with fear and trembling* let us *work out our salvation*,# knowing without doubt that *we still have this great treasure in earthen vessels.**

---

*Matt 22:40
*Tob 4:16
*Acts 15:23

*Matt 7:12

*Jas 3:2

*Matt 13:41

*Ps 147:14

*see Col 3:13

*Matt 22:40

*Matt 5:24

*Matt 18:32-33

*Rom 14:17; see also 1 Cor 13:13
†Luke 17:21
#Eph 6:5; Phil 2:12
*2 Cor 4:7

Sermo 19

Concerning Romans 14:17: The Kingdom of God is not food and drink[1]

1. The apostle Paul is usually brief in words, rich in meaning. Saint Jerome, who was known for his eloquence as well as his gifts of wisdom, considered each of Paul's words to be as thunder. Paul, you see, expressed it all so clearly and so thunderously with *spirit and power.** He wonderfully taught in a sequential order and a fullness of meaning in each connection. *The kingdom of God is not*, he says, *food and drink but justice and peace and joy in the Holy Spirit.** What do you say to this, you who are gluttonous and wanton, *whose God is the belly,** whose every enjoyment is either in the belly or beneath the belly, about whom, as the same apostle says, *in riotousness you have nourished your hearts* and your bodies?* Listen, listen: *Food for the belly and the belly for food, but God shall destroy both it and them.** *Woe to you who sleep upon beds of ivory and are wanton on your couches, who eat the calves from the midst of the herd, who drink refined wine and anoint yourselves with the best ointments.** Oh, you sons of men, how long will you be dull of heart because you are fat of body, *why do you love vanity** *and despise truth?*

*Luke 1:17

*Rom 14:17

*Phil 3:19

*Jas 5:5

*1 Cor 6:13

*Amos 6:1, 4, 6

*Ps 4:3

---

[1] Written by Nicholas of Clairvaux.

Fat of flesh, delights of body, fullness of belly: either they shall abandon you before death, or you shall leave them behind at death. *For when one shall die*, says the saint, *one shall take nothing away, nor shall one's glory descend with him.** *They are laid in hell like sheep. Death shall feed upon them.** It is right to say *like sheep* because, once stripped of their fleece (i.e., worldly wealth), they are harshly oppressed and sheared, and then assigned naked to everlasting flames. *Death shall feed upon them* because they shall always die to life and live for death. Therefore, in this world, the flesh is given to worms; in the next world the soul is assigned to fires until again the unfortunate body and soul partnership shall be rejoined. Then they shall be joined in punishing torments, this body and soul who were partners in vice.

*Ps 48:18
*Ps 48:15

2. Oh you hedonist, you who are surrounded and confused by luxuries and wealth, you can expect shame and death.[2] *The kingdom of God is not food and drink,** nor purple and fine linen, for that rich man who was dressed in purple and linen descended at once into hell.*

*Rom 14:17

*see Luke 16:19-22

If not food and drink, what then? It is *justice and peace and joy in the holy Spirit.** Do you strive and struggle because joy is at the end? *So foolish children* of Adam,* with a headlong leap, jumping over justice and peace, you wish to convert and corrupt the end to the beginning? For there is no one who does not want to be glad. *It shall not stand, and this shall not be,** because just as *there is no peace for the wicked*, so also no joy, *says the Lord.*† *Not so the wicked, not so.*# The first goal is to do justice; *seek after peace and pursue it,** and so eventually seize joy—more correctly, be embraced by joy.

*Rom 14:17
*Dan 13:48

*Isa 7:7
†Isa 48:22; 57:21
#Ps 1:4
*Ps 33:15

---

[2] *Surrounded . . . confused . . . shame*: Nicholas plays on the words *circumfusus, confusus, confusionem*.

So the angelic assembly first did justice when it stood in truth* and deserted the deserter of truth. After this, by that peace they were strengthened, that *peace which surpasses all understanding*;* because although the angels are enveloped by various ranks of honor, none would complain, none would envy.

*see John 8:44

*Phil 4:7

3. *Praise you, the Lord, O Jerusalem. Praise your God, O Zion, because he has strengthened the bolts of your gates, he has blessed your children within you, he who has placed peace on your borders.** Praise, and redouble your praises, because your gates have been closed with the safest bars and unshakable bolts. No enemy enters, and no friend exits. *He has blessed your children within you** with every spiritual blessing in heavenly places with Christ.* There is now no fear on your borders, because he has *placed peace on your borders.** You have no temptations, no squadron of thoughts upsets you, because that perverter and shape-shifter is far away from your walls and from your children. And the one who is always the *selfsame** consolidates and unites with the same identity, which is *compact together,** as Scripture says.

*Ps 147:12-14

*Ps 147:13
*Eph 1:3

*Ps 147:14

*Ps 101:28
*Ps 121:3

This is now the third time that they shall draw waters with joy out of the Savior's fountains.* And to the naked eye, so I should say, they gaze upon the essence of divinity, not deceived by any imagination of corporeal phantoms. Behold joy *in* the end but *without* end.

*John 21:14
*Isa 12:3

4. Having been expelled from that happy region, we wretched people have descended into this vanity, or, more correctly, we *fell* into vanity. *The noble Children of Zion*, says the prophet, *and they who were clothed with the best gold, how are they considered as earthen vessels?** *Children of Zion*, meaning children of that contemplative city, obviously, *the Lord has built up Zion so that he may be seen in his glory.** *Children of that heavenly Jerusalem which is free, which is our mother.** We have been nobles by the dignity of our creation, *clothed with the best gold* by our divine image. How therefore from these nobles have

*Lam 4:2

*Ps 101:17
*Gal 4:25-26

we in fact been regarded *as earthen vessels*? How have we degenerated into these clay and fragile bodies?

For the angels demonstrate, dearest brothers, justice to God, peace among themselves, and joy for themselves. So also you, human being, must not first seize what is yours, nor may you spurn both justice that is for God and the peace that you owe to your neighbor. Justice is the virtue by which one renders to each his due. You do not owe merely one justice to the Creator, but many and various [acts of] justice. *For the Lord is just and has loved justice.** *Your justice is as the mountains of God;** rightly *as the mountains*, because he has heaped many piles of his compassion upon you.

*Ps 10:8
*Ps 35:7

5. And of course he first created you along with and among other creatures, not without a privilege of great dignity. With regard to all creatures, *he spoke, and they were made.** After that, in his majesty, having been inflamed with a most vehement love for you, he redeemed you. Was this redemption accomplished in a word? No, rather in thirty-three years *he wrought salvation in the midst of the earth,** nailed to a cross, doomed to death, regarded as a laughingstock. Your God was made your brother, not the brother of angels, because *nowhere does he take hold of the angels, but of Abraham's seed he takes hold.** Indeed, you have this in common: that you were made, that you specifically are his brother.

*Ps 148:5

*Ps 73:12

*Heb 2:16

He has added something more special to us as well, because with his finger he has dragged us from the *wide and broad way that leads to death,** and put us *in the council of the just and in the congregation.** *What should he do more that he has not done?** Who indeed would not feel their hearts of stone softened* in the face of such a great and admirable multitude of benefits, from so great and so wonderful a benefactor? Therefore whatever you are, whatever you can be, you owe to your Creator, to your Redeemer, to the one who calls you.

*Matt 7:13
*Ps 110:1
*Isa 5:4
*see Ezek 11:19

6. But once you have made justice, then make peace. For as long as we are in this earthen vessel* and the

*Lam 4:2

fragility of human association, we cannot be found entirely immune from scandals. *If therefore you remember that your brother has anything against you,** may you be humble enough to beg pardon. If you have something against a brother, then may you readily forgive, and all members shall be in peace.*

*Matt 5:23

*RB 34.5

Insofar as we are most prepared for these two, charity and humility, we cannot experience conflict. *Learn from me*, says the Lord, *because I am meek and humble of heart.** The meek heart pertains to charity because *charity is patient, is kind.** The humble heart is self-explanatory.

*Matt 11:29
*1 Cor 13:4

So *joy in the holy Spirit* will be for those who advance.* I say what the expert knows but the inexperienced does not know: For *the sensual man perceives not these things that are of God's Spirit.** Does it not often happen that, when we pray, we are shaken to the core at the memory of the joy in the *Jerusalem which is above, which is our mother,** and a wave of tears washes over the face of those who meditate?

*Rom 14:17

*1 Cor 2:14

*Gal 4:26

Oh, if it would last! *If I forget you, O Jerusalem, let my right hand be forgotten. Let my tongue cleave to my jaws if I do not remember you, if I make not Jerusalem the beginning of my joy.** The heavenly Jerusalem is truly the beginning of happiness, because that is where happiness is finally restored.

*Ps 136:5, 6

7. When, Lord Jesus, *will you cut my sackcloth and surround me with gladness so that my glory sings to you and I need not repent?** The beginning of that joy that we sometimes experience here is a drop, a little drip falling from that river whose flow *makes the city of God joyful.** When will the time come that we may be plunged more deeply into that spring of divinity with everlasting joys, when wave follows wave without interruption and alteration? *When shall I come and appear before the face of God?** When *shall I go over into the place of the wonderful tabernacle, even to the house of God?** When *as we have heard, so shall we see in the city of the Lord of hosts?**

*Ps 29:12-13

*Ps 45:5

*Ps 41:3
*Ps 41:5
*Ps 47:9

Look therefore, brothers, let us faithfully pursue this happy threesome,‡ and may we always be mindful of this saying: *Friend, why have you come?*# For we have not come to kill the king with a pretense, but to serve him *who is blessed forever.*‡

‡peace, justice, joy in the Holy Spirit
#Matt 26:50

‡Rom 1:25

Sermo 20

Concerning Luke 14:11:
Everyone who exalts himself shall be humbled, and one who humbles himself shall be exalted

1. *Everyone who exalts himself shall be humbled and one who humbles himself shall be exalted.** If we were to consider the stages of human beings carefully, brothers, we would find that there are four: the highest happiness, I say, is in heaven, to which we aspire, the middle happiness is that in Paradise, from which we have fallen, and similarly the middle unhappiness that is in this world on account of which we grieve, and finally there is the extreme unhappiness in hell that we rightly dread. I can say it even more briefly: life and the shadow of life, the shadow of death,* and death.

*Luke 14:11

*Ps 87:7

Since we have been put in neither the highest nor the lowest place, we fear to go any lower. Rather, we want to ascend, and we are so much the more anxious because we seem closer to the lowest than to the highest place. And behold the Lord says to us, *Everyone who exalts himself shall be humbled, and one who humbles himself shall be exalted.* What is the meaning of this inverse relationship between exaltation and humiliation?

So is it not enough, Lord, that *in your truth you have humbled us,** yet you still require human beings to humble themselves?* And indeed there still remains that place to which we can be humiliated, but *one who*

*Ps 118:75
*see Ps 9:39

falls to that place *shall no longer seek to rise again,** and one who has been humiliated down to hell would hope in vain for exaltation, as Scripture has it: *You have humbled us in the place of affliction, and the shadow of death has covered us.** If we have come to the point where *our life has drawn near to hell,** how shall we be humiliated further? *What profit is there in our blood if we go down to corruption?** Sensible people know that there is nothing else below us except that irreparable corruption. After the shadow of death, nothing remains except death; after *the place of affliction,** the only thing left is the place of death.

2. *One who humbles himself,* says the Lord, *shall be exalted.** If the Lord had said, "One who has been humbled shall be exalted," then certainly I would have exulted insofar as I had most definitely been humbled, and exceedingly so. Now, however, when he says, *Whosoever shall exalt himself shall be humbled,** then *I have trouble on every side.** Not that I am ignorant of what I would choose, but what I would do. I want to be exalted because it is exceedingly necessary, because indeed *I have not here a lasting city,** and it would not be good to remain here* even if it were allowed.

What is more, to go lower still is to perish. For I hold already the lower place, and for one who has only the lowest place below, [going lower] means hell. If I humble myself to that place, then there is no hope of exaltation. If I do not humble myself, then I continually despair of exaltation because *one who shall humble himself shall be exalted,** and only that one. *If I do this thing, it is death to me, and if I do it not,* then *I shall not escape the hands** of death, having been excluded from exaltation. If this is difficult to understand, then let us at least consider the previous saying.

3. The Lord says, *Everyone who exalts himself shall be humbled.** How does one whom Truth humbles exalt himself? Here we do not say where, but how, for there

*see Jer 8:4; Ps 40:9

*Ps 87:7
*Ps 87:4

*Ps 29:10

*Ps 87:7

*Luke 14:11

*Matt 23:12
*Dan 13:22

*Heb 13:14
*see Luke 9:33

*Matt 23:12

*Dan 13:22

*Luke 14:11

seems to be no lack of place, but rather lack of strength. I say again, where one can exalt oneself is not lacking to a human being, but what is utterly lacking is one who is able. There is indeed much will, but no ability.

To be sure, whether human beings are willing or not, the voice of the whole community of Adam, of the whole human race, is, *In your truth you have humbled me.** But whoever is humbled in truth is truly humbled, unless he is falsely exalted. Moreover, to be falsely exalted cannot be real exaltation.

*Ps 118:75

Thanks be to the Lord because he did not say, "Everyone who exalts himself shall be exalted." If we believed that, then we would try in vain to be exalted, for even now despair of ever achieving exaltation does not restrain our appetite for exaltation. As luck would have it, this is what he said: *One who exalts himself shall be humbled.** This does not pertain to the results of self-exaltation, which comes to nothing, but to the desire, which is stupid.

*Matt 23:12

4. For how many people do we see humiliated but not humble? How many are *stricken*, but *not grieved*?* How many are cared for by the Lord but not healed by the treatment itself? Such are those who *count it delightful to be under the briers*,* ignoring sins‡ that they frequently commit, ignoring the slippery path in which they falter, the darkness by which they are blinded, the traps among which they walk, ignoring the place of affliction† that they inhabit, the *body of death*# that they bear, the *heavy yoke*‡ that they carry, the heavier conscience that they hide, ignoring the most heavy judgment that they await. Such was that person to whom John was ordered to write in Revelation, *You say: I am rich and have need of nothing, and you know not that you are wretched and miserable and poor and blind and naked.**

*Jer 5:3

*Job 30:7
‡Wis 11:24

†Ps 87:7
#Rom 7:24
‡Sir 40:1

*Rev 3:17

It is no wonder if the exaltation of the children of human beings is vain and false, since indeed *they* are vain and false.* Truth humbles them, vanity exalts

*see Ps 61:10

them: *And they loved darkness rather than the light,** embracing vanity, which exalts them, and they seek after lying.* In turn, they kick against truth that humbles them, with any vows and devotions possible, with dissembling and useless efforts.

5. Have we accomplished anything? We have found, I think, how human beings might actually humble themselves. People can cling, I say, to the truth that humbles them, not dissemble, but cooperate with the truth by an affection of devoted loving-kindness. Hence in turn I shall beware hardness of heart* as carefully as I can; I shall feel and *lament my sorrow** lest, if perhaps I have been unfeeling, my wound might even be incurable. I shall be a *man seeing my poverty by the rod of his indignation,** lest my soul come to be associated with those of whom Truth says, *I have struck them, and they have not grieved,** and similarly, *We have cured Babylon, but she is not healed.**

This humiliation is a heavy cure, but heavier is that sickness pride. I wish my pride would be cured in order to be healed by this treatment! Therefore I agree with my adversary, I submit to my judge,* and finally I yield to the pressing thorn lest I be stung twice. For so I reckon myself to be what the Lord says: *Everyone who exalts himself shall be humbled, and one who humbles himself shall be exalted.** And if he says, whoever *kicks against the goad** is stung twice, then the one who feels it is spared, and *he gives place to wrath.**

*John 3:19
*Ps 4:3
*Matt 19:8
*Job 10:20
*Lam 3:1
*Jer 5:3
*Jer 51:9
*see Matt 5:25
*Luke 14:11
*Acts 9:5
*Rom 12:19

Sermo 21

Concerning Wisdom 10:10

1. *She conducted the just one through the right ways, and showed him the kingdom of God, and gave him the knowledge of the holy things, made him honorable in his labors, and accomplished his labors.** The *just one* is the one who *is the first accuser of himself,** and the *just one* is the one who lives *by faith;** the *just one* is also the one who is *without dread.** The first is indeed good because he approaches the way; the second is better because he runs through the way;* the third is the best because he already approaches the way's goal.

*Wis 10:10
*Prov 18:17
*Rom 1:17
*Prov 28:1

*see Ps 118:32

Here, however, let us take the first *just one,* whom we can find more quickly. It is the Lord, and no other, who led this first *just one,* because it is God's place to lead people back from the way of iniquity to the way of truth* and to guide them along the way.

*Ps 118:29-30

Through the right ways, he says. The ways of the Lord are right ways, beautiful ways,* full ways, level ways. Right ways without error because they lead to life, beautiful without dirtiness because they teach cleanness, filled with a multitude because the whole world already enters the net of Christ,* level and without difficulty because the right ways give sweetness. *For* his *yoke is sweet and* his *burden light.**

*Prov 3:17

*see Matt 13:47

*Matt 11:30

And showed him the kingdom of God. The Kingdom of God is relinquished, promised, shown, secured. The Kingdom is relinquished in predestination, promised in calling, shown in justification, secured in glorification.*

*see Rom 8:30

That is why the Lord says, *Come, you blessed of my Father, possess you the kingdom.** For thus says the apostle, *And whom he predestined, them he also called. And whom he called, them he also justified. And whom he justified, them he also glorified.** In predestination is grace, in calling power, in justification happiness, in praise glory.

*Matt 25:34

*Rom 8:30

2. *And gave him the knowledge of holy things.** Knowledge of holy things means being temporarily tormented in this life and delighted in eternity.* But knowledge of wicked things turns that backward. One part of wickedness is the knowledge of the world, which teaches vanity, and the other part is knowledge of the flesh, which teaches pleasure. The first is like a father; the second is like a mother to us. For just as a mother prefers rest for her son and by all means blocks every toil from her son, so is the flesh: *fat and thick and gross,** not allowing even the smallest fingers to be touched. On the other hand, just as the father wants his children to dash about here and there so that they can learn where and when they can gain status, so also the world wishes to entangle human beings in many labors so that they may learn how they can take pride, how to be puffed up, and how by vanity they may act foolishly.*

*Wis 10:10

*see Luke 16:25

*Deut 32:15

*Ps 61:10

The horse leech has two daughters: the horse leech is self-will, which is like the root; the two daughters are vanity and pleasure, shouting: *Bring, bring!** These two *are never satisfied; they never say: It is enough.** If any extinguishes these completely in themselves, not without merit will they be able to join that voice: *For my father and my mother have left me*, he says, *but the Lord has taken me up.**

*Prov 30:15
*Prov 30:15-16

*Ps 26:10

3. *She made him honorable in his labors.** Are we not also made honorable in our labors when we join all things that we do to the bond of unity,* so that *diverse weights and diverse measures* are not among us, because *both are abominable before God?** Are not also these cheap, common possessions, these belts and scapulars, honored

*Wis 10:10

*see Eph 4:3

*Prov 20:10

and revered by the princes of the earth? Pity us if we should rejoice in anything other than Christ and for Christ! Pity us if we should offer a poverty that is for sale!

And she accomplished his labors,* either in perseverance on earth so that he does not abandon justice before the end of life or hereafter in glory so that he may rejoice in eternity. Both are a happy fulfillment when, on earth, the just die full of days,* and after death they rise *unto length of days.** Fulfilled in both places: both grace here and glory hereafter, because *the Lord will give grace and glory.** Amen.

*Wis 10:10

*see Gen 25:8
*Ps 22:6

*Ps 83:12

Sermo 22

Concerning the Quadruple Debt

    *Matt 7:14
    *Pss 106:7; 17:31
    ‡see Ps 106:4;
     Dan 3:28
    #Gal 4:26

1. You are on *the way*, brothers, *that leads to life,** *on the right and undefiled way** that leads to that holy city Jerusalem,‡ *which is above, which is free, which is our mother.*# Arduous indeed is its ascent, since the ascent is cut into the very summit of the mountain, but this more advantageous way both eases and lessens the intensity of your toil.

    *see Ps 118:32
    *see Matt 11:28

What is more, you walk as much by a happy ease as by an easy happiness. You not only walk but you run,* because you have been unburdened* and well prepared, carrying no weight upon your backs. *Not so* the others,

    *Ps 1:4

*not so,** those who pull chariots and loads of gear. They must settle for circling around the base of the mountain, and usually they fall down the slope of the mountain so that they scarcely find their life's goal. Therefore you are the fortunate ones, you who have left behind yourselves and your possessions, everything without the least exception, because *you make a way* to the peak of the mountain *for him who ascends upon the west, the Lord is

    *Ps 67:5

his name.**

    *see Exod 16:3
    ‡Ps 106:4

On the other hand, although they have fled Egypt, those who still sigh, in their weakness, for various goods of Egypt* *found not the way to a city for their habitation.*‡ Rather, weighed down by the most heavy baggage of their self-will, either under the burden or with the burden, they fall, or they scarcely arrive at the intended course.

2. For in what way—thanks be to him whose grace has created all this—does your life not represent the apostles' life? They left all things,* and in the Savior's school, gathered under his presence, *they drew waters with joy out of the savior's fountain;** drinking in that fountain, they drank the source of life himself.* *Blessed are the eyes that have seen.** Have you not done something similar, though not in his presence, rather in his absence,* and not at the words of his mouth but rather at the voice of his messengers? Defend for yourselves this privilege: what they believed by vision and word, you have believed by hearing and proclamation.*

*Matt 19:27
*Isa 12:3
*Ps 35:10
*Matt 13:16

*Phil 2:12

*see Rom 10:16

So, my dearly beloved brethren, stand fast in the Lord* so that just as the apostles held the royal way* *in hunger and thirst, in cold and nakedness, in labors and fasting, and in keeping vigils,** and in all the other observances of justice, so also you, although you are not their equal in merit, are made their equal by your training (at least to some extent), so you may say to the Lord your God, when you have come before the throne of his glory, *We have rejoiced for the days in which you have humbled us: for the years in which we have seen evils.** *In truth I say to you** that in truth you are on the right way, on the holy way which leads to the holy of holies.

*Phil 4:1
*Num 21:22

*2 Cor 11:27; see 2 Cor 6:4-5

*Ps 89:15
*Luke 4:25

I would be lying—I say this for your consolation—if I said that out of the hands of this sinner, the souls of monks, of novices, and of lay brothers have not flown to heavenly joys, as free as those freed from our prison of mortality. If you ask how I know this, know that very certain signs have occurred and been shown to me.

3. It is not therefore that I should fear for you or on your behalf because of the powers of Satan and his servants,* since I know that his strength, by the wounds of the Redeemer, has been exposed to ridicule and reduced to nothing.† For in a spirit of fortitude# *the stronger crushes the strong,*‡ *shattering gates of brass and iron*

*see 2 Cor 11:14-15
†Ps 14:4
#Isa 11:2
‡Luke 11:21-22

bars.* I fear for you because of Satan's cunning and tricks, partly because of his natural subtlety and partly because he has learned about fragile human nature by experience over time for thousands of years. In whichever direction he turns, he is not ignorant.* So that insatiable murderer* did not assign bears or lions or strong animals of the earth to our first parents, but a twisting and crafty serpent,* who was in the habit of hiding among his twisting coils, now his head with his tail, then his tail with his head. In fact Scripture says not that the serpent was stronger, but that it was *more cunning than any of the beasts of the earth.**

So the serpent began in his first inquiry, searching the woman's mind, knowing that he must work by a clever trick rather than by force, saying, *Why has the Lord God commanded you that you should not eat of the tree of knowledge of good and evil?** And she answered, *lest perhaps we die*,* as certainly God had ordained, saying, *In what day soever you shall eat of it, you shall die the death.** She now places that under doubt, saying *lest perhaps* if we have eaten, then *we may die*. And hear the clever trick and malice of the serpent: *By no means*, he says, *shall you die.** God affirms, the woman doubts, Satan denies. So also I fear that just as the serpent seduced Eve by his trick,* so also *your minds should be corrupted from chastity which is in Christ Jesus.**

4. Do you think there is anyone among you to whom Satan says in his thoughts, "Why has God commanded you to keep this Rule?" For, depending on your spiritual vigor,* Satan suggests a relaxed lifestyle to this tepid monk, and to that fervent monk he proposes a more strict life. In each case he wants and expects only this: to take the monk from *the council of the just and the congregation** by any means. Surely the spirit that suggests this is a lying spirit,* a spirit that has power, that envies your place.* The wise one was not ignorant of this matter, for he says, *If the spirit of him who has power ascends upon you, leave not your place.**

*Ps 106:16

*see 2 Cor 2:11
*John 8:44

*see Gen 3:17; Isa 27:1

*Gen 3:1

*Gen 3:1; 2:17
*Gen 3:3
*Gen 2:17

*Gen 3:4

*see 2 Cor 2:11
*2 Cor 11:3; see Rom 8:39

*see Dan 14:35

*Ps 110:1
*1 Kgs 22:22
*Eccl 10:4; see Luke 11:22
*Eccl 10:4

Sermo 22

Far be it that the spirit of truth* who led you here should wish to lead you away, because it is not in his mouth to say, *Yes and no, but yes in him.** It is yes, just as the indisputable authority attests: *no one*, says the apostle, *speaking by the Spirit of God, says Anathema to Jesus.** Jesus is the savior or salvation itself; *anathema* is understood to mean separation. In fact, one who quietly murmurs to you about separation from salvation is neither the Spirit of God nor from God.† For the Holy Spirit knows not scattering, but gathering,# he who always *calls back the scattered of Israel into his land.*‡

5. What? Does someone seek a more vigorous life? I say to you that this is the most vigorous life, and it corresponds in every way possible, if you will face facts, to that first school of the Savior. Or do you dare to descend to a more relaxed life at least in your thoughts? Oh, *if you had also known** how much and to how many you are indebted, then you would see that what you do is nothing, nor does it count the least bit in comparison to your debt. Do you wish to know what and to whom you owe?

In the first place you owe all your life to Christ Jesus, because he laid down his life for your life.* He also sustained bitter tortures lest you sustain perpetual tortures. What could be terrible or hard to you when you recall that he who was in the form of God* *in the day of his eternity, in the brightness of the saints, begotten before the day star,** *the brightness and the figure* of God,† came to your prison and to your mud, *stuck fast*, as Scripture says, up to his elbows *in the mud of the deep.**

What is not sweet to you when you add up all your Lord's bitter experiences, when you remember first indeed those needs of his infancy, and then the labors that he endured in preaching, his weariness during his wanderings, temptations in fasting, giving up sleep for prayer, tears of compassion, treacherous traps in discussions, and finally the dangers he suffered among false brothers:* verbal abuse, spitting, beatings, floggings,

*John 14:17

*2 Cor 1:19

*1 Cor 12:3

†see John 9:16, 33
#see Luke 11:23
‡Bar 2:34, Isa 11:12; 56:8

*Luke 19:42

*see 1 John 3:16

*Phil 2:6

*Ps 109:3
†Heb 1:3
*Ps 68:3

*see 2 Cor 11:26-27

derision, mockery, reproaches, nails, and these similar sufferings that he labored and suffered with in his thirty-three years *in the midst of the earth** for the salvation of our race?

*Ps 73:12

Oh, how undeserved this mercy, how freely given and therefore how genuine the love, how unexpected the honor, how awe-inspiring the sweetness, how invincible the clemency! The king of glory* to be crucified for a most despicable slave, no, rather, for a worm!* *Who has ever heard such a thing? And who has seen the like to this?*† *For scarcely for a just man will one die,*# yet Jesus died for the unjust and for enemies,‡ choosing to live in exile from heaven in order to carry us back to heaven, a kind friend, a prudent counselor, a strong helper.*

*Ps 23:7
*see John 19:15
†Isa 66:8
#Rom 5:7
‡1 Pet 3:18

*Ps 70:7

6. *What shall I render to the Lord for all the things he has rendered unto me?** If all the lives of the children of Adam,† and all the days of old,# and the labors of all the human beings who have ever existed, who are and who shall be, were brought together in me, would it not be as nothing in comparison to his singular and amazing body? It is amazing even to the powers above: the conception by the Holy Spirit, the birth from the Virgin, the innocence of life, the flood of learning, the gleaming miracles, the revelations of sacraments.

*Ps 115:12
†Jer 32:19
#Mal 3:4

You see therefore: *As the heavens are exalted above the earth, so is his life exalted above our life.**[1] Yet his life was laid down for our life. Just as you cannot compare nothing to something, so also our life has no proportion to his life. For, you see, his life cannot be more dignified, and our life cannot be more wretched. May you not think that my words exaggerate the matter, because here every tongue fails, nor is a soul capable of gazing upon a mystery of such great dignity. When therefore I shall have devoted to him whatever I am and whatever

*Isa 55:9

---

[1] Bernard here paraphrases, as he often does, substituting "life" (*vita*) for "ways" (*viae*).

I am able to do, is it not just like a star to the sun, a drop to a river, a stone to a tower, dust to a mountain?

I have nothing except two paltry mites,* no, rather, the very smallest coins, that is, my body and soul. Or better, one paltry mite: my will. And shall I not give even that to his will, he who is so great, who preceded me with such great benefits, though I am so very small, who purchased the whole of me with his whole self? In any case, if I retain my will, with what face, with what eyes, with what mind, with what conscience do I go to the mercy of our God?* And dare I dig through that strongest of ramparts that protects Israel?* Do I dare to divert not just drops of his blood* but also streams from the five parts of his body into the price of my redemption?

Oh *perverse generation and unfaithful children!* What will you do in the day of the calamity which comes from afar? To whom will you flee for help?*

*Mark 12:42

*Luke 1:78
*Ps 120:4
*Luke 22:44

*Deut 32:20

*Isa 10:3

7. But is it possible that I am in debt to him alone to whom I am scarcely able to repay anything remotely sufficient? My past sins demand from me my future life, so to *bring forth fruits worthy of penance,** and *to recount all my years in the bitterness of my soul.** And *who is so sufficient for these things?** "I have sinned beyond the number of the sands on the seashore, and my sins have multiplied, and I am not worthy to see the heights of heaven because of the multitude of my iniquity, seeing that I provoked your wrath, and I have done evil before you."² *For evils without number have surrounded me; my iniquities have overtaken me, and I was not able to see.**

*Luke 3:8
*Isa 38:15
*2 Cor 2:16

*Ps 39:13

In that case, how shall I count what is beyond counting? How can I make satisfaction when I am forced to *repay the debt to the last farthing?** But also, *who can understand sins?** Saint Ambrose, that heavenly flute, says, "I have more easily found those who have preserved their

*Matt 5:26
*Ps 18:13

---

² *Peccavi*, response for Sundays after Pentecost, from the prayers of King Manasseh 9–10; see SCh 496:39n.d.

innocence than those who have done sufficient penance."* But also, however much one may repent, however much one may afflict and exhaust oneself, it is *for your name's sake*, not because of the merit of penance, *Oh Lord, that you will pardon my sin*, says the just one, *for it is great.** So when you have dedicated whatever you live, whatever you understand, whatever you have, whatever you can do to repentance alone, could it possibly count for something?

*De paenitentia 2.10.96

*Ps 24:11

A little earlier, you rendered your life to Christ for his life, and now again recollection of past sins demands your whole life. Can it be that, as is commonly said, you have arranged two husbands for one daughter?

8. What if I were to show you a third creditor who just as keenly as truly demands your life for himself? I think that you, too, long to possess citizenship from that place where, as Scripture has it, *Glorious things are said of you, O city of God,** that *glory that eye has not seen nor ear heard; neither has it entered into the heart of a human being,*† *the kingdom of all ages,*# to live forever *into everlasting eternity.*‡ I believe that you wish to be *as the angels of God in heaven,** to be even *heirs of God, and joint heirs with Christ,** to sing *alleluia* perpetually in the streets of the heavenly Zion,* and even to see what that might be *when Christ shall have delivered up the kingdom to God and to the Father, and God shall be all in all,*° and finally *to be like God* and *to see him as he is.**

*Ps 86:3
†1 Cor 2:7, 9
#Ps 144:13
‡Dan 12:3
*Matt 22:30
*Rom 8:17
*Tob 13:22
°1 Cor 15:23-24, 28
*1 John 3:2

Nor do I doubt that you also desire to receive the retiring shadows and the daybreak* when that solemn day shall dawn and cast out the clouds of worldly affairs, when the day shall no longer be far spent* but shall be eternal noon full of warmth and light, the sun standing still, shadows banished, swamps dried up, and foulness repelled.

*Song 2:17

*Luke 24:29

Does it not behove you to give your whole self along with whatever you can collect from whatever source to buy this? And when you have completed all of this, may you nevertheless reckon *that the sufferings of this time* or of your body *are not worthy to be compared with the glory to come that shall be revealed in us.** Can you be so shameless or so foolish that you dare to count your paltry mite toward this debt, even when both the life of Christ and your repentance for sins compete in snatching it up?*

9. What will you say if I bring up yet a fourth creditor into the discussion, one who by right comes first and wants the other three to give up their superior places? *Behold, he who made heaven and earth is at the door;** he is your Creator, you are the creature; you are the servant, he is the Lord; he is the potter, you are the pottery.* Therefore, you owe the whole of what you are to him from whom you have all, to him who is above all, the Lord who both made you and who has benefited you, who attends to the course of the stars, the proper mixture of air, the fecundity of the earth, the abundance of the fruits.

In fact, he must be served with your whole self right down to the marrow, with the whole of your powers, lest perhaps he regard you with an eye of indignation and despise you and crush you unto eternity and forever and ever! But I do not suppose that so great a madness has overcome you that in this case you presume also to mention your paltry mite, still less to count it.

Now then, explain to me, to which of these four creditors would you propose to *pay back what you owe*, when each one is so important a collector that any one of them could choke you to death?* See, *Lord, I suffer violence, answer for me.** *Into your hands I commend my paltry mite.** Pay all my creditors! Free me from them all! Because *you are God, and not a human;** because for *humans this is impossible, but for you all things are possible.** *I have done what I could.*† Lord, *hold me excused,*# because *your eyes have seen my imperfect being!*‡

*Rom 8:18

*see Matt 11:12

*Matt 24:26, 33; Ps 120:2

*see Rom 9:20-21

*Matt 18:28
*Isa 38:14
*Ps 30:6
*Hos 11:9
*Matt 19:26
†Mark 14:8
#Luke 14:18
‡Ps 138:16

Who therefore will groan further, saying, "We work too much, we fast too often, we keep vigil too long," when all that cannot answer to one thousandth, no, not even the least bit of one's debt?

This is perhaps, brothers, your true Lent, not exterior but interior, which contains not the skin of the sacrament but the fat. For if you owe to each of these four creditors, both through them and on their behalf, every perfection of the Ten Commandments, certainly four times ten makes your forty days of Lent, which we must keep *all the days of our lives.** And the one who assembled you in this place preserves your life in holy work, so that *when he who is your life shall appear, then you also shall appear with him in glory.** Amen.

*Ps 22:6; see RB 49.1

*Col 3:4

Sermo 23

Concerning the Discernment of Spirits; Concerning the Seven Spirits

1. Paul, the teacher of the Gentiles, on account of the spiritual nature by which we live, prompts his disciples to the spiritual way of life, saying, *If we live in the Spirit, then let us also walk in the Spirit.** It is as if he were saying, If *the flesh profits nothing* and *it is the spirit*, rather, *who gives life* to flesh,* then it is necessary to distinguish the precious from the worthless* and to put first the more worthy part so that we may *walk according to the spirit, not according to the flesh.**

*Gal 5:25

*John 6:64
*Jer 15:19

*Rom 8:4

For indeed the flesh must be converted to the spirit so that the flesh serves, and is not served by, the spirit. So it is proper that the spirit says to its servant, *Come, and she comes. Do this, and she does it.** If the flesh will remain *on the sides of our house,** that is, in a concealed and humble place, then so indeed shall *our wife be like a fruitful vine,** and *she shall be saved through childbearing,*‡ that is, through good works. May the soul, on the other hand, reside within the house like a lady, like the head of the household, like a judge. Thus shall it be as Scripture has it: *My soul is continually in my hands.** Accursed indeed is that spirit who makes his own portion worse. Accursed is the person who *feeds on barren women and has done no good for the widow.** Finally, as the same apostle testifies, *if we live according to the flesh, then we*

*Matt 8:9
*Ps 127:3

*Ps 127:3
‡1 Tim 2:15

*Ps 118:109

*Job 24:21

129

shall die,* because *those who walk according to the flesh cannot please God.** And *those who sow in the flesh shall reap corruption from the flesh.** *If*, however, *by the Spirit we mortify the deeds of the flesh, then we shall live, for whosoever are led by the Spirit of God, they are children of God.** And *those who sow in the spirit from the spirit shall reap life everlasting.**

*Rom 8:13
*Rom 8:1, 8
*Gal 6:8
*Rom 8:13-14
*Gal 6:8

2. Consequently, brothers, we wisely choose a spiritual life, *and it shall not be reputed as foolishness for us;** it is wise indeed *to chastise the body* and to subject it to servitude,* and *to adore God, who is a spirit, in spirit and truth.**

*Ps 21:3
*1 Cor 9:27
*John 4:24

But, because there are diverse types of spirits, it is necessary for us to discern spirits,* especially since, as we learn from the apostle, *not every spirit should be trusted.** It can seem to the less educated, and to those who have not sufficiently *exercised their senses,** that every thought is a conversation within the human spirit itself rather than with another. The reliable truth of faith proves that isn't so, as does the witness of divine Scriptures. *I will hear*, says the prophet, "not what I myself shall speak," but *what the Lord God will speak in me.** And another prophet says, *the angel who spoke in me,** etc. And in the psalm we learn that *indignation and wrath* are *sent by evil angels;** so accordingly does the apostle fear that *just as the serpent deceived Eve by his cunning,** so also the hearts of his disciples to whom he speaks might be deceived‡ by the devil.

*see 1 Cor 12:10
*1 John 4:1
*Heb 5:14
*Ps 84:9
*Zech 1:9
*Ps 77:49
*2 Cor 11:3; see Gen 3:13
‡see Deut 11:16

Paul himself was certainly not ignorant of the devil's devices,* so he also says, *For our struggle is not against flesh and blood but against principalities and powers, against the rulers of the world of this darkness.** However, when he testifies that certain people are puffed up by their own *carnal spirit,** the same apostle plainly points out that a spirit of flesh is not good. He also declares that there is even *a spirit of this world* when he *boasts in the Lord* on behalf of himself and equally on behalf of his

*2 Cor 2:11
*Eph 6:12
*Col 2:18

disciples because they have not received that worldly spirit, *but* rather *the Spirit that is from God so that we may know,* he says, *the things that are given to us from God.**   *1 Cor 2:12; 1:31

3. So these are the two accomplices of that spiteful prince of darkness: the spirit of the flesh and the spirit of this world, which are controlled by the spirit of wickedness.* Therefore, whichever of these three spirits speaks to our spirit, let us not believe it, because they thirst for blood, certainly not the blood of bodies but, because it is more important, the blood of souls. Since the nature of all three is spiritual, *by their* words *we shall know them.** And whichever spirit it may be who speaks, the suggestion itself shall reveal them: for the carnal spirit always speaks of comforts, the worldly spirit speaks of vanities, and the malicious spirit always speaks of bitter things.   *see Eph 6:12   *Matt 7:16

Therefore, as often as carnal thoughts ruthlessly strike the mind, as usual when, for example, thinking about food, about drink, about sleep, and about other similar things pertaining to care of the flesh, we burn with a certain human desire, certainly it is the spirit of the flesh who speaks to us. Let us repel that spirit as an enemy, saying, *Get behind me, Satan, because you understand not the things that are of God,** but rather, your *wisdom is an enemy to God.**   *Mark 8:33   *Rom 8:7

However, when thoughts that are not about incitements of the flesh but about worldly ambition,* vain thoughts about boasting and arrogance and other similar things, turn over and over in our hearts, then it is the spirit of the world who speaks, a more dangerous enemy by far that must be repelled with greater care.   *1 John 2:16

Sometimes however, when these accomplices turn their backs, the prince himself, *having great wrath,** like *a roaring lion,** rises up against us. This happens, of course, when we are provoked not to pleasure of the flesh or to vanity of the world, but to anger, to impatience, to envy, to bitterness of soul. He ruthlessly forces   *Rev 12:12   *1 Pet 5:8

a way in if any word or action seems less discreet or less friendly. Or if any occasion for indignation seems to be given either in a sign or in work, then it becomes material for suspicion. Therefore this thought must be resisted as if it were none other than the devil himself;* nor should it be avoided as anything other than perdition itself. For Scripture has it, *In your patience you shall possess your souls.**

*see 1 Pet 5:8-9

*Luke 21:19

4. Still, it sometimes happens that our spirit is frequently overcome by one or another of these three spirits and, tragically, reduced to slavery! For once overcome, the soul works out her own destruction, doing the work of the wicked spirits, so that now without any suggestion from another spirit, the soul on her own gives birth to thoughts of pleasure, vanity, or bitterness. Now, in fact, I do not suppose that one easily distinguishes between one's own spirit's speaking and really hearing any of the other three spirits speaking. But what does it matter who speaks, since what they say is one and the same? What difference does it make to know the identity of the speaker, since we agree that what the speaker says is dangerous? If it is an enemy, then courageously resist the enemy; if it is your own spirit, then argue with it, and then lament with compassion, because it has come into such great wretchedness and such wretched servitude.

5. But on the other hand, as often as a wholesome thought turns in the mind, thoughts about castigating the body, humbling the heart, preserving unity, and showing charity to the brothers, or acquiring, preserving, and increasing the other virtues, then without doubt it is the divine Spirit who speaks,* either by himself or through his angel.

*see Matt 10:20

And just as we said about the human and the spiteful spirit, so also concerning the angelic and divine Spirit; it is not easy to discern who speaks or to ignore the danger, especially since it is certain that a good angel never speaks on his own, but it is God who speaks in him.* *see Ps 84:9

6. That being the case, last but more attentively, let us consider how we should hear suggestions from those spiteful spirits, or rather, with how much indignation we should cast them aside. We must turn away *our ears lest we hear blood** or the "wisdom" that *flesh and blood reveal*.* Likewise, right from the start, we must *take the little children of Babylon* (which are worldly thoughts, of course) *and dash them against the rock*,* casting away the spiteful spirit along with his temptations, away from the perception of our hearts and reducing him to nothing.* *Isa 33:15 *Matt 16:17 *Ps 136:8-9 *see Ps 14:4

When, however, with the whole of our devotion we take up those thoughts that remind us of justice and truth, then let us have gratitude for the divine honor. Let us not at any time be found ungrateful for the kindness, knowing that *it is* he himself *who speaks justice*,* *it is he whose word is truth*.* *Isa 63:1 *John 17:17

For how great is the temerity, or more correctly, how great is the madness, if perhaps, while the Lord of majesty calls upon us, we insanely turn away an ear, and instead we turn our souls to I know not what stupidity? How great is this offense, and how seriously should it be punished when a most worthless worm refuses to hear the Creator of the universe shouting to him?

But truly, how great and how ineffable is the honor of divine goodness that daily receives us unfaithful people who avert our ears, who harden our hearts;* yet nonetheless God shouts at us, and continually *he calls out in the streets*.* Rightly he shouts in the streets because of the breath of his love. *Ps 94:8 *Prov 1:20-21

For behold, *Lord, you have no need of my goods*.* Yet nevertheless you say, *Be converted* to me, *Oh you children of humans*.* And again you call out: *Return, return, Oh Sulamite woman, return. Return so that we may behold you*.* *Ps 15:2 *Ps 89:3 *Song 6:12

7. Therefore I beseech you, most beloved, *you who are mindful of the Lord, hold not your peace, and may you give him no silence,** hearing continually what the Lord God may speak in us, for he will speak peace.* And so blessed and happy is the soul who perceives the veins of divine whispering in silence,* frequently repeating as did Samuel, *Speak, Lord, for your servant listens.**

*Isa 62:6-7
*Ps 84:9

*Job 4:12
*1 Sam 3:9

Here therefore let our daily talk come to an end so that in silence we may listen to God speaking *and exhorting about the kingdom of God** within us, as useful as it is subtle, by internal inspiration. If however the Lord's own voice were even now to suggest anything about the necessity of listening, then we shall discuss it in another sermon, especially so as not to burden your minds by the length of a discourse on such a useful and spiritual topic.

*Acts 19:8

Sermo 24

Concerning the Versatile Usefulness of God's Word

1. You recall, I trust, how in yesterday's sermon we urged you to care about discernment of spirits,* which is absolutely necessary for us. So you must strive to stop up the ears* of your heart against the poisonous hissing of the ancient serpent,* against the deadly songs of the siren. That way you shall not hear the spirit of the flesh speaking about pleasures, nor the spirit of the world suggesting vanities, nor the spirit of wickedness insinuating bitter feelings and sowing scandals.* It is especially necessary to know the cunning of this last spirit; it behoves you not to be ignorant of his thoughts.*

*1 Cor 12:10
*see Ps 57:5
*see Rev 12:9

*see 1 Cor 2:12

*2 Cor 2:11

In fact, sometimes that spiteful and *wicked spirit transforms himself into an angel of light** so that he causes even more harm by a pretense of virtue. But even in this case, if we look closely, he never scatters anything but seeds of bitterness and discord. For instance, he persuades some people to a particular, individual fasting by which their neighbors are scandalized. The wicked spirit does this not because he loves fasting, but rather because he delights in scandal.

*2 Cor 11:14;
Acts 19:15

Likewise, the wicked spirit habitually conveys many counsels in this manner, which are easily discerned by divine wisdom if we keep Saint James's apostolic definition before our eyes. *Wisdom*, he says, *that is from God, is first indeed chaste and then peaceable.** Every thought therefore that does not concur with these two virtues is without doubt alien to the wisdom of God. On the other hand, if a thought seems chaste, if it does not openly draw you to sin but displays an image of virtue, then finally you may know that it is from God, provided that it is also peaceable. And it truly is peaceable if it is approved by the judgment of your superiors and spiritual brothers, for *the Lord God does nothing without revealing it to his servants.**

<small>*Jas 3:17</small>

<small>*Amos 3:7</small>

2. We already said, in yesterday's sermon, in part, with how much devotion, how much humility, how much care a wholesome thought should be taken up as though it were nothing less than a divine honor. So also in today's sermon we shall likewise try to persuade you a bit more fully.

Blessed, in fact, *are they who hear the word of God and keep it.** You wish to know how blessed? First, the divine *voice sounding in the ears** of the soul certainly upsets, frightens, and judges, but if you *do not turn away your ear,** then at once the voice brings you to life: it melts,‡ warms, illuminates, and cleanses the soul. Finally, it is also our food and a sword and medicine and encouragement and rest, also resurrection and our consummation. May you not be amazed that now the word of God is already found *to be all in all** with regard to justification since the word is also going to be *all in all* to our glorification.*

<small>*Luke 11:28
*Song 2:14

*Lam 3:56
‡see Song 5:6

*1 Cor 15:28

*see Rom 8:30</small>

May the sinner listen *and his heart be troubled*. Let the carnal soul *tremble at the voice.** *The living and effectual word, the discerner of hearts and of thoughts** probes and discerns all secrets of the heart. Thus, though you be *dead in sin*,* *if you will hear the voice of God's son then you shall live.** That is to say, *The word that he speaks is spirit and life.*† If your *heart is hardened*,# then remember that Scripture says, *He shall send out his word and shall melt them.*‡ And similarly, *My soul melted as my beloved spoke.*°

<small>*Hab 3:16
*Heb 4:12; see 1 Cor 2:10, 15
*John 8:21
*John 5:25
†John 12:48; 6:64
#Exod 7:13
‡Ps 147:18
°Song 5:6</small>

If *you are lukewarm* and you fear *being vomited out*,* then do not depart from the Lord's speech, so it will enkindle you, for his speech contains fire.* What is more, if you lament the darkness of ignorance, then attentively *hear what the Lord God speaks in you*,* and *the word* of the Lord shall be *a lamp to your feet and a light to your paths*.*

    3. On the other hand, perhaps you grieve so much the more, having been enlightened, as you recognize more clearly even the smallest sins. Rest assured, the *Father shall sanctify you in truth*, which is certainly his word.* And so, with the apostles, you can merit to hear, *Now you are clean by reason of the word which I have spoken to you*.* Now truly, since *you will wash your hands among the innocent*,† behold, he *has prepared a table before you*,# so that *not by bread alone do you live, but from every word that proceeds from the mouth of God*.* And *in the strength of that food*,‡ you *run the way of his commandments*.°

    When *if armies in camp should stand together against you* and *a battle* of temptation *should rise up*,* then take up *the sword of the Spirit which is God's word*,* and you shall easily triumph with it. Because, as is common experience in this struggle, one might possibly be wounded at some time: *Then he shall send his word and heal you and deliver you from your destructions*.* Thus in you also may be fulfilled the words of the centurion whose faith was so superbly commended: *Lord*, he says, *only say the word and my servant shall be healed*.* Even if you still falter, then confess and shout, *But my feet were almost moved; my steps had well nigh slipped*.* And he shall *strengthen you in his words*,* so that by experience you say, *By the word of the Lord the heavens were established and all their power by the spirit of his mouth*.*

    4. Persevere in these and other temptations! Continually practice in such struggles until *the Spirit says that you may rest from your labors*!* At his word you shall rest sweetly and be given pleasant sleep until he comes,*

*Rev 3:16

*see Pss 96:3; 118:140

*Ps 84:9

*Ps 118:105

*John 17:5, 17

*John 15:3
†Ps 25:6
#Ps 22:5

*Matt 4:4
‡1 Kgs 19:8
°Ps 118:32

*Ps 26:3
*Eph 6:17

*Ps 106:20

*Matt 8:8, 10

*Ps 72:2
*Ps 118:28

*Ps 32:6

*Rev 14:13
*1 Cor 11:26

when *all who are in the graves shall hear his voice and shall come forth.* But to where? Some indeed come forth *into judgment,* but others *into eternal life.** *And yet, who knows whether one is worthy of love or hatred?** Then *be especially mindful of your word to your servant,* Lord, *in which you have given me hope,*† so that *I might not fear the evil report.*# Rather, may the blessed report‡ conduct me to that vision in which you shall say, *Come, you blessed of my Father.** For *whosoever shall confess me before human beings,* says the Lord himself, *I shall confess* in the presence *of my Father and the holy angels.*° May *he who was appointed to be judge of the living and of the dead* deign to confer this upon us.◊

*John 5:24, 28–29
*Eccl 9:1

†Ps 118:49
#Ps 111:7
‡see Luke 11:28

*Matt 25:34

°Matt 10:32; Luke 12:8; see Mark 8:38

◊Acts 10:42

Sermo 25

Concerning Four Types of Prayer

1. It seems to me that the words of the apostle express four ways to pray when he says, *I want, first of all, that supplications, prayers, intercessions, and thanksgivings be made.** Some people are frightened and tormented by remorse for sin. They have not yet received the virtue of resistance. But then as soon as the Spirit of truth* shines upon these who lie in the mud of their sins, and the Spirit raises them and makes them ashamed and afraid as they see the enormity of their crimes and their lack of merits, they become frightened as if hell itself were burning right in front of them. Seeing that they find nothing good within themselves, they grope about for cover. That is to say, they know that it is not safe *to appear empty before their Lord* God,* as is contrary to the precept of the law, and much less do they dare to obey the law with hands full of dung. Therefore, because they fear, and rightly do they fear to approach by themselves, they strive to supplicate as it were through others.

Supplication is the type of prayer that we are accustomed to use when we say, "Saint Peter, pray for us" and the like. But this type of prayer is especially manifested in the supplication, "Lord, free us through your cross and suffering" and the other prayers using this formula. This seems to be the type of supplication employed by a robber who has been arrested; when his hanging is near, he deeply despairs, nor does he find

*1 Tim 2:1

*John 14:17

*Exod 23:15

within himself any excuse to beg for mercy, so he extends his arms and says that Christ also suffered in this way.* That way the souls of those who hold him are moved to pity.

2. I believe that one can say about this type of supplicant, *The kingdom of heaven suffers violence, and the violent bear it away.** *The publican* was doing violence to the kingdom of heaven; even though he would dare *not raise his eyes to heaven,** yet he was able to bend heaven toward himself.

That woman who had an issue of blood seems to have done something similar. Even though she was afraid to approach Christ, she still made *power go out from him.* For she secretly *touched the hem of his garment** and she was cured of her infirmity.‡ As a result, the Lord's response to her seems indignant when he says, *Who touched me?** And he adds, *I sensed that power went out from me.**

I do not believe there is such a one among us, but perhaps there are some people with worldly attitudes or lifestyles who could sometimes experience what I am talking about, as they unwillingly suffer an issue of blood. *Blood,* I say, that *shall not possess the Kingdom of God.** And indeed *whosoever commits sin is the servant of sin,** nor shall sinners be able to control themselves by their own power even when they will it. Therefore it is not the least bit expedient for such sinners to approach Christ on their own. Rather, it is better to touch Christ's hem if one finds it. In other words, Christ considers the person whom he sees as more humble and on the fringe of the church, which is the garment of Christ.† I say it is proper for Christ to consider the one who *has chosen to be subservient in the house of God,*# because such a one is truly the hem placed on *the garment's edge,* to which the whole spiritual abundance of oil runs down, *dripping down from the head.** If sinners touch the garment's hem by some kindness or by a

---

*see Luke 24:46

*Matt 11:12

*Luke 18:13

*Mark 5:25-30; Luke 8:44
‡see Luke 5:15

*Luke 8:45
*Luke 8:46

*1 Cor 15:50
*John 8:34

†see John 19:23-24
#Ps 83:11

*Ps 132:2

humble prayer or by a pure confession, so that they prompt the Lord's feeling of affection toward them and an outpouring of compassion for them, then they have faith and will without doubt be cured.* However, the garment's hem will know that not from itself but from Christ power has gone out, from him, who also testifies that he was touched on the hem.* *see Jas 1:6; see Jas 5:14, 16*

*see Luke 8:46

I have now expressed to you, as much as I could, for what type and what soul supplications are necessary.

3. However, once we have received the virtue of restraint and have become self-aware, then we approach confidently, seeking pardon for past transgressions. And we use prayer, which is, of course, reasoning of the mouth,[1] because we now speak to God with our own mouths.

That is why Mary Magdalene, although not less humble than the woman with the issue of blood, also did not fear to approach Jesus, but *she washed his feet with tears and wiped them with her hair, anointed them with the ointment, and kissed his feet** with a devout mouth. Whence we have enough proof that she had already resolved in her heart* to abstain from sin entirely thereafter,* as if her *issue of blood* had stopped.

*Luke 7:38

*see Prov 24:32
*see John 8:11

If you also have achieved this grace already, then the first thing to do is *recount all your years in the bitterness of your soul*,* speaking in prayer to the Lord himself.

*Isa 38:15

4. Next, after persevering in tears of repentance for a considerable time, you will receive a certain cheerfulness and confidence in your forgiveness. Then you may approach intercessions so confidently, insofar as you have been received into the Lord's grace, that you dare to ask what is necessary for yourself and for your fellow servants.*

*see Matt 18:33

---

[1] The word for prayer here is *oratio*, which Bernard seems to relate to the words for "mouth" and "reason," i.e., *oris* and *ratio*, respectively.

But then, perhaps you would ask how or from whom you can know whether you have obtained this forgiveness. No doubt, in order to preserve the grace of humility, divine kindness usually ordains that the more people accomplish, the less they notice their own accomplishments. For even up to the highest step of spiritual exercises, if anyone accomplishes that much, some of the first step's imperfection remains, so that even the first step seems scarcely attained.

Be that as it may, I know what it said in today's gospel. Jesus said to the paralytic, *Be assured, son, your sins are forgiven you,** and this was considered blasphemy on Jesus' part.† But Jesus, to whom no doubt *a human being's thought is revealed,*# says, "*Why do you think evil in your hearts?*‡ You blaspheme by calling me blasphemer, and in your attempt to explain away* my power to make a visible healing, you claim that I usurp an invisible power. But I rather expose your blasphemy by proving my invisible power with a visible sign": *So that you may know that the Son of man has power on earth to forgive sins,* he then said to the paralytic man,* *Arise, take up your bed and walk.*‡

*Matt 9:2
†see Gen 15:6; Rom 4:3
#Ps 75:11
‡Matt 9:4
*see Ps 140:4

*Mark 2:10; Matt 9:6
‡John 5:8

And therefore, if you now arise with desire for heavenly realities, if you take up your bed, raising your body from earthly pleasures so that your soul is no longer carried by her concupiscence but rather, as is proper, your soul rules your body and bears it to where it would not choose, eventually, if you walk *forgetting the things that are behind, and stretching forth yourself to things that are before** with the desire and goal of finishing, then you need not doubt that you have been cured. For you would not be able to rise if you had not been somewhat relieved of your burden, or to pick up your bed unless you were somewhat unburdened. Nor is it possible to walk with the fervor of conversion with a heavy burden of sins.

*Phil 3:13

5. That is why such people can now confidently make intercessions. Only let them beware lest perhaps they ask for what should not be asked, or ask excessively for what should not be asked from God, or seek tepidly what ought to be sought with the whole of their passion and at every time.

You ask and receive not, says Saint James, *because you ask wrongly in order to spend it on your desires.** Things such as the death of enemies are what worldly people usually ask for in their prayers, and other similar things that are not appropriate. On the other hand, temporal things, if they are lacking, are indeed to be requested insofar as human necessity requires. Still, according to the opinion of blessed Gregory, these things are not to be sought overmuch.[2] Also in this category are those spiritual goods without which salvation can be assured just the same, such as a word of wisdom,* the grace of healing,* and all those graces that we are not certain really help us. For example, suppose a temptation wears you down; it is then necessary to plead that it may be removed from you, but not too resolutely. For in such cases we must always remember the opinion of the apostle: *For we know not what we should pray for as we ought.** So let us be entrusted to God rather than rashly assert something among ourselves.

These however should be requested in intercessions at all times and with one's whole passion; these are the things for which your desires shout to God without ceasing and as strenuously as they can: that you may keep God's good grace and you may be pleasing in the eyes of his loving-kindness, and in him you may live and in him die so that you may merit to see his glory* and to enjoy him in perpetuity. For concerning these graces it has been said, *Pray without ceasing.** So also the

*Jas 4:3

*1 Cor 12:8
*1 Cor 12:28

*Rom 8:26

*John 1:14

*1 Thess 5:17

---

[2] Gregory the Great, *Regula pastoralis curae* 3:26 (SCh 382:438–47).

prophet says, *My face has sought you. Your face, O Lord, will I still seek.** And elsewhere he says, *One thing I have asked of the Lord; this will I seek: that I may dwell in the house of the Lord all the days of my life.**

*Ps 26:8

*Ps 26:4

6. Next, I believe that very few people attain the fourth type of prayer, which is thanksgiving, and it is more precious for being more rare. For by all means we have come to copious grace before God when, according to his promise, God responds before he is called.* And *the Spirit gives testimony to one's spirit*, the Spirit that we have from God,‡ because our desire has been heard;# we are so confident in God that we can no longer pray, but rather give thanks. For so you have it in the resuscitation of Lazarus, when the Lord, although he had not first prayed, says, *Father, I give you thanks, for you have heard me.**

*see Isa 65:24; 58:9
‡Rom 8:16; 1 Cor 2:12
#see Ps 9:38

*John 11:41

Therefore the first type, that is, supplication, happens with a feeling of shame. The second, which we properly called prayer, happens with pure feeling so we do not conceal sins* nor flatter ourselves, knowing that that is the way all people find mercy before God if their own harsh judge is found within. The third type, that is, intercession, strives for generous feeling and breadth of faith. It is written, *Let everyone ask in faith, nothing wavering.** That is also the sense, I believe, of the saying, *Every place that your foot shall tread upon shall be yours.** In other words, we extend the foot of faith insofar as we receive by asking. The fourth type, which is thanksgiving, should itself be utterly filled with devotion and flowing with delights.*

*see Wis 11:24

*Jas 1:6

*Deut 11:24

*Song 8:5
*RB 20

7. However, since "Reverence in Prayer"* was read in chapter today, since the authority of the Rule has just encouraged you, I thought something should be said about prayer on this occasion. Still, I shall speak briefly.

Some people, I notice, occasionally experience dryness and a certain dullness of mind in prayer, as though praying with the lips only;* they don't pay enough attention to what they say or to whom they speak. That is because they have come to prayer out of a certain habit rather than worthy reverence and concern. *see 1 Sam 1:13

For what else should a brother imagine while entering into prayer than the prophetic saying, *I shall enter into the place of the wonderful tabernacle, even to the house of God?** Indeed it altogether behoves us to enter into the heavenly court at the time of prayer, that court in which "The King of kings sits on his starry throne,"³ surrounded by an innumerable and indescribable army of blessed spirits. Thus also the prophet who had seen them said, because he found no greater number, *Thousands of thousands ministered to him, and ten thousand times a hundred thousand stood before him.** *Ps 41:5

*Dan 7:10

Therefore, with how much reverence, how much fear, how much humility should a common frog approach the heavenly court as he comes forth, crawling from his swamp? How much trembling, how suppliant, how humble, and finally how concerned and intent with one's whole soul can a wretched little human appear before God's majestic glory, *in the council of the saints and in the congregation?** *Ps 110:1

8. Consequently, vigilance of spirit is necessary in the whole of our actions, but especially in prayer. For, just as we read in our Rule,* although *the eyes of the Lord observe* us *in every place** and at every hour, yet most especially in prayer. For granted, we are always seen by him, but in addition, at prayer we present and show ourselves as though speaking *face to face with God.** *RB 19
*Prov 15:3

*Exod 33:9, 11

What is more, however much God is everywhere, we must nevertheless pray to him as in heaven, and we must imagine him in heaven at the time of prayer, so that our mind is not hindered by the roof of the chapel,

---

³ Office of the Virgin Mary, first Vespers of the Assumption

or by the intervening space of the air, or by the thickness of the clouds, according to that formula that was handed down to us from Christ,* where he says, *Thus shall you pray: Our Father who art in heaven.** For heaven, by a certain prerogative, is even called the *seat** or *throne of God*,* because compared to that vision by which the holy angels and the souls of the elect see God in heaven, we wretched *strangers on the earth** scarcely seem to have even the name.

*see Rom 6:17
*Matt 6:9
*Isa 66:1
*Matt 5:34

*Heb 11:13

Therefore let him who prays, pray thus:* as though he had been taken up and presented to God *who sits upon a throne high* among the angels (certainly not the fallen angels). Pray as though you are raised up‡ among human beings like *the needy*, whom *God raised up from the earth and lifted up the poor out of the dunghill.*# Thus, I say, let him reckon himself and pay attention as though presented to the Lord of majesty,* so that he can say with Abraham, *I will speak to my Lord, though I am dust and ashes*,* and because I am so commanded by your precept and formed by your instruction, I perform it, Lord, source of loving-kindness.

*see Matt 6:9

‡Isa 6:1; see
  Isa 14:12;
  Rev 12:9
#Ps 112:7

*see 1 Cor 2:8

*Gen 18:27

Sermo 26

How One's Will Ought to Be Subject to God's Will

1. Brothers, you have just heard Christ's teaching about humility from our Rule.* Every time this is read, I wish with my whole soul that you would pay close attention. Whoever trusts in any value in life, trusting in whatever piety or wisdom, is foolish and sick unless he trusts in humility alone.

*RB 7

Before the Lord, brothers, we cannot have any rights, seeing how *in many things we all offend.** Nor can we deceive him, *for he knows the secrets of the heart.** And how much more conspicuous are our deeds? Certainly we must not resist God's power, seeing that he is omnipotent. What therefore remains except to take refuge in the remedy of humility with one's whole mind? And whatever we lack in others, we can make up in humility. O, how astonishing the foolishness of our hearts' vanity, whose ambition and stiff-necked emotion even the power of humility fails to repress perfectly or to tame completely, for even earth and ash may yet be proud!*

*Jas 3:2
*Ps 43:22

*Sir 10:9

2. What is more, the height of humility seems to consist of our will being subject to the divine will, as is only proper according to the prophet, who says, *Will not my soul be subjected to God?** I know indeed that all creatures, whether they wish it or not, are subject to the Creator. What is more, a voluntary subjection is expected from rational creatures in order that they make willing sacrifice to the Lord and confess his name:

*Ps 61:2

not because his name is terrible and holy,* not because it is omnipotent, but because *it is good*.* Even this subjection must be triple, so that we always want what is certain to be God's will. Likewise we must also detest what is certainly against God's will.

There are, however, some things about which we are uncertain whether God wills them or not, so we must not really want them or deeply reject them. Brothers, it is certainly here in the middle that the whole danger lies for religious persons. We seduce ourselves by faithless flattering and coaxing in order to pretend that we are seeking the Lord's will while also doing our own will, and we want to make ignorance another excuse. For what monk is so wretched that he would dare to deny what is certainly God's will or presume to want that which is certainly against God's will? No, the real danger is in this middle area for those who, having already left worldly life, dwell in the place of conversion as in a Paradise of pleasure, just as the tree of transgression was placed in the middle of Paradise, that by which our first parents sinned. It was the tree of knowledge of good and evil, not so much of good or of evil alone, but of good *and* evil.*

*Ps 98:3
*Ps 53:8

*Gen 2:8-9

3. Therefore I ask you, brothers: pay close attention, because it seems to me that there is nothing more useful for you to hear. When the will of God is certain, then let our will follow wholeheartedly. In those matters about which we find some certainty in Scriptures, or when the Spirit himself shouts loud and clear in our hearts that we should embrace virtues like charity, humility, chastity, and obedience*—to these things let us consent and strive without hesitation. We know without question that they please God. By all means we must also hate the vices that God surely hates, such as apostasy, fornication, injustice, and impatience.

*Rom 8:26; Gal 4:6

Truly in those matters about which we can find nothing certain, let our will set no certain limits. Let us weigh each option, or at least let our will not cling firmly to either side. Let us always consider that perhaps the other way pleases God more, so we may be prepared to follow his will to whichever side we find virtue to be inclined.

Let no one hesitate over things that are certain. Let no one admit doubtful things as though certain. Let no one decide dubious matters for oneself or prejudicially express an opinion. Rather, let us try what is written: *There is much peace for those who love your law, and to them there is no stumbling block.** For whence are stumbling blocks, whence tribulation, except when we follow our own will and rashly choose what we determine in our hearts? If somehow our choice happens to be prohibited or impeded, at once we lapse into impatience and grumbling, into scandal, not considering that *all things work together to the good for those who, according to his purpose, are called to be saints.**

*Ps 118:165

*Rom 8:28

Even those things that seem like accidents to us, are they not indeed a lesson from God, indicating his will to us? Yet whoever keep their hearts open when choices are not clear, to whichever side they are later turned, cannot stumble in the end. Or if they consider doing anything about which they have no certain instructions, if they keep their will open until they can ask the superior, whom they obey in the Lord's stead and from whom they seek the Lord's will, then they will not be disturbed, however they are advised, seeing that *There is much peace for those who love your law, and to them there is no stumbling block.**

*Ps 118:165

4. Back when I spoke about the need to keep one's will open or to submit one's will to the divine will, I was not talking about carnal longings or about irrational feelings. For that is impossible while the soul is held in this *body of sin,** in this *body of death.*‡ For would it not be eternal life itself to follow the divine will in all things with the whole of one's feelings? But it is

*Rom 6:6
‡Rom 7:24

necessary to subject our consent to the divine will if we desire to have peace in this life, just as Scripture has it: *My peace I give to you, peace I leave with you.** ⁎John 14:27

Lord, says the prophet, *in the light of your face they walk, and in your name they rejoice the whole day.** ⁎Ps 88:16-17 For some people walk in the light of your face, careful to do your will and to reflect upon what pleases your heart.* ⁎1 Cor 7:32-33; Eph 1:9 Others walk in a human light, by which they are always eager for what pleases human beings and judgments of the world; regarding their day the prophet says, *I have not desired the day of man, Lord, you know.** ⁎Jer 17:16 *Dismay and unhappiness in their ways, and the way of peace they have not known. There is no fear of God before their eyes.** ⁎Ps 13:3 For those who always have the fear of God before their eyes, *Their ways are beautiful ways and all their paths are peaceful.** ⁎Prov 3:17

Come to me, he says, *all you who labor and are burdened,** ⁎Matt 11:28 you who are oppressed by the harsh slavery of your will or that of another, *and you shall find rest for your souls. For my yoke is easy and my burden light.** ⁎Matt 11:29-30 For how much kinder and sweeter is divine mercy than human mercy? It is obvious that his yoke is easier than other burdens.

Besides, people who strive to please themselves or other people are confused.* ⁎Rom 15:1-3; Ps 52:6 But those who walk in the light of your face, Lord,‡ ‡Ps 88:16 considering only how to do your will and striving to please you with their whole heart,* ⁎see 1 Cor 7:34 even now *they will rejoice in your name the whole day.*† †Ps 88:17 There will be no stumbling block for them.# #Ps 118:165 They rejoice in your justice alone when,‡ ‡Ps 144:7 stripping off their weaknesses and entering into your power, they will be mindful of your justice alone,° °Ps 70:16 so ever after they attain without toil what they now struggle to follow.

Sermo 27

Against the Most Wicked Vice of Ingratitude

1. **M**y most beloved brothers, *great is our God's mercy upon us*, a very great mercy.† By an ineffable power of his Spirit,* by an inestimable gift of his grace, he rescued us from our empty way of life in this world,# a life in which we sometimes wandered as though without God,‡ or, what is certainly more detestable, against God, not just out of ignorance but even contempt.*

†Ps 85:13; Luke 1:78
*Luke 1:35; 4:14
#1 Pet 1:18; 2 Pet 2:7
‡Eph 2:12-13

*see Rom 2:4

If only the disgraceful image of that worldly life, or rather that death—for *the soul which has sinned is itself dying**—if only that disgraceful image would turn frequently before the eyes of our hearts. How great indeed was the blindness! How great the perversity!

*Ezek 18:4

By considering, in conscientious meditation, the weight of our wretchedness, we could then estimate the greatness of God's liberating mercy, if not perfectly then nonetheless approximately. Now if any of us thoughtfully consider not only the manner in which we have been rescued but also where we have been placed,* not only what we have avoided but also what we have received, not so much from where we have been recalled but also to where we have been called, then we shall realize beyond doubt this massive accumulation of mercy that far exceeds the quantity of the prior measure.

*Acts 7:10

For God has not shown such mercy to any other nation,* in such a way that he reveals not only his judgments but also his counsels to them. For truly *the Lord has done great things for us.** He not only hired us as servants, but he even chose us as friends.* *For we have not chosen him; rather he chose us himself, and he placed us here so that we may go and bear fruit.** I say not only the nondestructive fruit that is produced by servants who are compelled by God's judgment, but the imperishable fruit that results from counsel and is revealed to friends.

2. The fact is, we have not been put here* to serve sin,* for that itself is destructive toil. Likewise we are not here to serve this age, like those whom we see subjected to worldly cares (if not to worldly vices) and to bodily needs (if not to criminal entanglements). These secular people labor in the fashion of this world *that passes away,** laboring for their own immediate sustenance and that of their household. At any rate, their labor may not lead to damnation, but it scarcely lends to salvation, so even if they have maintained a moral foundation, in the end they will suffer loss of the transient goods upon which they built. *They themselves may be saved, but only as through fire.**

But what does the Lord say to us? What advice does he give to friends? *Let us not work for bread that perishes but that which endures unto eternal life.** Let us not cease to work for this bread even when we are occupied with earthly tasks or with the dictates of obedience or with the considerations of fraternal charity, seeing how our motivation is different from that of those whose labor is passing away, as we said before. Consequently, similar labor that is connected to a dissimilar root need not similarly perish so long as it is rooted in that which never perishes: eternity.*

3. Suppose we were to pursue what is not forbidden but also not edifying: perhaps, having abandoned previous fornication, we were to remain in conjugal chastity, not taking up the celibate life, which we know is a

*Ps 147:20

*Ps 125:3
*see John 15:15

*John 15:16

*1 Thess 3:3
*Rom 6:6

*1 Cor 7:31

*1 Cor 3:12-15

*John 6:27

*see Eph 3:17;
 1 Cor 13:8

counsel given.* Or suppose we were to abstain from robbery and fraud and we used our own property within the law, but not yet attaining evangelical perfection, as it is written: *If you wish to be perfect, go and sell all that you have and come follow me.** Then how great a loving-kindness would this be, if, after being entangled even in many crimes, as some of us have been, we considered ourselves answerable to death,* judgment, and certain damnation, yet we had nevertheless been given a reprieve on some lower step?

*see Matt 19:11; 1 Cor 7:25

*Matt 19:21

*2 Cor 1:9

Certainly the prodigal son was too afraid to count himself among the sons; he reckoned himself blessed if he could just merit to be counted among the hired men. Much less could he deserve paternal loving-kindness if [his father] had not showed him so much mercy that his elder brother, who had never left his father, could envy the prodigal.* So also, most beloved brothers, *having abundantly poured our God's mercy upon us*,‡ the Father not only received us from the sons of wrath and disobedience# into the number of the elect, but he even called us to the college of the perfect.

*see Luke 15:19-30
‡Titus 3:6; Luke 1:78
#Eph 2:3; 5:6

For even if perhaps the negligence of a few brothers falls short of perfection, they will have to see what excuse they can offer for themselves, seeing that we all have professed the apostolic life, we have all together signed on for apostolic perfection. I am not speaking about the glory of holiness that the apostles have merited to undertake for the whole world (and not just for themselves), as it is written, *Let the mountains receive peace for the people and the hills justice.** Rather, I am talking about their avowed profession that Peter proclaimed before all, saying, *Behold, we have left everything, and we have followed you.**

*Ps 71:3

*Matt 19:27

4. But now this is what really disturbs me, my brothers: what does it mean that divine clemency should now seem less generous toward us, since he has bestowed so much on those who did not ask, on those who did not desire, perhaps even on those who refused?

Now to us who beg, who pray, and who petition most often,* or continuously, rather, he seems to deny the very smallest things.

*1 Tim 2:1

What should we think, dearest brothers? *Has the hand of the Lord become short?** Or has perhaps his store of grace run out? What, I say, are we to think? Has his will changed or his ability diminished? Of course we are not allowed to make judgments about God; nor is it ethical to believe such things about God's omnipotent and immutable majesty. What therefore does God wish, with us incessantly begging, praying, interceding,* when he does not heed those to whom he previously granted such gracious mercy?

*Isa 50:2; 59:1

*1 Tim 2:1

If any of you were to offer the same answer given to the apostle Paul, that the *grace of God is sufficient* for us,* clearly you would be utterly mistaken. For you see, sufficient grace is the primary reason for all our begging, praying, and interceding,* lest *we walk in great matters or wonders beyond us.** Let us beg that humility be given to us, however much is proper—I say not so much humility as befits the saints,* but as befits monks who are sinners. Let us pray that patience be given for our part. Not, I say, as is found among the martyrs, but as is necessary for our profession. Let us make petitions for charity. Not, I say, so much charity as befits angels, but as for our fathers, who were human beings like us, vulnerable to feelings and suffering.* Let us pray for charity as befits us sinners, who recognize that charity is bestowed by divine gift, as Scripture bears witness.

*2 Cor 12:9

*1 Tim 2:1
*Ps 130:1

*see Eph 5:3

*Jas 5:17

5. Woe to this wretched generation* for its imperfection, to whom moral poverty—if not destitution—seems sufficient! Is there anyone who even seems to aspire to perfection, which the Scriptures advocate? Yet such an aspiration is well founded, because the beginning of our conversion is the same as that of our fathers. But how regrettable that we find the results of our conversion very different.* For we read that the fathers

*see Matt 12:45

*RB 73.1-2

progressed from day to day* and they completed their course,‡ but today one is counted as great among us if he merely maintains the virtue of his initial conversion: if he is not less humble or reverent, not less careful and prudent, not less fervent of spirit,* not less patient and meek* in mid-life than at the outset of his conversion. For how many people are apparently forgetful of their sins as well as unmindful of God and his kind favors, in such a way that they not only fail to redeem their time, but they even waste time,* so that in the end scarcely any mention may be made about their habits and affections?

*Isa 58:2; 2 Cor 4:16
‡2 Tim 4:7

*Rom 12:11
*see 2 Tim 2:24

*Eph 5:16

What else shall I say about the behavior of these monks who think nothing of dirty jokes and slander, who think nothing of words of boasting and insensitivity, who easily sadden their neighbors or, rather, the Spirit of God in their neighbors.* They reckon placing stumbling blocks for the little ones to be a small matter.* At the rebuke of others, either they seem asleep by some carelessness or they burst into a flaming rage. Despite this, *like the nation that has done justice,*￼ they shamelessly go to church; they sing with others but not in spirit or with presence of mind.* I do not know what trifles they think about at the time of prayer, and they do not fear to participate in the sacrament of the Lord's Body, which makes even angels tremble. What else should I say they are doing, other than presuming an intimacy that secures their position in their Lord's grace, being too confident in the Lord's grace, which they assume that they have long since merited? This indeed is what is meant by the common proverb, "An easy master nurtures a foolish servant." But where is it, my most beloved, that you so often sing: *For I am a stranger before you and a sojourner as were all my fathers.*

*Eph 4:30; 1 Cor 6:19
*Matt 18:6

*Isa 58:2

*1 Cor 14:15

*Ps 38:13

More regrettable still, no one is found who would come back and give thanks to God except this foreigner.* *Were not ten made clean? And where are the*

*Luke 17:18

nine?* You recall, I believe, that these are the words of the Savior when he rebuked nine of the lepers for their ingratitude. We have read that it is good indeed to have prayed, to have begged, to have made intercession* for those who raised their voices, saying, *Jesus son of David, have mercy on us.** But the fourth part is lacking, which the apostle added: *giving thanks*,‡ since they did not come back and give thanks to God.

 6. Even today we see many people brashly asking for what they know they lack, but we know exceedingly few who seem to give proper thanks for kind favors already received. We should not be blamed if we pray insistently, but clearly, if we are ungrateful, then the petition's effect is negated. Perhaps even this is also a kindness: to refuse us ungrateful sinners what we ask lest we be judged the more gravely for our ingratitude, for then we would prove to be even more ungrateful for more accumulated benefits. Therefore it is an act of mercy in this case to withhold mercy, and equally an act of wrath and indignation* to show mercy, about which the Father of mercies* has said through a prophet, *Let us have pity on the wicked, but he will not learn justice.**

 Brothers, how many monks do we see and weep over who suppose that all is well for themselves so long as they remain in the habit and tonsure? These wretched monks fail to consider how the worm of ingratitude eats away their interior instead of the exterior rind for all to see. The worm is careful not to pierce through the rind lest these monks recognize and blush, and correct themselves out of shame! The worm of ingratitude sometimes presumes that the whole interior has been consumed, and so he does not fear to stick his venomous head outside the rind. If such ingrates have not obviously been falling away from God,* then we assume that they have suddenly become wicked rather than failing little by little over time, as when *strangers devour their strength, and they know it not.**

7. So you see, brother, that it is not necessarily beneficial for everyone to cleanse the leprosy of a worldly life where sins are more obvious: for some monks the worse the ulcer of ingratitude springs up in secret, and the more internal the ingratitude, so much the more dangerous it becomes. And well does the Savior ask in the gospel, where are those nine,* because *salvation[1] is far from sinners*.* For so also God asked the first man, Adam, where he was after he had sinned.* Likewise on Judgment Day, the Lord will not recognize the workers of iniquity,* for we read in the psalm, *For the Lord knows the way of the just, and the journey of the wicked shall perish*.*   *see Luke 17:17 *Ps 118:155 *see Gen 3:9 *Luke 13:27 *Ps 1:6

Not without cause are the ungrateful lepers nine in number, those who did not return to the Savior, for nine is the joining of four and five, and it is not good to mix the fivefold bodily senses with the fourfold gospel tradition. For then, usually, we wish to obey the four gospels in a way that would equally satisfy the five bodily senses.

8. That grateful Samaritan, moreover, was the happy one,* for he knew that he possessed nothing that he had not received.* Therefore he kept what was entrusted to him,* and by the act of giving thanks he gave it back to the Lord. Happy is the one who returns each gift of grace to him in whom is the fullness of all grace.* So long as we do not betray ourselves as ungrateful to God for what we have received, we make a space for grace within us so that we merit to receive still more.   *Luke 17:16 *1 Cor 4:7 *2 Tim 1:12 *see John 1:16

Surely our ingratitude alone impedes us from progress in our conversion, since the giver supposes that what he gives is in a sense lost if it is received ungratefully; so he is cautious about giving more, lest the more

---

[1] *Salus* (salvation) can also mean "health."

he confers to the ingrate, the more he loses. Hence he who considers himself to be a foreigner is happy,* for he responds to even small kindnesses with large gratitude, neither doubting nor ignoring that it is a free gift bestowed upon a foreigner and stranger.

*Luke 17:18

In our beginning, however, sad and wretched, while we still counted ourselves foreigners, we were found to be sufficiently reverent, sufficiently devout and humble. So easily and so soon do we forget that whatever we receive is a gift and wrongly take for granted our friendship with God. We do not face what we may deserve to hear: that the Lord's enemies are among his household.* We more easily offend God because we know that if we receive too lightly, then we shall be judged more gravely, as we read in the psalm: *For if my enemy had reviled me, I would indeed have borne with it.*

*Matt 10:36

*Ps 54:13

And so I beseech you, my brothers, let us humble ourselves more and more under the powerful hand of God most high,* and let us especially strive to keep far away from this most wicked vice of ingratitude. For if we turn with complete devotion to giving thanks, then we gain for ourselves the grace of our God, which alone is able to save our souls.* Not only *by word or tongue, but in deed and truth** may we show ourselves grateful. For God expects from us not just lip service but genuine acts of thanksgiving—our Lord, who is blessed forever. Amen.*

*1 Pet 5:6

*Jas 1:21
*1 John 3:18

*Rom 1:25

Sermo 28

Concerning Job 5:19:
In six tribulations he shall deliver you, and in the seventh evil shall not touch you

1. It is very appropriate and the rule of fairness certainly requires that those for whom *the Kingdom is prepared from the foundation of the world** should diligently prepare themselves for the Kingdom. Otherwise, after the Kingdom has been prepared, those who were destined to reign might be found unprepared. For so we read concerning a certain dinner, when the Lord says, *The dinner is ready but those who were invited were not worthy.** We ask, therefore, how those who are going to be kings should prepare for the Kingdom that has been prepared. And if we ask devoutly, with the prophet of the Lord, then certainly we shall hear from the Lord with the prophet, *Lord, who shall dwell in your tabernacle? Or who shall rest in your holy mountain? He who walks*, he says, *without blemish.**

*Matt 25:34;
see Luke 14:16

*Matt 22:8;
see Luke 14:24

*Ps 14:1-2

But this preparation, you will say, seems to apply to Christ alone. For *no one* among all others *is clean of filth, not even an infant whose life is but one day upon the earth.** Therefore Christ alone shall enter,* he who alone is the Lamb without blemish,* who alone could not be accused of sin* because he has not sinned, nor was any sin found in him.* Clearly my high priest alone has not been defiled by father or by mother,* as the law says,

*Job 14:4 LXX
*see Matt 22:12
*Exod 12:5
*see John 8:46
*see 1 Pet 2:22
*Lev 21:10-11

having indeed no Father but God, having also a virgin mother. Whence also he alone enters the holy of holies,* and no one ascends into heaven except him who descends from heaven, the Son of Man, who is in heaven.*

2. Then what about us? Shall we then despair without further evidence? On the contrary, we shall henceforth hope all the more. Granted, Christ enters alone, but surely he shall enter whole, and none of his bones shall be broken.* The Head shall not be found in the Kingdom without his members if however the members have been both conformed and joined to their Head.* The members are conformed to the Head by morals; they are joined by faith. For even at a young age, people have a conformity to Christ as they can, and they also have the joining, so long as they are also *planted together in the likeness of his death** by that triple immersion and accept faith in that folded garment that children are not yet able to unfold by themselves. Certainly *the Spirit of wisdom is benevolent,** and one whom Wisdom tied up with an inherited fault he unties, having bestowed with justice.

But on the other hand, *He shall not free one who is cursed by his own lips.** *There remains no sacrifice for sin*‡ for one who willfully sins after acknowledging grace. So he shall not liberate people cursed by their own lips in the same way that he liberates one cursed by the lips of others. A curse, brothers, is a heavy stain, and we know that *not that which goes into the mouth defiles a person but what comes out of the mouth.** So from there comes the stain, from there comes the curse from one's own lips, but it is not always from one's own. In fact, infants' own original fault does not come from their heart,* for an infant cannot only not yet consent but in this interim[1] cannot even understand sin.

*Heb 9:3, 6-7
*John 3:13
*John 19:36
*see 1 Cor 12:12
*Rom 6:5
*Wis 1:6
*Wis 1:6
‡Heb 10:26
*Matt 15:11
*see Matt 15:18

---

[1] *interim*: Bernard uses this term four times in this sermon, apparently in a technical sense; see SCh 518:114n3.

Still, how is it that *the Spirit does not liberate one who is cursed by his own lips,** or *for those who sin willfully there is no remaining sacrifice** unless Christ is not crucified once more for him,* nor is the sinner again *planted together in the likeness of Christ's death* through *baptism?** Now sinners' own wave of tears is forced out by Christ; they must carry their own cross,* mortify their own members,* and sacrifice their own victim. Otherwise they would say in vain, "I believe." It is proper for the curse of one's own lips to be expiated by one's own lips. For it is necessary *to enter into the kingdom of God through many tribulations.** And no one enters except through tribulations, either one's own or another's.

*Wis 1:6
*Heb 10:26
*see Heb 6:6
*Rom 6:4-5

*Luke 14:27
*Col 3:5

*Acts 14:21

3. Of course, only the second Adam's tribulation cleanses those who are corrupted by the single offense of the first Adam.* Not that one's own satisfaction for an offense can suffice for anyone. For what is all our repentance if not this: unless we suffer with Christ then we cannot reign with him at all?* For Christ himself supplies what is lacking in us. Nevertheless, God does not let us hold back that little bit of ours, however small it is. Because if uniting to Christ by faith without conformity of morals never saves adults, far less could works without faith save us.* For a member, if it is deformed, is more easily reformed while attached to the head than a separated member, however similar, is joined. And this deformed member must either *be made conformed to the image of God's son** and of his head, or else in the end be separated from the head and *be anathema from Christ,** lest a member be found in some way shameful in that fullness of his body.

*see 1 Cor 15:45-47

*Rom 8:17; 2 Tim 2:12

*see Heb 11:6

*Rom 8:29
*Rom 9:3

4. Therefore, where there is individual stain, justice likewise requires individual purification. And if the contamination is multiple, then there is need for multiple tribulations. For when does tribulation come if not while we resist contamination and oppose concupiscence? In fact, what can be found in a human being

that is pure of this stain, immune from this contagion? A destructive venom flows from within, *comes out from the heart*,* and then occupies the whole body. The venom afflicts the mind with desires; it infects the members with enticements: thence itching of the ears, wantonness of the eyes, thence pleasures of the sense of smell, thence such inappropriate delights of the mouth, thence feeling of softness throughout the whole body and pernicious lust for touching. Thence within the soul come that drunkenness of desires and a certain furnace of ambition, of avarice, of envy, of stubbornness, of wickedness, and finally of all vices vigorously burning with passions.

That is to say, the just person suffers as many tribulations, endures as many temptations, as the body seems to have enticements and the world has sources of pleasure. And to the extent that anyone walking in the flesh* is gladdened by pleasure of the senses *and counts it delightful to be under the briers*,* so also everyone who *desires to sow in the spirit** strives more to uproot than to propagate thorns and thistles, which the individual and cursed land inevitably brings forth.* Obviously, one turns in anguish as often as the thorn sticks in.*

5. Therefore, while I resist this multifaceted pestilence in every way, shall tribulation be any less varied? *From the sole of the foot to the top of my head, there is no health in me.** Concupiscence infects the whole person; the law of sin is found in all one's members.* *Death* hastens *to enter through the windows** from all sides, and within me firewood of every wickedness rages more dangerously, doing evil more cruelly. Nevertheless, one must not at all yield to weakness or desperation in such multiple distresses. For even though our tribulations for Christ abound, so also our consolations through him abound.*

Finally, listen to this consolation. *Sin is present at the door*,* but unless you yourself open, sin shall not enter.

*Matt 15:18

*2 Cor 10:3
*Job 30:7
*Gal 6:8

*Gen 3:17-18
*Ps 31:4

*Isa 1:6
*Rom 7:23
*Jer 9:21

*2 Cor 1:4-5

*Gen 4:7

Appetite itches in your heart, but it is beneath you;* unless you willingly submit, it hurts nothing. **Gen 4:7*

Listen to this consolation. Withhold consent so that these evils do not prevail. Do so and you shall be without stain,* so that you may *walk without blemish* and you yourself *shall dwell in God's tabernacle* and *rest in the holy mountain* of the Lord your God.* *If they shall have no dominion over you, then shall you be without spot, and you shall be cleansed from the greatest sin.** Clearly it is the greatest sin because it overtakes the whole person, both the interior and exterior.* **Ps 18:14* **Ps 14:1-2* **Ps 18:14* **see Rom 7:22*

Listen still to this consolation. *In six tribulations you shall be delivered*, it says, *and in the seventh, evil shall not touch you.** If you are a Hebrew child, then *six years shall you serve; in the seventh you shall go out free.** You have six tribulations against the desires of your heart and against the fivefold pleasure of bodily sensuality. But in these six tribulations, you shall be freed from the seventh, not that the evil will not come, but it shall not harm you or injure you or touch you. **Job 5:19* **Exod 21:2*

Death indeed shall come, for death itself is the seventh tribulation, but it shall be the sleep of the Lord's beloved, and behold, his inheritance.* Death shall be the door of life: it shall be the beginning of rest, it shall be the ladder of that holy mountain* and entry *into the place of the wonderful tabernacle** that God has made, and not a human being. And so *in the seventh, evil shall not touch you.** **Ps 126:2-3* **see Gen 28:12* **Ps 41:5* **Job 5:19*

Certainly evil is triple because, in the seventh tribulation, evil awaits those who fail to be freed perfectly by the six tribulations during this interim. Nor are they thoroughly purified by the six water jars,* so that at the wedding of the bridegroom, *they might present themselves not having spot nor wrinkle.** For a trembling dread awaits them at their departure, suffering in their crossing over, shame *in the sight of the great God's glory.** **John 2:6* **Eph 5:27* **Tob 3:24; Titus 2:13*

6. How have we come to this pretense, my brothers? Whence this tepidity that is so dangerous? Whence this accursed carelessness? Why do we wretched folk deceive ourselves?* Perhaps we have already become rich; perhaps we already rule.*

Will not those horrible spirits besiege the doorway of our home? Do not those ghostly faces lie in wait for our exit? How great shall be that panic, oh my soul, when everything has been given up, everything that is so pleasant for you at present, such as the pleasant view and our familiar cohabitation! How great shall be that panic when you go out alone deep into the unknown country, when you shall see hordes of the foulest monsters rushing to destroy you! Who will run to meet you in such a day of need? Who will protect you *from those who roar, prepared to devour*?* Who shall console you? Who will lead you away?

My little children, *let us remember our last end so that we do not sin.** For we must also cross over through fire, *and the fire shall test the quality of everyone's work.** In that place our gold shall be *turned into dross*;* there all impurity shall be revealed, there Truth herself shall judge righteousness* at the appointed time because we think little of this interim that has been given to us. But over there, what shall *all our righteousness* be considered if not as *the rag of a menstruating woman*?* Whatever we now pass over as a small matter, whatever we cover with caresses, whatever we neglect by pretending ignorance, so much the more shall the avenging flame consume with torture in that place.

Rather, if only now *someone would give water to my head and a fountain of tears to my eyes.** For perhaps then the burning fire would not find what the flowing tears have washed away in this interim.

7. Now really, after that fire, do you suppose any remains shall be found in us? Or shall there be so much remaining that we would dare to offer it in the face of

*1 John 1:8
*1 Cor 4:8

*Sir 51:4

*Sir 7:40
*1 Cor 3:13, 15
*Isa 1:22
*Ps 74:3

*Isa 64:6

*Jer 9:1

majesty, or to stand in his sight? What shall be that shame or confusion, after so many favors, to appear so empty, so tepid, so imperfect before the face of the Lord our God?* Adam fled to hide himself from God after a taste of just one forbidden fruit.* So what should we anticipate after so much disgrace, after so many crimes?

*Exod 23:15; Ps 41:3
*see Gen 3:6, 8

When shall the eye of the heart be cleansed of this confusion* so that, undazzled, it may be strong enough to gaze upon the rays of that true sun? I mean the heart's eye to which we now fail to pay attention. *Just as wax melts before the fire, so the sinners shall perish at the presence of God.* And so *let rottenness enter into my bones and swarm under me so that I may rest in the day of tribulation* and in this *seventh tribulation, evil shall not touch me,*† this triple evil of dread, of suffering, and of shame.

*Eph 1:18

*Ps 67:3

*Hab 3:16
†Job 5:19

If indeed the soul who confidently *speaks to his enemies in the gate* is happy, then, "What are you doing here, savage beast? In me, deadly one, you shall find nothing."² More happy the one whose work shall not burn, whom that swarm shall find *to have built upon gold, silver, precious stones.* Most happy is the one who, without any cloud of confusion, *beholding* deep within *the glory of the Lord with face revealed, shall be transformed into the same image* and shall be like God, seeing him as he is,† by all means, God blessed over all things,# *both worthy of praise and glorious for ever.*‡ Amen.

*Ps 126:5

*1 Cor 3:12-15

*2 Cor 3:18
†1 John 3:2
#Rom 9:5
‡Dan 3:56

---

² See Sulpicius Severus, Ep 3:16 (SCh 133:343). Sixth reading of the second nocturn of the office of Saint Martin in the Cistercian and Roman breviaries.

Sermo 29

Concerning the Triple Love of God and the Necessity of Loving God

1. *L*ove not the world nor the things which are in the world. For all that is in the world is the concupiscence of the flesh, and the concupiscence of the eyes, and the pride of life, which is not of the Father.* What then? Are there some things from the Father that compensate us? There are indeed; they are altogether more sweet and more lovely than worldly passions, but these blessings are not entrusted to servants, much less to enemies. *Whosoever therefore will be a friend of this world becomes an enemy of God.** The Lord entrusts his plan to his friends, to whom he says, *because all things whatsoever I have heard from my Father, I have made known to you.**

*1 John 2:15-16

*Jas 4:4

*John 15:15

Blessed Gregory explains that love itself is knowledge.* Love therefore is triple, love that excludes that triple worldly passion that is not from the Father. And besides, three times, I believe, Peter was asked by Christ, *Do you love me, do you love me, do you love me?** Perhaps this love about which the Law teaches is also triple: *You shall love the Lord your God with your whole heart, and with your whole soul, and with your whole strength.** That is, you shall love sweetly or affectionately, you shall love prudently, you shall love bravely.

*Homiliarum in Evangelia 27.4 (CCSL 141:232)

*John 21:15-17

*Mark 12:30

Accordingly, the heart's love has a certain similarity to carnal love, for feelings are said to be proper to the heart. But here the soul denotes something a bit more superior, so the soul is also said to be the seat of wisdom in that it seems proper to attribute prudent love for God to the soul.

2. Thinking about Christ's incarnation certainly strengthens the heart toward that more affectionate love about which we are speaking. What is more, thinking about the whole economy of salvation that Christ bore in the flesh, and especially his passion, strengthens love. For when God saw human beings becoming utterly sensual, he exhibited so much sweetness to them in the flesh that only someone with the hardest of hearts could not love him with all affection.

Since he wished to restore his noble human creature, God said,

> If I compel someone against his will, then I have a donkey rather than a human being. For he will not come freely or willingly, so that he could say, *I will freely sacrifice to you.** Shall I give my Kingdom to donkeys? Or *would God take care for oxen?** Therefore, in order to have a willing creature, I shall frighten him, so perhaps he may be converted and live.* And he has been threatened by the most grievous things that can be devised: eternal darkness,* undying worms, and inextinguishable fire.*

*Ps 53:8

*1 Cor 9:9

*Jer 26:3; Ezek 18:23
*see Matt 8:12
*Mark 9:42-44

When, however, a human being is not revived by threats, God says, "Humans are not only fearful, but also wanton. I shall send to them what seems eminently desirable." Human beings desire gold and silver and the like, but above all these they desire life. This is obvious and very obvious. God says, "If they so much desire this wretched, laborious, and momentary life,* how much more shall they love a tranquil, eternal, and blessed life?" And so God promised eternal life; he promised *what eye has not seen, nor ear heard, neither has it entered into the heart of humans.**

*see 2 Cor 4:17

*1 Cor 2:9

3. However, seeing that fear accomplished nothing, God says, "One thing still remains. There is not only fear and desire in a human being, but also love; nothing in human beings draws them more vehemently." Accordingly, he came in the flesh, and he presented himself as so lovable that he employed for us that *love greater than which no one has, that he laid down his life for us.** [*John 15:13]

To be sure, anyone who would not willingly be converted on account of this great love shall certainly deserve to hear this reproach: *What should I do for you that I have not already done?** And truly in nothing else has God so *commended his charity** as in the mystery of his incarnation and passion; in nothing else does he so reveal his loving-kindness, in nothing else is his kindness so evident as in his humanity, as the apostle testifies when he says, *The goodness and kindness of God our Savior appeared.** [*Isa 5:4; *Rom 5:8; *Titus 3:4]

For indeed his power was hidden because he came in weakness.* So Habakkuk says, *There his strength is hidden*, without any doubt on the cross whose *horns are in his hands.** *Wisdom is* likewise *hidden*‡ and incarnate: *For it pleased God by the foolishness* of the Word *to save those who believe.** Did he not make himself somehow foolish, he who *has delivered his soul unto death and has borne the sins of many,** and *then did he pay that which he took not away?** Was he not drunk with the wine of charity* and unmindful of himself, against the advice of Peter, who said, "Take care for yourself"?* So also *his strength is hidden,** and the incarnate wisdom is especially covered, but his kindness* could not be more fully revealed, not more abundantly expressed, not more obviously commended. [*see 2 Cor 13:4; *Hab 3:4; ‡1 Cor 2:7; *1 Cor 1:21; *Isa 53:12; *Ps 68:5; *see Eph 5:18; *see Matt 16:22; *Hab 3:4; *see Titus 3:4]

4. What is more, we have said that this mystery certainly reaches to the heart's affectionate love. For it also seems that men and women are so emotional about this sort of thing that they are scarcely without tears when they hear or recall it. Therefore this love coun-

teracts concupiscence of the flesh.* For how could carnal sweetness compare to the genuine sweetness of Christ's passion? *see 1 John 2:16

However, this sweetness can be deceptive if it lacks prudence. And besides, poison in the honey can be avoided only with difficulty. In that case, prudence must be present, by which we can diligently investigate interior mysteries, so that *we may be ready always to satisfy everyone who asks for a reason.* This prudent love prevents curiosity. Indeed this earnest soul cannot be curious about worldly matters, saying with the prophet, *O how have I loved your Law, O Lord! It is my meditation all the day.* *1 Pet 3:15

*Ps 118:97

5. The third way is so that each of us loves bravely: to the extent that we cannot be deceived, so also we cannot be compelled; thus we are prepared to suffer all things for the sake of justice.* For everyone knows that the King of heaven did not seek earthly rule and honors, but rejected them instead. What is more, *Blessed are they who suffer persecution for justice's sake, for theirs is the kingdom of heaven.* *1 Pet 3:14

*Matt 5:10

And so it was that Peter was questioned about these three types of love, for earlier he had been found wanting.* You see, when he first heard about the Lord's passion, he could not bear it. Though he loved Christ sweetly, as it were, he said, *Far be it from you,* for he loved foolishly. So he also deserved to hear, *Get behind me, Satan, because you understand not the things that are of God.* There was similar confusion among the apostles to whom Christ said, *If you loved me, you would indeed be glad because I go to the Father.* More precisely, they suffered because they loved. They both love and do not love; they love sweetly, but they do not love wisely. *Dan 5:27

*Matt 16:22

*Mark 8:33

*John 14:28

But on the night in which the Lord was to be handed over, both sweetly and wisely was Peter loving when he said, *Lord, I am ready to go with you both into prison and to death.* But he was not loving bravely, because *Luke 22:33

"He that is fallen low did never firmly stand."* *The power from on high*† had not yet come, which, once accepted, Peter did not refuse, but using his liberated voice, he said, *You be the judge whether we ought to obey God rather than human beings.*#

Is it not fitting that Peter, who was put in charge of feeding the flock, was asked to give an account of his love?* For one who is intoxicated and burning with the wine of charity‡ should lead others, unmindful of himself, so that he *seeks not things that are his own but rather things that are Jesus Christ's.** And note that when Peter was asked if he loved more than these others, he only answered that he loved. He was upset, for he dared not assert what he had rashly said before.* And perhaps for that reason *he was deeply grieved,*† for he had said before, *Even if all shall be scandalized in you, yet not I.*#

Marginal notes:

*Boethius, Consolatio philosophiae 1 (CCSL 94:1)
†Luke 24:49
#Acts 4:19; 5:29

*see John 21:15-17
‡see Eph 5:18

*1 Cor 13:5; Phil 2:21

*see John 21:17; Mark 14:29
†John 21:17
#Mark 14:29

Sermo 30

Concerning Wood, Hay, and Stubble

1. There is no security anywhere, brothers: not in heaven, not in Paradise, much less in the world. For in heaven the angel fell under the very presence of divinity; in Paradise, Adam fell from *the place of pleasure*;* in the world, Judas fell out from the Savior's school. I have said these things lest anyone flatter himself about this place,* for it is said: this *place is holy*.* What is more, the place does not sanctify human beings, but rather human beings sanctify the place.   *Gen 2:10; see Gen 3:23   *i.e., Clairvaux   *Ezek 42:13

For there are actually three types of people among us who are quite unsuited for our order and even unsuited for a person who has entered this way of life. There are those who began well but faltered right away.* And there are those who never really began but continued in their own softness,* and they continue to stay. Finally there are those who are snatched up by a spirit of levity, slow to hear, swift to speak,* and very ready hastily to enumerate what they do, as if they do anything!   *Ps 72:19   *see 1 Cor 3:12, 15   *Jas 1:19

Then has God actually *rejected* these *people?** Not if they persevere on the foundation: *But they shall be saved, yet so as by fire.** By what fire? The apostle says, *For another foundation no one can lay but that which is laid, which is Christ Jesus. Now if anyone build upon this foundation: wood, hay, stubble, then he shall suffer loss, but he himself*   *Rom 11:1   *1 Cor 3:15

shall be saved, yet so as by fire.* *The foundation is Christ.*‡ Wood is fragile; hay is soft; stubble is light.[1] The wood represents those who begin strong, but once broken they are not rejoined. Hay represents those who are too frightened to flee in their softness, nor have they been willing to raise a fingertip, as they say, to take up the arduous labors. The chaff represents those who are blown about by the motility of their levity, so they *never continue in the same state.**

*1 Cor 3:11-12, 15
‡1 Cor 3:11

*Job 14:2

2. And we must indeed fear for these monks. But let us not despair, because, if they have Christ as a foundation, that is, if they finish their life in this way, then *they shall be saved, yet so as by fire.**

*1 Cor 3:11, 15

Fire has three elements: smoke, light, heat. The smoke causes tears; the light illuminates the surroundings; the heat burns. So also this type of monk must have smoke, which is bitterness, in his mind because he is tepid, because he is lax, because he is not serious,[2] because he undermines and troubles the Order insofar as he has it in him. But in confession also he must declare himself with such light in his mouth as reflects his condition of mind. Likewise he mourns as his conscience sharpens his tongue and his tongue discloses his conscience. He must also feel the heat in his body, that is, the distress of repentance, perhaps not in many ways, but to some extent at least.

Do you think that God, *who wants every person to be saved** and wishes no one to perish, will reject sinners who are so contrite at heart, who have confessed with their mouth, and who are weary of body?

*1 Tim 2:4

There are also others who *build upon this foundation: gold, silver, precious stones,** who begin vehemently, who make progress more vehemently, and who finish most

*1 Cor 3:12

---

[1] *Levis* ("light in weight") has the same root as *levitas* ("levity").
[2] *Levis est*, "he is light"; see previous note.

vehemently, not attending to what the flesh can do but what the spirit wills.* *see John 6:64

Sermo 31

Custody of Thoughts

1. Blessed Benedict urges us, brothers, to be careful about our thoughts,* following indeed the advice of a wise man who suggests, *With all watchfulness keep your heart, because life issues out from it.** Consequently three types of thoughts come to mind that must be avoided with great care *by those who are converted to the heart** and by those who hasten to present a worthy temple for God within themselves.* That is to say, at times there are some thoughts deep within that are idle and to no purpose.* The soul can reject these thoughts as easily as accepting them, provided that she dwells with herself in her heart and *stands before the Lord of the whole earth.**

2. There are other more impetuous and persistent thoughts, namely those that pertain to the necessities of nature and those taken up from the same mud, as it were, from which we were made.* If they sink in even a little bit then they cannot be extracted without injury and difficulty. For often a carnal thought about food, about drink, or about clothing* so afflicts us that it can scarcely be uprooted from our hearts. This is because such thoughts are made from the same material as ourselves; they are muddy and viscous in a way, so they find in us the same muddy and sticky earth. For good reason it was said that human beings were formed not from earth, but from mud.* For see how muddy the body is; it also clings so strongly and tenaciously to the

*RB 7

*Prov 4:23

*Ps 84:9
*see 1 Cor 3:16

*Eph 5:4

*Zech 4:14

*see Gen 2:7

*see Matt 6:25, 28

*Gen 2:7

spirit itself that only with much torment and difficulty can it ever be separated.

So what should be done when that muddy thought sinks into the mind? Clearly we must cry out with holy Jacob and say, *Reuben, my firstborn, you shall not grow, because you climbed into your father's bed.** For this type of carnal and bloody concupiscence is red.¹ The concupiscence climbs into our bed when memory not only strikes up a thought but also enters the couch of the will and pollutes it with perverse pleasure.

*Gen 49:3-4

Rightly is that carnal appetite called our first born; this appetite evidently sprouts within us from the very beginning of our life, whereas the other vices, in the passage of time, are brought into the mind from the wickedness of this world and various opportunities. Therefore we must suppress whatever appetite we cannot extinguish: as quickly as it enters our bed, let us not allow it to increase at all, *but let it be under us*, just as Scripture says, *and we shall have dominion over it.**

*Gen 4:7

3. Now indeed the third type of thought is extremely impure and malodorous, and we must not allow it entrance for any reason. Rather, we should sense its stench from a distance and repel it with all our strength, drive it back with our whole soul, and at once turn away and groan, with tears and sighs invoking *the Spirit who helps our infirmity.** Thus the spiteful enemy will no doubt withdraw in confusion. Thereafter, so long as we resist vigorously, the enemy won't so easily dare to convey or cause anything similar.

*Rom 8:26

I say moreover that those impure and stinking thoughts deep within that pertain to lust, to jealousy, to vainglory, and to the other vices must be averted. For it is necessary, if we wish to keep our souls pure, to resist those thoughts with much indignation while

---

¹ Bernard plays on the word *rubea*, "red," which sounds like the name *Reuben*.

they are still acting in the distance and blow them away from us, so that no access is given to them.

Even the first type of thoughts, those idle and *to no purpose*,* are dirt, but a simple dirt that is not sticky or smelly, unless perhaps they linger in us for a longer time and through our carelessness and negligence turn into another type of thought that we experience daily. For while we spurn them as idle and trivial, we slip away toward shameful and degrading thoughts.

However, the second type of thoughts are not simple dirt, but, as we already said, they are sticky and muddy. So obviously the third type should be avoided, not like dirt or mud but like the filthiest and smelliest mire.

*Eph 5:4

Sermo 32

Concerning Three Types of Judgment

1. *Let a human being consider us as ministers of Christ and the dispensers of God's mysteries.** A minister of Christ should live in such a way that the composition of the interior soul, which is not seen, may be evaluated by the person's exterior behaviors, which are seen. The minister cannot be judged by another, nor even by himself; rather, let him say with the same apostle, *To me it is a very small thing to be judged by you or by any human authority, but neither do I judge my own self. He who judges me is the Lord.**

*1 Cor 4:1

*1 Cor 4:3-4

In these words we should note three judgments: human judgment, self judgment, and divine judgment. Humans can indeed judge exterior matters that are perceived by the senses of the body, but one cannot judge interior matters. So it is written, *For who knows a human being's secrets if not the spirit of the human that is within him?** On that account, *the spirit of the human that is within him* is able to judge these matters within the person. Yet God's judgment in these matters is far more important. The apostle confesses that he has not yet evaded divine judgment. He has, however, dismissed both human judgment and his own judgment.

*1 Cor 2:11

Further, the apostle paid little heed to human judgment when he said, *But to me it is a very small thing to be judged by you or by any human authority.** But neither did he fear his own judgment when he said, *But neither*

*1 Cor 4:3

do I judge my own self. For I am not conscious to myself of anything.* Therefore divine judgment stands alone, concerning which he says, *He who judges me is the Lord.**

2. Nevertheless, all people, insofar as they can, should present themselves blameless: first indeed in God's presence and then in the presence of human beings.* This of course is what the same apostle says in another place: *Providing good things not only before God, but also in the presence of human beings.** One must also note that good things are provided in the presence of human beings in three ways, that is: by attitude, by action, by speech. By attitude, lest it be noticeable; by action, lest it be blameworthy; by speech, lest it be contemptible.

There are even three ways in God's presence: thought, affection, and intention. For even thought should be holy; hence it is written, *Holy thought shall protect you.** Likewise affection must be pure and intention upright. These three (that is, thought, affection, intention) are in the soul, but in the soul each seems distinguished by its own location as well. For thought is in the memory, affection in the will; intention exists in the reason.

3. And now, so we can see more clearly their respective functions and differences, let us take an example concerning exterior matters.

Take bodies: if any ugly color stains only the skin, then the body is rendered more unsightly, but its health is not diminished. On the other hand, if some festering wound or some livid swelling should set in, then not only the beauty of the body but also the health is disturbed. For you see, if feebleness increases, then it seizes the inner bones along with the flesh, and thence one may rightly despair.

Similarly, in the soul, if sin is suggested to the memory through a thought yet the will does not allow feeling nor deliberation itself allow consent, then I confess that that is indeed a deformity, and that soul does not merit to hear, *You are all fair, O my love.** Still, even if this is a stain, it is not a disease.

*1 Cor 4:3-4
*1 Cor 4:4

*Col 1:22; Rom 12:17

*Rom 12:17

*see Prov 2:11

*Song 4:7

If the will itself is now also afflicted by a sense of pleasure, the deliberation of the reason nevertheless still resists. The soul is indeed weakened, but she is not yet dead. It is necessary, however, for her to cry out,* *Heal me, O Lord, and I shall be healed.*‡ For the soul is said to die when the reason itself is bent to sin through its intention. Truly this is the sin about which is said, *The soul who sins, the same shall die.**

*see John 11:6, 14, 43
‡Jer 17:14

*Ezek 18:4

David deplores this third stage, saying to the Lord in the persona of a sinner, "By banishing me from Paradise to be a wanderer in this wide world, *your hand has been strong upon me.** And seeing that carnal desires° are punishments of sin, *There is no health in my flesh because of your wrath.** At that point there is not even the stronghold of reason: *There is no peace for my bones because of my sins.*"*

*Ps 37:3
°1 Pet 2:11

*Ps 37:4

*Ps 37:4

On the other hand, in the persona of a just man, David sings about the same stages, saying, *I remembered God, and was delighted, and was exercised.** For he was delighted through the will; he was exercised through the reason.

*Ps 76:4

4. Therefore, lest a numerous crowd of intruding thoughts expel God from one's memory, thoughts that usually flow forth like a common mob in a palace hall, a porter is placed at memory's gate whose name is "recollection of one's own profession." So when the mind senses that it is weighed down by shameful thoughts, it rebukes itself and says to itself, "Should you think about these things, you who are a priest, you who are a cleric, you who are a monk? Should one who cherishes justice allow any thoughts of this nature within oneself? Is it proper for a servant of Christ, lover of God, to consider any such thing even for a moment?" By saying these things, one's mind shuts out the flow of illicit thought through recollection of one's own profession.

Similarly at the gate of the will, in which carnal desires* are accustomed to lurk, a doorkeeper is placed

*1 Pet 2:11

like a domestic servant in one's home, a doorkeeper who is called "recollection of one's heavenly homeland." For he is able to expel immoral desire, as wedge drives out wedge. This doorkeeper can accept without hesitation him who says, *Behold, I stand at the gate and knock.**

*Rev 3:20

Now, however, so excellent and so fierce a guardian must be employed at the bedroom of reason, a guardian who spares no one. Rather, should any enemy dare to enter either secretly or openly, the guardian keeps it at a distance. And this guardian is "recollection of Gehenna."

Among the first two, that is, memory and will, it is not so intolerable if at some time either the memory accepts a stray thought or the will accepts an impure affection. But this is most serious and utterly harmful: if ever the reason should lose uprightness of intention.

Sermo 33

Concerning Psalm 23:3:
Who shall ascend into the mountain of the Lord?

1. This is a word of exhortation,* my brothers, seeing as we all struggle to ascend, we all strive for the summit, we all aspire upward, we all endeavor to reach the heights. We are eager to ascend to that place where *it is good for us to be,** where it is secure for us to be, from where we ought not to fall, where we can stand firm.

    Not merely to provoke a person's desire does the prophet ask about the climber of this mountain,* but also to teach anyone who wants to ascend how to ascend. Happy is the one who *has set in his heart the ascent** of this mountain, *longing and fainting in the courts of the Lord.** If indeed this mountain is a fruitful mountain,‡ the peak of all good things, the mountain of eternal pleasure, then it is the house of God. *Blessed are they who dwell in your house, O Lord; they shall praise you for ever and ever.**

    Hear a faithful witness* proclaim that the mountain is God's house: *O Israel, how great is the house of the Lord and how vast is the place of his possession! It is great and has no end; it is high and immense.** More correctly, in fact, it is not only a mountain, but also the mountain of mountains, with many mansions in it,* many mountains. Finally, even *the foundations thereof are in the holy mountains.**

*Acts 13:15

*Matt 17:4

*see Ps 23:3

*Ps 83:6

*Ps 83:3
‡see Ps 67:16

*Ps 83:5

*Rev 1:5

*Bar 3:24–25

*John 14:2

*Ps 86:1

2. And not even holy Isaiah was silent about this: *The mountain of the Lord's house shall be prepared on the top of mountains,* he says, *and it shall be exalted above the hills.** How would *the mountain* of mountains be *founded with the joy of the whole earth** where there is such diverse abundance of all delights, where there is one plenitude of all abundance? For it shall be the mountain of peace, mountain of joy, mountain of life, mountain of glory, and all these mountains one mountain of complete happiness.

*Isa 2:2

*Ps 47:3

Will it not be the mountain of peace, peace beyond peace, *peace which surpasses all understanding?** Clearly a great mountain: peace in the heart, peace in the flesh, peace from unjust human beings, peace with all neighbors, peace from the demons themselves, peace with God, *and there shall be no end of peace.**

*Phil 4:7

*Isa 9:7

And there shall be joy, but the type that the Lord says is full,* a secure *joy that no one shall take from us.*‡ But also we are going to have life *and have it more abundantly,* because the arrival of so great a shepherd cannot be ineffectual, this shepherd who testifies that he comes to his sheep for this very purpose: *so that they may have life and may have it more abundantly.**

*John 16:24
‡John 16:22

*John 10:10

Does not the mountain seem to you also *an eternal weight of glory far above measure?** Rather, out of all these (if anything can be considered similarly desirable), a single *good measure* of blessedness is *pressed down and shaken together and running over,** as though you rendered many mountains into one mountain: one indeed gold, another silver, another from sapphire and emerald and the glory of all gems, another also from dyed fabric, purple, and linen, and other such wealth equally heaping up. For everything shall be given back to us multiplied. And one who *builds upon this foundation—gold and silver, precious stones**—shall be amazed that a humble building grew into huge mountains, and from a little seed one shall reap not just big sheaves but heaps of big sheaves.

*2 Cor 4:17

*Luke 6:38

*1 Cor 3:12

3. *Who, therefore, shall ascend into the mountain of the Lord? Or who shall stand in his holy place? The innocent in hands and clean of heart.** Blessed is that person, at least if there is such a one. But who shall boast about innocent hands or about having a pure heart?* *No one is clean of filth, not even an infant whose life is but one day upon earth.**

One, however, is innocent among the guilty, clean among the impure; one is *free among the dead,** *and there shall be no other accounted* except for him.* It is he about whom you have read, *And no one has ascended into heaven except him who descended from heaven, the Son of Man who is in heaven.** For he was *innocent in hands*† who *did no sin,*# but *having done many good works,*‡ he said freely to the Jews, *Which of you shall accuse me of sin?*° But can anyone doubt that his heart was the purest, he who was personally united to Wisdom? For unto Wisdom *no defiled thing occurs,** and she *reaches everywhere by reason of her purity.**

But *he has not received his life in vain,** he who alone had power *to lay down his life and to take it up again.** He did not receive his life in vain when he was born; he did not lay it down in vain when he died; not in vain did he accept it in his resurrection.

4. But then how *has he not sworn deceitfully to his neighbor,* how *has he not received his soul in vain,** how has he not accomplished all that in vain, if Christ alone would receive blessing?* So *ought not Christ to have suffered, to rise again, and so to enter into his glory?** The glory was his own. *What profit is there in* his *blood, while* we all *go down to corruption?** What truth is in the promise if, as we recalled above, *no one has ascended into heaven except him who descended from heaven?** So be it: *he receives blessing,* but why *mercy?**

But not Christ alone shall receive. Or rather, he shall certainly not receive for himself only, if you are paying attention. That is, go through the sacred prophetic words and see how, as though secretly, he stands for the

*Ps 23:3-4

*Prov 20:9; Ps 23:4

*Job 14:4 LXX

*Ps 87:6
*Bar 3:36

*John 3:13
†Ps 23:4
#1 Pet 2:22
‡John 10:32
°John 8:46

*Wis 7:25
*Wis 7:24

*Ps 23:4
*John 10:18

*Ps 23:4

*Ps 23:5
*Luke 24:26, 46

*Ps 29:10

*John 3:13
*Ps 23:5

many. He was speaking about one when he said, *This one shall receive*,* but at once he transforms *this one* into *this generation*, when he adds, *This is the generation that seeks*.* So you are not to understand this as one person individually, but rather *unity of the Spirit*.* Of course *this one* is the bridegroom, and *this generation* is the bride. And we know who has said, *Now they are not two, but one flesh*.* So therefore this one shall ascend, *this one shall receive blessing*,* but they shall ascend with him, or rather in him, because they shall receive blessing from him. Hear this from the prophet: *For the lawgiver shall give a blessing; they shall go from virtue to virtue*.*

What is more, this is because *it behoved Christ to suffer and to rise again from the dead* so that *penance and remission of sins should be preached in his name*;* let penance substitute for innocence, forgiveness substitute for purity. For blessed is not one in whom he finds [no sin], but *to whom the Lord has not imputed sin*.* *I have found*, he says, *a human being according to my own heart*.* Could one possibly boast of having a pure heart?* No, because *the stars are not pure in his sight*,* but *a contrite and humbled heart God shall not despise*.* A contrite heart is nearest to a clean heart, and this is to be next to God's heart if indeed *he is near to them that are of a troubled heart*.* The Samaritan is a neighbor to him *who fell in among the robbers*.* *He shall not swear deceitfully* to this *his neighbor*,* but he shall do what he promised: *Amen, I say to you, that you shall also sit as judges*.*

5. Therefore, dearest brothers, let us also be followers of both hands of innocence and heart of cleanness, at least in our own small measure.* Above all else indeed let us take care to *decline from evil** as much as we can, not only evil actions, but also evil thought, even if we lack the power to avoid sin thoroughly on account of human frailty.

In addition, *lest we receive our* rational *souls in vain*,* let us train ourselves in good works and let us employ reason's advice. For how do people not receive a human soul in vain* when, like one of the irrational animals, they brood over bodily pleasures and follow only carnal appetite? *see Ps 23:4

The prophet also adds, *nor has he sworn deceitfully to his neighbor.** For just as it is appropriate to observe cleanness within ourselves and innocence toward our neighbor, so both within us and toward our neighbor works of virtue and works of piety should be practiced. Therefore let us not be useless to ourselves *lest in vain we receive our souls;** let us not be useless to our neighbors, lest we be held as having sworn in vain to them. *Ps 23:4 *Ps 23:4

The Spirit who speaks through the prophet* *knows how we are formed,** and he did not simply wish to remind us about usefulness to our neighbor. He confronts us about our oath so that we recognize our debt and so that we fear to nullify the promised faith.* For we have all been pledged to our neighbors, with whom we have come into the church's unity. And this is the profession of Christian faith: *that one who lives may not now live for oneself, but for him who died* for all.* *Acts 28:25 *Ps 102:14 *1 Tim 5:12 *2 Cor 5:15

6. Let no one say to me, "May I live for him, but not for you," because he not only lived for all but also died for all.* For how can someone who neglects those whom he so loved possibly live for him? How can someone who does not fulfill his law or keep his commandment live for him? Do you ask what law? Do you ask what commandment? *This is my commandment*, he says, *that you love one another as I have loved you.** And the apostle: *Bear one another's burdens and so you shall fulfill the law of Christ.** *see 2 Cor 5:15 *John 15:12 *Gal 6:2

Therefore do not suppose that the good that you present to your neighbor is gratuitous, as though you are even permitted to ignore [your obligation] if you wish. You are a debtor by a pledge of the sacrament, and you are held by your own profession.

He shall receive, therefore, *a blessing from the Lord and mercy from God his Savior.** *He,* because only *one receives the prize.** But may you not suppose that that means one *Ps 23:5 *1 Cor 9:24

human being: *This is the generation that seeks the Lord.** *He shall receive blessing,** because the Head and the Body is one Christ.* But *this is the generation*, because *we all meet* equally *unto the measure of the age of Christ's fullness.**

7. And perhaps the same Lord himself is *the mountain of the Lord*, concerning whom it is said, *Who shall ascend into the mountain of the Lord? Or who shall stand in his holy place?** Certainly he himself is that stone cut off without hands, which grew into an enormous mountain.* The Lord himself is *lifted up from the earth, draws all things to himself*,‡ *a curdled mountain, a fat mountain.*

Why, you Jews, *why do you suspect a curdled mountain, a mountain in which God is well pleased to dwell?** *By Beelzebub, the prince of devils*, they say, *he casts out devils.** A detestable suspicion and a reprehensible blasphemy! The prince is Christ and a great prince, whose rule even the demons themselves cannot flee. But their *kingdom divided against itself shall be brought to desolation.** His kingdom is whole and complete, *and of his kingdom there shall be no end.** So there is a difference between the prince and princes; there is no comparison between *the mountain curdled and fat* and the mountains merely curdled.*

Your Beelzebub himself is a curdled mountain, but not fat,* cursed rather by perpetual sterility. A mountain because he proudly raised his head, curdled because *his scales press upon one another,** and *their heart is curdled like milk.**

8. Christ the Lord is the mountain, *a curdled mountain, and a fat mountain.** He is a mountain by his superiority, curdled by the accumulation of many, fat by his charity.

And now see how *he draws all things to himself,** how all things are united to him by a unity that is substantive, personal, spiritual, sacramental. He has within himself the Father, with whom he is one substance; he has taken up humankind, with whom he is one person; he has a faithful soul adhering to himself, with which he is one spirit;* he has one spouse, the church of all the elect, with which he is one flesh.* And perhaps it seems that we should speak about this carnal union, but I prefer to say *sacramental*, having judged this term more suitable, especially when the apostle gives the precedent, where he says, *This is a great sacrament, but I speak in Christ and in the church.*

*see 1 Cor 6:17
*see Eph 5:31-32

*Eph 5:32

Clearly Christ is the fattest and most fruitful mountain, *in which God is well pleased to dwell,** if indeed *he has anointed him with the oil of gladness above his fellows.** Christ is the heavenly *mountain of aromatic spices,** a mountain of spiritual gifts, receiving not *the Spirit by measure,** but by all means obtaining fullness of grace.

*Ps 67:17
*Ps 44:8; Heb 1:9
*Song 8:14
*John 3:34

He is a great mountain, *in whom are hidden all the treasures of wisdom and knowledge,** in whom the whole truth of his humanity, the whole fullness *of his divinity dwells.*† He is high and immense,*#* *in whom are restored all things that are in heaven and on earth,*‡ so that God may be all in all.*°*

*Col 2:3
†Col 2:9
#Bar 3:25
‡Eph 1:10
°1 Cor 15:28

9. *Come*, brothers, *let us ascend* into this *mountain!*◊ And if the way seems arduous to us, then let us unburden ourselves. If the way is narrow, then let us not even refrain from emptying ourselves. If the way is long, then let us hurry so much the more. If the way is laborious, then let us cry out to him, *Draw us after you! We will run in the odor of your ointments.**

◊Isa 2:3

*Song 1:3

Happy is the one who *so runs so as to seize*, nay rather, so that he *is seized** and merits to be admitted into that great expanse of the mountain and *fullness of Christ's body.** Happy the one who so longingly and persistently ascends into that mountain of blessings, so that *in the holy place,** receiving one's station, one may appear to God the Father in his Holy One. At the same time, may one also see *his power and glory,** by no means, of course, a glory other than the same mountain of mountains itself, *a mountain curdled and fat,** Jesus Christ our Lord.

*1 Cor 9:24; Phil 3:12
*Eph 1:23; 4:13

*Ps 23:3

*Ps 62:3

*Ps 67:16

In Christ we have appeared undoubtedly from eternity, through predestination, to him *who loved us,** and

*Rom 8:37

he has graced us in his beloved son,* in whom he chose us before the foundation of the world.* But *then*, moreover, *we shall know even as we are known*,* when more fully and more perfectly that exalted, most high, and most fruitful mountain *will draw all things to himself*,* *who is over all things, blessed forever. Amen.**

*Eph 1:6
*Eph 1:4
*1 Cor 13:12
*John 12:32
*Rom 9:5

Sermo 34

Concerning a Teaching of Origen on Leviticus 10:9

1. I fear, perhaps, that some of the words that were read to us yesterday can do harm. I mean Origen's homily about that chapter in the law where Aaron and his sons are forbidden to drink wine before they approach the altar.* Origen's words might be harmful if one took them literally, at face value. "My Savior," he says, "mourns even now my sins, and he is in mourning as long as we persist in error."* Many other passages also speak in this manner, perhaps in language more verbose than well considered, more grandiloquent than sensible.

*see Lev 10:9

*Origen, Homilies on Leviticus 7.2 (SCh 286:311)

What is the meaning of these odd groans I hear? Or who among you whispers about I know not what? Indeed I know that those who are learned in the divine law ridicule such words. Still, I admit that I am a debtor to even the less wise.* The question is not merely about Origen's meaning. He could perhaps be speaking in hyperbole; that is his business and not our concern. Nevertheless, I would not be silent about this: the authority of the holy fathers tells us that obviously Origen has sometimes written contrary to the faith, and likewise warns that Origen is to be read with discretion.

*Rom 1:14

However, at present we do not seek what Origen himself thought. Rather, we want to spend some time on this matter so that all of you who understand sound doctrine[*] will not be the least bit disturbed by Origen's words.

2. Far be it from anyone to believe that there is any place for sadness in heaven. Likewise there is no place for blame. No one in heaven can do wrong; no one can mourn, just as there would be no punishment on earth unless iniquity preceded it. In heaven there is certainly only justice, likewise only joy. In hell there is only sin and the punishment for sin. What is more, between heaven and hell both justice and sin are found, and so neither is complete. We are offended in many things because *in many things we all offend.*[*]

Since there could be no place of suffering or pain in heaven, it follows that the Only Begotten of God the Father would redeem human beings by his suffering when he took up the flesh in which he would suffer. For he was not able to suffer in his divinity; so likewise *he was seen upon earth and conversed with human beings,*[*] so to humble himself[†] *in a place of affliction.*[#] The Son was therefore troubled.[‡] He also deigned to be frightened and weary,[°] *tempted in all things as we are, without sin.*[∞] On earth, I say, Jesus really wept,[◊] he really was sad,[*] he really suffered, really died, really was buried, but when he was resurrected *former things passed away.*[†]

Seek no further for your beloved in your bed:[#] *He is not here. He is risen.*[‡] It is the voice of the bride who says, *In my bed by night I sought him whom my soul loves. I sought him and found him not.*[*] It was Mary who sought the Lord in bed: she sought in a tomb; she did not find.[†] Rather, the watchmen found him,[#] and they said, *Why do you seek the living among the dead?*[‡]

He was indeed with the dead, but now he is not. He was among the dead, but even then he was free.[*] If indeed he was troubled,[†] still *he laid down his life* himself;[#] *he was offered up because it was his own will.*[‡] For every weakness was of his own will, not of necessity. So also *the weakness of God was stronger than human beings,*[*]

---

[*]2 Tim 4:3

[*]Jas 3:2

[*]Bar 3:38
[†]Phil 2:8
[#]Ps 43:20
[‡]John 11:33
[°]Mark 14:33
[∞]Heb 4:15
[◊]John 11:35
[*]Matt 26:37
[†]2 Cor 5:17

[#]Song 3:1
[‡]Luke 24:6

[*]Song 3:1
[†]see John 20:11–15
[#]Song 3:3
[‡]Luke 24:5

[*]Ps 87:6
[†]John 11:33
[#]John 10:17
[‡]Isa 53:7

[*]1 Cor 1:25

for then he was also great among the small, strong among the weak, *free among the dead.** *Ps 87:6

3. Sometimes it seems that there is also some freedom in our tribulations, namely when we sustain some labor of penitence with free and generous charity, weeping for sins of our neighbors, fasting for them, enduring blows for them, and *paying for that which we have not stolen.** Thus also Paul says, *Whereas I was free to all, I made myself the servant of all.** Yet this was nothing to Paul's freedom—Paul, who had no sin of his own, who owed nothing to death, who merited no tribulation. *Ps 68:5
*1 Cor 9:19

On the other hand, the neighbor cannot perhaps by right require from us those voluntary tribulations. God, however, does require. And if perchance anyone seems to give back more than he owes to his neighbor,* still, no one ever gives back to God the whole of what is owed.* *see Matt 18:28

*see Matt 22:21

But to me, says the apostle, *it is a very small thing to be judged by you or by man's day, but neither do I judge my own self.** Notice, if you will, what he says in another place: *If we would judge ourselves then we should not be judged.** And similarly, *The spiritual man discerns all things.** For he does not put *judge* here, but *discern,* which is certainly to discern and to prove, as he also says: *Blessed is the one who judges not himself in that which he approves.** *1 Cor 4:3
*1 Cor 11:31
*1 Cor 2:15

*Rom 14:22

And so for Paul *it was a very small thing to be judged* by them* to whom he knew that he owed no debt of service, nor had he sinned against anyone, but rather he surpassed all to such a degree that he said frankly and with a secure conscience, *Who is weak and I am not weak? Who is scandalized and I am not on fire?** For *he became to the Jews a Jew so that he might gain the Jews. And to them that were without the law, as if he were without the law.* And finally *he became all things to all people so that he might save all.** Rightly, in the same manner for him *it was a very small thing to be judged* by them* to whom he *1 Cor 4:3

*2 Cor 11:29

*1 Cor 9:20-22
*1 Cor 4:3

had thus far shown himself as without offense,* among whom *he had* so *honored his ministry.**

But *neither does he judge himself** *by that which he approves,*† even paying perfectly what he owed to himself:# chastisement of his body,‡ compassion for his soul, and every concern for guarding his heart° so that his conscience held no sin against him. *Yet am I not hereby justified*, he says, *but he who judges me is the Lord.** For by all means I cannot divert the Lord's Judgment. *And if* I shall have been *just, I shall not lift up my head,** because *all my righteousness* is *as the rag of a menstruating woman** *before him.* There is no one who *shall be justified* in *his sight;** *there is not even one.*‡

4. Indeed there is no one among others who need not say to God, *Against you have I sinned,** but great is one who can truly say, *Against you alone.** Yet again, Christ alone was completely free among the dead,* he who did no sin,* whose justice is like the mountains of God.* Moreover, he is no longer among the dead; rather, he was taken up from them,* changed in body, changed in heart, *having entered into the powers of the Lord** and deprived of every weakness, certainly having cast off those filthy garments in which he first appeared dressed before the prophet Zechariah and put on *splendid garments,** just as it says in the psalm: *You have cut my sackcloth and have surrounded me with gladness.**

In fact, because he took up the true substance of human flesh and soul, the true nature of each, the sufferings neither of the body nor of the soul were lacking to him, and out of this he is now glorified in both. I think that the prophet expresses glorification of body and soul in one short little verse, saying, *The Lord has reigned. He is clothed with beauty. The Lord is clothed with strength.** That is, beauty in the body of his splendor,∞ strength truly in his imperturbable state of mind.

Finally he says, *My soul is sorrowful* but *even unto death.** Thus *bowing his head, he said: It is finished,*◊ so that no weakness in him could be suspected.

---

*1 Cor 10:32
*Rom 11:13
*1 Cor 4:3
†Rom 14:22
#2 Cor 12:15
‡1 Cor 9:27
°Prov 4:23

*1 Cor 4:4

*Job 10:15
*Isa 64:6

*Ps 142:2
‡Ps 13:3

*Ps 50:6
*Ps 50:6
*Ps 87:6
*1 Pet 2:22
*Ps 35:7
*Acts 1:11

*Ps 70:16

*see Zech 3:3-4
*Ps 29:12

*Ps 92:1
∞Phil 3:21

*Matt 26:38
◊John 19:30

5. But Origen says, "If God's apostle *weeps for* certain people who *sinned before and yet have not done penance for sins that they have committed*,* then what shall I say about him who is called Son of Charity?" And then Origen says, "Therefore, since he sought things that are ours, does he now no longer seek us, nor does he consider things that are ours,* nor does he grieve about our errors, nor does he sob about our destructions and contrition, he who wept over Jerusalem?"* Origen says in a similar passage, "Now, because *merciful and compassionate* is *the Lord*,* with greater feeling than his apostle *he weeps with those who weep*,* and *he mourns those who sinned before*.* For one must not think that Paul mourns and weeps for sinners but that my Lord refrains from weeping."

    *2 Cor 12:21

    *see Phil 2:21

    *Luke 19:41

    *Ps 110:4
    *Rom 12:15
    *2 Cor 12:21

Shall I still say to accept this at face value, *in my bed I sought my beloved*?* The dead person knows not *to seek the one whom his soul loves** outside his tomb, the sick person knows not outside his bed, the infant knows not outside his cradle.

    *Song 3:1
    *Song 3:1

Certainly, as we recalled above, Christ is not glorified less in his heart than in his body (nay rather, so much the more since the soul is more spacious and has greater capacity for glory than the flesh); in the same way he cannot neglect his own, nor can he weep for them. But when can such human frailty grasp the affection that commiserates without misery and so loves and vehemently loves anyone who hurts or is at risk, while God himself neither hurts at all nor is disturbed? Still, it is far beyond our experience. *For God*, however, *nothing is impossible*.*

    *Luke 1:37

Therefore, he can bestow that delight not only for himself, but also for all his own; he clothed with strength* those who have laid aside the infirmity of the flesh, and he led them into powers.* His delight *rejoices with those who rejoice* but does not *weep with those who weep*.* And so those whom he loves most effectively and affectionately he supports so that love perseveres

    *Ps 92:1
    *Ps 70:16

    *Rom 12:15

imperturbable. No doubt God's love is far more excellent, just as we would judge a medicine, if there were such a thing, as more precious if it cured wounds without being diminished in its potency nor in its substance, that is, more precious than a medicine that is diminished or spoiled as it cures.

Granted, *the Lord wept over Jerusalem*,* but from then on he shall no longer weep at all, just as he died, but, *rising again from the dead, he dies now no more*;* just as he was in the bed, but, rising up, he is no longer found in bed.* *Luke 19:41 *Rom 6:9 *Song 3:1

6. Even now the Lord has indescribably more ample and more effective affection than those who weep for sinners,* or those who lay down their lives for their brothers,* even though, since Christ has certainly finished his work,* he shall no longer weep or lay down his life. *see 2 Cor 12:21 *1 John 3:16 *John 17:4

That is our weakness. We still *cast a net into the sea, and gathering together all kinds of fishes*,* we separate none at all. For Christ and not only Christ but also his apostles and the other saints who are with him* arrive at the shore indeed; they do not put the mixed variety of fish into vessels, but only the chosen and the good, for certainly they cast out the bad fish.* *Matt 13:47 *Rom 16:15 *Matt 13:48

For now, I myself am compelled to haul in many bad fish. How many troublesome and annoying fish have I gathered within my net since my soul was attached to you!* I rejoice with those who make progress, a congenial affection that is a good fish. I suffer with those who fail: *I weep with those who weep*,* I am in anguish with those who are at risk, *I am weak with those who are weak, I am on fire with those who are scandalized*.* Harsh and burdensome indeed are these bad fish. I say that they are bad not on account of guilt, but because of punishment. May God make it so that we be not overwhelmed by the multitude of bad fish, *by pusillanimity of spirit and a storm*,* until we arrive at our station on *see Gen 34:8 *Rom 12:15 *2 Cor 11:29 *Ps 54:9

the best shore, where we separate out the bad fish and seclude them from the good. So thenceforth *neither mourning, nor crying, nor any sorrow** nor even fear may be in our country, but *thanksgiving and the voice of exultation.**

*Rev 21:4

*Isa 51:3; Ps 117:15

Sermo 35

To the Abbots.[1]
How Noah, Daniel, and Job crossed the sea, each in his own way: on a ship, by a bridge, by the shallows

Printed in SBOp 5:288–93; English in Bernard of Clairvaux, *Sermons for the Autumn Season*, translated by Irene Edmonds, Cistercian Fathers 54 (Collegeville, MN: Cistercian Publications, 2016), 85–90.

---

[1] *Sermo ad abbates* (Abb)

Sermo 36

On the Occasion of the Preceding Sermon:[1] The Heart's Loftiness and Baseness

Printed in SBOp 5:214–16; English in Bernard of Clairvaux, *Sermons for the Summer Season*, translated by Beverly Mayne Kienzle, Cistercian Fathers 53 (Kalamazoo, MI: Cistercian Publications, 1991), 128–30.

---

[1] *Sixth Sunday after Pentecost*, Sermo 3 (6 Pent 3)

Sermo 37

On The Time of Harvest:[1]
Sermon 3.
*This is the generation of those who seek the Lord, of those who seek the face of the God of Jacob.**

*Ps 23:6

P rinted in SBOp 5:222–28; English in Bernard of Clairvaux, *Sermons for the Autumn Season*, translated by Irene Edmonds, Cistercian Fathers 54 (Collegeville, MN: Cistercian Publications, 2016), 7–13.

---

[1] *Sermo in labore messis* (In lab mess 3)

Sermo 38

On The Time of Harvest:[1]
Sermon 1.
How a Twofold Evil Works for Good

Printed in SBOp 5:217–19; English in Bernard of Clairvaux, *Sermons for the Autumn Season*, translated by Irene Edmonds, Cistercian Fathers 54 (Collegeville, MN: Cistercian Publications, 2016), 1–3.

---

[1] *Sermo in labore messis* (In lab mess 1)

SERMO 39

On The Time of Harvest:[1]
Sermon 2.
Of the Two Tables

Printed in SBOp 5:220–22; English in Bernard of Clairvaux, *Sermons for the Autumn Season*, translated by Irene Edmonds, Cistercian Fathers 54 (Collegeville, MN: Cistercian Publications, 2016), 4–6.

---

[1] *Sermo in labore messis* (In lab mess 2)

Sermo 40

Concerning Seven Steps of Confession

1. **Y**ou *have made known to me the ways of life. You shall fill me with joy with your countenance. At your right hand are delights even to the end.** Gladly indeed we approach you, Lord Jesus, as disciples to a teacher,* the sick to a physician, servants to a lord. For you are the teacher and lord* whose school is on earth, whose seat is in heaven. You are that extraordinary doctor, you who renew the universe by a word alone. *Show your ways to me, O Lord, and teach me your paths.** For your ways are *beautiful ways, and all your paths are peaceable.** Blessed are those who walk in your ways,† *Lord of hosts.*# Even more blessed are those who run the way of your commandments,‡ who run *in the odor of your ointments,*° *for you rejoice as a giant to run the way.*∞ And not only running, but even *leaping on the mountains, skipping over the hills.*◊
    The giants among philosophers have not rejoiced to run your way, but to seek vainglory, *growing weak in their thoughts,** not by humility in your powers but in their own. For *they have not known the way of wisdom, neither have they remembered her paths. It has not been heard of in Canaan, neither has it been seen in Theman.** Accursed are those who said to the Lord Jesus, *Depart from us! We wish not the knowledge of your ways.** We ourselves *seek you from day to day; we wish to know your ways.**

*Ps 15:11

*Matt 5:1
*John 13:13

*Ps 24:4
*Prov 3:17
†Ps 127:1
#Ps 68:7
‡Ps 118:32
°Song 1:3
∞Ps 18:6
◊Song 2:8

*Rom 1:21

*Bar 3:22-23

*Job 21:14
*Isa 58:2

2. You have two principal ways: confession and obedience. In confession all sins are washed; in obedience virtues are strengthened. Confession is good equipment for the soul; it both purifies the sinner and renders a just person more pure. If there are sins, then they are washed in confession; if there are good works, then they are commended by confession. When you confess your wicked deeds, *a sacrifice to God is an afflicted spirit.** When you confess God's kindness, you *offer to God a sacrifice of praise.** Without confession, the just person is declared ungrateful and the sinner is reckoned as dead. Confession therefore is life of the sinner, glory of the just. I see David saying, *I have sinned.* And he hears, *The Lord has taken away your sin and you shall not die.**

*Ps 50:19

*Ps 49:14

*2 Sam 12:13

I consider Mary, if not in words then at least in her actions, publicly confessing her offenses, and the Lord responding on her behalf, *Many sins are forgiven her, because she has loved much.** I reflect on the prince of the apostles denying Christ fearfully, then weeping bitterly when Christ looks back at him.* I look at the lucky thief accusing himself and excusing Christ, and the Lord promising, *This day you shall be with me in paradise.**

*Luke 7:47

*see Luke 22:57-62

*see Luke 23:41-42, 43

O, how sublime that confession by which from the gibbet to the Kingdom, from earth to heaven, from the cross to Paradise, the condemned and crucified thief ascends—a glorious confession that liberated the apostle Peter from the crime of denying three times and did not allow him to fall from the summit of apostleship. The faithful institution that forgave Mary much because she loved much* also distinguished Mary with the reputation for much love and allied her with the body of disciples. The illustrious mercy that cleansed the king and prophet of his flood of crimes also guided and led him back into the glory of venerable dignity. This is the way that never fails the traveler, the way that never forsakes anyone except those who abandon it.

*Luke 7:47

3. The paths to finding this way of confession are many and various, difficult to master, baffling to count.

Sermo 40

The first path, and the first step on this way, is self-knowledge. This decree fell from heaven: "Human being, know yourself!"[1] See if the Bridegroom in the Song of Love does not say the same to the bride: *If you know not yourself, O fairest among women, then go forth.** *Song 1:7
Knowledge of self consists of three parts: that people know what they have done, what they have deserved, what they have lost.

What is more vile, O noble creature, image of God, likeness of the Creator,* than to disfigure your flesh *see Gen 1:26
with carnal enticements and for the sake of a brief pleasure to lose a torrent of pleasure?* What is more *Ps 35:9
crazy than to let your mind be carried off by anger, lifted by pride, bothered by envy, and tortured by anxiety? *You who were brought up in scarlet, why have you embraced dung?** *Lam 4:5

Call to mind also what you deserve. Let the cauldron of Gehenna rise into your memory, the iron furnace* *Deut 4:20
of great Babylon,* the home of death, abode of anxiety, *Rev 4:8
ball of flames, anguish of cold, perpetual darkness. Consider the series of torments, faces of torturers, succession of punishments, infinite miseries. And with your mind's eye run through these torments, and you will be able to say, *It would be better* for me if I *had not been born.** *Matt 26:24

Turn your eyes and turn your attention to what you have lost. Recall what is the nature of the glorious city, heavenly dwelling, place of life, palace of sweetness, splendor of glory, magnitude of grace, infinite resplendence. Attend to the order of joys, faces of those who rejoice, vicissitude of rewards, and multitude of delights, and you can exclaim, "He who has lost you, Lord God, has lost all." If you will bind your soul with this threefold cord,* then you will understand and notice that *Eccl 4:12
the beginning of salvation is the recognition of sin.* *see Sir 1:16

---

[1] This maxim has a long history; see S 40 in SCh 518:210n2.

4. The second step is repentance. These two are mutually joined to each other in such a way that one cannot know oneself without repenting, nor can one repent without knowing oneself. Therefore, wounded by a javelin of compunction, let the soul repent with a threefold repentance, for she has lost her innocence, has not missed her lost innocence, and has ignored God's patience.*

I know, Lord Jesus, that in baptism you have given back to us our first robe* of innocence. And having been dressed in a snow-white cloak, placed on a throne of justice, *we have quickly strayed from the way which you have shown to us,** and we squander *the portion of inheritance that falls to us* with the prodigal son in the region of unlikeness.* The most vile spirits and the kings of eternal fires came to us: the filthy to the clean, the damned to those to be saved, the crooked to the upright, *and they said to our souls: Bow down so that we may cross over.** We heard them, and we were bent down. They crossed through us, and we lost innocence.

If it is an offense to have lost, what do you think it will be if you do not even miss the loss? When people lose something in this mortal life, they seek judges, call friends together, bring a lawsuit, leave no stone unturned, until they either find what is lost or restore what was taken away and preserve what is restored. We have lost our *inheritance that is incorruptible and undefiled and that cannot fade, reserved in heaven,** by the cunning of that insatiable murderer, and we do not miss it? And he has made us bend down, and we do not rise up again? *Let us arise and go to our father and say to him: Father, we have sinned against heaven and before you.** And acting out the whole text of the gospel narrative, let us offer to the Father repentance of mind and contrition of heart so that perchance *when we are yet a great way off, the Father might see us, and moved with compassion, and running, fall upon our neck, and let him kiss us with the kiss of his mouth.**

*see Rom 2:4

*Luke 15:22

*Exod 32:8

*Luke 15:12-13

*Isa 51:23

*1 Pet 1:4

*Luke 15:18

*Luke 15:20; Song 1:1

Perhaps he shall order that the first robe of innocence be brought forth and order us to be clothed with the garments of virtue and to be given the ring of secrets on our hand and shoes to be put on our feet,* *in preparation for the gospel of peace.* He shall perhaps order that the fatted calf be led forth and killed in satisfaction for those who are returning, to feast* and to rejoice and to be led back to the joys of the heavenly city in music and dancing,* where *there shall be joy for God's angels over one sinner doing penance.*

*Luke 15:22; see Isa 61:10
*Eph 6:15
*Luke 15:23
*Luke 15:25
*Luke 15:10

We know, Lord Jesus, that *you will not deprive of good things those who walk in innocence* or those who walk in repentance. In fact, only one *has done no sin.* *Blessed, however, is the one to whom the Lord has imputed no sin.* Everything that he ordained not to charge against me is as though it had never existed.

*Ps 83:13
*1 Pet 2:22
*Ps 31:2

Furthermore, consider with how much pride you have used, or rather abused, the patience of God. He saw you sinning, and he ignored it* as though not seeing. He was calling, and you were not listening. He was threatening, and you were not afraid. He was promising, and you paid no heed, nor were you enticed by the promises or struck with alarm. *Don't you know that God's patience leads you to repentance?* Be afraid with great fear, lest *you treasure up for yourself wrath in the day of wrath and of revelation of God's just judgment,* and remember that *it is a fearful thing to fall into the hands of the living God.* Therefore, bind the wound of your soul with this triple plaster of repentance* and say, *Have mercy on me, O Lord, for I am weak, heal me.*

*see Wis 11:24

*Rom 2:4

*Rom 2:5

*Heb 10:31
*see Isa 38:21
*Ps 6:3

5. The third step is sorrow,[2] but this step is also bound by a triple knot. Rightly, after thought and repentance, *my sorrow was renewed and in my meditation a fire* glows because I have offended my Creator. I have not feared my Lord; I have spurned my benefactor.

*Ps 38:3-4

---

[2] *Dolor*: Bernard uses this and related terms six times in this section, seeming to refer to pain, suffering, regret, sorrow, and grief.

The Lord says: *As is clay in the hand of a potter, are you not likewise in my hand?** If he himself made you a vessel of honor, why have you dared to make yourself into an insult?* *Should earthenware say to the potter, Why have you made me so?** You the creation have dared to challenge the Creator? The earthenware challenges its maker? The work the worker? Be mindful, you most worthless earthenware vessel, that *if you should fall on this stone, then you shall be broken. But if it shall fall upon you, it shall grind you to powder** with a frightful grinding, so that not the least trace remains. You, moreover, have mixed blood with blood,* both offending your Creator and not fearing your Lord.

You were a servant of that Lord *whose wrath no one can resist,** and in his teachings you had accepted his will. *You refused to understand so that you might do well,** but disobeying your Sovereign's command, you have decided to live by your own law within his state. Have you not heard about the punishment paid by the wicked servant* who, *knowing but not doing the will of his Lord*, was held down for *many blows?*†

Angels stand by,# *attentive to the voice of his orders*.‡ *Stars are called, and they say, Here we are.*° *The winds and the sea obey him,*∞ and all things uphold the law set before them with an unshaken firmness. *Are you only a stranger,*◊ and don't you care about the decrees of the imperial majesty? Listen! He is able *to cast* you *into outer darkness where weeping and gnashing of teeth** increase with everlasting unhappiness.

But if you are not moved by your Creator's displeasure or by reverence for his power, then at least be moved by your ingratitude, because you have scorned such a great benefactor and so many of his favors. Indeed, where will you find a similar benefactor who supplies for you the course of the stars, a proper mixture of air, fecundity of the earth, abundance of crops? Ultimately, in order to include the consummation of all life's benefits for you, *He spared not even his own Son;*

*Jer 18:6
*Rom 9:21
*Rom 19:20

*Matt 21:44

*see Luke 13:1

*Job 9:13
*Ps 35:4

*Matt 18:32
†Luke 12:47; see Jas 4:17
#see Dan 7:10
‡Ps 102:20
°Bar 3:34-35
∞Matt 8:27
◊Luke 24:18

*Matt 22:13

rather, *he delivered him up for us all*,* surrendering his Only Begotten for the adopted, the Lord for servants, the Just One for the impious.* *What more should he do for you that he has not done?** When therefore you have suffered the pain of realizing this, then you can say with the prophet, *My bowels, my bowels are in pain, my heart's senses are troubled within me.**

6. The fourth step is confession by mouth. After thought of oneself, after repentance of mind, after pain of heart, confession by mouth follows. In all these, *With heart one believes unto justice, but by mouth confession is made unto salvation.** But confession is also triple if it attains the virtue of salvation. That is, it must be true, bare, and personal.

The Most High seeks truth. Since he does not intend to deceive, when would he wish to be deceived? We both know and have experienced a great many people who, by coming to the grace of confession, went back to their sense of guilt more burdened than liberated from sin. For if they are priests, then they talk about what they did in their literary pursuits. If they are soldiers, then they talk about armed conflict so that they bring in pride under a cloak of humility. With the great seal of confession they condemn themselves, the seal under which the pinnacle of all human salvation depends.

There are some who are compelled to confess by fear. Others are led by pretense. For this reason they confess, so at least to keep up the appearance of confessing. But do you reckon this to be true confession, that which either fear wrenches out or pretense makes, when *the Holy Spirit of discipline flees from deceit*,* and the All Powerful seeks satisfaction with no strings attached? True confession is that which comes down from contrition of mind, not forced by fear or cloaked in pretense, but which brings forth that which one feels in an afflicted spirit.*

*Rom 8:32

*see Rom 5:6
*Isa 5:4

*Jer 4:19

*Rom 10:10

*Wis 1:5

*Ps 50:19

But confession must also be bare, stripped of the veil of all concealment. For what does confession accomplish by telling part of one's sins while hiding another part, to be cleansed in part but partly subservient to impurity? Can a vessel dispense *sweet and bitter out of the same hole,** tasteful[3] and tasteless? *All things are bare and open to God's eyes,** and you would conceal something from one who occupies God's place in so great a sacrament? Show and lay bare whatever rends your heart! Uncover the wound so that you feel the first aid of the healer. *In simplicity of heart** you must seek the Lord, not in duplicity, because woe to those who *speak with a double heart** *and walk the earth by two ways.*‡

*Jas 3:11
*Heb 4:13

*Gen 20:5

*Ps 11:3
‡Sir 2:14

Confession must also be personal. For there are a good many who count sins of others with great seriousness, and they tell about a companion's excesses with multifaceted oratory. They do not know their own sins, but they commit other people's sins to everlasting memory. Unfortunate and wretched are those given to lamenting the sins of others while leaving out their own! Have you not read that the *just one accuses himself in the beginning of his speech?** *Himself*, Scripture says, not *another.* Surely you have not forgotten the apostle who says, *Confess therefore your sins one to another.** *Your sins*, he said, not *another's. I know my iniquity and my sin is always before me.** The prophet said *my iniquity*, not *your iniquity.*

*see Prov 18:17

*Jas 5:16
*Ps 50:5

7. The fifth step is mortification of the flesh, but this also is consecrated by the number three. For it is properly done secretly, with permission, discreetly. Your tender limbs were reared with exquisite pleasures. Crush them with a long-lasting martyrdom so that to the degree that you recognize abstaining from what is permitted, to that same degree you will remember having done what is forbidden. But this must be done

---

[3] *Sapidum*: this is a play on words; "prudence" is the basic meaning.

secretly so that *your left hand knows not what your right hand does*.* For the preservation of so great a good is not in your mouth but in the secret of your heart, so that your *glory is the testimony of our conscience*.* We do not say this to prevent *your light* from *shining before*, to prevent *people* from *seeing your good works and glorifying your Father who is in heaven*.* Rather, we want to prevent you from covering your intention in a brief, worldly glory. For nothing is more unfortunate than to mortify the flesh by fasting in this life, to afflict oneself with night vigils so as to receive the glory here, only to suffer in Gehenna later.

*Matt 6:3

*2 Cor 1:12

*Matt 5:16

Certainly mortification must be done with permission, because anything made with the consent of a pastor is more agreeable in God's sight. And the Most High especially receives that sacrifice that comes not from will's opinion but rather that offered by a teacher's instructions. Indeed, excluding self-will greatly strengthens you in refuting pride. And one who loves the vanity of this world cannot eradicate pride.

Discretion, however, must be maintained in our strictness. For if we desire flagellation too much we might lose salvation; while we seek to subjugate the enemy, we might kill the citizen. Consider your body and your body's potential, look at the constitution of your flesh; impose a measure on your severity. Preserve your body unharmed so you can serve your Creator. We have seen many people who have so beaten their body as novices, have broken the locks of discretion, that they are rendered unfit for the solemnities of praise, and they end up spending a long time being taken care of in luxury.

8. The sixth step is correction of one's work. But this step is also consecrated by the number of the Trinity. That is: do no evil to yourself, do no harm to anyone else, and do not conspire with one who does harm.

You have experienced how temporary a plunge into pleasures is, and you would go there again? You have observed that the pleasure passed away, yet sin remained. Restrain your foot from the abominable roads of filthy wantonness! Submit your neck to the Most High's commands lest *there be iniquity in your hands!** Cut out the customary feasts for your raging throat, likewise vain conversation. *Turn away your eyes lest they see vanity,** *stop up your ears lest they hear blood!** And then you can say, *The chastising Lord has chastised me.**

*Ps 7:4
*Ps 118:37
*Isa 33:15
*Ps 117:18

But what is the profit in restraining your works within the limits of righteousness if you desire to harm others? One who does no *evil to his neighbor nor takes up reproach against his neighbors** *shall rest on God's holy mountain,** receiving *a blessing from the Lord and mercy from God, one's Savior.**

*Ps 14:3
*Ps 14:1
*Ps 23:5

However, do not assume that you are innocent unless, as much as you can, you refute with authority impious sinners who walk against virtue, and *you set yourself as a wall for the house of Israel** by chastising yourself, not harming others or conspiring with one who does harm. This saying is true indeed: "One who neglects to improve when he can no doubt sets himself up as a participant in sin."[4] For when God's cause is tossed into the air[5] and falsehood is put forth as truth, one who does not resist in proportion to his responsibility shall be condemned for his silence.

*Ezek 13:5

9. The seventh step is perseverance, but it is also hallowed by the holiness of the number three. For imitation of the saints, shortness of seasons, and frailty of bodies all make perseverance. For in fact, what could you not endure when you see young people, boys, little

---

[4] Publilius Syrus, *Sententiae*, ed. E. Woelflin (Leipzig, 1869), 100. Also quoted by fathers like Gregory the Great; see SCh 518:230n1.

[5] *Ventilatur in medium* ("winnowed"): the sense seems to be "called into question."

girls, old women, old and decrepit men not only accepting but even seeking various torments? Consider the youth of boys, fire of young people, tenderness of little girls, fragility of old women, infirmity of old men, and impotence of the decrepit, and wherever you turn your eyes you shall find in these times a multitude of examples that have run to the palm of martyrdom with manly vigor.* Were you not also *formed from the same mud*,* and did you not receive the same breath of life?‡ And perhaps persecution does not come violently so that you suffer martyrdom: you are not condemned if you serve Christ; rather you are praised and proclaimed by all.

*see Phil 3:14
*Job 33:6
‡see Gen 2:7

But if persecution is imminent, then you should consider it a small matter because of its short duration. For well does nature provide for us; it shows no suffering to be both long and great. If indeed it is great, then it cannot be long. For instance, the fellowship of body and soul does not sustain exquisite torments for a long time, but, when shaken by the magnitude of a shock, it is dissolved most quickly. Therefore it is characteristic of great souls to think little of great torments that, in a short time, beget a change so great that they make the long-suffering person fly away from toil to rest, from misery to glory.

We must also take into consideration the body's fragility. Often either some little fall or continual bouts with high fever can smother a body in a moment. Therefore, whenever you must, make a virtue of necessity; for a brief trial you shall win eternal reward.

10. So you see how difficult running the way of confession becomes, how complex and numerous are the paths that we must keep. It is true that so great a teacher of the church says, "I have more easily found those who have preserved their innocence than those who have done suitable penance."*

*Ambrose, *De Paenitentia* 2.10 (SCh 179:192)

We have said these things about the way of confession according to our little measure, saving the weight of sublime insights for more sublime thinkers. Still, we shall try to explain the way of obedience during another sermon, lest you grow sick of our Lord Savior's words, he *who is blessed forever.**

*Rom 1:25

Sermo 41

Concerning the Seven Steps of Obedience

1. **W**e are not able *to think anything by ourselves, as from ourselves, but our competence is from God.** I mean to say, in this earthen vessel* and in this fragile human condition, what could a spirit think, a spirit locked up in prison, corrupted by sin, weighed down by earthly affairs?* *For the corruptible body weighs down upon the soul, and earthly habitation presses down the mind that ponders many things.**

    However, *the Spirit of wisdom is benevolent,** and he even illuminates the imprisoned spirit and heals the corrupted and lifts up one who is weighed down. For indeed *the Spirit of loving kindness** *releases those who are fettered, enlightens the blind, and lifts up those who are cast down.** In addition, he is the *Spirit of truth* who *teaches us every truth*, but he not only *teaches* but even *suggests.** Obviously he suggests so that we ask, he teaches so that we understand.

    The Spirit is the very one whom the Lord Jesus, after *obedience* to his Father *unto death on the cross,** sent to his apostles,* to those who obeyed him. Does it not seem to you that they have ascended the summit of singular obedience? I mean those who have received freedom to remain in the city,* have been concealed within the walls of one little house, *and so persevered with one mind in prayer.**

*2 Cor 3:5
*Lam 4:2

*see Wis 9:15

*Wis 9:15
*Wis 1:6

*Isa 11:2

*Ps 145:7-8
*John 16:13; 14:26

*Phil 2:8
*see John 15:26

*Luke 24:49

*see John 20:26; Acts 1:13-14

213

Do you realize that the apostles *went from the presence of the council, rejoicing that they were accounted worthy to suffer reproach for the name of Jesus*?* O how great the powers of obedience on which they lean, they who rejoice to be dragged to the council for Christ's sake: they consider it an honor to be slain for Him; they seek glory to die for him! Souls blessed and flowing with abundant majesty of the Spirit, to whom, by a wonderful change, degradation seems like grandeur, reproach glory, endurance victory. *For their soul is greatly filled; they are a reproach to the rich and contempt to the proud.** You see their composure when they confront the priests to their faces, to the brow of the Pharisees,* to the uproar of the mob, saying, *One ought to obey God rather than human beings.** Consider those two great luminaries, Peter and Paul. Peruse the whole order of the apostolic elders, and there you shall see that they courageously persisted in firmness of obedience amid a multitude of torments.

*Acts 5:41

*Ps 122:4

*see Luke 4:29

*Acts 5:29

Was not the King's Son himself, King of that region that is illuminated by continuous joys, *made obedient to his Father unto death, even to the death on the cross,** and *he learned obedience from that which he suffered*?* You have heard the misery; hear also the crown. You have seen the danger; see the reward. You have paid attention to the infirmity; pay attention to the power. *For which cause*, it says, *God also has exalted him and has given him a name which is above every name.**

*Phil 2:8
*Heb 5:8; see Heb 11:8

*Phil 2:9

2. But for now, let us be silent about his obedience, which is signed and sealed* by a unique prerogative. Let that great patriarch come into our midst, that lamp of faith, model of obedience, supreme leader of justice, he who hears from the Almighty, *Go forth from your country, and from your kindred, and from your father's home, and come into the land that I shall show to you.** And at the voice of one command, he flees his homeland, abandons his parents, deserts his inheritance, and emigrates into a foreign country as a total stranger. This is a great

*see Rev 5:5

*Gen 12:1

event that consecrated him father of many nations, giving him the privilege and honor of being the first.* The first patriarch, first of all, renounces his own resources and runs the way of obedience with untiring speed. *see Gen 17:4

Finally, when he had received *a son in his old age*,* in whom blessing of the whole world was to be amassed,* God said to him, *Take your only-begotten son, Isaac, whom you love, and offer him to me as an holocaust.** O, how great the bitterness in those words, how great the severing of paternal love* from the father's heart! For he is ordered to kill his son, *bone from his bones and flesh from his flesh*,* son of the great promise, of his extreme age, of his very own wife, a son remarkably promised, happily born, nurtured in innocence. *Luke 1:36 *see Gen 12:2 *Gen 22:2 *pietatis *Gen 2:23

And lest any pain be lacking, *only-begotten* is added so that a most subtle flame of suffering permeates the father's organs. For in fact there are many sons, but not many are *only begotten*. So he is *that* son because he is *only begotten*. He is that unique son to his father, *only begotten* to his mother, reserved for the inheritance. Please do not consider Ishmael, because, you see, he had been born in servitude and from a slave girl, so he in no way pertains to freedom and inheritance.* *see Gal 4:22, 30

Even if there are both many and only-begotten sons, still there are not many beloved sons. So in order to magnify the distress in the father's heart and to confirm obedience in the mind of the just one, the Lord adds *whom you love*. And so to stimulate the father's tender feelings even more by reminding Abraham of the beloved name and to arouse the whole interior paternal love* by the sound of the beloved voice, the boy is named *by the name which he had been called* by the Lord *before he was conceived in the womb*.* *pietas *Luke 2:21

You see therefore how Abraham's paternal love* is stricken with great hammers of distress when he is ordered to take up his son, to kill his only begotten, to sacrifice one whom he loves, to strike down Isaac! He is greatly tried, greatly tested, greatly scorched. Sweet *pietas is the link of son to father, of father to son. Abraham forgets this sweetness and the feelings of all family bonds. He saddles his donkey, gathers some wood, kindles a fire, draws his sword. He does not ask the Lord why; he neither murmurs nor complains, nor does his face betray any trace of suffering. Rather, without sensitivity to all that God commands, he hurries to the death of his son with a godly cruelty.* Therefore, the virtue of obedience being so high and admirable in Abraham, it should be proclaimed with praise of singular excellence.

*see Gen 22:3-10

3. True obedience is a most powerful force, and one that cannot descend into a rational soul unless it is cleansed deliberately and purely of this world's corruption. In order to illuminate the way of obedience more clearly, let us show as best we can what is special obedience to God, what is proper obedience to humankind, and what obedience to God and to a human being have in common.

There are certain extreme evils; likewise extreme goods. The extreme goods are to love God, to love one's neighbor, to speak truth, *not to steal, not to bear false witness, not to commit adultery,** and to avoid many other sins that brevity prevents us from listing. The extreme evils are contrary to the goods, or sins similar to them. God commands that we do good deeds; he orders us to abstain from evil deeds. The holy and unchangeable authority of this precept cannot be refuted in any way, because it is authenticated with the seal of the one who says, *I am the Lord and I do not change.**

*Matt 19:18

*Mal 3:6

If therefore that person whom God *has set over our heads** chooses to understand differently, *counting darkness for light and light for darkness** so that he commands us to abandon good commandments or to cling to the aforementioned evils, then the authority of the superior giving such commands must be fearlessly refuted, and with a free voice one must say, *One must obey God rather than human beings.** This is the special obedience to God

*Ps 65:12
*Isa 5:20

*Acts 5:29

that the human will must never neglect but must preserve with unwavering resolve. Hold therefore to a certain rule so that you don't abandon good commandments by the authority of superiors or do evil deeds.

However, between extreme evils and extreme goods, there are certain intermediates that, considered among themselves, take up the name of good and of evil. The intermediates are to walk, to sit, to speak, to keep quiet, to eat, to fast, to keep vigil, to sleep, and anything similar, which, if they are done with a pastor's permission, await the highest reward. Consequently, we should be submissive and obey in these intermediate matters at the nod of our superiors, *asking no question for conscience's sake*,* because God puts no imperative in these matters, but he delegated regulation of such matters to the authority of our superiors. Let not an inexperienced master trouble you if his power seems undiscerning, but be mindful that *there is no power but from God*,* and *one who resists power, resists God's ordinance*.*

*1 Cor 10:25

*Rom 13:1
*Rom 13:2

This is the obedience proper to humankind, that which we owe to humans, we who have been placed under humans. This is common between God and humankind: that whatever obedience is shown to superiors is shown to him who says, *One who hears me, hears you*.* Therefore we say that one must walk this path with great caution, for many steps might be concealed in the same place; someone who neglects one step will keep the others without reward.

*Luke 10:16

4. So the first step is to obey willingly. Every generation *is prone to evil from its youth*,* and each one follows the will of his crooked heart.* In fact, from that narrow passage of the first transgression, love of one's own will was born into the human being. Self-will abandoned the will of her creator; in that place where she wished to dominate, she was subjected to servitude. Therefore it is difficult to relinquish one's own will and to be subjected to the will of another. What is more, however heavy it may be, one who has not made his own will

*Gen 8:21
*see Bar 1:22

that of one who gives orders cannot ascend the first step of obedience.

Just people take pride in entrusting themselves to the Lord with their own will.* And he says, *I will freely sacrifice to you.** Therefore it is the will alone that adorns the effect of one's whole work, the will without which nothing is done well, even if it seems to be good.

Therefore the orders of superiors should be accepted with one's will, and the heart itself must be detached from turning back to its own wishes until, having sacrificed its own will, it loves the command of one who gives orders. So this is to obey willingly: voluntarily to fulfill the will of superiors.

*see Ps 27:7
*Ps 53:8

5. The second step is to be sincerely* submissive: *He who walks sincerely, walks confidently.** Solomon *in the sincerity of his heart joyfully offered all things.** And Scripture teaches *to seek the Lord in sincerity of heart.**

*simpliciter
*Prov 10:9
*1 Chr 29:17
*Wis 1:1

We see many people asking many questions about the authority of the one giving orders and more often inquiring why, how, on what account, redoubling their frequent complaints, asking, "How does he order this? From where did this come? Who devised this plan?" Thence grumbling, thence words echoing the grumbling and indignation and reeking of bitterness. Thence constant excuse, pretense of impossibility, pleading to friends, not as Abraham did.*

*see John 8:40

Hear what the Lord testifies about a sincere people: *At the hearing of the ear*, he says, *he obeyed me.** Thus he shows that the authority of one who commands and the obedience of one who obeys proceed in one and the same moment. *Be not deceived, God is not mocked.** Do you grumble against your superior in the tabernacle of your body? God's right hand is raised to strike you down.*

*Ps 17:45

*Gal 6:7

*Ps 105:25-26

Therefore, advance sincerely in the mandates of obedience, adding sincerity to your will, illumination to your intention. For *the Lord's way is strength of the sincere;**

*Prov 10:29

because they put on strength, they march *sincerely* in the Lord's way, that is, obedience.

6. The third step is to obey cheerfully. *For God loves a cheerful giver. Not out of sadness,* says the apostle, *nor out of necessity.** A serene face and pleasant speech greatly color the obedience of one who complies. Thus also that pagan poet says, "Above all, with pleasant faces they approached."*

*2 Cor 9:7

*Ovid, Metamorphoses 8:677-78

For what is the place of obedience when irritation betrays sadness? Exterior signs generally show the will of the soul, and it is difficult for those who change their will not to change their expression. A body's gloomy manners and a face clouded with the darkness of sadness are signs that devotion has withdrawn from a soul. Consider David cheerfully dancing before the ark of the Lord,* how he sensibly checked the indignation of his disapproving wife. *I shall play,* he said, *and become even more common** in the presence of the Lord.

*see 2 Sam 6:14

*2 Sam 6:22

Therefore you discern how necessary and appropriate cheerfulness is in performing obedience. For who would gladly command a person who exudes sadness? Therefore, *If you wish to be perfect,** take up the order of one who commands cheerfully and with an enthusiastic expression, so that you add cheerful expression to the heart's will, to the work's sincerity.

*Matt 19:21

7. The fourth step is to comply swiftly. *God's word runs swiftly,** and he wants to have a swift follower. You see how swiftly the psalmist runs, who says, *I have run the way of your commandments.** One who obeys faithfully allows no delays, flees procrastination, and disregards slothfulness. Indeed such people anticipate the one who commands, prepare their eyes for seeing, their ears for listening, their tongue for speaking, their hands for work, their feet for a journey. They collect their whole self in order to collect the will of one who gives orders.

*Ps 147:15

*Ps 118:32

See the Lord promptly commanding and this person promptly obeying: *Zachaeus,* he says, *make haste and come* down, *for this day I must abide in your house. And he made haste and came down and received him with joy.** You have noticed that he both descends promptly and receives joyfully. You have heard obedience; hear also the reward for obedience. *This day salvation has come to this house.** Consider also the powerful mystery at the conclusion of his obedience, this judgment signed with the seal of mercy: *For the Son of man has come*, he says, *to seek and to save those who were lost.**

Have you not read how the children of Israel were ordered to eat the lamb in haste?* That of course, is a sign that the true Lamb should be consumed promptly, because those words, which he gave through the law, which he provided in person by himself, which he left to be handed down by the leaders of the church, are to be accomplished by swift obedience. And therefore when you have united will of heart, sincerity of deed, and cheerfulness of countenance, then add also swiftness, so that you will be, according to the apostle, *swift to hear** and more swift to fulfill.

8. The fifth step is to carry out obedience with vigor. *Act vigorously and let your heart be strengthened, all you who hope in the Lord.** There is no fortitude in going to disobedience, but rather, fortitude is to refuse to be lured from obedience. If tribulation thunders, if persecution resounds, if *sinners place a snare for you,** if spiteful people obstruct your journey, then may you not quit the way of obedience, but say, *I am ready and I am not troubled, so that I keep your commandments.**

For what use are these aspects of obedience listed above if fortitude is lacking? Fortitude assembles the virtues in the stronghold of perseverance, and there it fortifies virtues with a rampart where the attack of the furious cannot reach. *Have you put your hand to strong things?** You must act urgently, and you must obey consistently; you should not abandon the royal path amid harsh words or blows, but hold fast to the path with more tenacious fervor. And so we may briefly conclude

*Luke 19:5-6

*Luke 19:9

*Luke 19:10

*Exod 12:11

*Jas 1:19

*Ps 30:25

*Ps 118:110

*Ps 118:60

*Prov 31:19

the qualities of fortitude: it is a virtue that guards and fortifies virtues. Therefore join fortitude to swiftness and perseverance to urgency, and then you shall chant securely, *The hand of a sinner shall not move me.**   *Ps 35:12

9. The sixth step is to obey with humility. *For he who made us was mindful of us in our humiliation.** Humility is a great virtue. Without possession of humility, the virtue of fortitude is not only not a virtue, but it even erupts into the vice of pride. How bravely Saul used to run *when he was a little one in his own eyes!** How many battle lines of Philistine soldiers he struck down! With what power he employed his sword! However, after *pride held him fast** and *he crossed into his heart's affection,*‡ he became weak and inept; he easily fell, overthrown by weapons of the uncircumcised.*   *Ps 135:23   *1 Sam 15:17   *Ps 72:6   ‡Ps 72:7   *see 1 Sam 31:4

Consider the king in whom sublime humility and a humble sublimity begins to shine by a happy arrangement. *Lord,* he says, *my heart is not exalted nor are my eyes haughty.** Look back on his whole life's journey with painstaking attention, and wherever you turn your eyes, you shall find him sprinkled with flowers of humility.   *Ps 130:1

In fact, listen to what he says in another place: *I shall guard my strength in you.** How truly the just one speaks, the one who practices justice! For indeed there are many who guard their strength not in God but in vainglory,* those who *trust in their own virtue,*† who boast about receiving virtues *as if they had not received them,*# causing offense to their Creator, from whom comes *every best gift and every perfect gift.**   *Ps 58:10   *Phil 2:3   †Ps 48:7   #1 Cor 4:7   *Jas 1:17

Therefore, don't let fortitude cross over into pride. Fortitude must be seasoned with the salt* of humility, because nothing shall benefit a bold obedience if, unhappily, it is stained with haughtiness. Therefore *they guard their strength in God,** those who, when they have done what they should do, can say, *We are unprofitable servants because we have done only that which we should do.**   *Mark 9:48   *Ps 58:10   *Luke 17:10

10. The seventh step is to comply without ceasing. Not one who has begun, but *one who shall persevere unto*

the end, he shall be saved.* There are many who begin, few who persevere. Perseverance is the singular daughter of the high king, the goal of virtues and their consummation, repository of all good, a virtue *without which no one shall see God,** nor shall one be seen by God. It is *the end unto justice for everyone who believes.** By perseverance, the collected virtues consecrate their sacred marriage bed.

For what is the use of running only to quit the course before the goal? The apostle says, *So run that you may obtain.** O, how persistent was the foot of the one who completed the course and said, *I have finished my course!** O, what a long course was completed by that fortunate bandit, what repentance he found by perseverance,* who, *being made perfect in a short space, he fulfilled a long time!**

Again, the Lord of prophets speaks through a prophet: *If the just man shall turn away from his justice and shall commit iniquity, then all his righteousness shall not be remembered.** You see therefore how those virtues that are not marked with perseverance are buried with a profound forgetfulness. Perseverance alone leads the lover of obedience to the king's bedroom,* *so to see the king in his beauty,*‡ *on whom the angels desire to look.*# Consequently, *on this way in which we walk, the proud have hidden a trap for me.** This way is difficult and heavy with thorny twists, tied up with bonds of numerous chains.

But do you suppose there is any fruit in obedience when subordinates accept a command that they had requested with many promises, when they are instructed to do something that smells of dignity, flows with joy and happiness, and is supported by an image of power? On the contrary, wouldn't you grant merit to that obedience that, proceeding against adversity, frightens the soul of those who hear, is oppressive to hear, more oppressive to fulfill, most oppressive to master? It is not so. It must be done so that we are detached in our soul from success and embrace adver-

---

*Matt 10:22

*Heb 12:14
*Rom 10:4

*1 Cor 9:24
*2 Tim 4:7

*see Luke 23:40-43
*Wis 4:13

*Ezek 3:20; 18:24

*Song 1:3
‡Isa 33:17
#1 Pet 1:12

*Ps 141:4

sity with our soul if we wish to follow him who fled royal power and came voluntarily to his passion.* *see John 6:15; 10:18

11. You notice therefore that these ways are ways of life† leading to life.# Blessed are the meek,‡ because the Lord shall teach the meek his ways.° For the following pertains to them: *You shall fill me with joy with your face.*∞ Because as long as we are in the body, we wander from the Lord.* We are far from God's face, from the face of glory, from contemplation of majesty unless, generally speaking, the merciful and compassionate Lord* causes the light of his countenance to shine upon us.* This happens when the cloud has been removed, the cloud that was set before us so that our prayer might not pass through,* and we approach him and are illuminated,† beholding the glory of the Lord revealed face to face.#

†Ps 15:11
#Matt 7:14
‡Matt 5:4
°Ps 24:9
∞Ps 15:11
*2 Cor 5:6

*Ps 110:4
*Ps 66:2

*Lam 3:44
†Ps 33:6
#2 Cor 3:18

However, let us not take *revealed face to face* too literally, since *we* still *see through a glass darkly*,* and we are held in a bodily prison. *Revealed*, he says in fact, partially through the body's gloom. Thus that created spirit sometimes rises to the Creator of spirits and, *joining to the Lord, is made one spirit with him.** This contemplation is not significant, though, because the spirit, surrounded by a bodily enclosure, is knocked down by frequent thought of the flesh and, having been established above the creature, is at once found beneath the most vile of them.

*1 Cor 13:12

*1 Cor 6:17

But also the creator Spirit, *whose works are great, sought out according to all his desires,** sometimes comes to us when we do not know, and sometimes he slips away unnoticed, for *we know not whence he comes or where he goes.** And generally, the more frequently he is sought, the more quickly he withdraws, so accordingly he also said to the spouse, *Turn away your eyes from me, for they have made me vanish away.**

*Ps 110:2

*John 3:8

*Song 6:4

It happens also that the Spirit comes when he is not sought, though when he is sought, he flees, just as in the Song of Songs the spouse points out in various ways that she has sought and has not found,* she did not

*Song 3:1; 5:6

seek and yet she found.* It is not, however, his face itself, the face of the Lord's glory* that she found, the face that is above the cherubim, because the most pure and bright face is presented to the community of angels, but to us seekers he is only sketched out in shadowy images.

<small>*Rom 10:20
*2 Cor 3:7</small>

12. Because therefore we are not able here to see God's face just as it is,* we do not have fulfillment of joy† until he draws us to himself,# and the Head joins the Body, and God may be all in all.‡ Here is a taste; there shall be fulfillment. For here we taste and we see that the Lord is sweet,° but that taste does not cross into drink, because although we see, we do not yet enter. In taste the Lord is sweet; in fulfillment he is a miracle.

<small>*see Exod 33:20 and 1 John 3:2
†Ps 15:11
#John 12:32; see Song 1:3
‡1 Cor 15:28
°Ps 33:9</small>

However, souls of the saints, stripped of their earthly bodies, who already have flown to a heavenly residence, do of course drink but are nevertheless not fulfilled or yet intoxicated. For however much blessedness they enjoy, they still await the resurrection of their dead bodies, and when *they possess double in their land, then everlasting joy* shall be poured over them.* For now *separate white robes have been given to each one of them,* and they are asked to bear *a little time until** the wicked *are destroyed by a double destruction** and the saints are crowned with a twin blessedness. Since therefore they don't yet have what they desire to have, they cannot be intoxicated. But that vision is drink to them, so just as it is drink without toil, so it is rest without toil, until *they shall be satisfied when his glory shall appear.**

<small>*Isa 61:7
*Rev 6:11
*Jer 17:18
*Ps 16:15</small>

When, however, we shall rise up *into a perfect man, into the measure of the age of Christ's fullness,** and that glorious city shall be decorated with pearls,† and *the dwelling place within* it *shall be, as it were, of all rejoicing,#* then *he shall fill us with joy with his face,‡* because *we shall see him as he is.°*

<small>*Eph 4:13
†see Ps 86:3; Rev 21:21
#Ps 86:7
‡Ps 15:11
°1 John 3:2</small>

Then *we shall be inebriated with the plenty of his house, and he shall make us drink from the torrent of his pleasure,** and we shall hear, *Drink, and be inebriated, my dearly beloved,** because the soul shall possess illumination and the body possess glorification by a perpetual right.

13. The psalm continues, *At your right hand are delights even to the end.** This present life is God's left hand. We consider the present life to be on the left because anything that we care little about is regarded as on the left. In this life, the Lord permits his elect to be so afflicted by evil people that he even suffers them to be killed. Does it not seem to you that they are given to oblivion,* those who say, *For your sake we are killed all day long; we are counted as sheep for slaughter. Why turn away your face and forget our poverty?**

However, the blessed life is designated as being on the right. That blessed life knows nothing if not joy, concerning which we can say nothing except that *glorious things are said of you, O city of God.** In that city are those delights that *eye has not seen nor ear heard; neither has it entered into the heart of a human being what God has prepared for those who love him.**

Tribulations are on the left; delights are on the right. How long? *Until the end.* What is that end? *An end unto justice, Christ to everyone who believes.** Wisdom says concerning that end, *It reaches therefore from end to end mightily and orders all things sweetly.** For to see God is the consummation of the end. God himself is the end, to whom when we shall come, we shall thirst no more. Jesus Christ, spouse of the church, *who is blessed for ever. Amen.**

*Ps 35:9
*Song 5:1

*Ps 15:11

*Ps 30:13
*Ps 43:22, 24

*Ps 86:3

*1 Cor 2:9

*Rom 10:4

*Wis 8:1

*Rom 1:25

Sermo 42

Concerning Five Businesses and Five Regions

*Luke 19:13   1. *C*onduct business until I come!* The Father's Word, God's Only-Begotten, the *Sun of*
*Mal 4:2   *Justice*,* that supreme businessman, has provided the price of our redemption from the farthest
Prov 31:10   frontiers of heaven. This business is faithful *and worthy*
*1 Tim 1:15   *of all acceptance** in which the king, son of a king, becomes a businessman: gold is handed over for lead; the just one is given in exchange for a sinner.

> O how undeserved is this mercy,
> how gratuitous and therefore genuine this love,
> how unexpected the honor,
> how astonishing the sweetness,
> how invincible the clemency;
> how mean is this business
> when God's Son is handed over for a servant,
> the Creator is killed for a creature,
> the Lord is condemned for slaves!
> Yours, Christ, are these works!
> You who have descended from heaven's light to hell's darkness,
> from the right hand of majesty to the misery of humanity,
> from the Father's glory to death on a cross,
> by illuminating hell, by redeeming humankind,
> by overcoming death and the originator of death.
> *You are one and you have no second:**
> your own kindness incited you to redeem us,

*Eccl 4:8

your compassion drew you,
the truth by which you had promised to come compelled you,
the purity of a virgin's womb received you;
your power brought you from a virgin's protected integrity,
your obedience influenced you in all things,
your patience armed you;
love revealed you by your words and miracles.

May *the merchants from the land of Theman* be far away. May *the children of Agar who seek prudence** withdraw. Keep away from me *those who were called giants by their generation, those who were great in stature from the beginning, experts in war. The Lord has not chosen them, nor did they find the way of discipline, and so they perished.** But the Lord *gave wisdom to Jacob his servant and to Israel his beloved.** For *you have hidden these things,* Lord, *from the wise and prudent,*† *from those called giants,*# who were made great in their own eyes, of course,‡ and *you have revealed them to little ones*° *and to your humble ones.*

I freely embrace your business because it is my business. My soul ruminates on these goods with the utmost sweetness. Moreover, my soul not only ruminates but also recalls your rumination. My soul both understands what it loves and commits to memory what it has chosen. In these business affairs you instruct my soul to become like *a merchant's ship bringing her bread from afar.** I shall conduct business *until you come.** I shall happily run to meet him who comes, and I hope to hear, *Well done, good servant.**

Yours are the heavens and yours is the earth.* Secure in your regions, I shall conduct business having you alone as my guide on the journey, my protector in dangers, my partner in tribulation.

2. You have five regions in which your merchants make the rounds to do business, where your elect seek you and your beloved find you.

*Bar 3:23

*Bar 3:26-27

*Bar 3:37
†Matt 11:25
#Bar 3:26
‡see 1 Sam 15-17
°Matt 11:25

*Prov 31:14
*Luke 19:13

*Luke 19:17

*Ps 88:12

The first region is the region of unlikeness. That noble creature was fashioned in the region of likeness because *he was made in God's image.** *When he was in honor, he did not understand,** and he descended from likeness to unlikeness. How extremely vast is this unlikeness: from Paradise to hell, from angel to beast,* from God to a devil! A detestable conversion: to convert glory into misery, life into death, peace into battle by a perpetual captivity! An accursed descent: to descend from wealth to poverty, from liberty to servitude, and from rest to toil!

We are wretched and born wretchedly, we to whom it is given to be born in sorrow, to live in toil, to die in pain. We have been begotten, and we still beget, as sinners from a sinner, debtors from a debtor, the corrupted from one corrupted, the subjugated from one subjugated. *A sinful nation, a people laden with iniquity, a wicked seed, sinful children, increasing transgression.** Behold, *we are before Him as though we have no existence. We are counted as nothing and void** while *thinking ourselves to be something when we are nothing.** We have been wounded by entering into the world, by passing our life in the world, by departing from the world: *From the sole of the foot to the top of the head, there is no health in us.** That sublime prophet knew this, he who, deploring the state of human misery, blurted out these words: *A heavy yoke is upon the children of Adam from the day of their coming out of their mother's womb until the day of their burial into the mother of all.**

3. In this region of unlikeness, Lord God, what business should we conduct? I see the human race making the rounds in this world's markets *from the rising of the sun to its setting.** Some seek riches, others covet honors, others are swept up by the charm of a popular breeze.

But what about riches? Are they not acquired by toil, possessed with fear, lost with pain? *You store up, and you know not for whom you shall gather these things.** See how much toil you have accumulated for riches that shall

*Gen 1:27
*Ps 48:13

*Ps 48:13

*Isa 1:4–5

*Isa 40:17
*Gal 6:3

*Isa 1:6

*Sir 40:1

*Mal 1:11

*Ps 38:7

perish. You cross oceans, and by navigation you open up another world for yourself, according to Wisdom: three inches away from death.* You flee your homeland, you abandon parents, you do not know your sons, you are separated from your wife, and you have forgotten all your family obligations; you seek in order to acquire, you acquire in order to lose, you lose in order to suffer.

*see 1 Sam 20:3

O you sons of men, how long will you be dull of heart? Why do you love vanity and seek after lying?* What is that madness, children of Adam, to wander the seas, to walk about the lands,* to be snatched out of the world, *in many more labors, in intense vigils, in constant hunger, in frequent deaths?** Behold, such are riches.

*Ps 4:3

*see Matt 23:15

*2 Cor 11:23, 27

But what about honors? In a high place you have been put: *They have made you a leader.** See if you are not to be judged by all, watched by all, harassed by all.

*Sir 32:1

If you are a soldier, then you sleep out on the prince's doorstep to acquire a chief command; dressed in a suit of armor, you are closer to a wound than honor, to death than life, to danger than reward. If your lot is with the Lord, then does not a bishop fear the Roman pontiff, the archdeacon or deacon fear the bishop? See also whether *you shake your hands from all bribes,** lest with Simon you should hear, *You have no part or lot in this matter because you wished to possess the Holy Spirit's gift with money.** It is not our part to judge the church's leaders. Let the friends of the Spouse‡ see for themselves when he who *judges the world in equity*# begins to settle accounts with the bride. Is it possible for anyone to be in honor without pain, in leadership without tribulation, in a high place without vanity? Behold, such are honors.

*Isa 33:15

*Acts 8:20-21; see Acts 2:38
‡John 3:29
#Ps 9:9

Then what about glory? From where is your glory, you stinking dust,* mud of earth,† you vessel made for common use?# *Not to you, not to you, but to the Lord's name give glory.*‡ Relinquish his glory to him who *is glorious in his saints.*° Praise him *whom the angels praise*

*Gen 3:19
†Gen 2:7
#Rom 9:21
‡Ps 113:9
°Ps 67:36

on high.* Is not glory itself empty* when it is nothing other than an empty swelling of ears and it can scarcely be had without envy? Look back on those whom you surpass and consider how you have provided seeds of envy for all. Therefore all are inflamed with pitiless eyes against you, tortured by your good fortune, burned by your glory. Behold, once glorious, then offensive, once exalted, then lowly, once carefree, then worried. Notice that if you run amid glory, then you run into envy. If you seek good fortune, then you are ruined by misfortune. You see, therefore, that *in vain is every person confounded.** °Ps 148:1-2
*Gal 5:26

*Ps 38:12

This is the merchandise that one finds in the region of unlikeness. Therefore, a prudent dealer who sees toil in riches, retribution in honors, envy in glory, makes contempt for the world his burden and flees.

4. The second region is a cloistered paradise. The cloister is truly a paradise, a region fortified with the rampart of discipline in which there is a fruitful fertility of precious merchandise. A glorious matter, human beings *of one manner dwelling in a house;** *how good and how pleasant it is for brothers to dwell in unity.** You may see someone weeping for his sins, another rejoicing in God's praises. This one ministers to all; that one teaches others. This one prays; that one reads. This one shows mercy; that one punishes sins. This one burns with love; that one is strong with humility. This one is humble in prosperity; that one is exalted in adversity. This one toils in activity; that one rests in contemplative pursuits. And you shall be able to say, *These are the camps of God.** *How terrible is this place! This is none other than God's house and the gate of heaven.*

*Ps 67:7
*Ps 132:1

*Gen 32:2

*Gen 28:17

What therefore, faithful soul, should you consider in this marketplace? Make the rounds among the virtues of those who dwell together in the Lord's house of virtues, and thence make your burden this form of living. You who were previously dwelling in the region of death's shadow,* cross over to the region of life and of truth!

5. The third region is the region of expiation. The souls of the dead are assigned to three locations according to various merits: hell, purgatory, heaven. In hell are the wicked, in purgatory those to be purified, in heaven the perfected.

Those who are in hell cannot be redeemed, because in hell there is no redemption. Those who are in purgatory await redemption, first to be tormented by heat of fire or bitter cold or some other affliction of pain. Those who are in heaven rejoice with joy at the vision of God, Christ's siblings in nature, coheirs in glory,* like Christ in a delightful eternity.

Because therefore the first group does not merit redemption and the third group needs no redemption, it remains for us, through compassion, to cross over to the middle group, to whom we have been joined through our humanity. I shall go into this region *and see this great sight,** how the loving Father left his children who are destined for glorification in the hand of a tempter, not for killing but for purification, not for wrath but for mercy, not for destruction but for preparation so that they might no longer be *vessels of wrath fitted for destruction*, but vessels of mercy prepared* for the kingdom.

Therefore I shall rise up and come to their aid. I shall break in with groans. I shall beg help with sighs. I shall intercede with prayers. I shall make satisfaction with a singular sacrifice, as if perhaps *the Lord may see and judge,** so he turns toil into rest, misery into glory, beatings into a crown. For their punishment can be cut short by kind services such as these; toil can be ended, punishment reduced. Therefore, whoever you are, faithful soul, run through the region of expiation and see what happens in it. And in this marketplace make your burden a feeling of compassion.

*see Matt 4:16

*see Rom 8:17

*Exod 3:3;
see Dan 10:8

*Rom 9:22-23

*Exod 5:21

6. The fourth region is that of Gehenna. O region cruel and oppressive, region that must be dreaded, region to be fled! Land of forgetfulness,* land of afflictions, *land of miseries, land of darkness in which there is no order, but where everlasting horror dwells!** It is a deadly place in which fire burns, where there is freezing cold, the immortal worm,* intolerable stench, blows of a hammer,‡ palpable darkness,# shame of sins, bondage with chains, horrible faces of demons! I tremble and shudder all over at the memory of this region, *and all my bones are shattered.**

How have you fallen, O Lucifer, you who have arisen in the morning?* *Every precious stone was your covering,*‡ but now *under you the moth is spread and worms are your covering.** O God, how great the distance between a covering of precious stones and a blanket of worms, between the delights of Paradise and the moth of hell! I know that *fire was prepared for the devil and his angels** and for humans like them, where they shall be ended without end, die without death, be tormented without relief. Therefore *go down alive into hell!** With your mind's eye run through the torture chambers; flee crimes and vices for which criminals and sinners perish! *Have hatred for iniquity and love* the Lord's *law,** and in so frightening a marketplace make your burden hatred of sin.

7. The fifth region is a super-celestial Paradise. O blessed region of heavenly virtues in which the blessed Trinity is seen face-to-face by those who are blessed,* where those sublime processions never stop proclaiming with sublime waving of wings, *Holy, holy, holy, Lord God of hosts!**

It is a place of pleasure* where the just *drink from a torrent of pleasure,** a place of splendor where *the just shall shine like the splendor of the firmament,*‡ a place of joy where *everlasting joy shall be upon their heads,*# a place of abundance where *nothing is lacking to those who see him,** a place of sweetness where the Lord appears sweet

*Ps 87:13

*Job 10:22

*see Mark 9:43
‡Prov 19:29
#see Exod 10:21

*Ps 21:15

*Isa 14:12
‡Ezek 28:13

*Isa 14:11

*Matt 25:41

*Ps 54:16

*Ps 118:163

*1 Cor 13:12

*Isa 6:3
*Gen 2:10
*Ps 35:9
‡Matt 13:43; Dan 12:3
#Isa 35:10

*Ps 33:10

to all,* a place of peace where *his place was made in peace*,* a place of admiration where *his works are wonderful*,* a place of satiation where *we shall be satisfied when his glory appears*,† a place of vision# where a great vision shall be seen.‡

*Ps 144:9
*Ps 75:3
*Ps 138:14
†Ps 16:15
#see Gen 22:2
‡Exod 3:3

O sublime region full of riches! We sigh for you from a valley of tears,* for in you shall shine wisdom without ignorance, memory without forgetting, understanding without error, reason without obscurity. A region that the Lord shall pass through, ministering to his elect;* that is, he shows himself as he is. In that place *the Lord shall be all in all*,* where a universe of realities are wonderfully arranged and shall give glory to Creator and joy to creature.

*see Ps 83:7

*see Exod 12:11-12; Luke 12:37

*1 Cor 15:28

Run therefore, spiritual soul, with the eyes of desire through this region and see the glorious *king of glory in his beauty*,* surrounded with legions of angels, adorned with processions of saints, *putting down the mighty, exalting the humble*,* condemning demons, redeeming human beings, and say, *Blessed are those who dwell in your house, O Lord. They shall praise you for ever and ever.** Therefore when you have perceived with your mind so precious a marketplace, such illustrious merchandise, pack your burden, love of God.

*Isa 33:17; Ps 23:8

*Luke 1:52

*Ps 83:5

You have seen the regions, you have observed the marketplace, you have packed your burden, and you have been blessed. Conduct business, therefore, until your Lord God comes,* so that you can say to him, *Lord, you have given to me five talents; behold I have gained another five over and above.** And may you merit to hear, *Enter into your Lord's joy*,* Spouse of the church, *who is blessed forever. Amen.**

*Luke 19:13

*Matt 25:20
*Matt 25:21
*Rom 1:25

Sermo 43

The Lord's Ascension:[1] Sermon 5.
Courage, forbearance, and concord

Printed in SBOp 5:149–50; English in Bernard of Clairvaux, *Sermons for the Summer Season*, translated by Beverly Mayne Kienzle, Cistercian Fathers 53 (Kalamazoo, MI: Cistercian Publications, 1991), 55–56.

---

[1] *Sermo in ascensione Domini* (Asc 5)

Sermo 44

On the Resurrection of the Lord:[1]
Sermon 4.
On the days of the resurrection: How Christ has not yet been born for some

Printed in SBOp 5:110–11; English in Bernard of Clairvaux, *Sermons for Lent and Easter*, translated by Irene Edmonds, Cistercian Fathers 52 (Collegeville, MN: Cistercian Publications, 2013), 175–76.

---

[1] *Sermo in die paschæ* (Pasc 4)

Sermo 45

Concerning the Divine and the Human Trinities

1. That blessed and eternal Trinity, Father and Son and Holy Spirit, one God of course, highest power, highest wisdom, highest benevolence, *created* a certain trinity *in his own image and likeness,** that is, the rational soul. Rational souls bear a certain vestige of that highest Trinity in that they consist of memory, reason, and will. Moreover, God created souls in such a way that, by remaining in him, they would be blessed by participation. But having turned away from him, everywhere they turn they remain wretched.

*Gen 1:26-27

But this created trinity chose rather to fall by a movement of self-will than to stand firm by the free choice provided by the gift of creation. She fell, therefore, through suggestion, pleasure, and consent from that high and beautiful Trinity that we know as power, wisdom, and purity into a certain contrary and dirty trinity that we know as weakness, blindness, and foulness. That is to say, memory has been made impotent and feeble, reason foolish and dark, the will impure and foul.

It follows that memory, which was standing firm contemplating the power of simple divinity, fell from that divinity and, as though crashing upon rocks, was shattered and burst into three parts, that is into affectionate, laborious, and idle thoughts. I call those thoughts *affectionate* in which one is affected, as in concerns about necessities: of eating, of drinking, and of innumerable others. *Laborious* thoughts might be about managing external matters. *Idle* thoughts are those by which one is neither afflicted nor burdened, but nevertheless through them one is distracted from contemplation of eternal matters, as when one might think about, for example, a running horse or a flying bird.

2. The fall of reason is also triple. Indeed, reason's role is to weigh good and evil,* true and false, beneficial and detrimental. In these matters that reason must discern, it is blinded by so much gloom that it often leads to a contrary judgment, undertaking evil for good, false for true, harmful for beneficial, and vice versa. However, reason would never be mistaken in these matters if it were never deprived of the light by which it was created. But since reason has fallen out of light, then beyond doubt it finds nothing other than the darkness of its own blindness.

*see Gen 3:5

As a result, reason has also lost the instrument by which it manages, certainly, that trivium of wisdom: Ethics, Logic, and Physics, which we can express in other terms: Moral Science, Speculative Science, and Natural Science. Accordingly, through Ethics, good is chosen and evil is rejected.* Through Logic, true and false are recognized. Through Physics, beneficial and detrimental, that is, what should be accepted for use and what should be rejected.

*Isa 7:15

3. Next comes the will, whose ruin is likewise in three parts. In fact, the will should have clung to the highest benevolence and purity and loved that alone. Through its own iniquity, the will has fallen from the heights into these lowest depths: it *loved the concupiscence of the flesh and the concupiscence of the eyes and ambition of the world.* What could be reckoned as more wretched than a fall where, by ruining memory, reason, and will, the whole of the soul's substance has perished?

*1 John 2:15-16

4. Nevertheless, that blessed Trinity, *mindful of his mercy*,* forgetful of our guilt, has repaired this fall of our nature, a fall so grave, so dark, so dirty. So God's Son, sent by the Father, has come and given faith. After the Son, the Holy Spirit was sent, and he both gave and taught love. And so through these two, that is faith and love, hope of returning to the Father was made.

*Luke 1:54

And this indeed is a trinity: faith, hope, and love.* By this trinity—as if by a trident—that immutable and blessed Trinity led back from *mud of the deep** the mutable, fallen, wretched trinity to that lost blessedness. And faith certainly illuminated reason, hope raised memory, love truly cleansed the will.

*1 Cor 13:13

*Ps 68:3

So when God's Son came, as we said, he was made human. He who was God, like a good physician, gave teachings that, when heeded, restore lost health. Truly, in order to induce faith in these teachings, he shows signs. In order to persuade us about the usefulness of these same teachings, he promised blessedness.

5. So there is one faith of teachings, another of signs, another of promises. That is, faith by which we believe unto God, by which we believe God, and by which we believe in God. Through faith of teachings, we believe unto God. But to believe unto God is to hope unto him and to love him. Through faith of signs we believe God, who is capable of such great things and is capable of all things. Through faith of promises we believe in God, who truly fulfills whatever he promises.

Similarly, hope is also triple and proceeds from the aforementioned triple faith. For from faith of teachings rises hope of pardon, from faith of signs, hope of grace, from faith of promises, hope of glory.

In the same way, love is counted as triple: *from a pure heart and a good conscience and a sincere faith*.* We owe purity to our neighbor, conscience to ourselves, faith to God. Moreover, purity is so that whatever we do, it may be done either for a neighbor's advantage or for

*1 Tim 1:5

God's honor. And purity must be shown especially to neighbors because *we are* in every way *revealed to God*,* but to neighbors we cannot be except insofar as we open our heart to them. **2 Cor 5:11*

Two virtues, penitence and self-control, make a good conscience in us. That is, through penitence, we punish sins that we have committed, and through self-control thereafter we do not commit punishable sins. We also owe this to ourselves.

After these, there remains sincere faith. A sincere faith must be vigilantly presented to God so that we not offend him or carry out his commandments with any less obedience on account of a neighbor to whom we devote ourselves nor on pretext of conscience's sake.* **1 Cor 10:27* For we wish to guard our conscience in humility through penitence and self-control. And that is sincere faith. However, sincere faith is distinguished as different from dead faith and from insincere faith. *It is a dead faith that is without works.** Insincere faith is that which *be-* **Jas 2:17, 20* *lieves for a while, and in time of temptation falls away.** So **Luke 8:13* it is said to be insincere, that is, fragile.

6. We can more briefly summarize all these so we can more easily commit them to memory. So let us say that there is the creator Trinity, Father and Son and Holy Spirit, from which a created trinity—memory, reason, will—has fallen.

There is a trinity through which the created trinity has fallen: by suggestion, pleasure, consent. There is a trinity into which it fell: impotence, blindness, dirtiness. In turn, this fallen trinity, that is, memory, reason, and will, each in itself has a three-part fall. Memory fell into three types of thoughts: affectionate, laborious, idle. Reason fell into a triple ignorance: of good and evil, of true and false, of beneficial and detrimental. The will fell into *concupiscence of the flesh, concupiscence of the eyes, and ambition of the world.** **1 John 2:16*

There is a trinity through which the fallen trinity is restored: faith, hope, and love.* Each of these has three subsections. For there is faith of teachings, of signs, of promises. And there is hope of pardon, of grace, of glory. And there is *love from a pure heart and a good conscience and a sincere faith.*

*1 Cor 13:13

*1 Tim 1:5

Sermo 46

On the Solemnity of the Assumption of the Blessed Virgin Mary:[1] Sermon 6.
To establish "full of grace" in Mary in three ways

Printed in SBOp 5:260–61; English in Bernard of Clairvaux, *Sermons for the Autumn Season*, translated by Irene Edmonds, Cistercian Fathers 54 (Collegeville, MN: Cistercian Publications, 2016), 53–54.

---

[1] *Sermo in assumptione Beatæ Virginis Mariæ* (Asspt 6)

Sermo 47

Concerning a Quadruple Pride

*Luke 1:28

*see Luke 1:48
*Ps 137:6

*Job 41:25

*Song 6:12

*Sir 23:5
*Isa 5:21

*Ps 11:4

*Ps 100:7

*H*ail, Mary, *full of grace:** very full because she is pleasing to God and to angels and to human beings. That is, to human beings by fruitfulness, to angels by virginity, to God by humility. In her humility alone she testifies that the Lord regarded her,* because it is he who *looks on the low, and the high he knows afar off.*

For just as the eyes of Satan see everything high,* likewise the Lord's eyes behold everyone humble. Thus he says in the Song of Songs, *Return, return, O Sulamite woman; return, return so that we may behold you.** He says *return* four times because of the quadruple pride by which she was turned away from the Lord and was not seen. For there is pride of heart, pride of mouth, pride of deed, pride of dress.

Pride of heart is when people are great in their own eyes. Against this, Wisdom prays, saying, *Give me not haughtiness of my eyes.** And in another place, *Woe to you who are wise in your own eyes!** Pride of mouth or of tongue, which is also called boasting, is when people not only feel great things about themselves but even say as much. Thus the psalmist says, *May the Lord destroy all deceitful lips and the tongue that speaks proud things.** Pride of deed is when people act with a certain pride so that they appear great. Concerning this, the same psalmist says, *One who works pride shall not dwell within my house.** Pride of dress is when people adorn themselves with expensive clothes in order to seem glorious. *Not in expensive clothing,** says the apostle. And the Lord says to his disciples, *Those who are dressed in soft garments are in the houses of kings,** where pride abounds.

However, the Lord offers five things to the rational soul as a remedy for such a deadly plague: place, body, temptation of the devil, preaching of Christ, and Christ's way of life. Place because it is exile, body because onerous, temptation because Christ scourges, preaching of Christ because he edifies, and Christ's way of life because he shapes.

With these, God accomplishes humility in the soul as in the five senses. For just as the soul is the body's life, so also God is the soul's life. And just as the body is dead if it is not invigorated by the soul through the five senses, so also the soul is dead that is not humiliated by the Lord in these ways.

*1 Tim 2:9

*Matt 11:8

Sermo 48

Concerning Voluntary Poverty

*Luke 10:38

Jesus *entered into a certain fortified town, and a certain woman, named Martha, received him into her home.** The *fortified town* where Christ entered is voluntary poverty, which protects its inhabitants from twin attacks that assault lovers of this world: one's own envy, of course, and that of another. You see, poverty, as long as it is considered wretched, is not envied by others. And because poverty is voluntary, it envies no one anything.

*Luke 10:41

These two sisters signify the two lifestyles of those who love poverty. Certain careful people, with Martha,* prepare two dishes, that is, correction of works with the salt of contrition, and works of piety with the seasoning of devotion. But those who, with Mary, give all their time to God alone, contemplating what God is in the world, what in human beings, what in angels, what in himself, what in the condemned, contemplate God as ruler and pilot in the world, liberator and helper of human beings, flavor and beauty of angels, beginning and end in himself, terror and horror of the condemned: wonderful in creatures, lovable in human beings, desirable in angels, incomprehensible in himself, intolerable in the condemned.

Sermo 49

Concerning the Triple Word

Day unto day utters a word.* Day unto day is the angel to the Virgin.* Day is an angel on account of blessedness; the Virgin is a day by virtue of her integrity.

And night unto night shows knowledge.* The serpent is night because of his wickedness. The woman is night on account of her ignorance.*

Day unto day utters a word: divinity to virginity, from the womb of paternal majesty in the womb of maternal integrity. In another way: *Day unto day utters a word*, God the Father to a rational soul illuminated by faith.

And night unto night shows knowledge, a rational creature to a rational soul not yet illuminated by faith. So therefore the apostle says, *From the creation of the world, the invisible things of God are clearly seen, being understood through things that were made.**

So we also speak of the word revealed, word inspired, word uttered.* The first made knowledge, the second made conversion, the third gave life. The first is an obstacle, the second has no benefit, the third lives. The first is an obstacle *because when they knew God, they did not glorify him as God or give thanks, but became vain in their thoughts.** The second has no benefit because *there has not been a law given which could give life.** The third lives because he redeems us through the flesh. The first is wholly external, the second is both external and internal, the third is wholly from within.

*Ps 18:3
*see Luke 1:28

*Ps 18:3

*see Gen 3:1

*Rom 1:20

*Ps 44:2

*Rom 1:21
*Gal 3:21

And note that, because he is uttered from the fullness of him who utters,* he is brought forth with a certain taste of his substance. And therefore incarnate Wisdom is said to have all fullness in himself,* knowledge in miracles, conversion in doctrine, life in his passion.

*see Ps 144:7

*Col 1:19

Thus says the prophet, *Come and let us return to the Lord, for he has taken us and he will heal us. He will strike and he will cure us. He will revive us after two days*, of course, after the day of knowledge and of conversion: *on the third day he will raise us up* by the voice of the incarnate Word through his first resurrection. *And we shall live in his sight*, revived by his passion. Illuminated, we shall know by knowledge of miracles. *And we shall follow so that we may know the Lord*,* instructed by conversion of doctrine.

*Hos 6:1-3

Sermo 50

Concerning Rightly Ordered Affections

1. *G**o forth, daughters of Zion, and see king Solomon.** It does not say Ecclesiastes or Idida. For King Solomon was also called by those names, and this Scripture verse signifies the true Solomon, our Jesus Christ. Jesus was Solomon, that is, peaceable* in exile. He was Ecclesiastes, that is, a preacher in judgment. He was Idida, that is, the Lord's beloved in his reign and everywhere king. In exile he was ruler of morals, in judgment discerner of merit, in his reign distributor of rewards. In exile he was gentle, in judgment just, in his reign glorious. In exile he was lovable,* in judgment terrible, in his reign admirable.

In the diadem with which his mother crowned him.* This is also the crown of compassion, and in this we can imitate him. His stepmother also crowned him with a crown of suffering, and in this he was despised. I speak of the synagogue, which revealed herself to him not as a mother but as a stepmother. His family shall crown him with a crown of justice,* and in this he is frightening. His Father crowned him with a crown of glory,* and in this he is desirable.

Therefore, sinners see him in a crown of suffering—that is, thorns—and they repent.* Daughters of Zion, sensitive souls, see him in a crown of compassion and imitate him. The wicked shall see him in a crown of

*Song 3:11

*see Song 8:12

*see 2 Sam 12:25

*Song 3:11

*2 Tim 4:8
*1 Thess 2:19

*Mark 15:17;
Ps 4:5

justice, and they shall perish. The saints shall see him in a crown of glory, and they shall perpetually rejoice.* *see Ps 106:42

2. *Go forth, daughters of Zion,** delicate souls, from sense of the flesh to an understanding of the mind, from servitude of carnal concupiscence to liberty of spiritual intelligence, *and see King Solomon in a diadem with which his mother has crowned him.** Indeed his other imitators are also crowned, but, through grace, they are helped by their diligence. He alone was crowned by his mother, because he alone *as a bridegroom coming out of his bridal chamber** came from his mother's womb with ordered emotions. *Song 3:11 *Song 3:11 *Ps 18:6

These four emotions, moreover, are well known: love and joy, fear and sadness. Without these the human soul does not exist, but for certain people they bring a crown; for certain other people they bring confusion.[1] For once purified and ordered, they render the soul glorious in a crown of virtues. Once disordered through confusion, the soul is disgraced and dejected.

What is more, they are purified as follows. If we love what should be loved, if we love more what should be loved more, if we do not love what should not be loved, then love will be purified. So also concerning the others.

Again, emotions are ordered as follows. In the beginning fear, then joy, after this sadness: love in the consummation. The arrangement is like this: prudence is born out of fear and joy, and fear is the cause of prudence; joy is the fruit. Temperance is born from joy and sadness, and sadness is the cause of temperance; joy is the fruit. Fortitude is born from sadness and love, and sadness is the cause of fortitude; love is the fruit. The circle of the crown is closed. Justice is born from love and fear, and fear is the cause of justice; love is the fruit.

---

[1] In this context, *confusionem* is difficult to translate concisely into English: it implies shame, trouble, and sin.

3. Consider therefore how these ordered emotions are virtues, but when disordered, disturbances. If sadness follows fear, then it generates despair. If joy follows love, then it generates laxness. Therefore let joy follow fear, because when fear bewares of the future, joy rejoices about the present, for joy possesses the goal of prudent caution. Therefore, let joy test fear. A tested fear is nothing other than prudence.

Let sadness accompany joy, because one who reminisces with sadness embraces joyful matters with moderation. Therefore let sadness temper joy. Temperate joy is nothing other than temperance.

Let love be joined to sadness, because one who desires through love what should be loved bravely puts up with sad situations. Therefore let love comfort sadness. Truly a comforted sadness is nothing other than fortitude.

Let love be joined to fear, because one who does not ignore what should be properly feared clings to what should be loved. Therefore let love set fear in order. An ordered fear is nothing other than justice.

Two emotions, joy and sadness, do not extend themselves to other realities, for we are happy in ourselves and we are sad in ourselves. [In contrast] love and fear extend themselves to other realities. For fear is a natural emotion that joins us to the higher through the lower part and keeps itself for God alone. Love is an emotion that joins us to the higher and to the lower and to the equal; it keeps itself for both God and for neighbor. In these two also consist perfect justice,* that we fear God on account of power, and we love him on account of goodness and the neighbor on account of common nature.

*Matt 22:40; see 1 John 4:12

Sermo 51

Concerning the Purification of Mary and Circumcision of Christ

*see Luke 2:22

*see Luke 2:21

Why do we say that blessed Mary is purified?* Why indeed do we say that Jesus himself is circumcised?* Certainly she has no more need of purification than he needs circumcision. Therefore it is *for us* that he is circumcised and she is purified, offering an example to those who repent so that, abstaining from vices, we are first circumcised through our abstinence and then are purified from vice through repentance.

*see Matt 1:18
*see Matt 2:14, 21
*see Luke 2:28

Why is it, however, that Mary carries Jesus in her womb,* Joseph carries him on his shoulder going into Egypt, and of course, after they return from there,* Simeon carries him in his arms?* For these three signify three orders of the elect: Mary preachers, Joseph ascetics, Symeon those who do good. For those who preach the Gospel carry Jesus as though in their womb so that they give birth to him for others, or rather give birth to others for Jesus. Blessed Paul was of this type; he used to say, *My little children, with whom I am in labor again until Christ is formed in you.**

*Gal 4:19

*Matt 5:10

Those who grow weary with toil for Christ, *who suffer persecution,** who inflict evil on no one but patiently bear impositions from others, are deservedly said to carry him on their shoulders, those to whom Truth herself says, *If any man will come after me, then let him deny himself and take up his cross and follow me.**

*Matt 16:24

However, if there is anyone who offers bread to the hungry and drink to the thirsty and carefully practices the other works of compassion for a needy person,* then does he not seem to carry him in his arms? For on Judgment Day the Lord is going to say of such a one, *As long as you did this for one of my least brothers or sisters, you did it for me.**

*see Matt 25:37

*Matt 25:40

Sermo 52

Concerning the Home of Divine Wisdom; Concerning the Virgin Mary

1. **W**isdom has built herself a home,* etc. Wisdom might be understood in many ways, so one must ask, "Which wisdom has built herself a home?" For one speaks of *wisdom of the flesh* that *is an enemy to God,** and *wisdom of this world* that *is foolishness before God.** Each of these, according to the apostle James, is *earthly, sensual, devilish.** According to this wisdom, it is said, *they are wise to do evil but they are ignorant to do good.** And in their own wisdom they are convicted and ruined, as it is written: *I will catch the wise in their own cunning.** And, *I will destroy the wisdom of the wise and I will reject the prudence of the prudent.** And Solomon's maxim certainly seems to me suitably and properly applied to the worldly wise, where he says, *There is evil which I have seen under the sun*: a man who seems to be wise in his own conceit.*

No such wisdom, either of the flesh or of the world, builds; rather, it destroys whatever home it inhabits. Therefore there is another: *the wisdom that is from above, first indeed it is chaste, then peaceable.** It is *Christ the power of God and the wisdom of God,** concerning whom the apostle says, *he who was made wisdom and justice and sanctification and redemption for us by God.**

*Prov 9:1

*Rom 8:7
*1 Cor 3:19
*Jas 3:15

*Jer 4:22

*1 Cor 3:19
*1 Cor 1:19

*Eccl 6:1; see Prov 26:12; 3:7

*Jas 3:17
*1 Cor 1:24

*1 Cor 1:30

2. And so this wisdom that was of God, and was God,* coming to us from the Father's bosom,* *built herself a home*,* Christ's own mother of course, the Virgin Mary herself, in whom *Wisdom has hewn out seven pillars.**   *John 1:1
*John 1:18
*Prov 9:1
*Prov 9:1

What is it, however, *to hew out seven columns* in her, if not to prepare for Wisdom a dwelling worthy of faith and works? No doubt the number three pertains to faith on account of the holy Trinity; the number four pertains to morals on account of the four principal virtues. Scripture bears witness that the holy Trinity was within blessed Mary (I mean by the presence of majesty), within whom was the Son alone through the humanity that he had taken up. The heavenly messenger, who revealed hidden mysteries to her,* said, *The Holy Spirit shall come upon you, and the power of the most High shall overshadow you.** Behold, you have the Most High, you have power, you have the Holy Spirit, that is, you have Father and Son and Holy Spirit. Nor can one say that there is either Father without Son, or Son without Father, or the Holy Spirit without both, proceeding from both, as the Son himself teaches: *I am in the Father and the Father is in me*, and again, *The Father abiding in me, he himself does the works.** It is obvious that faith of the holy Trinity was in the Virgin's heart.   *see 2 Cor 12:4
*Luke 1:35
*John 14:10

3. Whether Mary also possessed the four principal virtues, like four columns, it seems, is worth exploring. So let us first see whether she had fortitude. How indeed could any virtue be lacking to her, to her who, having rejected worldly status and spurned carnal pleasure, planned to live for God alone in virginity? Unless I am mistaken, this Virgin is she about whom we read in Solomon's writings: *Who shall find a steadfast woman? Far and from the uttermost countries is her price.** She was so steadfast that she struck the head of that serpent to whom the Lord said, *I will put enmity between you and the woman, and between your seed and her seed; she shall crush your head.**   *Prov 31:10
*Gen 3:15

Further on, we can confirm more clearly, by the angel's conversation and with light from her response, that she was self-controlled, prudent, and just. Obviously, having been greeted so reverently by the angel, *Hail, Mary, full of grace, the Lord is with you,** she did not raise herself as one who was blessed by a singular privilege of grace, but she grew quiet and pondered within herself what this unusual greeting was.* What is that if not self-control?

*Luke 1:28

*Luke 1:29

But truly, when she was taught about heavenly mysteries by the same angel, she attentively inquired how she would conceive and give birth, since indeed she had not known a man.* And in this without doubt she stands out as prudent.

*Luke 1:34

What is more, she offers a sign of justice when she confesses herself as *handmaid of the Lord.** That this is indeed a confession of the just is attested by him who said, *But as for the just, they shall confess to your name, and the upright shall dwell with your countenance.** And in another place it is said to the just, *And in confessing, you shall say, All the Lord's works are very good.**

*Luke 1:38

*Ps 139:14

*Sir 39:20-21

4. Therefore the blessed Virgin Mary was steadfast in purpose, self-controlled in silence, prudent in inquiry, just in confessing. And so, in Mary, heavenly Wisdom set up for herself a home with four columns of morals and with the aforementioned three columns of faith. Wisdom filled Mary's spirit* to such a degree that even her flesh would be made fruitful with regard to fullness of spirit. And by a singular grace, the Virgin gave birth to this same Wisdom, who had been covered by flesh and whom she had previously conceived with a pure mind.

*Lat *mens, mentis*

If we also wish to become a home for the same Wisdom, it is necessary that we be set up with the same seven columns, that is, that we should be prepared for Wisdom by faith and morals. And even in morals I think that justice alone suffices, supported however by the rest of the virtues. And so as not to be deceived by an error of ignorance, let prudence lead the way. Henceforth let there be self-control and fortitude, lest perhaps one fall by straying either to the right or to the left side.

Sermo 53

Concerning Names of the Savior

1. *A**nd his name shall be called Wonderful, Counselor, God, Mighty, the Father of the world to come, Prince of Peace.** Wonderful in his birth, Counselor in his preaching, God in his work, Mighty in his suffering, Father of the world to come in resurrection, Prince of Peace in everlasting blessedness.

*Isa 9:6

These names can also be aptly assigned to him in the work of our salvation. In the first place, it says *Wonderful* in conversion of our will, which *is the change of the Most High's right hand* alone.* Afterward, it says, *Counselor* in revelation of his will when he reveals what the converted should follow. Thus Paul, after his conversion, said, *Lord, what will you have me do?**

*Ps 76:11

*Acts 9:6

But it is necessary for the converted to feel remorse for past transgressions, in whose forgiveness it says *God* alone *is to forgive sins.** For this reason, while our Savior was on earth forgiving sins, the Jews said that he blasphemed, as if he would take for himself what was God's alone.*

*Luke 5:20-21

*see Luke 5:20-21

Fourth it says *Mighty*, for according to the opinion of the apostle, it is necessary that *all who will to live devoutly in Christ Jesus shall suffer persecution.**

*2 Tim 3:12

2. But who would withstand if Christ did not help? Thus David says, *Unless the Lord had helped me, my soul would have nearly dwelt in hell.** When therefore he protects us in tribulation,* when he wards off and repels from us *the powers of the air* themselves,* then what else

*Ps 93:17
*see Ps 90:14-15
*Eph 2:2

in this work can be said if not *Mighty?* Thus it has been said, *The Lord who is powerful and mighty, the Lord powerful in battle.** *Ps 23:8

And because conversion itself and our life must be lived in Christ, not to see temporal realities but with hope *of good things to come,** therefore *Father of the world to come* is put in fifth place. *Father* indeed in regeneration of our bodies. *Heb 10:1

To be sure *we shall all indeed rise again, but we shall not all be changed.** In order to distinguish the change of the just from the resurrection of the unjust, *Prince of Peace* is placed in the sixth place. *1 Cor 15:51

Once it has been obtained, the whole perfection is completed; nothing else remains any longer to be desired. For it is this peace itself about which the psalmist sings in exultation, saying, *Praise the Lord, O Jerusalem. Praise your God, O Zion, because he has strengthened the bolts of your gates; he has blessed your children within you, he who has placed peace in your borders.** *Ps 147:12-14

The angel speaking to Joseph briefly and elegantly expresses the logical consequence and virtue of these six names with one name: *And you shall call his name Jesus.** Explaining the reason for this name, he says, *For he shall save his people from their sins.** *Matt 1:21
*Matt 1:21

Sermo 54

Concerning the Appearance of Christ

*see Titus 2:11-12
*see 1 Cor 1:24

God's Son appeared in order to help and to teach us,* as he can do because he is the Father's Power and Wisdom.* Power helps; Wisdom teaches and forms. Help is necessary for weakness; blindness has need of teaching and doctrine. Wisdom certainly taught us, making us reject *impiety and worldly desires* so that *we should live soberly and justly and piously.** Impiety was unbelief, because we did not believe God or worship him. For just as it is pious to worship God, so it is also impious to reject him.

*Titus 2:12

Worldly desires are *concupiscence of the flesh and the concupiscence of the eyes and pride of life,** which draw and degrade us to love of the world. Having rejected these, a person lives soberly, restraining *concupiscence of the flesh and the concupiscence of the eyes and pride of life*. But after we begin to be more sober, we put double sobriety against double intoxication. Exterior intoxication is a profusion of pleasures; interior is a preoccupation with curiosities. The opposite, exterior sobriety, is restraining of pleasures, interior sobriety of curiosity. Thus people live *soberly* with respect to themselves, *justly* with respect to their neighbor insofar as they provide what is their own and what is just. Justice is in two parts: innocence and kindness. Innocence begins justice; kindness finishes it.

*1 John 2:16

Piously concerns our relationship with God. Piety is in two parts, so that we not presume about ourselves; rather, we trust perfectly in God so that we conquer all the world's impediments through him. One must not doubt God but must act with security and confidence. [Christ] himself, just like a pious and praiseworthy physician, first drank a cup that he prepared for his own people; that is, he sustained suffering and death. And thus he received the health of immortality and of impassibility, teaching his own people so that they confidently drink the cup that generates health and life. And he who lives after suffering lives by eternal life. He gives hope to us so that, by him, we likewise hope securely.

Sermo 55

Concerning Six Spiritual Water Pots

1. *There were set out six stone water pots according to the Jews' manner of purification.** We understand these six water pots placed there to be six observances put forth for God's servants, observances in which they should be purified like true Jews. These six are silence, psalmody, vigils, fasting, manual work, purity of the flesh.

*John 2:6

In the water pot of silence we are purified from sins that we committed by excessive talking. This vice has eight types because words might be stupid, empty, false, idle, deceitful, slanderous, unchaste, or self-justifying. No doubt this pestilence is born from talkativeness, and by the command of silence it is either reversed completely or at least restrained from doing much harm.

Confession is doubled in psalmody when a sinner both feels remorse for faults and *gives praise* to God *for the judgments of his justice.** So by this water pot, all Jews who confess rightly are certainly purified from the unclean spirit of blasphemy to which they were subjected before conversion. For as long as they praised themselves and accused God, what were they if not blasphemers? Are they not blasphemers who say, *The way of the Lord is not right?** And is not the blasphemer stupid when he *says in his heart: There is no God?** But once he has converted and confessed and been in-

*Ps 118:164

*Ezek 18:25
*Ps 31:1

structed by sacred songs, his corrected life corrects his words. And by accusing himself, he reflects his own evils back to himself, but by praising God, any good that he sees in himself he attributes to God and not to himself. And the whole of this is sung in psalmody. Through psalmody, accept whatever is done for God with a melody of mind, whether psalms, or hymns, or any song.* *see Col 3:16

2. I have placed the third water pot, vigils, next in order. Eagerness in prayer must always accompany vigils. Thus we also read in the gospel that the Lord *passed the whole night in prayer.** And exhorting his disciples, he likewise united vigils and prayer, saying, *Keep watch and pray so that you enter not into temptation.** Vigils of this sort purify us from any uncleanness that we committed by drowsiness; when we have become lax by a certain forgetfulness, then we become lukewarm and slothful, straying from the way of salvation. *Luke 6:12 *Matt 26:41

The fourth water pot is fasting, concerning which no one doubts whether it also purifies. That saying is true that opposites are cured by opposites.* If therefore we have sinned through appetite and gluttony, then what remains except to be renewed through self-control and fasting? Not only does fasting purify gluttony, but, in addition, we acquire the power to expel demons, as the Lord says: *This kind can go out by nothing other than prayer and fasting.** *Hippocrates; Gregory the Great, Evang 32.1 (CCSL 141:277) *Mark 9:28

3. The fifth water pot follows; it is called manual work. If you seek to know whether it purifies in some way, then you can easily find many [examples]. Still, to pass over most because I strive for brevity, let this alone [show] how worthy of proclamation and how much a grace it is: Who would not respect living one's life by one's own labor and desiring nothing from anyone? And lest anyone think that I offer this more rhetorically than factually, then listen to our *teacher in faith and truth,** the apostle Paul, writing to the Thessalonians, teaching *1 Tim 2:7

and preaching these things: *We entreat you, brethren,* he says, *that you thrive even more, and that you give attention to being quiet, and that you conduct your own business, and work with your own hands as we commanded you, and that you walk honestly toward those who are without, and that you want nothing belonging to another.**

*1 Thess 4:10-11

And listen to the same apostle practicing what he preached: *For you yourselves know,* he says, *how you ought to imitate us, for we were not disorderly among you. Neither did we eat anyone's bread free, but in labor and in toil we worked night and day lest we should be a burden to any of you.** Likewise, listen to Paul preaching what he practiced: *When we were with you, this we declared to you: that if anyone will not work, then neither let him eat.** Now we charge those who are such, and beseech them by the Lord Jesus Christ, that working with silence, they would eat their own bread.*

*2 Thess 3:7-8

*2 Thess 3:10

*2 Thess 3:12
*1 Tim 2:7

You see how carefully the *teacher of gentiles** taught that manual work must be heeded? Why did he care about this so much if not because, just like a good and diligent shepherd, he foresaw this as most expedient for salvation of the flock?*

*see John 10:2, 14

4. The last water pot remains, purity of flesh. By this, purification comes from that fivefold enticement of the body: sight, hearing, taste, smell, touch. And indeed, the observances discussed above, that is, silence, psalmody, vigils, fasting, and manual work can all be practiced without that purity, but then they provide no benefit. And indeed they can rightly be called *burning lamps.** But if one's *loins be* not *girt,*‡ that is, if one's flesh lacks purity, what shall the *burning lamps* benefit? So then, one must gather how purification of the six water pots is necessary; purification alone obtains the force of salvation equivalent to all those mentioned above.

*Luke 12:35; see John 5:35
‡Luke 12:35

And one should note that, among all these observances, the first four we owe to ourselves, the fifth to our neighbor, the sixth to God. For each person should practice the following for his own sake: silence, psalmody, vigils, and fasting; these are for one's own discipline. Manual work is for one's neighbor *so that we may have something to give to those who suffer need.** Purity of flesh is for God so that we may please him and do his will. Thus it is written: *For this is the will of God, your sanctification: that you should abstain from fornication; that each one of you should know how to possess his vessel in sanctification and honor.**

*Eph 4:28

*1 Thess 4:3-4

And as for these observances being called *stone* water pots,* this signifies that they cannot be observed without some difficulty, and that *the way that leads to life* is hard and rough.* Certainly they are also called *stone* because of their strength; they can neither break nor be dissolved so that the fluid of internal grace that is contained in them spills out, as could certainly easily happen if they were made of clay or wood or some other fragile material.

*John 2:6

*Matt 7:14; see RB 58.8

Or if of stone by the stone, Christ,* that is, [if they are] Christian, then indeed they become [stone] by the faith of Christ.

*see Acts 4:11 and 1 Cor 10:4

Sermo 56

Concerning the Sacred Water Pots that Are to Be Filled with a Threefold Fear

1. *C**ontaining two or three measures apiece.** The first thing one should know is that water pots of this kind are sometimes empty, and sometimes they are full. Sometimes, however, they are filled with poison, sometimes with water, and occasionally with wine.

Obviously they are empty and vain when they are for vainglory* or for some temporary benefit. They are full of poison if they are used with murmuring and a grudging soul. They are said to be filled with water when they are observed* for fear of God, if indeed by *water* one understands *fear.* Whence one reads in Solomon, *Fear of the Lord is a fountain of life to avoid the ruin of death.** But these water pots are filled with wine when fear turns into love, when *charity casts out fear,** when that which was previously observed in fear of punishment is now practiced with enjoyment and love of justice.

When these water pots are empty or corrupted with poison, the Lord does not will it. When however they are filled with water, then it is the Lord who orders it. But when the water is turned into wine, then it is the Lord who does it.*

But whom does the Lord command to fill the water pots with water? By all means, servants, *whom he* also

*John 2:6

*see Gal 5:26

*see S 55

*Prov 14:27
*1 John 4:18

*see John 2:7-9

Sermo 56

set over his family to give them their measure of grain in due season,* whom Mary has first advised, saying, *Do whatever he tells you.** This example acknowledges that no one should usurp for himself the office of preaching except those whom Mary, that is mother grace, has first instructed. Otherwise it shall be said to them, *They have reigned, but not by me; they have come forth as princes, and I knew not.** *Luke 12:42
*John 2:5

*Hos 8:4

So the servants fill the pots with water:* they preach about the wonderful sweetness of the Kingdom, they threaten with the horrendous terror of punishment. So for their listeners, a supreme, twofold fear is aroused: fear of being cheated of the Kingdom or of getting beaten by punishment. Hence *the water pots contain two measures.**   *see John 2:7

*John 2:6

But what is meant by *or three*?* A third fear is added to those two, and the water pots contain three measures. And indeed those two fears about the future mentioned above are very useful. But another fear about the present is much more commendable, a fear by which *a person fears* and *is always afraid** of being forsaken by internal grace. Accordingly, whoever has been filled by this fear has surely added a third measure to the two.   *John 2:7

*Prov 28:14

2. However, one must note that when the water pots have been filled *to the brim,** then water has been turned into good wine. Certainly the order of reason demands that *if fear is the beginning** of charity, then likewise fullness of love follows perfect fear.* Whence also *the chief steward says to the spouse: Everyone at first sets out good wine, and when guests have gotten drunk, then wine that is worse. But you have kept the good wine until now.**   *John 2:7
*Ps 110:10
*see Rom 13:9-10

*John 2:10

It is the way of worldly people that when they desire to obtain some honor, they first acquire supporters for themselves through love. But when the honors have been obtained, those who are exalted with power promptly make their supporters subject to themselves through fear. That is, previously, when they were ordinary citizens, they gave not fear, but love to their supporters. They set out *first the good wine*, that is love, *and when they have gotten drunk*, that is enticed by love, *then the wine that is worse*, that is fear.

Our spouse does just the opposite. For he always *saves the good wine* for last, for truly he puts out first what is worse by comparison, saying, *Son, when you come to the service of God, stand in fear.** If out of fear you have made yourself his servant, then he shall make you his friend out of charity.* And thus water of fear shall be changed into the wine of delight. That is to say, it is for this that you are purified by the waters of fear in those six water pots; for this you approach him in fear, like a servant to his lord, so that you advance from being a servant to being a son.

*Sir 2:1

*see John 15:15

Sermo 57

Concerning Seven Seals

1. *B*ehold *the lion of the tribe of Judah, the root of David, has prevailed to open the book and to loose its seven seals.** The seven seals are temporal nativity, circumcision according to the law, purification of the mother, flight into Egypt, needs of the flesh, baptism, passion. These are indeed marks of a certain true humanity by which the incarnate *Wisdom of God* willed himself to be held and bound.* This of course is a third person in the Trinity. Even though the Father and Son and Holy Spirit together made the same incarnation, nevertheless, neither Father nor Holy Spirit was incarnate, but only the Son. Certainly both Father and Holy Spirit fulfilled the Son's flesh, from whom neither of them could be separated, but each fulfilled it by his majesty rather than by taking it upon himself.

    And so the Son, in the flesh, showed the Father's power through his works; he showed the goodness of the Holy Spirit by redeeming sins. And because he was his own, rather because he was himself, that is Wisdom, he hid himself by those signs named above. Consequently, a wonderful and astounding event has happened. Supreme power was weakened, and so I would say, if it were allowed to be said, and I say it nevertheless with all due respect: it is as if Wisdom has been made a fool. Nor do I blush to say what the *Doctor of the gentiles** teaches. So he truly believed, so he taught, and so he left in writing. *We,* he says, *preach Christ crucified,*

*Rev 5:5

*1 Cor 1:24

*1 Tim 2:7

to the Jews indeed a stumbling block, and to the Gentiles foolishness. But to those who are called, both Jews and Greeks, Christ the power of God, and the wisdom of God. For the foolishness of God is wiser than humans, and the weakness of God is stronger than men.* *1 Cor 1:23-25

2. Nevertheless, this power had to be hidden and completed in humility so that the prophecies of all prophets would be fulfilled. Therefore our impassible God suffered on a cross, and God's immortal Son died and was buried in our mortal flesh. But behold: on the third day he rose from the dead, and he who appeared as a lamb in suffering became a lion in resurrection. He rose up, and *the lion from the tribe of Judah prevailed,** because, in rising by virtue of his power, he trampled upon death, which he endured by reason of our weakness.* For, *rising from the dead, he dies now no more; death shall no more have dominion over him.** However, by rising and ascending into heaven, *he opened the book,** that is, he has openly made known, from the authority of Sacred Scripture, that he was God. Thus it is written, *Be exalted, O God, above the heavens, and your glory above all the earth.**

*Rev 5:5

*see 2 Cor 13:4
*Rom 6:9
*Rev 5:5

*Ps 56:12
*Rev 5:5

He also *loosed the seven seals of the* same *book** when he opened understanding of Sacred Scriptures[1] to minds of the faithful. And whatever mysteries the Law and Prophets had predicted under allegories, concerning that which he has borne in the temporal world as a human being, these things predicted about himself, and in himself and through himself fulfilled, he revealed more clearly by his light.

---

[1] *sacri eloquii*, e.g., "sacred eloquence," "sacred speech," "sacred pronouncement"

Sermo 58

Concerning the Three Women at the Tomb

1. What does it mean that, after his death, those three holy women *bought aromatic spices so to anoint him and place him in the tomb?** What do they leave in their actions for us to imitate? For, as blessed Gregory says, what they did signifies something that should be done in Holy Church.* Therefore, if we perceive that Christ is dead in the heart of any brother or sister, that is, if faith in Christ is dead,* then we must approach with purchased aromatic spices to anoint the dead body. Now these three women signify three capacities within us that acquire for themselves suitable aromatic spices. What are they? Mind, hand, tongue.

*Mark 16:1; Luke 23:53

*Gregory, Evang 21.2 (CCSL 141:174)
*Jas 2:17

Everyone who buys both gives and receives something, and what people give, they lose, so that they may possess what they receive. Consequently, the mind gives the coin of self-will and acquires the feeling of compassion, the zeal of justice, and the discretion of counsel. The hand gives obedience and buys self-control in the flesh, patience in tribulation,* and perseverance in work. The tongue gives the coin of confession and receives measure in correction, abundance in exhortation, and effectiveness in persuasion.

*Rom 5:3

2. Having prepared such ointments, while the women were coming to the tomb together, they were discussing among themselves *and said: Who shall roll back for us*

269

the stone from the door of the tomb?* This stone is either excessive sadness or laziness or insensitivity; as long as it obstructs access to the heart, it is in vain that the mind or hand or tongue comes with any sort of aromatic spices so to anoint the dead. But it is written, *Your ear has heard the preparation of his heart,** *they saw the stone rolled back, they entered into the tomb,** and they heard that the dead one, whom they wanted to anoint, had arisen.

    Who announces this? Who proclaims this? Certainly an angel is a witness of the resurrection. It seems indeed that the person to whom Christ has risen has a happier face, a more attractive appearance, a purer speech, a more modest gait, and a spirit more eager *for every good work.** What are all these signs? Are they anything other than a sort of cheerful herald of an internal resurrection?

    The others that were also done or said in Christ's resurrection, such as finding the napkin and seeing the Lord in Galilee, and others which the gospel history recounts, can obviously be interpreted allegorically, so that what precedes historically in the Head is also believed to happen morally in Christ's Body.

*Mark 16:3
*Ps 9:38
*Mark 16:4–5
*2 Tim 3:17

Sermo 59

Concerning Three Loaves

*F*riend, lend me three loaves. Our friend is come to us from his journey;* that is, any neighbor who has been converted should be refreshed with three loaves of bread. The first loaf is self-control, by which the body is restrained lest eventually it die away through deadly pleasures. The second loaf is humility, by which the soul is instructed lest she take pride in her own self-control. The third loaf is fervor of charity, by which the spirit is kindled so that each, that is, body and soul, is preserved steadfastly in chastity and humility.

*Luke 11:5-6

A person of God is refreshed and strengthened by these three virtues, that is, chastity, humility, and charity, like three loaves of bread, so that, according to the apostle, in the day *of our Lord's coming, his spirit and soul and body may be whole.** I call *spirit*, however, the strength that is grace, which, according to the same apostle, *helps our infirmity* lest we fail*, until *we reap in due time the good that we have sown.**

*1 Thess 5:23

*Rom 8:26
*Gal 6:8-9

What is more, the first loaf is called carnal or bodily, the second rational, the third spiritual. These daily loaves are lacking; they must be sought from God. Rightly, moreover, three are sought because three come to be refreshed: the soul like a husband, flesh like a wife, spirit like a servant of both.

And one should note that he does not say, "Give," but *lend me three loaves,** as though he is going to give them back. For, certainly, a priest ought to obtain grace

*Luke 11:5

271

from heaven for a repenting sinner, but he does not owe the fruit of that same grace to himself but ought to refer it back to God.

Sermo 60

Concerning Christ's Descent and Ascent

1. *No one has ascended into heaven except him who descended from heaven, the Son of man who is in heaven.** *John 3:13

Our Lord and Savior Jesus Christ, wishing to teach us how we might ascend into heaven, himself did what he taught:* he ascended into heaven, of course. Whereas he was not able to ascend unless he first descended, and whereas the simplicity of his divinity would not allow him to descend or ascend, and naturally his divine simplicity could not be diminished or increased or varied by any means, he therefore took up our nature into the unity of his person. That is, he descended and ascended in his human nature, and he showed to us the way by which we would ascend. All of this is indicated by the words of the holy gospel cited above. *Acts 1:1

For Christ's assumption of human nature is expressed in that verse, *No one has ascended except him who descended.* Moreover, in what is added—*who is in heaven*—is shown the changeless nature of his divinity. These words likewise acknowledge that he himself is the life* through which we ascend, himself the fatherland where we remain, the way indeed for those who cross over, the fatherland for those who arrive. *John 14:6

Remaining therefore what he was in his own nature, he descended and ascended in ours for our sake, *reaching,* no doubt, *from end to end mightily and ordering all things sweetly.** Accordingly he descended to where he could not go lower; he ascended to where he could not properly go higher. He made this descent mightily because he was Power; he arranged his ascent sweetly because he was Wisdom.* Moreover, it says that he *descended*, not *fell*, because one who falls does not fall in stages, but one who descends places his foot step by step.

*Wis 8:1

*see 1 Cor 1:24

2. While there are steps in descending, there are also steps in ascending. And in descending, the first step indeed is from highest heaven* to the flesh, the second step to the cross, the third step to death. Behold how far he has descended. Could he have descended lower? Our king certainly could already say and proclaim by the very fact of what he did, *What more is there that I ought to do that I have not done?** *Greater love than this no one has: that he lay down his life for his friends.**

*Ps 18:7

*Isa 5:4
*John 15:13

We have seen the descent; let us see also the ascent. But the ascent is also triple: its first step is glory of resurrection, the second power of Judgment, the third sitting at the Father's right hand. And he merited resurrection for his death; he merited power of Judgment for the cross. Because he was judged unjustly in the crucifixion, he therefore obtained the lawful office of Judge, as he said after his resurrection: *All power is given to me in heaven and on earth.** He truly exalted above all the heavens‡ the resuscitated form of a servant,# that is, the flesh in which he suffered and died; he even exalted it over all choruses of angels, up to the Father's right hand.

*Matt 28:18
‡Eph 4:10
#Phil 2:7

What is more sweet than this arrangement where *death is swallowed up in victory*,* where disgrace of the cross is turned into glory, so that the saints say about it, *God forbid that I should glory save in the cross of our Lord Jesus Christ*,* where even the flesh's humility *should pass out of this world to the Father*?* Nothing is more sublime than this ascension; nothing more glorious than this honor can be said or contrived. Thus through the mys-

*1 Cor 15:54

*Gal 6:14
*John 13:1

tery of his incarnation the Lord descended and ascended, *leaving for us an example for us to follow his steps.* *1 Pet 2:21

3. Let us take from the mystery of the incarnation an example for our way of life: *For one who says he abides in Christ ought himself also to walk even as he walked.* *1 John 2:6
Let us descend by way of humility, and let his first step be set for us, that is his first success, to be unwilling to dominate. His second step is to be willing to be made subject. His third step is to suffer calmly any harsh abuse that is inflicted in his subjection.

Lucifer in heaven lacked that first step, he who *said in his heart,* *Ps 13:1
I will ascend into heaven. I will exalt my throne above the stars of God. I will sit in the mountain of the covenant, in the sides of the North. I will ascend above the height of the clouds. I will be like the most High. *Isa 14:13-14
Saying these things, he fell irreparably from heaven,* *Isa 14:12
and this is perhaps because wishing to dominate is an utterly intolerable pride.

The first human beings in Paradise lacked the second step. Although they preferred to misuse their own will rather than be subjected to their Creator, they did not presume to dominate others who shared their lot. And therefore their fault and their punishment are much different from the devil's pride and fall. Thus also they merited to be renewed by divine mercy one day.

Those who *believe for a while and in time of temptation fall away* *Luke 8:13
do not have the third step.

4. We say these things so that we know whom we should avoid imitating. For the devil and the human being each wished to ascend out of turn: the human to knowledge, the devil to power, both to pride. Let us not wish to ascend that way! Let us rather listen to the prophet who asked how he should ascend: *Who,* he said, *shall ascend into the mountain of the Lord? Or who shall stand in his holy place? The innocent in hands and clean of heart who has not taken his soul in vain and not sworn deceitfully to his neighbor.* *Ps 23:3-4
Note here that he established

a threefold step of ascent. The first step is innocence of deed, the second purity of heart, the third fruit of devotion. We find these steps wonderfully manifested in the steps of descent discussed above.

In the steps of descent, of course, there was the third step, tolerance of injuries. This is what proves the first step of this ascent, that is, innocence in deed. The second step of descent was patience with subjection, and this produces purity of heart, which is the second step of ascent. For to this purpose we have teachers as superiors, so we may purify our hearts, as the Lord says: *Now you are clean by reason of the word which I have spoken to you.** Likewise the first step of descent was disdain for dominating others; this third step of ascent is the fruit of devotion. Anyone, moreover, who does not seek to dominate certainly ought to be in charge of the others who are to be instructed fruitfully.

*John 15:3

Sermo 61

Concerning Four Mountains to Be Ascended

1. *Who shall ascend into the mountain of the Lord?** Christ indeed bodily ascended one time above the heights of heaven, but he now also ascends spiritually every day in the hearts of the elect. If therefore we wish to ascend with him, then we must ascend into the mountains of virtue from the valleys of vices.

There are, however, twin species of these vices. For there are some that hurt us, others that hurt our neighbors. The first are called scandals; the second are called crimes. And all these are referred to as a valley of tears,* because everyone must lament a life of sins with a river of tears.

From the valley of scandals one ascends to the mountain of chastity by a threefold self-control: control of one's members, of one's senses, of one's thoughts. In the first, action is restrained by self-control. In the second, looking is avoided. In the third, feeling is curtailed.

Likewise, from the valley of crimes one ascends into the mountain of innocence. Here a ladder is erected: *See that you not do to another what you would not have done to yourself.** And three steps of fear are placed on the ladder: of those who suffer, of course, lest they pay back in retaliation—either of superior power, lest they inflict revenge, or of the internal Judge, *who renders to every*

*Ps 23:3

*Ps 83:7

*Tob 4:16

*Rom 2:6

*see Rom 1:17

*see 2 Tim 3:12

*person according to his works.** When, however, people have ascended to this mountain, they are already just and live [by faith],* but it is necessary for them, according to the apostle, to suffer persecution.*

2. And so one must flee from the mountain of innocence to the mountain of patience, and here also is erected a ladder of three steps. The first step is suffering of the Lord; second is the courage of martyrs; third is the importance of the reward. These steps can sensibly be called steps of shame, just as they were [called steps] of innocence and of fear.

And note that this mountain of patience, according to these steps, is steep, thorny, and arid. It is steep on account of the difficulty of imitating the Lord's passion. It is thorny on account of barbs of temptations, which happen in many ways: by the loss of property, by verbal insults, by bodily pains, by all sufferings that test the holy martyrs. It is arid on account of the payment of the rewards; they are not [paid] in this world, but entirely hoped for in the future.

After this mountain remains another mountain to be ascended, indeed the mountain of mountains. When one has arrived at this mountain, then God already rests

*see Ps 14:1

*Ps 75:3

*Matt 7:12

in that person.* Thus it is written, *His place was made in peace.** But in this mountain of peace the ladder of charity is erected; thus the Lord says: *Whatsoever you would have other people do to you, do you also to them.** We do indeed want to be rewarded, we want to be pardoned, we want gifts to be given freely.

SERMO 62

Concerning John 12:26

*A*nyone who ministers to me, let him follow me.* Certain people do not follow Christ but flee instead. Others do not follow but rather precede. Some follow but do not catch up. Others truly follow and attain.

*John 12:26

Those who still persist in their sins do not follow but flee; concerning these it is written, *Every one who does evil hates the light.** And the prophet says, *Behold those who keep away from you shall perish.**

*John 3:20
*Ps 72:27

Those who prefer their own opinions to those of their masters do not follow Christ; rather, they precede him. Peter represented this type when he rebuked the Lord, who wished to suffer for our salvation, *saying: Far be it from you, Lord; this shall not be for you.**

*Matt 16:22

Those who act half-heartedly and lackadaisically follow, but they do not catch up. Or *not persevering to the end,** they turn back in the middle of their journey. The apostle says to such as these, *Lift up your hands which hang down and your feeble knees, and make straight steps with your feet so that no one who wavers may go astray, but rather be healed.**

*Matt 24:13

*Heb 12:12-13

Those who steadfastly imitate Christ's way of humility with devoted feeling of mind do follow and attain. Such as these truly follow the Lord: *Anyone who ministers to me, let him follow me,** that is, let him imitate me. For what benefit? *Where I am,* he says *there also is my minister.** And

*John 12:26
*John 12:26

so the benefit of this imitation is an eternal dwelling of blessedness.

Sermo 63

Concerning Matthew 16:24

*Anyone who wishes to come after me,** through me, to me. After me because I am Truth, through me because I am the way, to me because I am the life.* *Matt 16:24

*see John 14:6

Any who wish to come after me, let them deny themselves and take up their cross and follow me.* Christ, the power of God and the wisdom of God,* messenger of great counsel,* proposed three things to the rational soul made in the Trinity's image: servitude, worthlessness, severity.

*Matt 16:24
*1 Cor 1:24
*Isa 9:6

Servitude is indicated by denial of self, worthlessness by enduring of the cross, and severity by imitation of Christ. Thus a soul who has fallen from a state of triple happiness by disobedience may arise from a humiliated torment of triple misery by obedience. She had indeed fallen from herself, from the fellowship of angels, from the vision of God, that is, from freedom, from dignity, from blessedness.

Let her listen therefore to counsel so that by denying herself, that is, denying self-will, she may restore freedom of herself. By taking up her cross, that is, by crucifying her flesh with its vices and concupiscence,* by the good of self-control, she restores her fellowship with angels; by following Christ, that is, by imitating his passion, she restores the vision of his clarity, because if we suffer with him, then we shall also reign with him.*

*Gal 5:24

*Rom 8:17;
2 Tim 2:12

Sermo 64

Concerning Psalm 15:15

1. ***P****recious in the sight of the Lord is the death of his saints.** Sometimes the saint's life makes it precious, sometimes the saint's purpose,* sometimes the saint's life together with purpose. The life of confessors who die in the Lord* makes death precious. Among martyrs who die for the Lord, their purpose alone sometimes makes it precious, but sometimes their purpose equally with their life. And indeed the death that life commends is precious; more precious is that made precious by the martyrs' purpose; truly most precious is that which life precedes along with purpose.

*Ps 115:15
*causa

*Rev 14:13

2. *Precious in the sight of the Lord is the death of his saints.** Three virtues make a person holy: sober living, just action, pious sense.

*Ps 115:15

Our living shall be sober if it is with self-control, with fellowship, with obedience; that is, we shall have lived chastely, charitably, and humbly. For one acquires chastity by self-control, charity by fellowship, and humility by obedience. And this last virtue is that which makes a soul live perfectly submissive to God, secure *under the shadow of his wings.**

*Ps 16:8

Action will be just if it has been honest, discreet, and fruitful: honest by its good intention, discreet by its measure of what is possible, and fruitful by its usefulness to neighbors.

Sense will be pious if our faith perceives God as supremely powerful, supremely wise, and supremely good, so that by his power we believe our weakness is helped,* by his wisdom we believe our ignorance is corrected, by his goodness we believe our iniquity is cleansed.

*Rom 8:26

Three things make the death of saints precious: rest from toil, joy of restoration, and the security of eternity.

Sermo 65

Concerning Matthew 13:44: *The kingdom of heaven is like a treasure hidden in a field*

1. The triple parable in this one reading recommends for us three steps. The field is one's body.* So long as the passions of desire dominate, the body lies uncultivated and liable *to a curse; it sprouts forth thorns and thistles;** anything hidden within is not known. For who at this time considers the body suitable to bear *fruits worthy of penance?**

*see Matt 13:38

*Gen 3:17-18

*Luke 3:8

Why, soul, do you so foolishly expose your body? Do you not know what is hidden within it? What, if not the Kingdom of heaven?* Your task is to discover works of salvation in the body by which you shall be able to gain the Kingdom of heaven. Therefore purchase the field* and claim for yourself your body from your worldly desires by truly paying the price for what instigates and what gives occasion to worldly desires.

*Matt 13:44

*see Matt 13:44

2. But once you have dug up the treasure,* then right away be *a merchant* and *seek precious pearls.** If *you shall have found one most precious*, then again *sell whatever you have and buy it.**

*see Matt 13:44
*Matt 13:45

*Matt 13:46; Mark 10:21

What, however, is the one so precious? It is indeed no wonder if *he sold all that he had** for the treasure, that is, for *the riches of salvation,** and gave up both sins and whatever instigates sin. For certainly these were all he had before.

*Matt 13:44
*Isa 33:6

284

Now however, when we find this treasure, how do we seek good pearls and sell everything for just one? I myself think this one is nothing other than unity. Those however who seek good pearls are people who are not content with inferior goods in the work of salvation but seek everywhere whatever is highest and more excellent. Therefore, finding nothing more precious than unity, on account of it they do not spare all the rest: they boldly prefer unity to fasting, vigils, prayers.

3. But I wish that such a person would not only remain in unity but also remain as one with all and not as one apart from all. May his bosom open, may he enclose within his heart* people of every type† of disposition, *may he become all things to all people,*# prepared both to rejoice with and to suffer with them: *to rejoice with those who rejoice, to weep with those who weep.*‡

*viscera, "internal organs"
†see Matt 13:47
#1 Cor 9:22
‡Rom 12:15

For when he shall come to the shore, then *he shall remove bad fishes from the net* of charity, and whatever is troublesome *shall be cast out.**

*Matt 13:48

Sermo 66

For the Feast of All Saints: The Beatitudes as Remedies for Sins

1. The remedy for a fault follows the same order by which the fault preceded.
    The first sin happened in heaven through the pride of that transgressor angel who said *in his heart,** *I will ascend into heaven. I will exalt my throne above the stars of God. I will sit in the mountain of covenant, in the sides of the north. I will ascend above the height of the clouds. I will be like the most High.** He was fearful within himself, and, having been cast out from the lot of blessed spirits, he lost the Kingdom of heaven. Against this sin it has been said, *Blessed are the poor in spirit, for theirs is the kingdom of heaven.**

    The second sin was committed through the disobedience of the woman in Paradise.* From this sin, the flesh was made rebellious toward the spirit so that, because its spirit has not been subject to its Creator, neither is the flesh subject to the spirit. Against this sin it has been said, *Blessed are the meek, for they shall possess the land.** The Lord conceived a remedy for these two sins, saying, *Learn from me because I am meek and humble of heart.**

    The third sin happened because this woman also dragged her husband along with herself into the fault.* Certainly she should have wept for her sin rather than

*Ps 13:1

*Isa 14:13-14

*Matt 5:3

*see Gen 3:6

*Matt 5:4

*Matt 11:29

*see Gen 3:6

adding sin upon sin.* But in this she supposed that she would be consoled, that is, if she made her husband a participant in her sin. For it is natural that each person wishes to involve his or her partner in either sins or virtues. Against this sin is the treatment: *Blessed are those who mourn, for they shall be comforted.**   *Isa 30:1

*Matt 5:5

2. Adam, who consented, committed the fourth sin. For Adam, as the apostle says, was not seduced, but the woman, being seduced, was in the transgression.* She sinned through ignorance; he sinned through weakness. Moreover, he sinned by loving his wife too much, not because he did her will, but because he preferred her to the divine will. So the Lord also said to him, *Because you have hearkened to the voice of your wife* more than mine, *cursed is the earth in your work.** For certainly justice requires that he should do the will of him to whom he owed more. Who in truth would call into question that he owes more to his Creator than to his wife? For this reason he was obliged to his wife only through love, but to God through fear together with love. These two links should therefore have been strong enough to make him observe God's commandment rather than his one and only affection for his wife.

*1 Tim 2:14

*Gen 3:17

Against this fourth sin, a treatment is applied: *Blessed are those who hunger and thirst after justice, for they shall have their fill.** Adam indeed had justice, having been created just by a just God. But because he did not love justice by his own free will, he easily drifted away from justice through the same free will. In contrast, it is said about Christ through the psalmist, *You have loved justice and hated iniquity.**

*Matt 5:6

*Ps 44:8

He who flung back his own fault onto his wife likewise committed the fifth sin when he said, *The woman whom you gave me as a companion gave to me from the tree, and I did eat.** In the first place, he who excused his own sin was cruel to himself; in the second place, he was cruel to his wife whom he accused. Actually, it was

*Gen 3:12

a revenge appropriate enough for the woman's sin when he accused her for whose love he sinned. Against this sin it has been said, *Blessed are the merciful, for they shall obtain mercy.** ⁎Matt 5:7

3. Eve caused the sixth sin. When the Lord rebuked her, asking why she did this, she answered him, *The serpent deceived me, and I did eat.** ⁎Gen 3:13 Thus she also strayed into words of malice to make excuses in sins,* ⁎Ps 140:4 pouring fault back upon the serpent as if exempt from blame, since the serpent's suggestion would have done no harm if she had denied the assent of her own will. And perhaps some emotion of pride within her had preceded, so therefore she deserved to be seduced by the serpent. Against this it has been said, *Blessed are the clean of heart, for they shall see God.** ⁎Matt 5:8

The seventh sin happened outside Paradise when Cain rose up against his brother Abel and killed him.* ⁎Gen 4:8 Now, ever since then, it is a long-standing fact that evil people rise against the good and oppress them. Here is the treatment for this sin: *Blessed are the peacemakers, for they shall be called children of God.** ⁎Matt 5:9 Because if evil people have refused to stop their unjust attack, then the just patiently endure them, hearing the consolation that follows and says, *Blessed are those who suffer persecution for justice's sake, for theirs is the kingdom of heaven.** ⁎Matt 5:10

Behold how necessary was the coming of Christ, who subjected flesh to spirit, who made peace between humans and himself, and who reconciled God with humans.* ⁎see Col 1:20

Sermo 67

Concerning the Twofold Precepts of the Law, Moral and Figurative

For *the law was given by Moses; grace and truth came by Jesus Christ.** I find two types of precepts in the ancient law, for there are certain moral precepts, such as *you shall not covet, you shall not commit adultery, honor your father and mother,** *and such like.*† There are even certain precepts that are figurative and foreshadow,# such as the sacrifice of bulls and blood of goats.‡ However, those carnal people could neither fulfill the former° nor obtain salvation by the latter.∞ Whence also the Savior in the gospel reproaches the Pharisees with the precepts of the law, because *they made void the commandments of God on account of their own traditions,** no doubt those that edify morals. For concerning the others, he says through the prophet, *I gave them commandments not good,** clearly those that would be *a shadow of things to come.**

For what logical consequence of reason suggests that, when a person sins, a ram is punished and might say with the prophet, *Then I paid for that which I have not stolen?** It is right and sensible that the people who were not good did not receive good precepts, as the prophet says: *With the holy, you will be holy, and with the perverse, you will be perverted.** For the Lord knew the carnal hearts of the Jews, so he also handed them carnal sacraments *which could not, as to the conscience, make perfect one who serves in justice of the flesh.**

*John 1:17

*Rom 13:9;
Matt 19:18-19
†Gal 5:21
#see Heb 10:1
‡Heb 9:13
°see Acts 15:10
∞see Heb 9:9

*Matt 15:3;
Mark 7:9

*Ezek 20:25
*Col 2:17

*Ps 68:5

*Ps 17:26-27

*Heb 9:9-10

Therefore our Lord Christ came *full of grace and truth*,* so that, from this, morals may now indeed be fulfilled through grace. Those however that had been mysterious and had foreshadowed were revealed by truth and then observed not literally but understood spiritually according to the spirit.*

Therefore a ram or bull is no longer sacrificed when a person sins; rather, a living offering of one's body, a rational* and acceptable sacrifice: by fasts and labors one merits pardon and grace equally.

*John 1:14

*see 1 Cor 2:13-14

*Rom 12:1

Sermo 68

A duplicate of Sermo 32, above, on pages 177–80.

Sermo 69

Concerning the Triple Renewal of Triple Oldness

1. *Just as we have borne the image of the earthly human, let us bear also the image of the heavenly.** *1 Cor 15:49

There are two human beings, old and new: Adam old, Christ new. The former is earthly, the latter heavenly; the image of the former is oldness, the image of the latter is newness. There is on the one hand a triple oldness, and on the other hand a triple newness. For there is oldness in heart, in mouth, in body. In these three ways we sin: in thought, word, and deed.

Carnal and worldly desires are in the heart, that is, love of the flesh and love of the world. Similarly, in the mouth is a twin oldness: arrogance and disparagement. Likewise twin in the body: debauchery and crimes. All these are the image of the old human being, and all of these must be renewed in us.

If there were not oldness in the heart, the apostle would not say, *Be renewed in the spirit of your mind, and put on the new human, who according to God was created in justice and holiness of truth.** Likewise if there were not oldness in the mouth, then Scripture would not say, *Let old matters depart from your mouth.** And the apostle says, *Let no evil speech proceed from your mouth, but that which is good to the edification of faith so that it gives grace to the hearers.** But he also makes mention of the body's oldness when he says, *Just as you have yielded your mem-

*Eph 4:23-24

*1 Sam 2:3

*Eph 4:29

bers to serve uncleanness and iniquity to iniquity,* and concerning the body's renewal he also adds, *So now yield your members to serve justice for sanctification.**   *Rom 6:19
    *Rom 6:19

2. Therefore let our heart be renewed, so that by shutting out carnal and worldly desires, God's love may be introduced, as well as love for the heavenly homeland. Let arrogance and disparagement keep away from our mouth, and let true confession of our sins and a positive view of our neighbors follow in place of those vices. In place of debauchery and crimes, which are oldness of body, let us take up self-control and innocence so opposite vices may indeed be driven out by opposite virtues.

Christ, who dwells in us through faith,* makes this renewal mentioned above, as Christ himself says: *Behold, I make all things new.** Thus he says to the bride in the Song of Songs, *Put me as a seal upon your heart, as a seal upon your arm.** Wisdom is therefore dwelling in the heart, truth dwelling in the mouth, justice dwelling in the body.   *see Eph 3:17

    *Rev 21:5

    *Song 8:6

Sermo 70

Concerning Reflection

*1 Cor 4:9

*W*e are made a spectacle to the world and to angels and to human beings,* so clearly to both the evil and the good equally. For the passion of jealousy incites the former and mercy's sympathy incites the latter so that they unceasingly study us. The evil indeed desire our failure; the good desire our success. No doubt we are on probation; in a meantime, we stand in the middle between Paradise and hell, as though set up between the cloister and a worldly life. What we do is carefully considered on both sides. It is said on both sides, "If only he would cross over to us!" Their intentions are indeed different, but perhaps their desires are not so disparate.

But if the eyes of all are thus upon us, then where have *our* eyes gone? Or rather, why have our eyes alone turned away from us? That is to say, we have been watched from both the right and from the left with so much zeal, yet we alone avoid inspecting our life. We alone neglect to look at ourselves; we do not fear those who deceive or even revere ministering spirits.* *The just wait for me until you reward me,** and similarly, *The sinners have waited for me to destroy me.** From here a crown is prepared for me, from there Gehenna. And between this crown and that Gehenna, the middle is pleased to play the fool and enjoy loafing? I am to the point where I am neither drawn by desire nor frightened by danger, neither completely desirous nor terrified, and in both

*Heb 1:14
*Ps 141:8
*Ps 118:95

more has been necessary. Most dangerously still, [I am] insensitive to both.

Let us arise before it is too late, brothers; let us not receive our souls in vain,* souls for which others keep watch with so much zeal, either for good or for evil. It is not a small matter for which the enemies pursue with hostility and fellow citizens thus stand ready.

*Ps 23:4

Sermo 71

Concerning the Entrance of the Sons of Israel into the Land of Egypt

1. Vigorous and complete morality consists chiefly in two activities: avoiding vices and eagerly striving for virtue, because it does not suffice to abstain from evil if we do not do good. Hence the psalmist sings, *Turn from evil and do good.** Therefore let us flee vices and embrace virtues. So let us briefly sample some biblical stories in order to reap the fruit of morality.

*Ps 36:27

Famine forced Israel to immigrate to Egypt.* Very soon they get a new ruler there, and he turns freedom to slavery. Living in that region results in their subjection to the power of Pharaoh, who orders the baby boys to be killed and the girls to be spared.* Israel is harshly afflicted by works in brick and clay. Pharaoh serves straw to the laborers, who were compelled by hunger.*

*Gen 42:1-5

*Exod 1:16

*Exod 1:13-14

2. It was not hunger for bread or thirst for water that forced so many to enter Egypt. It was hunger and thirst for hearing the word of God.* This word of God is *the true light which enlightens every human being who comes into this world.** That is why the psalmist says, *The precept of the Lord is luminous, enlightening the eyes.** One who follows this light does not walk in darkness but has the

*Amos 8:11

*John 1:9
*Ps 18:9

light of life.* Such a one crosses over from the light of precepts to the lamp of rewards. *John 8:12

Those who suffer a lack of this divine word are forced to enter Egypt, that is, darkness. For they are enveloped in the darkness of ignorance and subject to the dominion of Pharaoh, that is, the devil who is the leader of Egypt, of darkness, according to the apostle: *For our struggling is not against flesh and blood, but against principalities and power, against the rulers of the world of this darkness, against the spirits of wickedness in high places.* *Eph 6:12
Works done under the yoke of Pharaoh become clay, that is, useless and filthy. Straw is given by Pharaoh, that is, light thoughts. This cognitive straw easily catches fire and is consumed in a moment. Thus bad thoughts sent by the devil are quickly kindled in our minds while the weakness of the flesh gives consent. But if we courageously strive to resist, with God's help, at once these thoughts are extinguished. Once the straw caught fire, the clay was cooked and solidified into bricks. Little thoughts, which are the clay, catch fire when they take pleasure in the straw. When the thoughts cross over into action, then they cook. When they in fact become a habit, then they solidify.

Sermo 72

Concerning Psalm 1

1. **B**lessed is the one who has not walked in the counsel of the ungodly.* The pious are those who believe in God and worship him, for piety is the worship of God. This worship is threefold: faith, hope, and charity, which are invisible. The impious, who do not worship God, lack these three; their counsel is to put the visible before the invisible, the earthly before the heavenly. The head and leader of the impious is the devil, who was the first to abandon piety. Also, having become impious, he used his fraud to cast down from that same piety even the humans who were placed in Paradise, wishing to have them as companions in his error and as sharers of iniquity. For he seduced Eve, and through her he subjected the man to himself.

*Ps 1:1

Similarly, the demon still makes suggestions to the flesh, and then the flesh to the spirit, so it too becomes the counsel of the impious. For they say among themselves, *Let us all have one purse.** Therefore they all place in the memory, as if in a purse, their own coin: the demon of course places suggestion, the flesh pleasure, the spirit consent. So it follows that, as from a common fund,* they acquire for themselves their particular nourishment. The flesh acquires a burning, a fire that is never extinguished. The spirit acquires a bad conscience, which is the worm that never dies.* The demon, however, gains the blood of both.

*Prov 1:14

*Prov 23:21

*Mark 9:43

2. One comes to this counsel of the impious in four ways. Some are dragged unwillingly. Others, once en-

ticed, are drawn to it. Still others are seduced without realizing it. Finally, some follow by their own will. Four virtues are necessary by which, once so armed, we may resist submission to the counsel of the impious. Fortitude is necessary for the unwilling; by fortitude they resist unto death even threats, torture, and injury. Those who are easily enticed and drawn to impious counsel lack temperance; temperance calms illicit desires, does not yield to promises, and is not softened by enticements. For those who are seduced unaware, there is need for prudence, which discerns what is useful from what is useless and shows what should be retained and what should be rejected. Those who follow of their own will require justice. Justice is uprightness of the will, which does not love to sin or consent to sin.

Justice and fortitude have their dwelling in the will, because the will ought to be just and resolute. Justice puts the will in order thus: refusing what is evil and putting better things before good things. Adam seems not to have had this ordered justice, because he consented to evil[1] and forsook what was useful.

Prudence and temperance have their dwelling in the reason, because the reason ought to be prudent and temperate. Prudence, once educated by reason, by grace, of course, is to avoid what is contrary to justice for the sake of justice. [Educated reason] indeed avoids not only overt injustice but even whatever might be against justice, paying close attention not just to what is licit but more to what is expedient: avoiding wealth and certain other things, not because they are illicit, but because they are usually impediments to justice. The Lord adds *on account of justice* because of certain people who so behave out of hypocrisy. Justice is the perfection of a rational soul. The other virtues are for the acquisition

---

[1] Bernard plays here on the homonyms *malus* (evil, bad) and *malus* (apple).

or keeping of justice: fortitude, temperance, prudence; they maintain justice lest it be lost or diminished. Truly, after justice has been perfected and crosses into the affection of the heart, it likewise becomes those three, that is resolute, prudent, temperate.

3. [*Blessed is*] *the one who has not gone astray.** To go astray pertains to those who are fickle, those who can be urged on thoughtlessly. That is, certain people wish to avoid [the strait and narrow], becoming obstinate, acquiescing to no one's advice, holding stubbornly to their own purpose. And that is why the psalm adds, *nor has he stood,* so as not to be fickle or obstinate, of course. *The way of sinners* is the world, or self-will, which is the pride whence come all evils, in the same way that good things are from a common will.

Nor has he sat in the chair of pestilence.* One who sits, teaches, making others sin by his example. This is the chair, and it stands on four legs. The first leg is wickedness, second is contempt for God, third is irreverence, fourth is cunning. Wickedness means to love evil and to have a taste for evil, and it is to love evil for the sake of evil, as do the devil and some sinners. But because it sometimes happens that such people don't fear God with a good fear, but rather a fear of either losing property or suffering bodily pain, so that they become more evil, then they also despise God himself, and the second leg becomes contempt for God. Likewise it could happen that they love evil and they despise God, but the shame of other people with whom they live holds them back. Therefore irreverence, the third leg, follows, increasing evil so that they neither fear God nor respect other people.*

Cunning, the fourth leg, is truly near to the consummation of total wickedness; thus sinners know how to use the three aforementioned legs, mixing poison with oil and vinegar with honey. The prominent part of the chair, to which the seated sinner clings, is power. For

*Ps 1:1

*Ps 1:1

*Luke 18:2

if it is a powerful person who holds the aforementioned seat, then he does the most harm. Or if he is able to lure the powerful person to himself, seducing the powerful one with his advice, he then urges him to evil. Then a cushion is put in place so that he sits comfortably. The cushion is made from light feathers of birds, signifying vainglory and popularity, by which people who enjoy such things are exalted. A footstool is placed under his feet so that they don't touch the ground. For some such people do not do earthly deeds, but they pretend to do spiritual deeds so as to deceive even more. Their teaching is like a pestilence, overtaking and devastating many places.

4. *But his will in the law of the Lord.** In the previous verse, it says what should be rejected; in this verse, however, it says what should be sought. In the former it says, as it were, *decline from evil*; in the latter, however, *and do good*,* which certainly is to walk in the Lord's law. But, because this way is conducted not by steps of the body but by affection of the mind, it therefore says *his will in the law of the Lord*. For, as blessed Gregory testifies, to will is to go by mind.* Three types of people (either slave, mercenary, or son) advance through this way, as though they led a certain wagon. Moreover, two beasts named Threat and Promise draw the same wagon. A slave sits on Threat; a mercenary sits on Promise. Each of these pulls the wagon, one by fear, the other by desire, and each is driven by his own particular goad. The son alone, who is neither shaken by fear nor enticed by desire but driven by a spirit of love, without toil or injury, is conveyed in the wagon: *For whosoever are led by the Spirit of God, they are the children of God*,* and conversely, whosoever are children of God are led by the Spirit of God.

In addition, that wagon has four wheels, namely, those four well-known affections of the soul, love and joy, fear and sadness, which both the chosen and the

*Ps 1:2

*Ps 36:27

*Gregory the Great, Evang 27.5 (CCSL 141:233)

*Rom 8:14

condemned set in order for themselves, variously according to their own judgment. For the condemned put love and joy in the first place, and in last place fear and sadness. That is, they love temporal realities, and they rejoice when they act wickedly, but pain and everlasting sadness follow this love and this joy. But the elect, to whom it is said, *The world shall rejoice, and you shall be made sorrowful, but your sorrow shall be turned into rejoicing,** put fear and sadness as the front wheels, as the rear wheels love and gladness. I mean to say, for them fear is changed into rejoicing, sadness into everlasting joy.

*John 16:20

5. One should also note that this way of the Lord's law is completed within six days. And indeed the first day is called groaning of heart, second is confession of mouth, third is distribution of one's own property, fourth is physical labor, fifth is denial of self-will, sixth is disdaining death. On the seventh day one finds rest from all the above, looking forward to the eighth day of resurrection. *And on his law he shall meditate day and night.** In whatever situation people might find themselves, they should never slip away from the Lord's law, but in a day of goodness let them never forget evils, and in a day of evils let them always remember goods. Furthermore, *by day and by night* can be understood as the contemplative and the active life, both of which together are preserved in the Lord's law.

*Ps 1:2

Sermo 73

Concerning Psalm 13:1

*T*he fool has said in his heart: There is no God.* Although God is one, and he is singular, he seems to have different flavors to us depending on changes in our souls, not because of variations within God himself. He tastes of justice and power to one who fears him. He tastes of goodness and mercy to one who loves Him. Thus this same prophet said in another place, *God has spoken once; these two things have I heard: that power belongs to God, and mercy to you, O Lord.** Certainly to hear and to taste are the same, because both become one and very simple in the mind. And so *God has spoken once* because he begot one Word. But through the one Word we hear or we taste these two: *that power belongs to God, and mercy to you, O Lord.*

But certainly those to whom God tastes neither of fear nor of love are deeply foolish.* Let them learn as much as they want; I will not call them wise so long as they neither fear nor love God. For how shall I call them perfected in wisdom when I don't even see that they have begun? For *Fear of the Lord is the beginning of Wisdom.** Completion is love. Hope, however, claims for herself the time between. Therefore, those to whom God does not taste of justice through fear, or of mercy through love, say, *There is no God.* That is to say, those who suppose that God is neither just nor loving believe that he does not exist.

*Ps 13:1

*Ps 61:12-13

*insipiens, "foolish" or "without taste"

*Ps 110:10

Sermo 74

Concerning Psalm 13:1

*Ps 13:1

They have been corrupted and have become abominable in their devotions. There is not anyone who does good, no, not one.* The soul has its own corruption; the body also has its own. The soul's corruption is threefold; the body's is fourfold. And indeed the body consists of four elements, but the soul subsists in three powers. I mean the soul is rational, concupiscible, irascible.[1] Pride corrupts reason, whose health is knowledge of truth. Moreover, a corrupted reason is deceived in two ways: in knowledge of itself and in knowledge of God. Vainglory corrupts the concupiscible power; jealousy corrupts the irascible power.

Corruption of the body is called abomination, and it happens in four ways according to the four elements that make up the body. I mean, there are four [things] that corrupt the body: curiosity, talkativeness, cruelty, pleasure. There are, moreover, four parts of the body in which each particular element thrives best. For fire is in the eyes; air is in the tongue, which forms the voice; earth is in the hands, to which sense of touch is proper;

---

[1] *Rationalis, concupiscibilis, irascibilis.* This is a traditional formula. The middle term is the most difficult to translate in this context. *The Catholic Encyclopedia* says, "In its widest acceptation, concupiscence is any yearning of the soul for good; in its strict and specific acceptation, a desire of the lower appetite contrary to reason" (http://www.newadvent.org/cathen/04208a.htm).

water is in the genitals. The fourfold pestilence corrupts these four parts: curiosity of course the eyes, talkativeness the tongue, cruelty the hands, pleasure the genitals. Thus human beings become corrupted and abominable, corrupted in soul, abominable in body: corrupted before God, abominable before human beings. *There is not anyone who does good, no, not one.*

There are four types of human beings; none among these types does good, except one. I mean, certain types neither understand nor seek God, and these are dead. Some at least understand, but they do not seek, and these are impious. Others seek, but they do not understand, and these are foolish. Still others both understand and seek, and these are holy, about whom alone can it be said that they are saints who do good.

Sermo 75

Concerning Those Who Sin in the Hope of Confession *in Extremis*

*Ps 15:4

*1 Cor 15:52
*John 3:8

*Luke 23:39-43
*Ps 15:4

*Matt 8:10

Their infirmities were multiplied; afterward they made haste.* So why do people neglect to do penance in their life and presume [that they can make] a confession when near death? How can they hold the opinion that all the soul's members can be recalled within the effort of one hour, members that through concupiscence and desires were torn apart and scattered throughout the whole world, that have been stuck in all dregs and everywhere bound by the glue of cupidity. "I do not say," says the Lord, "that I am not able to save some such, to recall everything in a moment and in the blink of an eye* through the Spirit who not only blows where he wills but also when he wills,* to inspire the penitence and compunction in their hearts that others scarcely achieve with lifelong practice, just as I gave it to the thief.* But I say to you, *I will not join in their meetings for blood offerings.*"* That is, "from those who persist in blood offerings I shall not gather together multitudes of such types, nor shall I collect them by large quantities into my kingdom." Accordingly, you shall find only one in all canonical Scripture saved by that last-minute confession, and that one at the hour of the Lord's passion, since so much faith would not be found in all of Israel.*

Sermo 76

Concerning God's Triple Grace

You have preceded him with blessings of sweetness.* We have need of a threefold blessing: one that precedes, helps, and consummates. First is the blessing of mercy, second of grace, third of glory. Mercy precedes conversion, grace helps our way of life, glory perfects our consummation. If God has not given this threefold blessing, then our land cannot produce the fruit of salvation.* I mean, we cannot begin any good until we are preceded by mercy, nor do good until we are helped by grace, nor be consummated in good until we are filled with glory. Truly, among these three blessings, it is right that one of them tastes more sweet, that blessing that preceded not only [when we were] without merit, but even when we deserved bad things, so that while we were still children of wrath* and we performed the works of death, God would think thoughts of peace* concerning us, and he generously gives a good spirit,† a spirit of life,# a spirit of adoption‡ not just to those who entreat, but rather also to those who accuse, not to those who invoke, but to those who provoke, not to those who appeal, but even to those who spurn.¹ What would taste sweet for that soul to whom so much mercy has no taste? So a blessing of

*Ps 20:4

*Ps 84:13

*Eph 2:3

*Jer 29:11
†Luke 11:13
#Rom 8:2
‡Rom 8:15

---

¹ *petentibus . . . impetentibus . . . invocantibus . . . provocantibus . . . interpellantibus . . . repellentibus.* The wordplay can scarcely be conveyed in English.

sweetness is rightly called that which precedes, because what helps belongs to fortitude, what consummates belongs to fullness.

Sermo 77

Concerning Psalm 17:45:
A people that I knew not

A people that I knew not has served me.* It would be no great wonder if a people known by God were to serve him. But when an unknown people serves him and obeys when the ear hears, then they merit great praise. There are four different types among those who are known and those who are not known. For there are certain beings who are both known by God and also know God.* Others neither know nor are known. Others at least are known, but they do not know. Finally, others are not known, and yet they know.

When God knows a being, he makes the being happy. When human beings know, it means that they give thanks for the perceived happiness. Therefore, those who are known by God and who know God are holy angels. Those who have been made happy by him always have leisure for his praises and devote themselves to his service.

Those who neither know God nor are known by God are poor of necessity; neither wealth of temporal goods nor riches nor divine servitude blesses them. However, those who are known but do not know are the wealthy of this world.* Indeed, those who abound with the wealth that they have received but are overwhelmed by carnal desires never dedicate their heart to heavenly realities.

*Ps 17:45

*1 Cor 13:2; Gal 4:9

*1 Tim 6:17

However, those who are not known and yet know are the voluntary poor, those whom neither tribulation nor difficulty nor any other dangers can separate from the love of Christ.* And no doubt these are tested in many adverse ways and are wearied by harsh tribulations, as Scripture says: *The furnace tries the potter's vessels, and the trial of tribulation tests just people.** Likewise the psalm says in their personae, *God my God, look upon me. Why have you forsaken me?** Do not those who pray to be looked upon seem partially known? Nevertheless, although they are considered unknown, although they have been forsaken, still they know God. And in the personae of those who know, in the same psalm it is immediately inserted, *My God, I shall cry by day and you will not hear, and by night, and it shall not be folly in me.**

*Rom 8:35

*Sir 27:6

*Ps 21:2

*Ps 21:3

Now the divine voice says about these, *A people that I knew not has served me**—as if God were to say frankly to his angels, "Is it any wonder if you whom I make happy serve me, seeing that those whom I forsake in their poverty serve me? And is it any wonder if you who see my face obey me, when those who only hear me and do not see also obey me?" Of course angels see; human beings hear. Certainly they listen[1] and obey so that at some time when they have been made equal to angels* they might deserve also to see what angels see. And so listening is the dues for seeing, vision the prize for listening. And to listen is first, to see later, as it is written: *Listen, daughter, and see.** Therefore whoever desires to see God in the future surely must first listen to God in the present.

*Ps 17:45

*Luke 20:36

*Ps 44:11

---

[1] All the words for hearing and listening near the end of this sermon are forms of *audire*. "Listen" conveys the context of obedience or of gaining the vision of God.

Sermo 78

Concerning Three Tabernacles

There are three: tents, courtyards, homes. In tents are all the just people living and laboring in the flesh,* because tents belong to those laboring and in military service. A tent certainly has a roof but lacks a foundation. And it is portable, because the just in present circumstances are not established; rather they seek a city above that has foundations.* Even their faith, which is a foundation, is not in earthly realities, but in the Lord. They have a roof; it is the protection of grace and a shelter.

 Courtyards are spacious and near buildings. In these courtyards are holy souls who have shed their bodies, who are in wide-open spaces,* having deposited the narrowness of the flesh. Courtyards have a foundation but no roof, because souls that are in God's love do not fall; thus *our feet were standing.** Those who still expect advancement do not have a roof, a roof that will not exist except in the resurrection of their bodies. Really, after resurrection itself they will be with angels in a home that has a foundation and a roof. The foundation is stability of eternal blessedness; the roof is its consummation and perfection.

*Gal 2:20

*Heb 13:14; 11:10

*Ps 118:45

*Ps 121:2

Sermo 79

Concerning a Double Preparation of One's Heart

*Ps 56:8

*Num 21:22; 20:17

*Gen 21:10; Gal 4:30
‡Gal 5:19
#Gen 22:2

*Gen 22:13

My heart is ready, O God, my heart is ready. The royal road turns neither to the right nor to the left.* Still, you can find people who are prepared at least one time, but certainly not a second. If God were to say to someone, *Cast out this bondwoman and her son*—I mean works of the flesh‡—then that one would not hesitate. If God were to say, "Sacrifice for me your son whom you love, Isaac,"# then obviously that person could no longer listen to this patiently, seeing as the grace of fraternal utility or spiritual unity would seem to sustain devotional losses. Why wouldn't the servant of Christ easily toss away whatever pertains to bodily pleasure? But certainly, to be cheated of spiritual enjoyment calmly, when either obedience compels or the reason of fraternal charity demands—this plainly is to offer a great and pleasing sacrifice. Nevertheless, do keep in mind that Isaac is not to be slaughtered in this sacrifice, but the ram of stubbornness.*

Sermo 80

Concerning the Variety and Utility of Unity

1. *Behold how good and how pleasant it is for brothers to dwell in unity.** There is a natural unity, carnal unity, virile unity, moral unity, spiritual unity, social unity, personal unity, and principal unity. Natural unity is between body and soul. Carnal unity is between husband and wife, concerning which it has been said, *They shall be two in one flesh.** Virile unity is what connects the human being to itself, so that it does not flow out through various concerns, but, rather, with the prophet, virile unity begs just one thing from the Lord.* Moral unity is what connects us to our neighbor, so the psalmist says, *who makes people of one manner to dwell in a home.** Spiritual unity is what joins us to God, so the apostle says, *One who is joined to God is one spirit.** Social unity is among angels; personal unity is in Christ; principal unity, which is also essential, is in the Trinity.

*Ps 132:1

*Gen 2:24

*Ps 26:4

*Ps 67:7

*1 Cor 6:17

2. *Behold how good and how pleasant.** Certain things are good and pleasant; others are neither good nor pleasant; some are good and not pleasant; certain others are pleasant and not good. One arrives at good and pleasant things from what is good and not pleasant. One arrives at things not good and not pleasant from what is pleasant and not good. Good but not pleasant things are self-control, patience, discipline. Pleasant and

*Ps 132:1

not good things are pleasure, curiosity, and vanity. Jealousy, sadness, and *acedia*[1] are neither good nor pleasant. Honesty, charity, and purity are both good and pleasant.

Virile unity and moral unity are necessary to obtain the good and pleasant unity. Cowardliness and levity disturb the first. Cowardliness makes people abandon their intention; levity makes them change. Stubbornness, suspicion, and deceit disturb the second. Stubbornness does not accept the neighbor; suspicion does not trust a neighbor; deceit does not join itself to a neighbor. Hope of eternal realities drives out cowardliness; humble obedience drives out levity. Stubbornness is driven out with humility; suspicion and deceit are driven out with charity.

---

[1] *Acedia* is a sort of weariness that is sometimes counted among the deadly sins.

Sermo 81

Concerning Praise of Christ

*P**raise is not proper in the mouth of a sinner.** Praise even in the mouth of repenting sinners does not seem proper, because they still suffer shame from recollection and memory of sin, and thereupon they frequently feel remorse. But still, confession* in a sinner is useful and fruitful, even if praise is not proper and fitting.* In fact, after penitents make progress by God's favors, they adhere to divine praise.* They delight in praise and make progress so that nothing else pleases them; then proper praise of God is in their mouth. This is rather like a farmer who while he spreads manure in his field is completely in dirt and manure, and his labor is not pretty, although it might be fruitful. But when he collects bundles of grain,* then his labor is proper and sweet.

*Sir 15:9

*confessio, also meaning "praise"

*Ps 146:1
*1 Cor 6:17

*Pss 125:6-7; 128:7

Sermo 82

Concerning Custody of One's Heart

1. ***W**ith all watchfulness keep your heart, because life issues out from it.** Moreover, life issues from the heart in two ways: either because *with the heart one believes unto justice,** and *the just person lives by faith,** and God is seen by a pure heart,* that is, he is known, and *this is eternal life, that they may know you, the one God and Jesus Christ whom you have sent;** or because Christ shall then be our life,‡ he who now dwells in our hearts by faith,# when he has appeared, and we shall appear with him in glory, and he who now lies hidden in the heart shall then come forth as from the heart to the body, when *he will reform the body of our lowliness, made like to the body of His glory.** Thus also the other apostle says, *We are now God's children and it has not yet appeared what we shall be.**

*Prov 4:23

*Rom 10:10
*Rom 1:17
*Matt 5:8

*John 17:3
‡Col 3:4
#Eph 3:17

*Phil 3:21
*1 John 3:2

2. But one must consider how he says, *With all watchfulness keep your heart.** People in this world are used to saying "One who guards the body guards a good fortress." But not so for us; rather, "Anyone who guards the body guards a worthless dung heap," as the apostle testifies: *For one who sows in the flesh, from the flesh also shall he reap corruption. But one who sows in the spirit,* he says, *shall reap eternal life from the spirit.** And if he meant "cultivated," then all the more should the soul's castle be guarded, since eternal *life issues out from it.**

*Prov 4:23

*Gal 6:8

*Prov 4:23

But this castle is situated in a land of enemies* and attacked from all sides. On that account, *with all watchfulness*, that is, from every direction, it should be fortified with vigilant care: below, above, ahead, and behind, from right and from left. Carnal desire, which makes war against the soul, attacks from below because *the flesh lusts against the spirit.** God's Judgment threatens from above, for *it is a fearful thing to fall into the hands of the living God.** Behind is the deadly pleasure that arises from recollection of past sins, ahead urgent temptation. From the left, of course, the troubles from arrogant and murmuring brothers, from the right, fervor and devotion of obedient brothers, and the latter by two means: either by envying their deeds or by being jealous of their unusual grace.

3. Strict discipline therefore keeps watch against the flesh. Judgment of one's own individual confession [keeps watch] against God's Judgment, and let this be double: obvious faults from the obvious, hidden faults from the hidden. Therefore the apostle says, *If we would judge ourselves, then we should not be judged.** Moreover, frequent reading [keeps watch] against pleasure that issues from recollection of past sins; urgent and suppliant prayer [keeps watch] against urgent temptation. Patience and compassion [keep watch] against troubles from brothers. Congratulation and discretion [keep watch] against the fervor of obedient brothers. For congratulation drives out envy, and discretion drives out excessive jealousy.

*Bar 3:10

*1 Pet 2:11;
Gal 5:17

*Heb 10:31

*1 Cor 11:31

Sermo 83

Concerning Avoidance of Praise

*Prov 25:16

Y*ou have found honey? Don't eat too much, lest being filled you vomit it up.** In this context, what is called *honey* can suitably be understood as the acclamation of human praise. We are not prohibited from ever serving this honey, but from excess, and rightly so. I mean, we validly accept human praise as long as we have in view fraternal charity, and it is for the salvation of those who submit to us more easily on that account. By this frugality, therefore, moderate consumption of this honey shall do no harm. But any more

*Matt 5:37

than that is from evil,* and it will be turned into ruination. For when people find honey and eat it exces-

*Ps 61:11
*Deut 32:15;
Lat *impinguatur*, sometimes translated as *anointed* (with oil)

sively, entirely setting their heart on it,* then it is that they become puffed up, bloated, and fat* on the acclamation of human praise. The holy prophet begs to be guarded by the Lord against this acclamation about which we have been speaking, though he does not call it honey; rather he expresses it with the similar appellation, *oil*, when he says, *Let the oil of the sinner not fatten*

*Ps 140:5;
Lat *impinguet*

my head.*

Do you wish to know when intemperate people vomit their meal by feasting on honey that they took to satiety, when they exceeded the limit of frugality? Having been filled with praise, they seek no other enjoyment, but content only with human acclamation—then, no doubt, I say—with much anxiety they vomit the praise because they ate with destructive pleasure, while they pine with envy when they hear someone else being praised. For their mind has been surrendered to vanity, and, swelling with arrogance, they assume that the praise of another is disapproval of themselves.

Sermo 84

Concerning Higher and Lower Positions of the Soul

1. There are two positions for a rational soul: the lower, which she rules, and the higher, in which she rests. The lower position is the body, which the soul rules; the higher position is God, in whom she rests. What Scripture says about each position can correctly be understood: *If the spirit of him who has power ascends upon you, leave not your place,** that is, [leave] neither the lower position for ruling nor the higher for resting. But that which I have said first applies to people who are still immature and imperfect, to whom the apostle says, *I speak in human terms because of the infirmity of your flesh. For as you have yielded your members to serve uncleanness and iniquity unto iniquity, so now yield your members to serve justice unto sanctification.** The soul of course has to do three things in the body: give life, give senses, rule. But if life is withdrawn or the senses confused, then she incurs no guilt either way. But if, however, a living soul succumbs to the tempter, then that is regarded as a sin. Therefore Scripture told the soul not to leave her place when the spirit ascends upon her; this is so she will not provide her weapons of iniquity* for sin when temptation threatens.

2. One must note that it says, *If the spirit of him who has power ascends upon you.** Obviously a wicked spirit

*Eccl 10:4

*Rom 6:19

*Rom 6:13

*Eccl 10:4

cannot [act] against us unless it has been ordered or permitted. So even though a wicked spirit's will is always evil, it is never powerful unless justified. For indeed, his will is evil in and of itself, but it has no power from anywhere other than God. Nevertheless, the Lord always regulates any power, lest of course, out of the wickedness of will, a devil punish more than is merited by those who are to be punished. And let that be enough said about the lower position.

With regard to this higher position, when tempted by a devil, it is understood that one should not abandon the calm of mind that it has in God, but from wherever a devil might tempt, the mind firmly established in God remains unwavering. This last sentence applies to those who have been perfected, who can say with Elijah, *As the Lord lives, the God of Israel in whose sight I stand.** Also that saying from the apostle John: *because as He is, we also are in this world.** This sentence, I say, applies to those who have been perfected, who in their way of life already to some degree resemble the condition of eternity.

*1 Kgs 17:1

*1 John 4:17

Sermo 85

Concerning the Fall of a Tree or Death of a Person

*Eccl 11:3

*Jer 1:14
*Mark 8:24

*Ps 40:9

*1 Pet 2:11

If a tree fall to the south or to the north, in whatever place it shall fall, there shall it be. The south, with its warmth and mildness, usually has a good meaning in sacred Scripture. *From the north*, to be sure, *every evil spreads forth.** Further on, someone sees human beings as trees.* Therefore a tree is cut down in death, and wherever it has fallen, there it shall be, because God shall judge you in that place where he has found you. It shall be in that place, I say, unchangeably and intractably. Let the tree see where it is going to fall before it falls, because after it has fallen, *it shall rise again no more,** nor even turn itself.

If you wish to know in which direction a tree is going to fall, then pay attention to its branches. The direction in which there is a greater abundance and preponderance of branches—have no doubt that it is going to fall in that direction, if only it is then cut down. Our branches are in fact our desires, by which we are extended to the south if they are spiritual, but to the north if they are carnal. Certainly the middle of the trunk reveals which desires weigh more. In fact, the desires that weigh more heavily will drag the body along with themselves.

For thus our body is between the spirit, which we should serve, and *carnal desires which war against the soul,** or the powers of darkness,* as if you set a beast of burden between a robber and a peasant. Whatever the robber threatens, whatever he might stab at, if he will not lead the beast, then the defenseless farmer conquers the armored bandit. So however much the spiteful one rages, however much perverse desires torment, if the soul claims her vessel* for herself, then we must believe that she has conquered, just as the apostle says, so that sin might not reign in our mortal body.* And as he says in another place, *For as you have yielded your members to serve iniquity unto iniquity, so now yield your members to serve justice unto sanctification.**

*Col 1:13

*1 Thess 4:4

*Rom 6:12

*Rom 6:19

Sermo 86

The Difference between Creature and Creator

1. **Y**ou have created all things in measure and number and weight.* This saying points to a distinguishing characteristic of the divine essence. I mean, creatures have been made in weight and measure and number; the Creator alone lacks all these. Weight is considered in the worth of matter; however, worth consists in the appearance or utility of matter, for out of these one estimates how much each single matter has value. Therefore it was made *in weight*, which can be compared to matter of the same type, either according to more or according to less or according to equality. Weight, which every matter has, can be judged according to its value.

*Wis 11:21

However, measure is considered in place and in time. Because if we accept place as relating to physical matters alone, then the measure of incorporeal realities will be in time and not in place. For a soul cannot be in a physical place. Even the body itself, about which a soul seems more concerned, is not the soul's place. For how is a soul enclosed by a body, a soul that thus invigorates its exterior as well as its interior? Just as soul is found in surface of skin, so also in internal organs.

2. Inasmuch as from carnal affection and the experience of bodies, the soul goes so astray that she does not know herself except to imagine herself as corporeal. In

fact, where her treasure is, there also is her heart,* and by this she senses what she loves. If indeed she is both bound by and smeared over with earthy feelings, then she cannot contemplate her own face. She is stuck in deep mud,* and without seeing herself, she thinks her appearance to be that clay image that she carries.* But that is not at all the case. And the soul's measure is considered in a way other than by place. Indeed, for each single matter its place is the limit of its own substance. But the substance of a soul is in reason, in memory, in counsel, in judgment, and in the other similar powers, all of which are enclosed by their own limit. It is *in measure*, therefore, that every spirit has been made, except the Divine, because a spirit's reason and memory and all the others have their own measure. All things have been made *in number*, either according to composition of parts, as they are bodies, or according to variety and changeability, as they are also incorporeal. It is God alone into whom neither weight nor measure nor number falls at all. God is unique; there is nothing in the same category to which he can be compared. He alone is unique, totally beyond estimation, eternal and also immeasurable, indivisible, and utterly invariable.

*Matt 6:21

*Ps 68:3
*1 Cor 15:49

Sermo 87

Concerning Three Kisses

*Song 1:1

1. *Let him kiss me with the kiss of his mouth.** There are three kisses: first of feet, second of hands, third of mouth. When we are first converted, we kiss the Lord's feet. Moreover, the Lord has two feet:

*Ps 24:10

mercy and truth.* God imprints both of these feet on the hearts of those who are converting. And any sinner, if truly converted, embraces both feet. For if sinners were to accept mercy alone without truth, then they would fall through presumption. And in turn, if sinners were to accept truth without mercy, then likewise they would be lost through despair. But in order for us to become saved, we prostrate ourselves humbly at both feet, so that we condemn sins through truth and we hope for pardon through mercy, and this is the first kiss.

The second kiss happens when we aspire to good works after the first kiss of repentance. That is to say, we then kiss the Lord's hands when we offer to him our good works or when we accept from him gifts of the virtues. But in fact, the third kiss then happens when, after grief of penitence has been consumed, after gifts of virtues have been received, the mind, inspired by desire for heaven and impatient for love, desires to be introduced to the secret joys of the interior bedroom. With sweet sighs interrupting the soul's voice, with devout affection of heart, she chants, *Your face,*

*Ps 26:8

O Lord, will I seek.* And so out of vehement desire the Bridegroom becomes present to one's mind, he whom one so loves, so desires, for whom one so sighs. And so the first kiss happens in forgiveness of sins and is called reconciling. The second happens in gifts of virtues and is called rewarding. The third happens in contemplation of the heavenly and is called contemplative.

2. One should also know that there are two types of contemplation. I mean, there are certain people who ascend and fall, but others who are snatched up and descend. They ascend just like those about whom it is written, *When they knew God, they did not glorify him as God nor give thanks.** They gave no thanks, because they attributed what God revealed to them to their own powers and talent.* Therefore their fall followed: *And they became vain in their thoughts. For professing themselves to be wise, they became fools.** The elect, however, are snatched up, just like Paul and those like him. But they also descend so they can tell little ones*—in whatever way they can comprehend—what they have seen by transcendence of mind.

*Rom 1:21

*Rom 1:19

*Rom 1:21, 22

*1 Cor 3:1

Paul is snatched up when he says, *Whether we be transcending in mind, it is for God.* He descends when he says, *Or whether we be sober, it is for you.** A perfected soul desires to be snatched up by this latter type of contemplation into the purest embraces of her Bridegroom, saying, *Let him kiss me with the kiss of his mouth.* It is as if she were to say, "I cannot by my own powers or by diligence or by merits rise to my Lord's joys that should be contemplated, but *let him kiss me with the kiss of his mouth.* That is, let it happen by his grace, not through doctrine, nor through nature, but through his grace *let him kiss me with the kiss of his mouth.*"*

*2 Cor 5:13

*Song 1:1

Moreover, Scripture elegantly expresses in a wonderful way the grace of the actor and the deed and the manner of deed. For when he says *let him kiss*, grace of the deed is revealed. What is more, when he subjoins *with the kiss*, the deed itself, that is, contemplation, is designated. But when he adds *of his mouth*, the manner of deed, by what manner contemplation happens, of course, is vividly expressed. Indeed, by *mouth*, the Word is understood.

3. Contemplation, moreover, happens by God's Word condescending to human nature through grace, and exaltation of human nature to the Word himself through divine love. It should not seem absurd to anyone if we make this distinction in contemplation of God's Word since the gospel also testifies that the same Word's incarnation happened in the same order. As a matter of fact, in that gospel, grace is sent ahead when the Virgin is greeted by the angel: *Hail*, he says, *full of grace.** And whose grace it is, and how great the grace itself is, he subjoins, saying, *The Lord is with you.* And he also inserts the act of that same grace when he says, *Blessed is the fruit of your womb.**

*Luke 1:28

*Luke 1:42

The fruit of your womb is in fact the Word's incarnation. Truly the manner of so great a deed is taught clearly where it says, *The Holy Spirit shall come upon you, and the power of the most High shall overshadow you.** From these deeds of the Word, either by these that we drew from the gospel or by those from the Song of Songs that we explained, it is evident both that the incarnation happened only by the abundance of divine grace and that the former, that is, contemplation, never happened by human will but can only come about by divine gift.

*Luke 1:35

4. One must also note that this contemplation is distinguished in three ways according to various situations of the times. And indeed it is first called food, second drink, third intoxication. Thus also, in what follows, the elect are invited by the Bridegroom's voice saying, *Eat, O friends, and drink and be inebriated, my dearly beloved.** First they eat while they still live on in corruptible flesh. But afterward, having laid aside the body and been conveyed into heaven, they are now said to drink the same that they had previously eaten, because

*Song 5:1

now they contemplate by sight* without toil. [They contemplate] that which they had previously believed through faith while they were living in the body and were sojourning away from the Lord,* while they fed on their own bread by the sweat of their own face,* just as we more easily partake what we drink than what we chew, because in food sometimes there is toil; in drink is a smooth swallowing.

*2 Cor 5:7
*2 Cor 5:6
*Gen 3:19

Therefore, saints who are put in this position can indeed drink, but they cannot be inebriated, because they are somehow delayed from the most perfect contemplation of divinity while they still wait for resurrection of their own body in the final age. After the body's resurrection, the body so clings to the mind and the mind to God* that there is no longer anything that can call it away* from the internal intoxication of contemplation. And so at the first invitation, in which they eat, they are called friends, that is beloved; in the second, by which they drink, more beloved; at the third, in which they are inebriated, most beloved.

*1 Cor 6:17
*Song 5:1

5. *For your breasts are better than wine.** The breasts of the bridegroom are two: one of congratulation, another of compassion. Wine here is taken to mean worldly knowledge, concerning which Scripture says, *Their wine is the gall of dragons and the venom of asps, which is incurable.**

*Song 1:1

*Deut 32:33

6. *Smelling sweet of the best ointments.** When it says *of the best ointments*, it implies that some ointments are good and others are better, all of which are surpassed by these best ointments. Therefore we say that there are three types of ointments. The first happens by recollection of sins, when we feel remorse for them and seek pardon. And this ointment is good, because God does not spurn a humble and contrite heart.* Moreover, this ointment is poured upon the Lord's feet and there receives a reward, indeed forgiveness of sins, when the Lord says, *Many sins are forgiven her because she has loved much.**

*Song 1:2

*Luke 7:38; Ps 50:19

*Luke 7:47

The second ointment happens out of recollection of God's kindnesses. And rightly this is poured upon his head,* because virtues are referred to God, by whom they exist. This ointment, moreover, is already more dear, because Scripture says this about it: *Why was this ointment wasted? For this ointment might have been sold for more than three hundred denaria and given to the poor.** But the Lord approves this waste when he says, *Let her alone. Why do you molest her? For the poor you have always with you, but me you have not always.** He not only approves, but he even rewards her when he says, *Amen I say to you, wherever this gospel shall be preached in the whole world, this also which she has done shall be told in her memory.**

*Mark 14:3

*Mark 14:4–5

*Mark 14:6–7

*Matt 26:13

The third ointment is composed of precious aromatic spices, just as it has been written about certain holy women who *bought sweet spices so to come and anoint Jesus.** But any pouring out or loss of this third ointment does not happen, because the Lord willed that it not be poured over his dead body but be saved for his living body,* that is, the Holy Church.

*Mark 16:1

*John 12:7

And so the first ointment is called ointment of compunction, and it is consumed in the fire of contrition. The second ointment of devotion is also consumed in the fire of charity. The third is called ointment of loving-kindness; it is not consumed but preserved whole.

Sermo 88

Concerning Four Ways the Holy Spirit Works in Us

1. It is as if there are two [facts] about Christ, one unknown to us, I mean of course his divine generation, about which it is written, *Who shall declare his generation?** The other fact is known, that is, his divine works. So also [two facts] about the Holy Spirit, one of which is hidden from our senses, that is, how he proceeds from Father and Son, since he is equal and co-eternal with the same Father and Son. The other fact, however, is manifested by his teaching, by which means he clearly works his grace in us.

*Isa 53:8

Naturally the work of the Holy Spirit is double. I mean, he does one work within us for our sake; he does another for sake of our neighbors. For our sake, that is, for our benefit, he works within us first compunction, by burning up sins; second devotion, by anointing and healing wounds; third by creating understanding (he encourages and strengthens us with bread, as it were);* fourth by increasing these gifts in many ways, and by pouring in love, he inebriates us as with wine. The remaining gifts, that is, wisdom, knowledge, counsel,* and the like, are given to us for the benefit of others.* Thus the apostle, when he spoke about the distribution of gifts, does not say simply, *To one* wisdom *is given through the Spirit*, to another knowledge, but he added, saying, *the word of wisdom, the word of knowledge,** in order

*Ps 103:15

*Isa 11:2
*1 Cor 12:7

*1 Cor 12:8

to show that gifts of this sort are given on account of others, so that others are indeed edified.

2. In these works one must beware a double danger, lest either we share with neighbors the gifts that are given for our sake or we reserve for ourselves gifts that are given for sake of neighbors. For if we take what is for the benefit of others and we retain it only for ourselves, then we have not charity,* and it is said to us, *Wisdom that is hidden and treasure that is not seen, what benefit is there in them both?* On the other hand, if we wish to make known God's gifts to human beings rather than please God in the secrecy of our hearts, then we lose humility, and rightly we are rebuked by that voice, *What do you have that you did not receive?* Thus we are endangered both ways, the latter by losing humility, the former by losing charity. And who can become saved without humility or charity?*

*1 Cor 13:1; 1 John 3:17

*Sir 20:32

*1 Cor 4:7

*Mark 10:26

Therefore, the order of our progress is proper, that is, we first strive to be fulfilled by those gifts, I mean compunction and the other virtues, and then if through grace of the Holy Spirit the others increase, that is, wisdom and knowledge,* then we take care for them to be distributed to our neighbors. So to be sure we shall obtain that gift of the Holy Spirit that is called discernment of spirits,* if also that which only pertains to us we reserve for us, and those gifts that were assigned to the benefit of others we give generously to ourselves and to neighbors.

*Isa 33:6

*1 Cor 12:10

Sermo 89

Concerning the Holy Spirit's Kiss

1. *Let him kiss me with the kiss of his mouth.** The mouth of the Father is understood to be the Son. *No one, however, knows the Son except the Father; and neither does any one know the Father, except the Son and to whomever the Son wills to reveal.** But truly, to whomever that revelation happens, revelation of either the Father or the Son, it does not happen except through the Holy Spirit. Hence it is that, when Peter had said to the Lord, *You are Christ, the Son of the living God,** he answered, *Blessed are you, Simon Bar-Jonah,* which is interpreted as "son of a dove," *because flesh and blood have not revealed it to you, but my Father who is in heaven.** And the apostle, when he had put forth, *What eye has not seen, nor ear heard, neither has it entered into the heart of a human being what God has prepared for those who love him,** at once added, *But to us God has revealed through his Spirit.**

    Therefore the bride seems to have grace of the Holy Spirit, through which she acknowledges the Son equal to the Father. Nor does she say, "Let him kiss me with his own mouth," which is only for the Father to say, not for any creature at all—a creature of course can in no way be equal to the Father—but *with the kiss of his mouth.* Furthermore, the mutual kiss belongs to both the one who kisses and the one who is kissed. If therefore the Father and Son kiss among themselves, what is their kiss if not the Holy Spirit?

*Song 1:1

*Matt 11:27

*Matt 16:16

*Matt 16:17
*1 Cor 2:9
*1 Cor 2:10

2. And so the bride burns to be kissed with this kiss, saying, *Let him kiss me with the kiss of his mouth.** Even Paul testifies that she has received this kiss when he says, *Because you are his children, God has sent the Spirit of his Son into our hearts, crying Abba, Father.** Even the Savior himself promised this kiss when he exhorted his disciples to the urgency of prayer: *If you then*, he says, *being evil, know to give good gifts to your children, how much more will your Father give the good Spirit to those who ask him?** From the impression of this kiss, the rational soul receives from her bridegroom, from God's Word, knowledge and love of virtue, which presses upon her like two lips: the virtue of God and the wisdom of God.* Accordingly, wisdom confers knowledge and virtue confers love.

*Song 1:1

*Gal 4:6

*Luke 11:13

*1 Cor 1:24

Similarly, the soul herself also has two lips with which she kisses her bridegroom, that is, reason and will. It is for reason to gain wisdom, the will to gain virtue. If reason alone were to gain knowledge of wisdom and the will did not have love of virtue, then it would not be a full kiss. Or if the will alone obtained love and reason gained insufficient knowledge, then likewise it would be half full. Then truly the kiss is full and perfect when both wisdom enlightens and virtue moves the will.

Sermo 90

Concerning the Lord's Two Figurative Feet and Three Mystical Ointments

1. There are two feet of God, mercy and judgment.* With these feet, he continually walks around and through* spiritual minds, *rejoicing like a giant to run the way.** If, however, his feet are like that, then with good reason he says about them, *I will dwell in them and walk among them.** Therefore, the sinful soul anoints these feet with the first ointment, which is called compunction. In fact, Mary, who was a sinner, anointed Jesus' feet.* Certainly this is no ordinary ointment about which is written, *And the house was filled with the odor of the ointment.** No wonder, when even in the heavens fragrance of such an ointment is sensed, as Truth confirms when she says that there is *joy in heaven over one sinner who does penance.**

*Ps 32:5
*Job 1:7
*Ps 18:6

*2 Cor 6:16

*Luke 7:37-38

*John 12:3

*Luke 15:7

Yet however precious this ointment may seem, still it is valued as common and cheap compared to that which is called devotion; it is accomplished by remembering divine benefits, by which the Lord's head is anointed.* In fact, concerning the former it is said, *A contrite and humbled heart, O God, you will not despise.** Concerning the latter truth, *The sacrifice of praise shall glorify me.** You anoint his head by this when you thank God for his gifts, since indeed *the head of Christ is God.** Therefore the divinity in Christ is anointed as often as

*Mark 14:3
*Ps 50:19

*Ps 49:23
*1 Cor 11:3

we remember his benefits so as to praise him, just as it is not so much his divinity as his humanity that we must ponder when we call to mind our sins rather than his gifts.

2. For in taking up flesh, he is recognized as having received those two feet (that is, *mercy and judgment*)* to this end: so that a sinner who does not have access to his head (that is, to divinity) would approach his feet (that is, humanity). For unless that foot that we have said is mercy pertains to the human being that has been assumed, Paul would not have said about it, *Tempted in all things like as we are, without sin,** so that he would become *merciful.** And if judgment does not pertain equally to the person, then the God Man himself would not have said about himself, *And he has given him power to make judgment because he is the Son of Man.** And so the sinner no longer hesitates to approach the feet of the man of sorrows,* those feet of knowing infirmity, and he says confidently, "Now with confidence we also approach the throne of his grace."* *For we have not a high priest who does not know to have compassion on our infirmities.** Therefore the sinful woman [approached] his feet; the justified woman approached to anoint his head.

Moreover, the ointment of the head should be valued as so much more precious than the ointment that was put on his feet, insofar as the types [of ingredients] that compose it are more precious than those [that anoint the feet]. Of course, we easily and without toil obtain these in our region. We are in fact all sinners. On the other hand, with difficulty and from very far away, namely, from God's Paradise,* we import ingredients, I mean *every best gift and every perfect gift is from above, coming down from the Father of lights.** What finally would be more excellent than this sort of ointment when even the apostles are said to have murmured about pouring it out, saying, *To what purpose is this waste? For this could have been sold and given to the poor.**

*Ps 32:5

*Heb 4:15
*Heb 2:17

*John 5:27

*Isa 53:3

*Heb 4:16
*Heb 4:15

*Ezek 28:13

*Jas 1:17

*Matt 26:8-9

3. But perhaps even now, when it seems that some people are at leisure for God, and such people might have such great devotion and grace that they are properly believed to anoint Christ's head, remaining continually in holy calmness and giving thanks and enjoying divine contemplation, then there is no shortage of people who say that this is a waste. And with justice (as it seems to them), they complain with a mutter because they who could be useful to many others rest for themselves. They complain not because they envy holiness, but rather because they care about charity. Yet Charity, God, often shows consideration to a soul of this kind whom he sees enjoying spiritual devotion, and especially if he knows her to be the type who is still a woman of timidity and feebleness, and he has not yet made her into a perfect man.* For God, who regards the heart, certainly discerns better than human beings who see only the outward appearance* and judge according to appearance.* *Eph 4:13
*1 Sam 16:7
*John 7:24

This is obvious when people pay too little attention to the fact that to rest devoutly and to be occupied fruitfully are not equally easy; to be humbly available and to be usefully present, to be ruled without complaint and to rule without blame, to obey voluntarily and to command discreetly, finally to be good among good people and to be good among bad people, or, more correctly, even to be peaceful among sons of peace* and to be seen as a peacemaker to those who hate peace [are not equally easy].* Jesus therefore knows who are* suitable to be entangled in responsibilities and who are not,* so on behalf of such a delicate soul, who he senses is still not quite sufficient for managing business because of her youthful tenderness, against those who feel otherwise and who so condemn her calmness as being fruitless, although with good zeal not according to knowledge,* Jesus answers them with effect, *Why do you trouble this woman?*‡ For even if, one

*Luke 10:6
*Ps 119:7
*John 6:65
*2 Tim 2:4

*Rom 10:2;
see RB 72
‡Matt 26:10

must admit, you try to bring her to something better, it is nevertheless a good work that she has done for me.* In the meantime, allow her to do the good that she can* while she is not yet able [to do] better. For I myself know that she is still a woman.

When, however, by a change of the Most High's right hand,* she has been made a man from a woman‡ (which also cannot be hidden from me whenever it shall happen, because it shall be moved forth by my calling forth, and also it shall be maintained by my preserving), then *the iniquity of a man* shall be *better than a woman doing a good turn* at present.* Thus I hope for that better, and in the meantime I do not spurn in the least this good. Nor do I consider the pouring out of this ointment a waste, in which both the devotion of the woman is indicated and my burial is prefigured.* Hither she approaches because so widely and all around she disperses her perfume, in such a way that wherever this gospel shall be proclaimed, what she has done also must be told in her memory.*

4. Now let us come to the third ointment. Clearly, when comparing either of the two previously discussed ointments, the second is recognized beyond every doubt to be better and by far more excellent than the first. It seems a wonder, however, if some third ointment can be found that ought deservedly to be placed before both, on a par with that best ointment, which, as the bride boasts, scents her breasts.* Otherwise they are not the best if they do not also exceed the better ointments, just as those that do not surpass the good ointments are not truly called better. What is more, that second ointment, which anoints the head, was found to be of such great superiority that I do not say that scarcely any riches are preferred to it; rather it seems that they cannot so much as be compared to it.

I myself, however, would not believe that the bride has lied, for certainly she is the kind who has Truth himself as a bridegroom, whose words she also speaks, who certainly, just as he refuses to deceive, also cannot be deceived. In any case, she who lies to Truth desires and sighs in vain to be united with embraces. For what fellowship has falsehood with truth?* Rather, in fact, Truth destroys all who speak falsehood.* *2 Cor 6:14 *Ps 5:7

5. Perhaps if we search in the gospel we shall find that the image of this has precedent. It says, *Mary Magdalene and Mary, mother of James and Salome, bought sweet spices, so that coming, they might anoint Jesus.** In the introduction to this chapter, don't you see how much even this material ointment should be valued, of which not one or two could suffice for combining the aromatic spices? One woman brought the first ointment; one also brought the second. The three came together, moreover, to combine and prepare this ointment, so that, clearly, at the same time they bought what each one could not by herself, and so *coming they anointed Jesus*. Not only his feet or his head alone, but, *coming*, it says, that *they might anoint Jesus*, that is his whole body. *Mark 16:1

But notice that Christ refused to allow the waste of such expensive ointment to happen, because not finding the body, they brought the ointment back, and they were commanded to provide for the living what they had prepared for the dead. So they also did; when they immediately reported the joy of the resurrection, they took care to soothe the sad hearts* of the disciples, who without doubt were Christ's members,* and were living members. Members indeed, whom if Christ had not loved more than his crucified body, he would not have traded his body to be crucified for them. It is clear, therefore, that this last ointment surpasses in excellence the first two, just as Christ holds as more lovable that Body that is the church,* to which this last ointment is offered, than his own body, which he did not want to be anointed by this last ointment and also wanted to offer for the redemption of his other Body (the church). *Luke 24:17 *1 Cor 6:15 *Col 1:24; Eph 5:27

Sermo 91

Concerning Three Types of Shoots

*Song 4:13
*Heb 12:22

1. **Y**our shoots are a paradise.* This is the voice of that heavenly Jerusalem* rejoicing with this one that sojourns on earth. There are, however, three shoots. First are those of penitents joined by marriage in the world. Second are those of ascetic converts in a cloister. Third are those of prelates, who preach and pray for God's people. Concerning the first shoot, that is, repentance, the angels, for whom *there is joy over one sinner doing penance,** say, *Who is she who goes up by the desert like a pillar of smoke from aromatic spices of myrrh and of frankincense and of all the powders of the perfumer?** This soul who repents is said to ascend *by the desert*—that is, a land where there is no road and no water*—by remembering her sins. *She goes up like a pillar of smoke* by humbly confessing the same sins.

*Luke 15:10

*Song 3:6

*Ps 62:3

Any confession is rightly said to become *like a pillar of smoke* because, through many kinds of sins, it is like smoke drawn from a thurible through many small holes.* And one should note that although smoke might never have splendor, nevertheless it can sometimes have an odor. Moreover, insofar as this smoke of confession has a certain odor of piety, it is acknowledged by the words that follow: *from aromatic spices of myrrh and of frankincense and of all the powders of the perfumer.** Myrrh and frankincense should always accompany confession, that is, mortification of flesh and

*Rev 8:4-5

*Song 3:6

prayer of heart. Indeed, either of them without the other is of little or no profit. For if anyone should mortify the flesh and merely pretend to pray, then she is proud, and it is said to her, *Shall I eat the flesh of bulls? Or shall I drink the blood of goats?** Likewise if she has prayed and neglected to mortify her flesh, then she will hear, *Why do you call me "Lord, Lord" and not do what I say?** And elsewhere: *One who turns away her ear so not to hear the law, her prayer shall be accursed.** Therefore each supports the other, since it is agreed that one without the other is rejected.

*Ps 49:13

*Luke 6:46
*Prov 28:9

2. It follows: *And of all the powders of the perfumer.** After recollection and confession of sins, after mortification and prayer, then fruit of alms should be produced. These alms are well called *powder*, because they are made from earthly substance, and *the perfumer*, because they emit the sweetest odor. Hence the angel said to Cornelius, who acted well, *Your prayers and your alms have ascended for a memorial in the Lord's sight.** For if alms did not give off some pleasant scent, then by no means would they ascend *in the Lord's sight*. Therefore it even says, *of all the powders of the perfumer*, because not only the large but even the smallest sins whatever are to be expunged by confession and washed away by compunction. Let this suffice about the first shoot.

*Song 3:6

*Acts 10:4

3. The second shoot is the life of ascetics in the cloister or hermitage. In this shoot there occurs no mention of desert or smoke or repentance, but rather of splendor's light and virtue. In fact, an angelic voice sings in praise of this shoot, *Who is she who comes forth like the dawn rising, fair as the moon, chosen as the sun, terrible as an army set in array?** A triple virtue is shown in these words: humility, chastity, charity. Dawn is of course the end of night and the beginning of light. Night moreover signifies the life of sinners. Light signifies the life of the just. Therefore, dawn, which chases away darkness and announces light, rightly designates humility. That

*Song 6:9

is because just as the dawn divides day and night, humility divides the just and the sinner.* For from this source, that is, from humility, any just person begins and thereafter finishes. Thus also the dawn itself is said to be rising, that is, as the structure of virtues rises by humility, it is erected on its own foundation, as it were.

So, in order to show her humility, it says, *like the dawn rising*, but that which follows, *fair as the moon*, demonstrates chastity. What is more, the moon is said not to have its own splendor from itself but to draw it from the sun, and the more the moon is placed in full view of the sun, the more a larger part of the moon shines by the light of the same sun. Similarly, if a holy congregation or any faithful soul to be considered is offered to the gazes of the True Sun, then without doubt she immediately receives from the vision of that Sun a certain grace of beauty and a charm of chastity. So it happens that from his light that increases and finishes, she is carried even to perfection, so that what follows it is rightly said about her.

4. *Chosen as the sun.** In what way *as the sun*? Is it because *the just shine like the sun, in the kingdom of their Father*?* But in that place, how will they shall shine like the sun, if not by the splendor of their nuptial garments?* For those to be dressed were in this garment while still on earth, those to whom it was said, *But you stay in the city till you be dressed with power from on high.** Those who have been dressed in this virtue of charity that that nuptial garment signifies and have it properly arranged on themselves shall without a doubt be *terrible as an army set in array* to their enemies.* For if people lack charity, then demons do not care how many other virtues they have. But when demons see charity that is *set in array*,* then they are at once driven headlong into flight. *Chosen as the sun*, as it says, can also be understood as the perseverance that belongs only to the chosen ones. Moreover, in the phrase that follows, *terrible as an*

*Gen 1:4–5

*Song 6:9

*Matt 13:43

*Matt 22:11

*Luke 24:49

*Song 6:3

*Song 2:4

army set in array, is discretion, mother of virtues,* by which demons are terrified and put to flight while virtues are acquired and preserved. Many other things can also be fittingly understood and said about this second shoot, but let it suffice to have said these few words about many aspects.

5. The third shoot pertains to holy preachers, concerning whose life and teaching that admiring voice is now put forth: *Who is this who comes up from the desert, flowing with delights, leaning upon her beloved?** It had been said about the first shoot, *she who goes up by the desert.** However, it says about this third shoot, *she who comes up from the desert*, because, no doubt, in that desert thorns through which the penitents march prick them, but here the teachers have trampled with sublime intellect anything they have been able to snatch away from the world. That is why it said, *from the desert, flowing with delights*.

But one must ask, "What are those delights with which they are said to flow?" And who is that beloved? Or why are they said to lean on him? And, in fact, they should not be valued as trivial, since they are called delights by heavenly citizens. Indeed such delights are of the mind not of the stomach, of the soul not of the body, of the spirit not of the flesh, of reason not of sensuality, of the interior not of the exterior person. If I may describe these partially and briefly, they are a copious inflow of spiritual grace. Blessed is that soul for whom such a grace is poured in, who is preceded in blessings of heavenly sweetness,* so that she becomes God's temple and the Holy Spirit's oracle. Certainly *riches of salvation, wisdom, and knowledge** cannot be lacking to this kind of soul, and the best treasure of the same salvation is *fear of the Lord.**

When she has overflowed with these delights and been filled, she will now exalt the Lord in the assemblies and praise him in the throne of elders.* What she

*RB 64.19

*Song 8:5
*Song 3:6

*Ps 20:4

*Isa 33:6

*Isa 33:6

*Ps 106:32

has heard in bedrooms she shall proclaim on the rooftops,* and thus she shall flow with delights. For it has been said that to flow is to persevere in the word of doctrine, to shine with the example of life, vehemently to practice spiritual work.

6. But it is necessary in all these for a soul to seek not her own glory but that of her creator. For he is her beloved, concerning whom it is written, *I to my beloved, and my beloved to me,** and concerning whom the Father says, *This is my beloved Son; hear him.** One must lean upon him, clearly, so that a soul's work may be ascribed to the help of his grace, by whom all things, through whom all things, and to whom all things are rendered.* Why however one should lean upon him [is that] the beloved himself, *who teaches the human being knowledge,** teaches us more fully. He says to his disciples, whom he filled with delights of this kind, *I am the vine, you the branches.** *As the branch cannot bear fruit unless it remains on the vine, so neither can you unless you remain in me.** And again he says, *Without me, you can do nothing.** And also, if he were to say it openly, "If you wish to flow with delights, then lean on me."

But now let us see how they flow and lean. Let that one outstanding preacher come into the middle on behalf of all.* Yes, most blessed Paul, flow with your delights! Surely when you had proclaimed the Gospel *from Jerusalem round about as far as Illyricum,** when you had delivered the Gospel without charge,* when you had paid out the sacrament and heavenly treasures of faith *to Greeks and to barbarians, to the wise and to the unwise,** as does a *wise and faithful steward,‡ when you had borne about in your mortal body the mortification of Jesus,*#* and among your many and wonderful mighty deeds that you were able to do and we can scarcely describe, and that with every authority, without any arrogance, when you were the least of the apostles* in your own judgment, you nevertheless dared to say, *The grace of*

*Luke 12:3

*Song 6:2
*Luke 9:35

*Heb 2:10

*Ps 93:10

*John 15:5
*John 15:4
*John 15:5

*1 Tim 2:7

*Rom 15:19
*1 Cor 9:18

*Rom 1:14
‡Luke 12:42
#2 Cor 4:10

*1 Cor 15:9

God in me has not been empty, but I have labored more abundantly than all of them.* They are great and delicious delights, thus I say! But so as not to lose them, lean on your beloved! Lean! *Yet not I*, he says, *but the grace of God with me.** Flow again, because as I might admit, such delights give great pleasure. *I can do all things*, he says. A second time, lean! *On him*, he says, *who strengthens me.** Likewise the apostle says, *He who glories, let him glory in the Lord.** That is, one who flows with delights, let him lean on his beloved.

*1 Cor 15:10

*1 Cor 15:10

*Phil 4:13
*2 Cor 10:17

7. We have said these things, with the Lord's help, about three shoots as a representation of three types of human being whom the holy church maintains in this life. According to Ezekiel, Noah, Daniel, and Job* also correspond to these shoots, although they could suitably be assigned to each and any one who has been perfected. And among these, likewise, the first shoot is repentance, the second justice, the third doctrine. For they are first converted by doing repentance; second, they practice justice by living rightly; third, if they have progressed well, justice itself, which they keep by their life, they teach by word. But because vices set traps for virtues, and they are positioned nearby so that anyone who has deviated from virtue runs into their traps, it is necessary that repentance be without shame, lest of course one be ashamed to confess sins that have been committed. Let justice beware of pretense. Let the prelate eliminate self-glorification.* For where there is greatness of gifts, there also is greatness of hazard.

*Ezek 14:14

*2 Cor 12:7

Sermo 92

Concerning Three Introductions

1. **C**ome *into my garden, my sister, my spouse.** It is said in another place, *The king has brought me into his storeroom.** It is said in another place, *into his bedroom.* This triple introduction is made for a rational soul by her spouse, by God's Word, of course, according to the triple sense of Scriptures: historical, moral, mystical. In the *garden* is the historical sense, in *his storeroom* is the moral sense, in *his bedroom* is the mystical.*

In the garden, that is, in history, the triple operation of the Trinity is comprised: creation of heaven and earth, reconciliation of heaven and earth, consolation of heaven and earth. Father has created, Son has reconciled, Holy Spirit has consoled. And one is a time of creation, another is a time of reconciliation, another of consolation, just as in a garden one time is for planting, another for gathering fruit, another for eating. Creation and reconciliation are of the present; consolation is of the age to come. In the beginning of time the Father created; in the fullness of time the Son reconciled;* after every present time the Holy Spirit will console.

The Son has said about the Father, *My Father works until now,** and concerning himself he adds, *And I work.*†
Similarly the Holy Spirit will also be able to say in the consummation of the age, "The Father and Son work until now, and from now onward I myself work." Then indeed the Spirit will have already made our bodies

*Song 5:1

*Song 1:3

*Song 4:12, 15, 16

*Gal 4:4

*John 5:17
‡John 5:17

spiritual, and the body will have been joined to spirit, and spirit to God. Then the same Holy Spirit shall thus console this very work, so then in turn, without any moment of intervening time, what was written might happen: *One who is joined to the Lord is one spirit.** The Old Testament instructs us about creation and promises reconciliation. The New Testament presents reconciliation and promises consolation.

*1 Cor 6:17

2. The second introduction is into the storeroom. This storeroom contains moral knowledge and has three separate quarters. The first is called aromatic, the second is fruitful, the third is a wine cellar. In the first are those who conduct themselves well with prelates; in the second are those who [conduct themselves well] with equals; in the third those who [conduct themselves well] with subordinates. So there is the first cell* of discipline, the second of nature, third of grace. For whoever strives to attain the pinnacle of perfect conversion first becomes a disciple and enters into the cell of discipline, in which one's morals are arranged into various virtues by a master, just as perfumers compose aromatic spices from various types. Thus this cell is also called aromatic,* because, as long as any such religious willingly embrace the labor of discipline, they pour out the best odor of imitation to others by their example.

*Lat *cella*, "storeroom"

*Song 4:16

Thence it follows that they enter the second cell, of nature, seeing that they can easily be compatible with the other fellow disciples who have learned to break their own will under a master. And this cell, where one lives in common with others, is aptly called the cell of nature, because nature begets all human beings as equals, but she has either put some in command of others on account of merit or made others subordinate. It is also called fruitful,* because it is of great utility if they would pass on the grace that they receive to one another.* So it is written, *A brother who helps his brother shall be exalted like a fortified city.** And likewise the

*Song 4:13

*1 Pet 4:10
*Prov 18:19

prophet says, *Behold how good and how pleasant it is for brothers to dwell in unity!** *Ps 132:1

But truly when they have been fully perfected in this second cell of nature, then at last they can enter the third, which is the cell of grace. So now too, those who have lived with the others justly and without complaint can be in charge of others who are to be trained in religion. And this cell is also called a wine cellar, as those who are in charge of others in this regimen do indeed burn with charity. It is also called the cell of grace, which is a name it could share with the other two cells. For both discipline and a life in fellowship are gifts of grace. This cell, however, specifically claims that name for itself, because indeed it is easier to be a subject or a member; on the other hand, it is rare and difficult for anyone to be capable of receiving the charge of others' regimen in a beneficial way.

3. In these three cells the morals of all human beings are reformed and sustained. That is, human beings are either prelates or equals or subordinates. But however they are chosen from the gardens, whatever is better is put in the storerooms, where they also have particular places in which they are preserved. Thus the moral sense is drawn from the historical and hidden, as it were, in the storeroom where every human life is instructed. In fact, prelates read in Scripture how they should present themselves toward subordinates, seeing that it says to them, *Not lording it over the clergy, but being made a pattern of the flock.** And again, *Not because we exercise dominion over your faith, but we are helpers of your joy.** And the Lord says in the gospel, *The good shepherd gives his life for his sheep.**

*1 Pet 5:3
*2 Cor 1:23
*John 10:11

Those who are equals also find in the same Scripture how they conduct themselves with others when they read, *Bear one another's burdens and so you shall fulfill the law of Christ.** And again, *Anticipating one another in showing honor,** and many other verses along this line. In

*Gal 6:2
*Rom 12:10

Scripture, the subordinates also find what comprises their morals, how indeed they should be placed under their betters. To subordinates it is said, *Obey your superiors and be subject to them. For they watch as though they will render an account on behalf of your souls.**   *Heb 13:17

Sermo 93

Concerning the Qualities of Teeth

1. *Y*our teeth as flocks of shorn sheep which come up from the washing, all with twins, and there is none barren among them.* As I understand it, the Holy Spirit, from whose hidden spring the river of Songs flows out, entrusts to us no small mysteries in these teeth. These teeth are not those about which it is said, *God shall break their teeth in their mouth*,* or concerning which the divine voice proclaims to a holy man, *His teeth are terrible round about*,* but rather, these teeth are whiter than milk.* They are indeed the teeth of the bride, whose beauty the Most High has desired,* who has neither spot nor wrinkle.* As the bride is entirely white, she is proven to be even whiter in her teeth. However, he concludes his praises of the bride with a new and unheard-of comparison when he says, *Your teeth as flocks of shorn sheep.**

What, I ask, in this parable is worthy of our belief that it has come down from heavenly secrets? It is truly important and should be understood superbly and with a great mind. I mean, it is the Spirit who speaks, he whom, when he speaks, not one iota can pass by without meaning.* Surely something is wrapped up in these teeth that, once unwrapped, might designate a secret of more sacred understanding.

2. Teeth, I mean, are white and strong. They do not have flesh, they lack skin, they can allow nothing within themselves, there is no pain like their pain;* they are

*Song 4:2

*Ps 57:7

*Job 41:5
*Gen 49:12
*Ps 44:12
*Eph 5:27

*Song 4:2

*Matt 5:18

*Lam 1:12

closed in by lips so as not to be seen. It is unbecoming when they are seen except when laughing, they chew food for the whole body, they have no sense of taste for food, they are not easily worn away, they are placed in order, some upper, and others lower, and although the lower ones can be moved, the upper ones never move.

I suppose that teeth of this kind are the people of monastic profession, who, choosing a more advantageous path and a more secure life, seem to be the whitest from among the whole body of the church, which is itself white. For what is whiter than those who avoid the dirt of all impurity of thoughts as well as action, and who also deplore sins? What is stronger than those for whom tribulation is regarded as consolation, insult as glory, poverty as plenty? These monks have no flesh because, forgetful of the flesh while in the flesh, they hear from the apostle, *You however are not in the flesh but in the spirit.** They lack skin because, lacking the polish and preoccupation of worldly cares, they fall asleep at once and rest peacefully.* *Rom 8:9

*Ps 4:9

They suffer nothing to stay between them, because they do not consider even a small offense to be tolerable either among themselves or in the conscience of an individual. This is the source of your useful lack of consideration,[1] by which you so often weary us that many times, even when it is not necessary, you expend much of the day in these. There is no pain like their pain,* because nothing is so dreadful and horrible as murmur and dissension in the congregation. Teeth are enclosed by the lips, lest they be seen;* so also we are surrounded by material walls lest we be open to the eyes and approach of secular people.

*Lam 1:12

*Matt 6:5-6

It is unbecoming if they are revealed, except now and then perhaps to laugh, because nothing is more

---

[1] *opportuna importunitas*: literally, "opportune importunity" or perhaps "opportune relentlessness."

disgraceful than a monk roaming about through cities and villages except when that which covers a multitude of sins* compels him. That is to say, charity is laughter, because it is cheerful, indeed happy, though not loose. Teeth chew food for the whole body because they have been established to pray for the whole body of the church, indeed for the living as well as the dead. Thus they should have no sense of taste, because they should attribute no glory to themselves, but rather say with the prophet, *Not to us, O Lord, not to us, but to your name give glory.** They are not easily worn down, because the more they age, the more fervent, and they run more rapidly to that place that brings them nearer the prize.

  They have been placed in order. For where has anything been well ordered if it is not here where food and drink, waking and sleeping, working and resting, walking and sitting, and all the rest are established in number and measure and weight?* There are upper and lower ranks—that is, there are prelates and subordinates among us, and thus superiors are joined to lower ranks so the subordinates do not stray from their superiors. Even though lower monks may be moved, superiors should never be moved, because even if subordinates are sometimes disturbed, it is for the prelates to endure with composure.

  As flocks of shorn sheep, he says. How well monks are compared to shorn sheep, because those are in fact shorn for whom neither hearts nor bodies nor anything worldly has been left to their ownership. *Which come up from the washing*: the washing is baptism, from which one who strives for the heights of a more perfect life comes up. On the other hand, one who surrenders to a disreputable life goes down. *All with twins* because they also give birth by word and by example. *And there is none barren among them*,* because none of them is unfruitful.

*1 Pet 4:8

*Ps 113:9

*Wis 11:21

*Song 4:2

Sermo 94

Concerning the Flight of Elijah from Jezebel

1. *Elijah feared Jezebel, and rising up he went wherever his will took him. And he came to Beersheba of Judah and dismissed his servant there, and he proceeded into the desert. And when he had come under the shade of a juniper tree and was sitting, he cast himself down and slept. And an angel of the Lord touched him and said to him: Arise and eat. He looked, and behold there was at his head a hearth cake and a vessel of water. Therefore he ate and drank, and he walked in the strength of that food forty days and forty nights as far as God's mountain, Horeb.**   *1 Kgs 19:3-8

By Elijah, you see (interpreted "the Lord" or "the mighty Lord"), is understood any just person who suffers persecution for sake of justice. In the same vein, that other verse: *Blessed are they who suffer persecution for the sake of justice.** Those who fear Jezebel, that is, the   *Matt 5:10 world's wickedness or the devil's tyranny, rise from the temptation of sins and go away to wherever the will conferred on them by the Lord might take them. And they come into Beersheba of Judah, into the holy church, which is called Beersheba, that is, the seventh well, on account of overflowing grace of the sevenfold Spirit, grace that is there divided for the faithful.* It is   *Gen 2:10 also called the well of fullness on account of the depth of God's mysteries and the refreshment of Holy Scriptures. Concerning this depth, we have in the psalm,

*Ps 17:12
*Ps 35:7

*Rom 11:33

*Ps 22:2
*Ps 35:9

‡Gregory the Great, *Moralia in Job*, "Ep Leandro. 4" (CCSL 143:6)
*Gen 2:15; Ezek 28:13

*Ps 131:14

*Matt 16:24

*Ps 91:14

*Ps 4:9

*Eph 5:23

Dark waters in the clouds of the air; and again, *Your judgments a deep abyss.* The apostle becomes frightened when contemplating the same well, and growing faint with alarm, he is compelled to shout, *O the depth of riches of wisdom and of knowledge of God*, etc.*

2. You read about this fullness in the psalm: *He has brought me up on the water of refreshment,* and similarly, *They shall be inebriated with the plenty of your house.* This kind of inebriation does not induce disgust but provokes an unfailing appetite for certain desires. On this sea of sacred reading, a lamb walks and an elephant swims.‡ On the table of catholic doctrine are placed sufficient foods according to some small measure of understanding for each individual. This is the Paradise of pleasures; this is the garden of all fruits.*

And so coming into Beersheba, into holy church, as was said, he runs to confession, which is recorded as by way of Judah, and there he dismisses his servant,[1] that is, childish perception or the weakness of former acts, and he proceeds into the desert; this is contempt for this world. After he comes there, he sits; that is, he rests from the commotion of the world, singing with the prophet, *This is my rest for ever and ever.* He throws himself down, that is, he considers himself worthless, renouncing his desires, according to that gospel: *Anyone who wishes to come after me, let him deny himself.* He fell asleep in the juniper's shade because in the courts of the Lord's house* he is completely free from all depravity with respect to the body's five senses, saying with the psalmist, *In peace shall I both sleep and rest.*

Then the angelic vision touches him, rousing him to do good work and aspire to higher realities. He looks to his head, that is, to Christ, who is Head of the church.* And behold a hearth cake, that is, sustenance

---

[1] Lat *puerum*, "servant" or "boy" or "child." Hence the following *puerilem sensum*, "childish perception."

of divine teaching, rough indeed on the outside but on the inside ineffably sweet and strengthening. And a vessel of water, that is, a spring of tears with compunction of heart.* He eats and drinks, that is, he fulfills what he hears. And he proceeds in strength to God's mountain, that is to say, to the height of beatitude.

*Jer 9:1

Sermo 95

Concerning Bitterness in Teaching that Should Be Tempered by Preachers

1. *There was a famine in the land and the children of the prophets dwelt in Elisha's presence.** Elisha had a stew set out for them, *and when they had tasted of the pottage, they cried out: Death is in the pot, O man of God. And they could not eat. But Elisha said, Bring some meal. And he cast it into the pot and said, Pour some out for the crowd. And he ate, and there was no longer any bitterness in the pot.** *Famine in the land* means scarcity of God's word in the human mind; *children of the prophets* means children of preachers. *Prophet* is translated "Seer."*

*2 Kgs 4:38

*2 Kgs 4:40-41

*1 Sam 9:9

And the holy preachers are not called prophets for nothing, for they contemplate the hidden mysteries of God, and, as they see the people's behavior, they employ methods of treatment. *Elisha* is translated as "the Lord's salvation," by which name any prelate or teacher of the church is appropriately counted, by whose wholesome persuasion salvation of the Lord is preached to the peoples and imparted by preaching. Such as these, out of the duty of their office, set out a large pot containing wild herbs for their subjects; that is, they spell out warnings about grave matters filled with bitterness, yet nevertheless burning with the Holy Spirit's fire. Therefore the subordinates shudder at the harshness of the sermons and shout, *Death is in the pot*, and they cannot taste it.

2. So a wise steward does not bring; rather he orders a meal to be brought, because he does not provide, but rather he encourages others to have charity. Charity, as a seasoning, renders sweet what previously seemed bitter. For in fact a preacher can make loud warnings about salvation for the ears of those who are gathered around him, but no one except God alone* has the power to pour a taste of charity onto the palate of the heart. So Gregory: "If it is not the Spirit who teaches within, then outwardly the tongue of a teacher works in vain."* One is a taste of heaven; the other is a taste of earth.

*Luke 18:19

*Gregory the Great, Evang 30.3 (CCSL 141:258)

By no means can a taste of heaven please us while we seek a taste from our cook.* Quail and manna were given in the desert, which are interpreted to mean the greater and lesser commands in a place of discipline. When *the children of Israel saw* the manna, *they said one to another: Manna! What is this! For they knew not what it was. And Moses said to them: This is the bread which the Lord has given you to eat.** The mystery of this fact is suitably explained in John's gospel when the Lord says, *Amen, amen I say to you: unless you eat the flesh of the Son of man*, etc. *Therefore many of his disciples, when they heard this, said: This saying is hard. Who can listen to it? After this, many of his disciples went back.**

*Exod 16:1-21

*Exod 16:15

*John 6:54, 61, 67

And so it happens this way: when some simple people come to monastic life, they are frightened by the severity of the Rule. If a sermon about contempt for the world is given to them, or a word about the conflict of virtues and vices, if great care for keeping vigil, attention to prayer, or temperance in fasting is required of them, then they say while complaining among themselves, "What is this? Who is capable of accomplishing so many and such challenging things?" For they don't know how great is the virtue of the

Order that they have taken up. The pastor, however, has to answer them in a comforting manner and urge them *to bring some meal.*

Sermo 96

Concerning Four Fountains of the Savior

1. **Y**ou shall draw waters with joy out of the Savior's fountains.* Christ the Savior has been restored to us in place of the Paradise that we have lost. So it follows that, just as four rivers are diverted from one spring in Paradise in order to irrigate Paradise,* so also four springs proceed from the secret of the Savior's heart. From these springs are drawn four types of waters, by which the entire church is irrigated throughout the whole world. Moreover, there are four springs: truth, wisdom, strength,* and charity. Therefore, various waters are drawn out of these springs, one each from each spring, of course. For instance, waters of judgment are taken up from the spring of truth, waters of counsel from the spring of wisdom, waters of protection from the spring of strength, waters of desire from the spring of charity. We learn what is permitted or what is not permitted in the waters of judgment. We discern what is advantageous or what is not advantageous in waters of counsel.

*Isa 12:3

*Gen 2:10

*virtus, throughout

But since temptations are not lacking for chosen people who are advancing rightly in these powers, such people are also tempted in two ways: I mean, they are either shaken by fears or seduced by flattery. For that reason they should be armed against fears with the protection of divine strength and against flattery with the desires of heavenly charity. In fact, desires for inferior things are overcome by desires for better things, as a certain saint has said.* We can indeed proceed as follows. What is the benefit in knowing what is permitted and advantageous—at least what judgments and counsels would indicate—if it turns out that we can scarcely accomplish it? That is why waters of protection should be sought after the waters of judgment and counsel. And again, what can we achieve if the goal of all these is not charity? And so rightly after judgment, after counsel, after protection, desire is drawn from the spring of charity so that, clearly, whatever we understand or say, whatever we do or experience, the goal of eternal life reaches fulfillment.

*see Gregory the Great, Evang 24.6 (CCSL 141:203)

2. But in order to illuminate more clearly what was just said about springs and waters, I think our words should be confirmed by the witnesses of Scripture, and the likenesses of gold that we have put forth should be inlaid with silver.* And what was said first, that those four springs flow from Jesus' heart, I suppose no one doubts. Still, how the previously mentioned waters are drawn from the same springs needs to be elaborated. Therefore let David come and say what judgments proceed from the spring of truth. He certainly seems to have realized this when he said, *Let my judgment come forth from your face.** For a holy man would not call a judgment his own if it did not come forth from the face of God, that is from truth. For he had learned that God's chosen ones are ruled by the judgments of truth, like an iron rod,* and he was realizing that he was himself under their direction; exulting he sang, *The judgments of the Lord are true, justified in themselves, more desirable than gold and many precious stones, and sweeter than honey and honeycomb.**

*Song 1:10

*Ps 16:2

*Ps 2:9

*Ps 18:10-11

So that they do not perhaps stray from them through carelessness, let them hear the Father's voice through the same prophet, who threatens, *If they walk not in my judgments*, he says, *and keep not my commandments, then I will visit their iniquities with a rod and their sins with flogging.** The keeper of the keys unlocked these mysteries of the heavenly Kingdom's divine Judgment when he said, *It is time for judgment to begin with the house of God. And if first with us, what shall be the outcome for those who do not believe the Gospel of God?** And this was said about the chosen.

 All the rest is another judgment about those who are condemned, which likewise proceeds from Truth himself. Thus it is also said through Paul, *For we know that the judgment of God is according to truth against those who do such things.** And indeed Truth himself embraces each judgment, saying, *For judgment I have come into this world so that those who do not see may see, and those who see may become blind.** However, he distinguishes each when he likewise says, *And these shall go into everlasting punishment, but the just into life everlasting.**

 3. If we have seen how judgments are drawn from the spring of truth, then let us see how counsels are served up from the spring of wisdom. Who would doubt that the apostle Paul is wise when his co-apostle Peter also confirms that wisdom was given to him,* and the whole series of the same apostle's words emits an odor of nothing if not wisdom? Therefore let him bring forth counsels and through them teach us what is advantageous to pilgrims and to those who hurry to the heavenly homeland. *Now concerning virgins*, he says, *I have no commandment of the Lord, but I give counsel, as one having obtained mercy from the Lord so that I am faithful. I think therefore that this is good for the present necessity, that it is good for a person to be so.** If he were to have a commandment about virgins, then nothing other than what is commanded would be permitted.

 But now, since both are permitted, either to marry or not to marry, what could be said more concisely than *it is good for a person to be so*, that is, to remain in

*Ps 88:31-33

*1 Pet 4:17

*Rom 2:2

*John 9:39

*Matt 25:46

*2 Pet 3:15

*1 Cor 7:25-26

virginity, especially when the urgency of necessity frequently has a way of overwhelming us and the brevity of time before we die hems us in and the form of the whole world is passing away.* Likewise, when he speaks about a widow: *More blessed*, he says, *shall she be if she remain so*, that is, unmarried, *according to my counsel.** And so as not to seem as though he had expressed this counsel from his own heart rather than from the spring of wisdom,* he adds, saying, *And I think that I also have the spirit of God.**

    But why concentrate on just a few examples when in his words every sex, every age, every situation may find salvation's counsel if one seeks diligently? But if anyone is willing to examine more carefully whether what was said is true concerning wisdom flowing with counsels, let that person read the books entitled Wisdom, where the whole fabric of the discourse seems to supply counsels. But if more advisedly and profitably one strives henceforth to *choose life*,* then let such a one hear Wisdom himself wholesomely inviting: *But if you wish to enter into life*, he says, *then keep the commandments.** Whose commandments, you ask? *Fear God*, he says, *and keep his commandments.** Let him listen, I say, to the same one crying out with maternal affection, *Give me your heart.** O how much I wish my heart also would hang upon Wisdom's word, from whose wonderful mouth I hear resounding such sweet counsels of life. Moreover, I also wish I could dip the pen of my tongue in his spring, by which I would be qualified to write down usefully what remains of the two springs, that is, the spring of strength and of charity.

    4. And since these four springs pour their taste from one to the other, so that anyone who drinks from one shall by a certain ineffable sweetness of delight be encouraged [to drink] another, it is a pleasure now to cross over from wisdom to strength. And insofar as I am helped by strength itself, may I show how waters

Margin notes:
- *1 Cor 7:31
- *1 Cor 7:40
- *Prov 18:4
- *1 Cor 7:40
- *Deut 30:19
- *Matt 19:17
- *Eccl 12:13
- *Prov 23:26

of protection are drawn from strength. Moreover, just as I have said above, there are twin judgments of truth because they do indeed show what is permitted or not permitted. So likewise the two counsels of wisdom show two things, that is, what is advantageous or what is not advantageous. So again here we recognize that waters of protection are to be drawn from the spring of strength in two ways, so that they may either wash the chosen from their offenses, or cool in torments.

Let us take up an example from both. Luke the evangelist reports that a certain woman who was suffering a flow of blood, having expended all her resources on physicians even though she had not been cured at all, approached from behind and touched the hem of the Lord's garment, and the flow of blood stopped at once, but Luke says that Jesus said, *Who touched me?* And when the disciples responded, *The multitudes crowd and press you, and do you say: Who touched me?* Again Jesus repeated, *Somebody has touched me, for I know that strength is gone out from me.** Behold what waters of protection the woman has drawn from the Savior's spring, by which she was cleansed of a flow of blood, she who could not be healed by any skill of physicians. But if anyone should object that the evidence we offered in no way pertains to the subject of the present work, that is, because the woman seems never to have been cleansed from her offenses but only from disease of the flesh, then he will recognize that it is the custom of divine strength to cure the heart before the body.

*Luke 8:43-46

So also in another place, when a certain paralytic is presented to him to be cured, like a good and loving physician, wishing to heal first what was more important, that is, the mind rather than the flesh, he says to the same paralytic, *Be assured, son, your sins are forgiven you.** Therefore, once the conscience has been healed, the body is consequently healed, since it is said, *Arise, take up your bed and go to your home.** So also, therefore,

*Matt 9:2

*Matt 9:6

Christ first cleansed this woman's heart interiorly through a gift of faith, through which she merited to be granted exteriorly health of body. In fact, the Lord himself acknowledges this when he says, *Daughter, your faith has made you whole; go in peace.**

*Luke 8:48

Moreover, those three boys who were put in the fire of the burning furnace, those boys for whom the flame itself became cool, also show that waters of protection may be drawn from this same spring of strength while in torments.* And especially that celebrated martyr Vincent, who, it is reported, when severely tortured, not only tolerated but even continually provoked his torturer with these words: "Rise up," he says, "and rage with the whole spirit of malice. You shall see that I who am tortured have more power—by God's strength—than you who torture."[1] More could be said, and more eloquently, about this spring of strength, but I pass over it briefly because I want to drink from the spring of charity rather than to write about it.

*Dan 3:21-50

5. We are invited to this spring by the voice of our Redeemer, who says, *If anyone thirst, let him come and let him drink, and out of his belly shall flow living water.* And next the evangelist explains to which spring he invites us, saying, *Now this he said about the Spirit which they who believed in him were to receive.** What Spirit if not the Spirit of charity, *whom the world cannot receive?** Rather, only those who truly believe in him receive him. Therefore, from this spring, let us draw waters of desires for ourselves; let us divide them into twin rivulets so that just as there are two precepts of one and the same charity, so also there are twin desires by which the same precepts are fulfilled. I mean, one desire is that by which God [is loved] for his own sake, another by which one's

*John 7:37-39
*John 14:17

---

[1] See "Sanctus Vincentius" 2:7, in *Acta Sanctorum*, ed. Jean Bolland et al. (Antwerp, Paris, and Brussels: Société des Bollandistes, 1643–1940), 395.

neighbor is loved in God or on account of God. In the former, God may be loved no way but from the whole heart, whole soul, whole strength;* in the latter, however, a certain way is prescribed when it says, *You shall love your neighbor as yourself.** By the former the prophet was aflame when he said, *As the deer longs for the springs of water, so my soul longs for you, O God.** And likewise, *My soul ardently desires and faints for the courts of the Lord.** The apostle demonstrated the latter for the Romans, to whom he wrote, *For I long to see you so that I may impart to you some spiritual grace.** And the Lord in the gospel to his disciples: *With desire I have desired to eat this Passover with you before I suffer.**

*Mark 12:30

*Matt 22:39

*Ps 41:2
*Ps 83:3

*Rom 1:11

*Luke 22:15

6. And one should note that the human mind is aroused and conveyed to that desire in particular by three affections, whence we are ordered to love God with a whole heart, whole soul, whole strength.* The first is indeed sweet, the second prudent, the third strong. Peter had the first when he was dissuading the Lord from going to his death;* that is to say, from his heart he was sweetly loving him whose passion he feared. But when he heard, *Go behind me, Satan, because you understand not the things that are of God, but that are of human beings,** he was corrected by these words and then understood what good the death of Christ held. He then began to love prudently with his whole soul the one whom previously he loved only sweetly with his whole heart, but he was not yet loving with his whole strength, because if he had been doing this, he would not have denied him when he was at risk of death. But on the other hand, after the resurrection and ascension, having been given the Spirit from above, then finally he loved with his whole strength, on which account he did not become afraid afterward even to endure the horrible punishment of the cross.

*Mark 12:30

*Mark 8:32

*Mark 8:33

We are also trained in charity for our neighbor in three ways, either to build up charity where there is none or to increase it where there is, or at least so that we take care not to let it perish or be diminished where it is. But whoever does this with a pure affection toward his neighbor without doubt deserves more abundantly that which is of God.

Sermo 97

Concerning Milk and Honey

1. *H*oney and milk are under his tongue.* That indeed is essential. Yet what is *on* the tongue sounds harsh. *The words of the wise are as goads, and like nails deeply fastened in.** There is another whose words are *smoothened beyond oil,** but let not the oil of a sinner anoint my head.** Instead, let a just person correct and rebuke me, for this is *in mercy*, rather than let that sinner's oil that contains treachery* anoint my head. For the words of either a wicked counselor or a counselor given to flattery are rightly said to be *smoothened* rather than smooth, because in them is not so much true and real sweetness as a superficial and simulated sweetness, since indeed *the same are darts.**

    What then, is *under* his tongue? Listen to the prophet: *toil and sorrow.** On the other hand, according to the same prophet, he who pretends[1] toil in a command* has honey and milk under his tongue. You are amazed that Truth pretends, for it is permitted to be amazed, not permitted to doubt. If you also seek another witness, then read in the gospel that *he pretended as though he would go farther.** What would he show to a pretense[2] if not a pretense? Since indeed *he knows our pretense,**

*Song 4:11

*Eccl 12:11
*Ps 54:22
*Ps 140:5

*John 1:47

*Ps 54:22

*Ps 9:28
*Ps 93:20

*Luke 24:28
*Ps 102:14

---

[1] *Fingit (fingere)*: the basic meaning is "to form" or "to create," but in this context the sense is "to pretend."

[2] *Figmentum* is related to *fingit* (see note above); the basic meaning is "a thing formed" or "a fiction."

in that [we are] intolerant of toil, impatient with delay, frail toward both, he piously provided that piety would have the promise of his life, which is both now and in the future.* He would not impose true toil, but rather pretend in the command.* Hear how he reveals that he himself pretends toil: *Take up my yoke upon you and you shall find rest for your souls. For my yoke is sweet and my burden light.** How could it not be pretended toil when only rest is found instead of toil?

2. So then, toil *on* the tongue, honey *under* the tongue. What is *above* the tongue? Inexpressible things *which no human person is allowed to utter.** Wretched are those people who only paid attention to and could only grasp what was uttered *on* the tongue, rather than what was hidden *under* the tongue or what was stored up *over* the tongue! *This saying is hard,** they say. It is hard indeed, but it is still the same word of life: *Whosoever does not carry his cross and follow me is not worthy of me.** *If anyone comes to me and hates not his father and mother and even his own life, he is not worthy of me.** What saying could be harder? Make no mistake. It seems a stone; it is bread. Hard on the outside but very sweet on the inside.

The Lord your God tests you.* That *pretense* of toil is a discipline of faith and a test of love. Still, let us consider it a stone. Don't you believe what even the devils believe?* *If you are the Son of God, then command these stones to be made bread.** We all know who said this. He does not doubt that the one whom he believes to be God's Son could make bread from a stone with a single word; nothing indeed would be easier than that. *It is permitted to learn from an enemy.** Let us also say to God's Son, *Command these stones to be made bread*. Because he who had come for the salvation of human beings, and certainly not for devils, thus refuted his adversaries in order to educate his little ones. I mean, he was not saying what he preferred, but what we needed to hear, obviously so that *this* stone would be-

*1 Tim 4:8
*Ps 93:20

*Matt 11:29-30

*2 Cor 12:4

*John 6:61

*Matt 10:38; Luke 14:27

*Matt 10:37; Luke 14:26

*Deut 13:3

*Jas 2:19
*Matt 4:3

*Ovid, *Metamorphoses* 4:428

come *our* bread, and not Satan's. *Not by bread alone does a person live, but by every word that proceeds from the mouth of God.** *Matt 4:4

3. Why do you murmur against this, you enemy of truth? Certainly you yourself admit and cannot possibly deny that God's Son has the power to command stones to become bread. When therefore Christ says about God's words, and he says generally, *Thus a person lives and the life of my spirit is in such things,** why do you hiss in my ear at any of God's words when you say, *This saying is hard?** What God's Son has said, and what has become life's nourishment, you would call stones, you who are not God's Son? I myself am not one who imagines you to be equal to God, as you yourself have imagined with totally reckless robbery,* so that, at your say so, bread would be turned back into a stone. You who are not God's Son, to no purpose do you command those breads to become stones. No less in vain do you serve up your stone instead of bread for us, a scorpion instead of an egg, a serpent instead of a fish.* Woe indeed to those who call a stone bread, bread a stone, *putting darkness for light, and light for darkness,** calling the yoke of Christ harsh* and believing that to be under thorns is pleasurable.

*Isa 38:16

*John 6:61

*Phil 2:6

*Luke 11:11-12
*Isa 5:20
*Matt 11:30

May I refuse these pleasures. I choose rather to taste and to see that the Lord is sweet.* For not in vain had he himself who gave this advice desired to experience this. He says in fact, *How sweet are your words to my palate!** And again, O *how great,* he says, *is the multitude of your sweetness, O Lord, which you have hidden for those who fear you!** Where do you suppose it is hidden? Under his tongue, to be sure, under the head, to be sure, of her who says, *His left hand is under my head and his right hand shall embrace me.**

*Ps 33:9

*Ps 118:103

*Ps 30:20

*Song 2:6

For granted that in the promise of her life that is now* sweetness and a multitude of sweetness, and also great sweetness, and however great that multitude may

*1 Tim 4:8

be, it is not perfection unless it is in the promise of the future. *You have accomplished,* he says, *for those who hope in you, in the sight of the children of humans.** What has he accomplished? This *speech is not on a tongue,** but *over* a tongue. I mean, for that reason, that ear does not hear, because tongue has not uttered what God has prepared for those who love him.* Nor will that consummation really be in secret, but *in the sight of the children of humans.* It is truly proper that it is not yet perfected, but he has already perfected for those who hope, since he says, *For we have been saved by hope.**

*Ps 30:20
*Ps 138:4

*1 Cor 2:9

*Rom 8:24

Sermo 98

Concerning the Triple Peace and the Square Stone

*His place has been made in peace.** There is a feigned peace, as in Judah; there is irregular peace, as in Adam and Eve. Neither of these is God's place. Only Christian peace alone, which the Lord leaves and gives to his disciples,* is that in which the Lord rests. This is offered to all humankind through the holy preachers; though certain people spurn it, others accept it. We, however, shaking the dust of our feet upon those who hate peace,* bring ourselves to the lover of that same peace. Some of them are said to be accepting peace, some are preserving peace, others are making peace.

*Ps 75:3

*John 14:27

*Matt 10:14; Ps 119:7

They can also be called by other names: peaceful, of course, long-suffering, and peacemakers. And these names are allotted according to the different situations of peace in which they are making progress. For through this peace the peaceful possess the land of their body because they are meek.* The long-suffering possess their own soul; to them it is said, *In your patience you shall possess your souls.** The peacemakers possess not only their own, but even those of others in whom they make peace. Thus they are rightly called children of God.* Therefore, those who accept peace are called peaceful; about them it is written, *If a child of peace is there, then your peace shall rest upon him.** But, because

*Matt 5:4

*Luke 21:19

*Matt 5:9

*Luke 10:6

they are little, disturbed by scandals, before long they ruin the peace that they had received.

On the other hand, the long-suffering are those who retain the peace that they have received; when irritated by any kind of injury, they do not lose their peace. The steadfast like these are ordered to *love peace and holiness without which no one sees God*.* But the peacemakers not only make peace in themselves and among others but even love [those who] wish to snatch it away, just as it is written, *With those who hated peace I was a peacemaker*.* Behold, these are the people in whom God rests and makes his dwelling.* Behold, these are the people whom God loves just like his children, and from whom Wisdom builds herself a temple as from living stones.*

*Heb 12:14

*Ps 119:7

*John 14:23

*Prov 9:1

With regard to this structure, since God himself both dwells in and equally works in it, so that these living stones cannot be shaken loose by any shock, like a stone they are made square in four ways, above, below, on the right, and on the left: above when they humbly and prudently subject their own will to the divine will, below when they rule their submissive flesh with moderation, on the right by justly cherishing good people, on the left, by bravely tolerating bad people.

Sermo 99

Concerning the Four Types of People who Possess the Kingdom of God

There are four types of people who possess the Kingdom of heaven. Some snatch it away with violence,* others purchase it, others steal, and others are forced to it. Those who disregard all things and follow Christ snatch it away; concerning these it is said, *Blessed are the poor in spirit, for theirs is the Kingdom of Heaven.**

*Matt 11:12

*Matt 5:3

There are others at a lower stage, by whom carnal things are harvested while spiritual things are sown for them, and to these the Lord says in the gospel, *Make friends for yourselves from the wealth of iniquity so that when you fail, they might receive you into everlasting dwellings.** These types are called merchants, because, in the present, they give away whatever temporal goods they possess so that they may receive eternal goods from them in the future, which they would not possess at all if not through them. In fact, it is necessary for all who are to be tried in the future Judgment either to be friends of the Judge or to have friends as intercessors before the Judge. Therefore, those who intercede have the first place of blessedness; those for whom they intercede have second place.

*Luke 16:9

There are others who do some good secretly for which they merit the Kingdom of Heaven, but still they are said to steal it because, avoiding human praise, they are content with the divine witness alone. The woman in the gospel held the example of these; she, who suffered from a flow of blood, thought within herself, saying, *If I shall touch the hem of his garment, I shall be healed.** Having said this, she approached secretly and touched, and she became saved.

*Matt 9:21

There are others who are forced: for example, those who are poor by necessity, who are indeed tested in this fire of poverty by God's arrangement, lest in the future the fire of Judgment punish them for their guilt. Concerning them it is written, *Compel them to come in so that my house may be filled.** For many are compelled when they are afflicted by various privations and oppressions; by God's wonderful providence, while they flee temporal death, once turned to God, they obtain eternal life.

*Luke 14:23

Sermo 100

Concerning the Manner of a Shepherd and a Flock

Insofar as a shepherd differs from his flock, so should a bishop differ from the people. The bishop stands elevated and upright; the people bend over with heads lowered toward the floor. Thus a certain poet has written, *While other animals look downward at the ground, he gave to human being an elevated face.** The bishop rules, and the people are ruled: the former feeds, and the latter are fed, so that from their actual manner and demeanor, they are distinguished. A bishop has in hand a staff with which he may strike, or preferably lead and bring back a sheep. But what does it mean to have a staff in hand if not discipline in action, so that he instructs his subjects more by example than by word? For disciples are ashamed to be proud if masters surpass them in humility. Thus it is written about the Lord, *Jesus began to do and to teach.**

*Ovid, *Metamorphoses* 1:84–86

*Acts 1:1

A bishop also has a stick with which he strikes a wolf: with a staff the sheep, with a stick the wolf. That is, he should gently correct the meek and obedient but severely accuse the hard of heart and shameless and, whenever it might be necessary, even to strike with the sentence of excommunication. He holds his dog with a leash, I mean, he holds his zeal with discretion lest he be one of those about whom it is written, *They have a zeal for God but not according to knowledge.** The good pastor also has bread in his satchel, that is, God's word in his memory.

*Rom 10:2

Sermo 101

Concerning Four Ways of Love

There are two loves, carnal and spiritual, from which four ways of loving are derived: to love the flesh carnally, love the spirit carnally, love the flesh spiritually, and love the spirit spiritually. A certain progress and ascent from the lower to the higher occurs in these. For God was made flesh* in order for human beings to make progress, so that humans (who had only known how to love the flesh carnally) could also love God spiritually. By speaking and keeping company with human beings,* God made himself first loved carnally by them.

Moreover, when he was willing to lay down his life for his friends,* they were already loving the spirit, but still in a carnal way. So even Peter responded thus to Christ when he spoke about his passion: *Far be it from you! Look out for yourself!** But when they recognized that through the same passion the mystery of redemption takes place, then in that passion they were already loving the flesh spiritually. When, however, he rises again and ascends, they love the spirit spiritually, and joyfully they sing, *And if we have known Christ according to the flesh, now we know him so no longer.**

We also love our flesh carnally when we carry out its desires;* the spirit carnally when we exhaust [the flesh] with weeping, sighing, and grieving in prayer; the flesh spiritually when, training the subjected flesh with good deeds, we watch over it with discretion. [We love] the

*John 1:14

*Bar 3:38

*John 15:13

*Matt 16:22

*2 Cor 5:16

*Gal 5:16

spirit spiritually when out of charity we postpone even our spiritual pursuits for fraternal benefit.

Sermo 102

Concerning the Triple Fall of the Human Being and the Triple Return

1. There is a certain way of returning to God that is opposite to the Fall of the first human. Adam, you see, after he was put in Paradise, first lost God's circumspection.* Blessed Augustine‡ bears witness that the tempter would never have driven out the human from Paradise if some pride had not preceded in the human soul, since most truthfully it is written, *The heart is lifted up before a fall.** Second, Adam lost justice when he obeyed his wife's voice more than the divine.* For justice is a virtue that renders to each her own. Third, he lost judgment, since having been corrected after his sin, he flung back his own fault onto his Creator (indirectly through the woman), saying, *The woman, whom you gave to me to be my companion, gave to me of the tree, and I ate.**

*Sir 14:22
‡*De civitate Dei* 14 (CCSL 48:436)

*Prov 16:18

*Gen 3:17

*Gen 3:12

Therefore a human being placed in exile must return by the same steps of virtue that humans lacked and so merited to be expelled from Paradise. Consequently, judgment must be done first, then justice practiced, and finally circumspection consulted. And certainly we owe judgment to ourselves so that we judge and accuse ourselves, practice justice to our neighbor, and give circumspection to God.

2. The prophet Micah shows to us this way of returning when he says, *I will show you, O mortal, what is good and what the Lord requires of you: Verily, to do judgment and to love mercy and to walk attentively with your God.** The apostle bears witness that Christ taught this way of salvation, saying, *For the grace of God our Savior has appeared to all human beings, instructing us that, denying impiety and worldly desires, we should live soberly, and justly, and piously in this world.** That would be soberly toward ourselves, justly toward our neighbor, piously toward God. Furthermore, he urges God's circumspection even more clearly when he says, *Looking for the blessed hope and coming of the great God's glory and our Savior Jesus Christ.**

*Mic 6:8

*Titus 2:11-12

*Titus 2:13

And in many other places in Sacred Scripture, if one seeks this way's order and life's arrangement, then it can be found, such as this: *Blessed is the man who shall continue in wisdom, and who shall meditate in his justice, and in his sense shall think of God's circumspection.** Accordingly, one remains in wisdom and is wise when he judges himself here so to avoid God's eternal Judgment. *But if,* says the apostle, *we would judge ourselves, then we should not be judged. But while we are judged, we are chastised by the Lord, so that we not be condemned with this world.** People are wise but not according to this world's wisdom*—rather, according to that which is drawn from secret places,* through which God's wonderful work is certainly done, so that all the chosen ones worn smooth by blows and forces here are presently built into the structure of the true Solomon without sound of hammer.*

*Sir 14:22

*1 Cor 11:31-32
*1 Cor 2:6
*Job 28:18

*1 Kgs 6:7

Sermo 103

Concerning Four Progressions of the Chosen

1. The progression of all the chosen can be divided into four steps. First, someone becomes a friend to his own soul; second, one becomes a friend of justice; third, of wisdom; fourth, one becomes wise. In the first progression, a person avoids all things that can offend the soul and loves that which can soothe the soul. Therefore one dreads hell and ardently desires heaven. Thus people can fulfill that divine precept received at their first conversion: *You shall love your neighbor as yourself.** For as long as you walk according to the flesh,* you can by no means [love a neighbor as yourself], but when directed by God's Spirit,* you easily can. For what advantage would people have if their neighbor burned in hell? Or what would people lose if their neighbor were with them in Paradise? For the inheritance of Paradise is not such that one's possession of it is diminished by the number. Therefore people love their neighbor whom they do not wish to suffer evil any more than themselves, and whom they wish to possess heaven just like themselves.

How could people naturally fear hell and also desire heaven by their own human spirit? But it *is* possible by the spirit of him to whom it was said, *If I ascend into heaven, you are there,** etc. The Spirit of Wisdom is in-

*Matt 22:39
*Rom 8:1

*Rom 8:14

*Ps 138:8

deed everywhere present; he knows what goes on in heaven and in hell. And when he has filled the human mind and instills fear about the punishments of hell in people, and pours in love of heaven, so also he makes people love themselves, and he says to them, *Have pity on your own soul, pleasing God.** Therefore to love yourself is first, and then your neighbor. For it does not say, "You shall love yourself as your neighbor," but rather, *You shall love your neighbor as yourself.** By this way you become a lover of your own soul through the Holy Spirit, whom you accept out of faith.

*Sir 30:24

*Matt 22:39

2. Having received this gift, one ought not to be content with the gift alone, but to be carried to greater things and to progress into what is better. Moreover, we live now through the Spirit. But *if we live by the Spirit,* says the apostle, *then let us also walk by the Spirit.** And he says in another place, *But as we all behold God's glory with unveiled face, we are transformed into the same image from glory to glory as by the Spirit of the Lord.** The psalmist also seems to have recognized this concerning the saints: *The lawgiver,* he says, *shall give a blessing; they shall go from virtue to virtue; the God of gods shall be seen in Zion.** And so let him also walk, this one whom we hold up as an example; let him go and progress until he arrives at the fourth step. Without doubt, on that fourth step, one who has become wise shall see the God of gods in Zion. Furthermore, as I have said above, he who loves his own soul ought also to love justice. In any case, if *he loves iniquity,* then obviously *he hates,* not loves, *his own soul.**

*Gal 5:25

*2 Cor 3:18

*Ps 83:8

*Ps 10:6

3. Moreover, by loving justice, one crosses over to the second step and hears that precept of Wisdom: *Love justice, you who judge the earth.** If you love justice perfectly, then you ought to bear patiently, for justice's sake, every punishment and whatever indignity might be inflicted. Indeed, justice gives us two orders: one is that we must do as we ought, the other is that we must suffer

*Wis 1:1

as we ought. Naturally, if we do not do the good that we ought, then we suffer the evil that we have deserved. Thus, in a wonderful way, when we forsake justice we are not also forsaken by justice, since through justice any guilt of transgression is punished. *There is no one, in fact, who can hide himself from his heat.** The just man* not only does not dread this punishment but even receives it gladly, since through punishment he faithfully believes that sins of his past life are cleansed. For hence it is written, *Whatsoever shall befall the just man shall not make him sad.** Therefore, he places in opposition to the various pleasures by which he came to grief counterbalancing remedies through which he lifts himself up. For example, he fell through disobedience; through toil of obedience he returns to life. He existed inconstant and dissolute; he is renewed through the devotion of self-control and the rigor of discipline. He suffers punishment from the very elements of the world,* the enjoyment of which, little by little, had flowed into pleasure.

When he has been tested by these tortures for a long time like gold in a furnace,* certainly he who *feeds us with the bread of tears and gives us tears in measure for our drink** shall judge how much is appropriate, so he begins now to be consoled, and he hears the voice of Isaiah saying, B*e comforted, be comforted, my people, says your God. Speak to the heart of Jerusalem, and call to her; for her evil* (that is, affliction) *is completed; her iniquity is forgiven. She has received from the hand of the Lord double for all her sins.** After he has truly accepted consolation, he is careful and seeks how he might please him for whom he tested himself. He does whatever good he does so that he pleases his Creator alone.*

4. We go over to the third step of progress as we naturally become friends of Wisdom, who, with maternal affection, speaks to us when she says, *My son, give me your heart.** Therefore, when one has arrived at this

*Ps 18:7
*vir iustus

*Prov 12:21

*Gal 4:3

*Wis 3:6

*Ps 79:6

*Isa 40:1-2

*2 Tim 2:4

*Prov 23:26

step, nothing else remains except to ascend to the fourth step, where one is said to be wise. But this happens because one now serves not just to please God, as one certainly did in the third step, but because God is pleasing, or because the very act of serving pleases God. Whoever is like this can surely sing that song of Wisdom with all confidence and security of conscience: *In all these I sought rest*, etc.*   *Sir 24:11

In fact, people to whom God is pleasing through all things rest in all things; they do not bend God's will to their own but learn to raise their own to God's. We shall also *abide in the Lord's inheritance*,* just as we are   *Sir 24:11 promised by the voice of the same Lord when it says, *I will give to you the land in which you sleep*.* That is,   *Gen 28:13 I shall make steadfast and perpetual for you that rest to which you have arrived by your toil and by my gift. What he also adds, *and to your seed*,* we can understand   *Gen 28:13 as not only the fact that tranquility might be given to the spirit, both here and in the future, but also *to your seed*; that is, glorification of your body shall be given for your services.

Sermo 104

Concerning Four Impediments to Confession

1. There are four impediments to confession: shame, fear, hope, despair. I mean, of course, shame hinders certain people who blush only because they are embarrassed to confess sins that they have committed. Concerning this, it is said through Solomon, *There is an embarrassment that leads to sin.* On the other hand, it says again concerning those who confess, *There is an embarrassment that leads to glory.** The prophet also commends those who confess when he says, *You have put on confession and beauty.** And in another place, *His work is confession and magnificence.**

*Sir 4:25

*Ps 103:1
*Ps 110:3

Fear hinders other types of people. In fact, they fear that if they were to confess, then a severe penance might be imposed upon them. Job also complains about this, saying, *Those who fear the hoarfrost, the snow shall fall upon them.** However, there are some people who still covet something in this world; they think that they will not obtain what they desire if they are exposed to human beings as they really are. Hope hinders the confession of these people, that is, passion for obtaining what they desire. The Lord threatens such as these in the gospel: *Woe to those who are with child and who are nursing infants in those days.**

*Job 6:16

*Matt 24:19

Besides these, there are others who fear none of that. Rather, they fear only this: after confession of sins they will not be able to abstain from their sins. And despair troubles these types. That saying can suitably be applied to them: *The sinner, when he comes into the depth of sins, shall keep away.** *Prov 18:3

To be sure, it sometimes happens that all these hinder confession simultaneously. But in fact, one who is overwhelmed by these four evils now lies properly in the tomb, and just like that man in the gospel, he stinks after four days.* For it is written, *Confession perishes from the dead as from one who does not exist.** Because if anyone who does not confess is dead, then certainly he or she who confesses shall be revived. So let Jesus come, and let him say, *Come forth!** And at his voice the dead person shall be awakened immediately. Let our dead one here follow this exhortation and not put off confession. *John 11:17, 39 *Sir 17:26 LXX *John 11:43

2. So let it be said to that person who is weakened by shame, "Why are you ashamed to tell your sin, which you were not ashamed to commit? Or why do you blush to confess to God, from whose eyes you cannot hide? Because if perhaps you are ashamed to expose your sin to one person who is perchance also a sinner, then what are you going to do on Judgment Day when your conscience has been exposed and shall be known to all?" And so these three disciplines are to be put forth against shame, namely, consideration of reason, reverence for our all-seeing God, comparison to a greater embarrassment.

Similarly there are three notions to be put in opposition to fear. I mean, we must consider how long is the punishment of hell, how grievous, how unfruitful. But in contrast, repentance in the present time is brief and light and fruitful. Likewise, there are also three beliefs that are put in opposition to hope, namely, that goods of the age to come are better than goods of the present life, more certain, more lasting. In comparison [to heavenly goods], whatever you can desire in this world is trivial and uncertain and, I should say, momentary.* So *2 Cor 4:17

against despair of ever conquering sin, there are three remedies: first is a special vigor that we obtain out of confession; second is God's grace, which we merit from humility; third is assistance that we have from the compassion of him to whom we confess.

Sermo 105

Concerning Remedies of Souls

1. Our salvation is comprised of two stages: justification and glorification. One is the beginning, the other its perfection. Toil is in the former, but the fruit of your toil is in the latter. And indeed justification now occurs through faith;* *2 Cor 5:7
glorification will be through seeing. But the human intellect can scarcely grasp how great is the glorification of the saints in the future life. About that it has been written, *Eye has not seen, nor ear heard, neither has it entered into the human heart what God has prepared for those who love him.** So having set aside glorification for the time *1 Cor 2:9
being, seeing that it exceeds our powers, for the edification of our brothers that seems necessary, let us say something about justification that is going on now.

For this is the very way through which the passage to glorification comes about, as the apostle says: *Those whom he predestined, them he also called. And whom he called, them he also justified. And whom he justified, them he also glorified.** For glorification could not be obtained *Rom 8:30
unless justification came first, since justification is merit and glorification is the reward. The Lord taught this in the gospel, he who when he proclaimed the Kingdom of God first proposed justice to them, saying, *Unless your justice exceed that of the Scribes and Pharisees, you shall not enter into the Kingdom of Heaven.** *Matt 5:20

2. One must note, however, that, just as in that reign of blessedness the Lord shows himself in person to his

elect for their glorification, so also he shows himself to the very same people on the way of pilgrimage for their justification. So those who are to be glorified by seeing him are previously justified by him through faith. And indeed there are three [evils] from which anyone who wishes to be justified should abstain. First, certainly, from immoral works, second from carnal desires,* third from worldly cares. Likewise there are three things that they should pursue that are also contained in the Lord's Sermon on the Mount: alms, fasting, prayer.* For thus justification is fulfilled* while they abstain from forbidden vices, and they faithfully practice good works that have been commanded. Therefore works of mercy are put in opposition to immoral works, fasts are employed against carnal desires, and worship follows in place of worldly cares.

*1 Pet 2:11

*Matt 6:1-18
*Matt 3:15

Sermo 106

Concerning Three States of a Soul

1. There are three states of the soul: when in the body, when the body has been set aside, when the body has been recovered. The first was given to the soul for doing penance; the remaining two are for having rest or punishment *according to how one has behaved* in the body, *whether* for *good or evil*, of course.* But there are three necessities for doing penance: time, body, and place. The apostle says which time is necessary: *Behold, now is the acceptable time. Behold, now is the day of salvation.** Similarly, the same apostle also writes about the body, *For we must all be manifested before the judgment seat of Christ, that everyone may receive the proper things of the body, according to how one has behaved, whether good or evil.** But Scripture also speaks about this place, saying, *If the spirit of him who has power should ascend upon you, leave not your place.** *2 Cor 5:10

*2 Cor 6:2

*2 Cor 5:10

*Eccl 10:4

Time is further divided into three: into past, into present, into future. Those who do penance properly waste none of these. For indeed they restore the past that they had wasted while reflecting on their years in the bitterness of their souls.* Moreover, they now keep the present through the practice of good works, but the future through a persistent good intention. The apostle speaks about the past when he says, *Redeeming the time because the days are evil.** To be sure, he urges us to good works in the present when he says, *While we have time, let us do good work to all people, but especially to those who*

*Isa 38:15

*Eph 5:16

are of the household of the faith.* The Lord admonishes us about perseverance into the future when he says, *And you shall be hated by everyone for my name's sake. But anyone who perseveres to the end shall be saved.**

    2. The body is also necessary for doing penance. We can of course both suffer harm in the body and do good works. That is to suffer for offenses committed and to do works so to obtain eternal rewards. So how could anyone who lacks a body have the power to make worthy fruits of penance?* And let us note that a penance that is borne through the body is brief and light. It is brief because it is limited by the body's death, light because it is more easily borne through the partnership of the body. Grievous indeed would it be if the mind were to carry it alone. But since the weight is shared with the mind's body, the more the body is thereby burdened, so much the more is the mind unburdened. The place also seems to be necessary and useful, namely, the church of the present life. In the church, anyone who neglects to do penance properly while living in the body will be able to obtain no remedy of salvation in future.

*Gal 6:10

*Matt 10:22

*Luke 3:8

Sermo 107

Ways of Praying to God

1. Just as a sick person is to a physician, so should a sinner be to his or her Creator. Therefore one who is a sinner should pray to God just like a sick person to a physician. However, a sinner's prayer is hindered in two ways: either by no light or by too much light. Those who do not see their sins are illumined by no light; nor do they confess. On the other hand, those who see their sin so much that they despair of receiving pardon for their sins are overwhelmed by too much light. Neither group of these sinners prays. So what then? Light must be adjusted so that sinners see their sins and confess and pray for them to be forgiven.

So first, sinners' prayer should be made with shamefaced affection. Sinners may pray this way when they do not yet dare to approach God by themselves;* instead, they seek some holy person, someone poor in spirit* who might be on the edge of the Lord's garment, on the hem, so to speak, through whom they might have access. That woman in the gospel represented the exemplar of this prayer, she who was suffering from hemorrhages; wanting to be healed, she approached, saying in her thoughts, *If I will touch the hem of his garment, then I shall be healed.**

The second prayer is made with pure affection. And naturally this happens when a sinner now approaches alone and confesses with his own mouth. That sinful

*Heb 11:6

*Matt 5:3

*Matt 9:21

woman leaves us an example of such prayer, she who washed the Lord's feet with her tears and wiped them with the hair of her head, concerning whom the Lord has said, *Many sins are forgiven her, because she has loved much.** *Luke 7:37-47

The third prayer is poured out with ample affection. And this happens when people who had prayed for themselves now pray for others. Thus the apostles prayed for the Canaanite woman who was asking on behalf of her daughter: *Send her away*, they said, *because she shouts after us.** *Matt 15:23

The fourth prayer bursts forth from devout affection; it is expressed with thanksgiving, from purity of heart, and without any hesitation. The Lord himself made such a prayer when he revived Lazarus, who was for four days dead in the tomb;* he said, *Father, I give you thanks because you have heard me.** The apostle taught us to make such prayers frequently, saying, *Pray without ceasing. In all things give thanks.** These four types of prayer that we have discussed, that is, shamefaced, pure, ample, and devout, the apostle calls by other names, and to them he exhorts us, saying, *I implore first of all that supplications, prayers, intercessions, and thanksgivings be made.** For supplications are made with shamefaced affection, prayers with pure, intercessions with ample, and thanksgiving with devout. *John 11:39 *John 11:41 *1 Thess 5:17-18 *1 Tim 2:1

2. We have spoken about types of prayers. Let us also say something about the purity with which one should pray. And indeed it seems to me that three necessities are here by which a prayer's intention ought to be tightly bound. For in fact, those who pray ought to consider both what they ask and whom they ask, and also consider themselves who are asking. What is more, in what they ask they ought to pay attention to two aspects: that what they ask is according to God and that they regard it with the highest affection and desire. For example, if they would ask in prayer for an enemy's

death, for injury or degradation of a neighbor, then such a prayer is not according to God, since he himself teaches and says, *Love your enemies; do good to those who hate you, and pray for those who persecute and calumniate you.** *Matt 5:44
And *you shall love your neighbor as yourself.** *Matt 19:19

But if such people should seek forgiveness of sins, if grace of the Holy Spirit, if virtue and wisdom, faith, truth, justice, humility, patience, gentleness, and the rest of the spiritual gifts, and if they ardently aspire to them with merely a thought, then this prayer is according to God, and it truly merits to be heard. In fact, concerning these types of prayers, God speaks through Isaiah: *Before they call, I will hear; as they are still speaking, I will hear.** *Isa 65:24

There are also other gifts that, when they are lacking, are sought from God and given by God, and they can either be or not be according to God. [These gifts are granted] only to the extent that the goal to which they lead participates in God's will, as are health of body, money, and abundance of other goods, which even if they might be from God, they nevertheless ought not to be highly valued nor held as an object of desire.

Likewise also in him whom one asks, two aspects should be considered: goodness and greatness: goodness, by which he freely wills, and greatness, by which he can obviously give whatever is asked. But also within themselves, those who petition should apply two [attitudes] as well, that is, they should suppose that they will receive nothing for their merits, but whatever they should ask, they hope to be granted only by God's mercy. So then a heart is called pure when a sinner considers these three that we have discussed and in that manner that we have said. And any who would pray with this purity and intention of heart, let them know that they are heard, because, just as the apostle Peter testifies, *God is not a respecter of persons, but in every nation, the one who fears God, and works justice, is acceptable to him.** *Acts 10:34-35

Sermo 108

Concerning Bloodletting

There are two reasons for bloodletting. Sometimes the quality is harmful, sometimes the quantity. Rampant excess is no less dangerous than disease. This is my treatise. My will is the blood of my soul. If indeed blood is said to be more akin to nature than the other fluids, and the life of the soul is in the will, then let ill will, which is the cause of spiritual sickness, be diminished. Let it be diminished, I say, as long as it cannot be thoroughly drawn out and drained dry. Let a vein be cut and opened with the steel of compunction, so that the consent of sin, even if not every sense [of sin], will surely flow out and be expelled.

But do you doubt that a useless abundance of useful blood is found in a soul? Listen to the wise physician, who also teaches the necessity of letting the blood of justice. *Be not*, he says, *overly just.** The teaching of the apostle is similar: *Do not be more wise than is necessary to be wise, but be wise unto sobriety.** What vein, do you suppose, should be spared if both justice and wisdom need to be diminished? For what is more useful than blood? However, remember that neither is too just, nor should inebriated wisdom, so to speak, be named wisdom. So no doubt it also happens in the body's blood that when it has increased too much, it no longer conveys nourishment for the body, but detriment. Consequently, if it still gives you pleasure to sin, then your

*Eccl 7:17

*Rom 12:3

blood is full of vice, and you should promptly diminish it. If you are willing to do penance, then it is necessary to chasten your members, to afflict the body, to judge yourself, so that you do not fall into the hands of the living God.* This is just indeed, but not any excess. Otherwise excess fervor is to be suppressed lest it harm unity, lest it serve indiscretion.

*Heb 10:31

Sermo 109

Concerning the Lamps of the Virgins in the Gospel

Let us beware, brothers, lest we be deceived by the empty splendor of our vessels in this life and late in the night we have cause to complain that *our lamps have gone out.** For I myself believe that the lamps that then seemed to be extinguished had not really been set alight. So indeed we have the parable, *The kingdom of heaven is like ten virgins who taking their lamps.** "They took," he said, not "they set alight." For how would those who *did not take oil with them** have lit their lamps? Or, where the fuel for fire is lacking, how was there fire? Chastity at least shines even of itself. But as much as a burning lamp is brighter than one without fire, so a chaste generation is more beautiful with charity.* And just as [virtues] seem to shine out from an inborn beauty even in the foolish virgins, so also self-control in the other pleasures, and patience in adversities, integrity in one's way of life, and foresight in speech, as well as alms giving and such works of piety seem to satisfy by a certain natural grace. But since they glittered more with a glassy than a fiery brightness, by the same token that they supposed that their lamps were extinguished they no doubt perceived that their empty splendor was rejected by the Eternal Light.

*Matt 25:8

*Matt 25:1
*Matt 25:3

*Wis 4:1

Sermo 110

Concerning a Person's Misfortune

How great is our misfortune, and how manifold our indigence! We even have need for words. And since each need is unfortunate, we should no longer wonder that [we need words] among us; rather it is a greater wonder that [we need words] even for ourselves. No one knows what is in a person except the spirit of the person that is in him.* A great chaos has been set between us* unless a certain passage between hearts is made between one another. This happens in the communication of thoughts by the intervening tool of words, as it were. Out of this necessity words were invented. Who doesn't know this? *1 Cor 2:11
*Luke 16:26

Still, it is also now necessary to speak to our very selves with words. *Shall you not be subject to God, my soul?* says the prophet, *for from him is my salvation.** And for whom is it not frequently necessary to recall one's soul, to invoke one's reason, to call together one's feelings? For whom is there no need to collect oneself often with words, to rebuke with threats, to motivate with advice, to urge with reproofs? Moreover, it is useful to persuade with reasoning, such as, *For from him is my salvation,** and at any time to console, according to this saying: *Why are you sad, O my soul? And why do you trouble me?** And now and then, for instance, to rouse oneself and to say, *Praise the Lord, O my soul.** *Ps 61:2

*Ps 61:2
*Ps 41:6
*Ps 145:1

And sometimes it is proper to remind [ourselves] more diligently concerning something, as in, *Bless the*

Lord, O my soul, and do not forget all his retributions.* Certainly *my heart has forsaken me*,* and I have need to speak to myself, or, more correctly, to another me. And all the more so for the present time, insofar as I have still returned too little to my heart,* returned into myself, united again for me myself. For no longer shall it be that we use words even among ourselves when we shall all meet the one perfect man.* Fittingly therefore *tongues shall cease*;* an interpreter between us shall not be required when that sole mediator shall cover over every middle with charity,* to a point that we are also made into one in them* who are for all ages truly one, in God the Father and in the Lord Jesus Christ himself.

*Ps 102:2
*Ps 39:13
*Ps 84:9
*Eph 4:13
*1 Cor 13:8
*Song 3:10
*John 17:22

Sermo 111

In Paschal Time, Concerning the Lord's Testimonies

1. No one who is at least nominally faithful doubts that the eternal happiness of the heavenly fatherland to which our sojourn aspires and the contrary tortures of hell prepared for the wicked both exceed every sense. They exceed not only every sense of the human body, but even the understanding of the heart. And if only that faith were living in all people and faith would follow belief, as is proper; from one comes desire, from the other comes fear! For why is it that we do not choose even amid swords, or, if it were necessary, to avoid such great misery half-burnt and hasten to so much glory, if not because our faith is insensible and dead?* \hfill *Jas 2:17

Our dead faith actually approaches a heap of misfortune, a hindrance to salvation, an occasion of our destruction, because indeed, in the assessment of each end, our affection does not agree with our judgment. Rather, when considering our ways, we do not even possess enough judgment of truth. It is no wonder if desire is not moved by the pleasure of virtues, because it is lethargic even concerning that eternal blessedness. It is no wonder if desire does not fear the present bitterness of sins, since it does not even fear the eternal punishments *prepared for the devil and his angels.** That is \hfill *Matt 25:41
because, in other matters, we have become accustomed both to seek pleasant things more vigorously and to

dread troubles whose experience is closer to us, even if they are less important by far.

2. I cannot marvel at this enough, why our faith, which seems so certain about the future, falters in the present time: *Children* of Adam, *so foolish,* not *judging or discerning what is true,** when *you have promises of* his *life which is now,* as well as *the life to come.** In this life that you presently experience, do you show yourselves so utterly unbelieving and unfaithful that it clearly seems to result in your faith in the future promise remaining only to accumulate condemnation? It is truly the same if we also consider the threat. For is he not the same one who asserts that the Kingdom was prepared for the chosen, and fire for the condemned?* By the same mouth and by the same truth does he not testify that whoever does not approach him *labors and is burdened,** but those who approach shall not grow weak* (as does the trepidation of human pusillanimity) but are to be refreshed by him?*

He who promises the inexpressibly delightful Kingdom testifies that his *yoke is sweet and burden light.** He who promises eternal blessedness in the fatherland also guarantees rest in the present and refreshment along the way. And then the prophet speaks, saying, *Eye has not seen, nor ear heard, neither has it entered into the heart of any human, what God has prepared for those who love him,** and we easily believe it all. The Lord of prophets himself speaks, *Come to me, all you who labor and are burdened, and I will refresh you. Take my yoke upon you and you shall find rest for your souls. For my yoke is sweet and my burden light*—*and how many turn away the ear of their heart? Yet now perhaps they dare not [turn away] the body's [ear]. What disbelief is that? Rather, what insanity? Indeed, as if wisdom could be deceived or truth could deceive! Or as if charity refuses to give what he offers, or omnipotence has no strength to deliver what he promises.

*Dan 13:48
*1 Tim 4:8

*Matt 25:34, 41

*Matt 11:28
*Matt 15:32
*Matt 11:28

*Matt 11:30

*1 Cor 2:9

*Matt 11:28-30

3. Indeed, who among humans are so devoted to pleasure and luxury that they would rather not choose sobriety and chastity if it were certain that they would be more enjoyable to him in the future? Who are so ambitious that they would not endeavor to be content with every worthlessness and extreme condition, if they knew, as in fact is true, that charity, which does not seek her own interests, is more delightful than all honors? Who are so greedy that they would not utterly spurn riches if they believed poverty to be more pleasing? Now, moreover, Christ shouts in vain about the lightness of his burden; he preaches to no purpose that his yoke is sweet,* since the devil's burden and the yoke of both the flesh and of this world are considered more enjoyable even by those who are counted Christian in name. *Matt 11:30

But, Lord my God, from where comes such a great a refusal to pay attention to you as that shown by nominal Christians? Why do you promise so publicly what you might so easily be caught not fulfilling? You assert that your spirit is sweet beyond honey,* and, behold, they found a sweeter flesh in the hunt. Flesh, for shame! Of a harlot, vanity of the world. Woe to these wretched people! They judge partially, and they disdain your hidden manna as bitter* because they have not tasted! *Sir 24:27 *Num 21:5

To be sure, those who examined both [God's spirit and manna], behold how they know that *God is true and every human being a liar.** Consequently, their testimonies should be extremely credible.* But along with your promises, the experience of your own people is also scorned and ridiculed. *Since indeed the sensual person perceives not these things that are of God's Spirit, rather it seems foolishness to him.** It is no wonder if a person who does not believe God when he makes promises also does not believe a human expert. Therefore we are considered insane, we who preach that Christ's cross is sweet, we who esteem the pleasure of poverty, we who *Rom 3:4 *Ps 92:5 *1 Cor 2:14

extol the glory of humility, we who shout the enjoyment of chastity. Let the prophet also be reckoned insane with us, he who says that he has been delighted in the Lord's testimonies *as in all riches.**

*Ps 118:14

4. May you prefer divine testimonies, you *who are wise in your own eyes!** Prefer them not to *all riches,*† but to whatever few riches you can beg for, so that your faith never has testimony! May it be in your power, in secret, in hiding, where not even your *Father who is in heaven** may see; rather, he would be able to say, *I don't know you.** You firmly believe God just, truthful, the one who rewards, all-powerful, supremely good, eternal. Present yourselves [as] *deaf snakes and stopping your ears** so you never hear the voice of him who reproaches, saying, *Show me your faith without works.** What is the value in believing yourselves? But don't undertake the way of testimonies,* because it is arduous, a rough and difficult walk. You wretched and unfortunate people who *found not the way of a city in which to dwell!** And therefore you *wander where there is no passing and it is not on the way!** Certainly the end of ways that seem good to you, that you judge to be enjoyable—for they have nothing of true pleasure—plunges to the depths of hell:* *there shall be weeping and gnashing of teeth.*#

*Isa 5:21
†Ps 118:14

*Matt 6:6
*Matt 25:12

*Ps 57:5

*Jas 2:18

*Ps 118:14

*Ps 106:4

*Ps 106:40

*Prov 16:25; see RB 7.21
#Matt 8:12
‡Joel 1:5

Awake, you who are drunk, and weep,‡ lest that perpetual weeping overtake [you] unaware. *For when you shall say: Peace and security, then* without warning *destruction shall come upon* you, *like upon a woman who is with child, and you shall not escape.** That is clearly well deserved, you who now knowingly let the time for flight slip away and escape the way of escaping.

*1 Thess 5:3

5. *Pray,* says the Lord, *that your flight be not in the winter or on the sabbath.** Flee while the time is acceptable° and the way seems agreeable. Flee during the six days in which it is permitted to work.* Flee in the testimonies of those six that we mentioned above: of justice, of truth, of recompense, of omnipotence, of supreme

*Matt 24:20
°2 Cor 6:2

*Luke 13:14

goodness, of eternity, lest perhaps you not give so much as unwillingly tolerate the seventh testimony, which is divine zeal. *You brood of vipers! Who taught you to flee from the wrath to come?** It is the way of death in which you run, the way of perdition, the way whose end plunges into the depths of hell.* However, there is still hope, because the end of the way, that is, of life, has not yet arrived. Hurry to arrive before the end, lest suddenly seized before it, *in whatsoever place you shall fall, there shall you be.** *Come, children, listen to me: I will teach you*‡ the way of salvation, the way of God's testimonies, in which you also shall be *delighted as in all riches.**

*Luke 3:7

*Prov 16:25

*Eccl 11:3
‡Ps 33:12
*Ps 118:14

6. Let the first step be all the way to the heart. Certainly the divine voice calls transgressors* to that place where the testimony of his justice brings forth compunction and fear. Henceforth, then, let it advance to confession of mouth, so that we not hesitate to give testimony to truth* even against ourselves. For whoever shall be ashamed of Truth in the presence of other people, of that one Truth also shall be ashamed in the presence of his Father.* Next, let detachment from possessions, distribution of resources, follow, as it is written: *He has distributed; he has given to the poor. His justice remains for ever and ever.** And similarly: *If you wish to be perfect, go and sell all that you have, and give to the poor, and you shall have treasure in heaven.** For in this generous outpouring of ownership, there is the testimony of the divine munificence and the plentiful recompense that he who distributes from his own free will seems to hope without doubt for more important things from the Lord's hand.

*Isa 46:8

*John 5:33

*Luke 9:26

*Ps 111:9

*Matt 19:21

And still it is also necessary that you offer a fourth testimony to omnipotence, I mean by affliction of the body. Obviously *a natural body is to be sown*, but *it shall rise as a spiritual body.** Therefore does it not seem to you that those who spare the body have doubts about their resurrection and transformation? So also those

*1 Cor 15:44

who do not feel their soul pierced with compunction about justice, and those who do not confess about truth, and those who are greedy about future retribution. One can also engage in similar reflections and the rest that follow. In fact, if you succeed to the point of renouncing self-will, then that is the most certain testimony of divine goodness. Coming truly *not to do your own will, but the will of Him*,* you superbly designate what you so prefer, shouting *not in word nor in tongue, but in deed and in truth*,* because *no one is good except God alone.*‡

7. It remains for you to strive for perseverance. For this is the consummation of the way, and it has the testimony of eternity. If indeed the image of divine eternity is perseverance in our way of life so that *as He is, so also are we in this* age,* so also we are in this world, imitating that immutability in the small measure of our capability. Hence Wisdom naturally says, *A wise person endures like the sun, but a fool changes like the moon.** So *this is the way*, dearest, *walk in it!** Because by ascending *from virtue to virtue, the God of gods shall be seen in Zion.**

To God's glory of vision, the Lord of virtues himself and the King of Glory* guides us, he who is *the way, the truth, and the life*,* Jesus Christ our Lord.

*John 6:38

*1 John 3:18
‡Luke 18:19

*1 John 4:17

*Sir 27:12
*Isa 30:21
*Ps 83:8

*Ps 23:10
*John 14:6

Sermo 112

Concerning the Fourfold Conscience

Turn, my soul, into your rest.* The soul works and rests in the conscience. That is, one conscience is good and not tranquil, another is tranquil and not good, another is neither tranquil nor good, another is both good and tranquil. The tranquil and not good is the conscience of those who sin in hope,* and *they say in their heart* that *God will not require it;** that belongs especially to adolescents. The good and not tranquil is the conscience of those who already have turned to God; *they recount their years in bitterness.** Neither good nor tranquil is the conscience of those who despair because of the multitude of their sins. Good and tranquil is the conscience of those who subdued their flesh to the spirit: *With those who hated peace they are peaceable.** This is the soul's bed; in this the soul takes rest, but not yet perfect rest. It is also necessary, so that the soul can make good its rest, to be not only a good and tranquil conscience, but also secure; thus he adds, *For he has delivered my soul from death, my eyes from tears, my feet from falling:** from death by giving a good conscience, from tears by giving a tranquil and good one, from falling by giving a secure one.

*Ps 114:7

*see Sir 5:4
*Ps 9:34

*Isa 38:15

*Ps 119:7

*Ps 114:8

Sermo 113

Concerning Three Secrets

*Ps 18:13-14

*From my secret sins cleanse me, Lord, and from [sins] of others spare your servant.** There are three secrets: illicit action, deceitful intention, shameless affection. Corrupt activity stains one's memory. Deceitful intention stains the reason or mind. Shameless affection stains the will. One's memory is cleansed through confession, one's mind through reading, one's affection or will through prayer. You shall be cleansed from others' sins if you don't insult [the sinner], if you don't withdraw, if you don't consent, if you don't ignore them. Not to consent, but rather to resist with rigor, belongs to justice. Not to withdraw, but rather to tolerate a neighbor's evils patiently, belongs to fortitude. Not to insult, but rather to have compassion along with restraint, belongs to self-control. Not to ignore, but with anxious concern to make provision for evils to cease, belongs to prudence.

Sermo 114[1]

Concerning Peace

So the peace of the body is the well-ordered arrangement of its parts. The peace of the irrational soul is the well-ordered rest of its appetites; the peace of the rational soul is the well-ordered agreement of understanding* and deeds. The peace of body and soul is the well-ordered life and health of the one living. The peace of the mortal person and of God is well-ordered obedience in faith under the eternal law; the peace of humans is well-ordered concord. The peace of the house is the well-ordered concord of ruling and obeying among those living together; the peace of the city is the well-ordered concord of ruling and obeying among the citizens. The peace of the heavenly city is the best-ordered and most-harmonious society, enjoying God and together in God. The peace of all things is the tranquility of order. Order is the arrangement of things equal and unequal, each in its own place.

cognitionis

---

[1] An excerpt from Augustine, *De civitate Dei* 1.19.13 (CCSL 48:678).

Sermo 115

Concerning the Threefold Heart

*Ps 63:7-8

*Isa 46:8

*Ps 83:6-7

*Rom 7:22; Eph 3:16

*Ps 30:23

*Man shall come to a profound heart and God shall be exalted.** There is a profound heart, a humble heart, and an intermediate heart. The prophet says, *Return, you transgressors, to the heart.** The first approach of a transgressor is that of servants to a humble heart, to which they are drawn through judgment. The second approach is that of mercenaries to an intermediate heart, to which they are called through counsel. The third is that of children to a profound heart, to which they are raised through desire. And then God is exalted, that is, he is elevated above one's heart so that, while he cannot be comprehended through reason, he is desired through affection and love. And note that these approaches or ascensions are conducted in the heart. Whence the prophet says, *In his heart he has laid out ascensions in the valley of tears.**

But sometimes the interior person* goes beyond reason and is snatched above himself, and it is said to be a rapture of mind.* So we say that there is also a fourth step of ascension: first to the heart, second in the heart, third from the heart, fourth above the heart. In the first the Lord is feared, in the second the counselor is heard, in the third the spouse is desired, in the fourth God is seen.

Sermo 116

Concerning the Twofold Death and Resurrection

If you have arisen with Christ, seek the things that are above.* There are two deaths‡ and the same number of resurrections. First is death of the soul; second is death of the body. Death of the soul is separation from God; death of the body is separation of the soul from the body. Sin causes death of the soul; punishment for sin causes death of the body.* Likewise, first is resurrection of the soul, second is resurrection of the body. The humble and secret advent of Christ caused the resurrection of the soul. The glorious and manifest advent of Christ shall perfect the resurrection of the body.

*Col 3:1
‡see Rev 20:6

*see Rom 6:23

But the invisible soul was created in God's image, whence Scripture says, *God made the human being to his image and likeness,** *[and God made him] right.*‡ So also the exterior human, that is, the body, is found to be right in its form, having life and sense, so that through this exterior and visible body we understood that interior* and invisible [self] that was made right in will, alive in knowledge, and capable of sensation in love. And just as the body, that is, the exterior human, shall receive life and sense in its resurrection, so also the soul, that is, the interior human, receives life and sense in her resurrection, that is, knowledge and love. Moreover, with respect to this, Truth testifies that knowledge is life, saying, *This is eternal life: that they may know you, the true God, and Jesus Christ whom you have sent.**

*Gen 1:26
‡Eccl 7:30

*see Rom 7:22;
Eph 3:16

*John 17:3

Accept also that love is the sense [of the soul]. Here is why. The exterior human is not divided up in life; that is, we live uniformly in our whole self. But our sense is separated into five well-known parts, namely, sight, taste, hearing, smell, and touch, because we sense differently in the eye, differently in the ear, so also in the rest. In the same way the interior human is not divided up in knowledge but rather in love. And just as the exterior is divided into five senses, so the soul is affected with respect to five invisible [qualities] of God, which are truth, justice, wisdom, charity, eternity. I mean that a soul is affected differently concerning truth, which she loves on account of freedom;* differently concerning justice, which she loves on account of equality; differently concerning charity, which she loves on account of virtue; and differently concerning eternity, which she loves on account of security.

*see John 8:32

Sermo 117

Concerning Four Spiritual Springs

A faithful soul has her own Paradise, spiritual rather than terrestrial, of course, and therefore the spiritual Paradise is more enjoyable and hidden than a terrestrial one. In this Paradise, a soul *is delighted as in all riches*.* Four springs come forth from this Paradise,* that is, truth, charity, virtue, wisdom. Healthful waters are drawn* from these springs for a distressed soul. A human soul in fact suffers from four sicknesses of vice: of fear, naturally, of concupiscence, of individual iniquity, of ignorance. In fact, a conquered soul is compelled into vice by fear; enticed by concupiscence, she is dragged into vice;* by her own iniquity she follows vice willingly; seduced by ignorance she slips into vice. The prophet comforts souls who suffer and groan under these evils, saying, *You shall draw waters with joy from the Savior's springs*:*

*Ps 118:14
*see Gen 2:10
*Isa 12:3

*Jas 1:14

*Isa 12:3

> against pusillanimity, which comes forth from the vice of fear, there is water of protection from the spring of virtue,
> against concupiscence of transitory pleasure, water of desires from the spring of charity,
> against malice of willing iniquity, water of judgments from the spring of truth,
> against deceit of ignorance, water of counsels from the spring of wisdom.

And *with joy* so that she who previously was groaning under the weight of vices may now rejoice in the attainment of virtues by acquiring for herself
prudence from the waters of counsels,
fortitude from the water of protection,
temperance from the water of desires,
justice from water of judgments.
In this way, during adversities, she may expel pusillanimity with fortitude,
so that in prosperity she may restrain wantonness with temperance,
in her duties, she may prevent iniquity with justice,
in uncertainty, she may instruct ignorance with prudence.

A soul refreshed by such waters* and equipped with virtues stretches herself and comprehends* *with all the saints what is the breadth and length and height and depth.* These four can be comprehended by God's two arms, truly by love and in fact by fear. By fear the height and depth, that is, power and wisdom, are comprehended; by love the width and length, that is, charity and truth. You see, God is feared because he is capable of all things by his power, and he is truly feared because nothing escapes his notice through his wisdom. God is loved because he is charity,* and he is truly loved because he is truth,* that is, eternity.

*Judg 15:19
*Phil 3:13
*Eph 3:18

*1 John 4:16
*John 14:6

Sermo 118

Concerning the Seven Steps of Ascension

Stand on the ways of the Lord and ask for his paths.* One who preserves the corporeal observances of good conduct stands in the way of the Lord. But because bodily exercise has limited value,* as Paul says, he therefore adds, *and ask for his* eternal *paths.* That is, may you desire the lives of holy Fathers, and then you shall find the *way; walk in it.** One who *returns to the heart** finds the way. One who *has disposed to ascend in his heart* walks in the way.* The first ascension of this way is contrition, second is confession, third is affection, fourth is casting out ownership, fifth is denial of one's own will, sixth is humiliation of a voluntary subjection, seventh is perseverance.

*Jer 6:16

*1 Tim 4:8

*Isa 30:21
*Isa 46:8
*Ps 83:6

Sermo 119

Concerning Three Aspects of the Incarnation that One Must Consider

The mystery of the incarnation includes three aspects within itself that ought to be considered, namely, the form of humility, the proof of love, the sacrament of redemption. The cry of the infant demonstrates the form of humility: his location the inn, lying down in a manger, wrapped up in swaddling clothes.* The proof of love is pious death, because *no one has greater love than he who lays down his life for his friends.** The sacrament of redemption shows three powers of the divinity, namely, he made something from nothing, he renewed what was old, he made something temporal into something eternal.

*Luke 2:7

*John 15:13

Sermo 120

Concerning a Threefold Ministry

The ministry of Christ's ministers* is threefold: the ministry of servitude, of charity, and of dignity. The ministry of servitude is chastening of the body,* of charity is devotion of mind, of dignity is consecration of the Body of Christ. The first happens in suffering, the second in cheerfulness, the third in humility. The first is a sacrifice of fear, the second of love, the third of praise.*

*see 1 Cor 4:1

*see 1 Cor 9:27

*see Ps 49:14

Sermo 121

Concerning Doctrines of Fear and of Charity

We are in the school of Christ, in which we are educated by a twofold doctrine, whereby that one and true teacher teaches part of the doctrine by himself and teaches another part through minsters: through ministers fear, by himself love. So it follows, when the wine runs out, he orders *the ministers to fill the jars with water.** Even so, *charity grows cold* every day,* so the *ministers* of Christ *fill jars with water,* that is, the minds of human beings with fear.

*John 2:3, 5, 7
*Matt 24:12

And one rightly understands water to mean fear, because just as water extinguishes fire, so also fear extinguishes passions. And just as water cleans dirt from our body, so also fear cleans dirt from our soul. Therefore let us fill our jars with that water, I mean fill our minds, because those who fear neglect nothing.* And those are well filled when they cannot fall by negligence. But because water weighs people down, that is, fear considers punishment,* we must approach him who makes wine from water; that is, he converts fear of punishment into a chaste fear so that we can hear what he himself teaches about love.

*Eccl 7:19

*1 John 4:18

He says in fact, *This is my commandment: that you love one another,** as if he were saying, "I teach many things through my ministers, but I entrust this in particular only through myself." And in another place, *By this all*

*John 15:12

shall know that you are my disciples: if you will have love for one another.* Therefore let us love one another so that we are proven to be disciples of Truth. And, with care, let us be vigilant in this threefold love, because *God is charity*.[1]* And we owe all our care to him;‡ that way love is born, thrives, is preserved.

*John 13:35

*1 John 4:16
‡1 Pet 5:7

Love is born if you feed your *enemy, if you give to him a drink,* because, *by doing this, you shall heap coals of fire upon his head.** Coals of fire are works of charity that are heaped upon the devil, who is the head of all the unjust. In that way, once the devil has been removed, God, who *is charity,** is born for them as their head.

*Rom 12:20

*1 John 4:16

Love thrives if you will come to help anyone who suffers need,* if you will provide for one who wishes to borrow,* if you will open your soul to a friend.

*Eph 4:28
**si volenti mutuare praestiteris,* Matt 5:42

Love is preserved if you satisfy the will of your friends by saying or providing even what does not seem necessary. Love is preserved and also increases by a pleasant face, by a kind word, by cheerful service. That way, a loving and cheerful service confirms charity, which one's face and word indicate, because setting an example by a deed is proof of love.

---

[1] In this sermon Bernard uses *dilectio* and *caritas* interchangeably.

Sermo 122

Concerning Two Vices to Be Avoided during Fasting

*Matt 6:17

But you, when you fast, anoint your head and wash your face.* The Lord said this on account of the double vice of vainglory, naturally, and impatience, which often subverts those who fast. By ordering us to wash our faces, he instructs us to keep our intention pure, because just as the beauty of the body is in the face, so also the beauty of all the soul's service rests in one's intention. By anointing one's head, by which what was rough is made smooth, he instructs us to keep a smoothness of mind while fasting. Our intention will be pure if in every one of our actions we seek either the honor of God or the benefit of a neighbor or our own good conscience.

Sermo 123

Concerning the Vision of Isaiah

1. ***W**alk in the spirit and you shall not accomplish the desires of the flesh.** There are those who walk in the flesh,* who put all their concern in this: how they might avoid troubling the flesh. These are people who, although they commend the virtues, at the same time want to completely avoid bothering the flesh, so they still cannot resist the flesh's sinful desires. The apostle says to this type of person, *Walk in the spirit,* that is, "Lay aside your concern about how to avoid troubling the flesh."   *Gal 5:16   *Rom 8:1

There are two steps in this way of the Spirit: superior and inferior. On the inferior step, people walk in their own spirit; on the superior step, they walk in God's Spirit. People walk on the lower step when, having returned to the heart,* concerned about their affections, they suppress within themselves what they know to be contrary to virtue. On this step, they offer *to God a sacrifice of an afflicted spirit and a humbled heart** through compunction.   *Isa 46:8; Ps 84:9   *Ps 50:19

Ascending from this step to the superior step, people begin to ponder God's kind gifts and, having turned to giving thanks, offer to God a sacrifice of praise through devotion.* On both steps one sees Christ: on the first, crucified; on the second, crowned with glory and honor.* Isaiah was on the first step when he said, *And we have seen him, and there was no splendor nor beauty in him.** He was on the second step when he said, *I saw*   *Ps 49:14   *Ps 8:6; Heb 2:9   *Isa 53:2

the Lord sitting upon a lofty throne.* And note that he said on the first step, "we have seen," and on the second, "I have seen," because the former belongs to many and to sinners; the latter belongs to few and to the prophet alone. Thus the apostle says, *For we know Christ in part, and him crucified, and we prophesy in part,** because we do not yet see him as he is. *We know*, in fact, *that when he shall appear, we shall be like him because we shall see him as he is.**

    The prophet has seen, but with a prophetic eye, *the Lord sitting upon a lofty throne*, that is, upon an angelic creature, a lofty creature, that is, above humans, because *he raises up the needy from the dust, and lifts up the poor from the dunghill so that he may sit with princes and hold the throne of glory.** And *every land was full of his majesty.*‡ Every land, that is, all the bodies of the chosen ones, were full of his majesty, when *he will reform the body of our humility, made like to the body of his glory.** And *those that were under him filled the temple.** After hypocrites and those who were invited but made excuses not to come have been cast into outer darkness,* the humble and those submissive to God shall fill the temple, seeing how he himself *will save the humble people, and will bring down the eyes of the proud.**

    2. *Upon it stood the seraphim: one had six wings, and the other had six wings.** Seraphim, that is the burning ones, signify those who serve God with fervor, whom *the Lord finds watching, and he shall place them over all his goods.** *The one had six wings, and the other had six wings*, because not only prelates but also subordinates have wings, and they are seraphim if they would be fervent.

    They covered his head *with two, and with two they covered his feet, and with two they flew.** Fervent souls have wings—hope and fear—with which they fly, because flying is sometimes to seek high places, sometimes to the lowest places. I mean they seek high places through hope because they dwell in the heavens. Thus some of

*Isa 6:1

*1 Cor 13:9; 2:2

*1 John 3:2

*1 Sam 2:8; Ps 112:7
‡Isa 6:3

*Phil 3:21
*Isa 6:1

*see Luke 14:18; Matt 8:12

*Ps 17:28

*Isa 6:2

*Luke 12:37; Matt 24:47

*Isa 6:2

them say, *Our conduct is in heaven.** Through fear, low places, for by lowering himself to the weak, he instructed them, *considering themselves lest they also be tempted.**

With two they covered his feet.* Their feet are their affections, by which they are united to their neighbors. But lest one be offended by the following two ways, namely, by casting down the weak with excessive rigor and by consenting to their vices with excessive lenience, seraphim veil them with two wings: against excessive rigor by consideration of their own fragility, against excessive lenience by zeal of righteousness.

With two they veiled his head.* The head is the intention of contemplation or of spiritual understanding. And the seraphim veil the head on account of enemies, on account of vainglory and secret pride, with two wings; against vainglory, one wing, namely, with love of truth; against pride, with zeal of humility.

*Phil 3:20

*Gal 6:1
*Isa 6:2

*Isa 6:2

Sermo 124

Concerning Four Steps of Good Will

1. The Word of God ought to perform two services, both to heal sinful souls and to admonish good souls. I do not call *sinful* all souls who are involved in vice, but those who consent to vice with their will and do not resist as much as they can. Truth speaks to such souls in the gospel, saying, *Be in agreement with your adversary as long as you are with him on the way*, etc.* He did not say *vice*, but *adversary*. This adversary is God's Word, who is always apposed to vices. We agree with God's Word when we can say with the prophet, *And my sin is always before me.**

*Matt 5:25

*Ps 50:5

I call *good souls* not only the perfect, but those who are beginning, those who, although they might have vice, nevertheless do not consent; rather they fight back. Such souls, although they often fall because of weakness or ignorance, as it is written, *A just person falls seven times in a day,** nevertheless they get up again through their will, which they keep good.

*Prov 24:16

For this is what makes a soul good, that, since there are many good faculties naturally instilled in a soul, such as good character, copious memory, an alert reason, and the soul's other goods, nevertheless only the will, if it would be good, makes the soul good. If it would be sinful, then sinful. But, as Job says, *a human being never remains in the same state,** for one either fails or succeeds. The accomplishment is in this will, because

*Job 14:1-2

Sermo 124

it is the way about which the prophet says, *This is the way, walk in it,** and the psalm, *Blessed is the man whose help is from you; in his heart he has arranged to ascend, in the vale of tears.** In the heart: that is, the will.

*Isa 30:21

*Ps 83:6-7

2. The first step of this way is a proper will, the second is strong, the third is devout, and the fourth is satisfied. On the first step the soul agrees to God's law with the mind, but while the flesh fights back,* the soul does not find the good that she loves to accomplish. Rather, through weakness, she often does evil that she hates.* In this, however, her will is proper, because *the will is in agreement with her adversary*;* within herself she hates what he reproaches in her.

*Rom 7:16, 18, 23

*see Rom 7:15

*Matt 5:25

On the second step the soul not only does the evil that she hates but also carries out the good that she loves, though with heaviness, nevertheless with bravery, saying with the prophet, *For the sake of the words of your lips, I have kept hard ways.**

*Ps 16:4

On the third step she now *runs the way of God's commandments with heart enlarged, and she is delighted* by them *as in all riches.** Because with her skin anointed with the oil of spiritual grace and knowing that *God loves a cheerful giver,** with cheerfulness stretching herself‡ to whatever good, she shouts with the prophet David, *I have run the way of your commandments when you enlarged my heart.**

*Ps 118:32, 14

*2 Cor 9:7
‡Phil 3:13

*Ps 118:32

On the fourth step there are angels who fully accomplish the good by that readiness in which they always will the good. A soul can at least desire this step, but she cannot ascend in her body, because she is weighed down by the body.*

*Wis 9:15

Those who do not yet have a proper will ought to know that a carnal intention hinders them. Those who have a proper will but not a strong will ought to know that corrupt habits hinder them. Those who have a devout but not yet satisfied will ought to know that their earthly dwelling hinders them.

If people's will remains sinful, then let them pray and say, *Thy will be done on earth as it is in heaven,** understanding themselves to be earth. But heaven is those who keep their will proper because, as far as heaven is from earth, so far is a proper will from a sinful will.

So let them pray, if they have a proper will but not a strong will, understanding themselves to be earth; but heaven is for the soul who is already strong. As for the remaining steps, since the soul strives always for progress, just as one who remains in a sinful will is condemned, so one who does not strive to make progress in the other steps is reprehensible.

*Matt 6:10

Sermo 125

On the Necessity of Giving Glory to God's Wisdom

1. *Glorify and bear God in your body.** In another place Scripture says, *Wisdom is justified by her children.** And in prayer we say, *Hallowed be thy name.** *Christ the power of God and the wisdom of God** is justified, sanctified, glorified by his children. Let us first say therefore how Wisdom is justified by her children. *God scourges every child whom he loves.** But in the beginning of the scourging, while the child is still God's servant under the law* and does not yet know how he will be a child of God, he murmurs. What is more, servants proclaim that they are innocent and God is truly cruel.

 Christ the power of God appears to this person, but not yet as Wisdom, because through scourging one feels the force of God's power but does not grasp the sweetness of Wisdom through understanding. Wisdom forcefully touches this type of person through scourging and arranges sweetly* through understanding, until he inspires in the person that understanding of the apostle, namely, to rejoice *in tribulations,* to know that *tribulation works patience, patience testing, and testing hope, and hope does not confound.** And now the child learns that he is punished not as a servant; rather, he is taught like a child through scourging,* so that he grasps the inheritance.‡ Proclaiming oneself to be a sinner and God to be truly just, one justifies Mother Wisdom within oneself.

*1 Cor 6:20
*Matt 11:19
*Matt 6:9
*1 Cor 1:24

*Heb 12:6
*see Rom 6:14

*Song 8:1

*Rom 5:3-5

*Heb 12:6
‡Heb 1:14

2. But what is gained by confessing sins amid scourging, if you do not refrain from the same sins through the holiness of self-control? Just as it is written, *Be holy as I am also holy** so that the child might be the same quality as the father. And in the sacredness of the children the name of the Father is sanctified.* And that is what we ask in prayer every day, just as the Father complains about certain corrupt and self-indulgent people, saying, *My name is blasphemed through you every day among the Gentiles,** so also through the saints it is sanctified.

*Lev 19:2

*Matt 6:9

*Isa 52:5; Rom 2:24

But lest you suppose that I made this up, that holiness is self-control, hear the apostle, who says to the Thessalonians, *For this is God's will, your sanctification.** And lest you suppose that sanctification is something other than self-control, hear what follows: *That you should abstain from fornication so that every one of you should know how to possess his vessel in sanctification.** Therefore we call saints those whom we see firm in their practice of self-control, abstaining not only from worldly actions that are forbidden, but even abstaining from shameless speaking. So it is written, *A holy man continues in wisdom like the sun; a fool is changed like the moon.**

*1 Thess 4:3

*1 Thess 4:3-4

*Sir 27:12

3. But because *a wise child is a father's glory,** it is necessary not only that Mother Wisdom be sanctified by the child through the stability of self-control, but that Wisdom also be glorified through producing fruit of good work, just as in the gospel Truth says, *So let your light shine before people so that they may see your good works and glorify your Father who is in heaven.** So the psalmist, describing a child of Wisdom, says, *Pleasing is the person who shows mercy and lends.** That is truly a brief and perfect definition of a wise person. For we are pleasing by confessing a fault amid scourging; we rejoice that through the present tribulation the fault is erased. *Pleasing God, he has pity on his own soul** through the beauty of self-control. We lend the fruit of good work to a

*Prov 13:1

*Matt 5:16

*Ps 111:5

*Sir 30:24

neighbor. And we are just when we give back to each what is his own: confession to God, mercy to ourselves, charity to a neighbor. So, moreover, *Wisdom is justified by her children** through confession of sins, sanctified through the good of self-control, glorified through producing fruit of good work. *Matt 11:19

The fear of God first has a conflict against negligence. I mean, fear rouses one to protect oneself, because if negligence prevails, it then generates curiosity. For while the heart's soil is uncultivated through negligence, *thorns and thistles sprout forth.** Thus negligence does not find rest in itself,* and it is compelled to wander outside. So curiosity, against which piety struggles, goes out from the heart. For piety is worship of God, and he who is known to dwell in the heart is worshiped in the heart. *Gen 3:18 *Matt 12:43

Curiosity, if it is not defeated, generates experience of evil, because while the mind wanders through many things, it easily finds where it might experience harmful pleasure. Knowledge fights against this, teaching what is safe to experience, what not. However, if experience prevails, it generates concupiscence so that *it passes into the affection of the heart.** *Ps 72:7

Scriptural Index

Column 1 indicates the book of the Bible, with the cited chapter and verses. Column 2 identifies the sermons and paragraphs in this volume where the citations appear.

Genesis		3:5	45.2	12:1	6.2, 41.2
1:2	1.4	3:6	28.7, 66.1	12:2	41.2
1:4-5	91.3	3:7	5.2	15:6	25.4
1:5	3.3, 3.4	3:8	5.2, 28.7	17:4	41.2
1:26	12.2, 40.3, 116	3:9	27.7	18:27	25.8
		3:12	11.2, 66.2, 102.1	20:5	40.6
1:26-27	45.1			21:10	79
1:27	9.2, 42.2	3:13	11.2, 23.2, 66.3	22:2	41.2, 42.7, 79
2:7	12.2, 31.2, 40.9, 42.3	3:15	52.3	22:3-10	41.2
2:8-9	26.2	3:17	11.2, 22.3, 66.2, 102.1	22:13	79
2:9	2.4			25:8	21.3
2:10	30.1, 42.7, 94.1, 96.1, 117	3:17-18	28.4, 65.1	27:40	13.3
		3:18	125.3	28:12	28.5
		3:18-19	1.6	28:13	103.4
2:15	2.6, 15.1, 94.2	3:19	3.5, 12.3, 42.3, 87.4	28:17	42.4
				29:16-30	3.4
2:17	22.3	3:23	12.2, 30.1	29:20	1.4
2:21-22	90.3	3:24	13.1	29:26	3.4
2:23	41.2	4:7	11.1, 28.5, 31.2	30:33	1.3
2:24	80.1			32:2	42.4
3:1	11.2, 22.3, 49	4:8	66.3	34:1-3	14.3
		4:12	1.6	34:8	14.3, 34.6
3:3	22.3	8:21	41.4	42:1-5	71.1
3:4	22.3	9:6	7.1, 9.2	46:6	8.3

429

49:3-4	31.2	**Numbers**		17	42.1
49:12	93.1	12:8	6.1	17:36-37	11.2
		13:24-25	18.2	20:3	42.3
Exodus		20:17	79	31:4	41.9
1:13-14	71.1	21:5	111.3		
1:14	8.3	21:22	22.2, 79	**2 Samuel**	
1:16	71.1			3:39	2.7
3:3	42.5, 42.7	**Deuteronomy**		6:14	41.6
3:14	4.2	4:20	40.3	6:22	41.6
5:21	42.5	6:5	10.3	11:1-12	4.5
6:30	17.2	11:16	23.2	12:13	40.2
7:13	24.2	11:24	25.6	12:25	50.1
10:21	42.6	13:3	97.2		
12:5	28.1	28:29	12.2	**1 Kings**	
12:11	41.7	30:13	10.1	6:7	102.2
12:11-12	42.7	30:19	96.3	17:1	84.2
12:46	6.3	31:16	11.3	19:3-8	94.1
15:23	2.4	32:13	9.1	19:7	1.4
15:25	2.4	32:15	21.2	19:8	24.3
16:1-21	95.2	32:20	22.6	22:22	22.4
16:3	22.1	32:24	4.2		
16:15	95.2	32:32	18.2	**2 Kings**	
20:9	18.2	32:33	18.2, 87.5	4:38	95.1
21:2	18.2, 28.5	32:39	4.5	4:38-41	2.4
23:15	25.1, 28.7			4:40	2.4
32:8	40.4	**Judges**		4:40-41	95.1
33:9	25.8	15:19	117		
33:11	25.8			**1 Chronicles**	
33:20	41.12	**1 Samuel**		29:17	41.5
		1:13	25.7		
Leviticus		2:3	69.1	**Esther**	
2:13	2.4	2:5	3.3	4:3	12.4
5:5	1.3	2:8	123.1		
6:12	2.4	3:9	23.7	**Job**	
7:2	34.1	9:9	95.1	1:7	90.1
10:9	34.1	15	42.1	1:21	3.3
11:3	16.7	15:17	41.9	2:10	3.4
19:2	125.2	15:22	2.5	3:24	18.1
21:10-11	28.1	16	42.1	3:25	1.3
		16:7	90.3		

4:12	23.7	1:6	27.7	15:11	1.4, 2.6,
5:7	2.1	2:9	5.3, 96.2		16.3, 40.1,
5:19	18.2, 28.5,	2:12	5.4, 8.6		41.11,
	28.7	4:3	19.1, 20.4,		41.12,
6:16	104.1		42.3		41.13
7:1	1.1	4:5	2.8, 50.1	16:2	96.2
7:4	3.4	4:9	93.2, 94.2	16:3	12.4
7:17	7.3	5:7	90.4	16:4	5.3, 124.2
7:18	3.1	5:11	16.4	16:8	64.2
7:19	18.1	6:3 ·	40.4	16:15	2.6, 41.12,
9:13	40.5	6:7	1.2, 2.8		42.7
9:28	14.1	6:8	16.2	17:12	94.1
10:15	34.3	7:4	40.8	17:26-27	3.9, 8.1, 67
10:20	20.5	8:6	123.1	17:28	8.1, 123.1
10:22	42.6	8:6-7	12.2	17:31	22.1
14:1-2	124.1	9:9	42.3	17:45	41.5, 77
14:2	30.1	9:12	2.4	18:3	49
14:4LXX	28.1, 33.3	9:21	2.1, 2.5,	18:6	40.1, 50.2,
17:2	8.8, 12.3		2.6		90.1
19:20	6.3	9:25	5.4	18:7	60.2, 103.3
21:14	40.1	9:28	97.1	18:9	71.2
24:21	23.1	9:34	112	18:10-11	96.2
25:5	33.4	9:35	2.1	18:13	22.7
26:11	16.5	9:38	25.6, 58.2	18:13-14	113
27:21	17.7	9:39	20.1	18:14	28.5
28:13	15.2	10:6	103.2	18:15	16.7
28:18	15.1, 102.2	10:8	19.4	19:4	17.5
30:7	20.4, 28.4	11:3	40.6	20:3	11.1
30:31	3.1	11:4	17.2, 47	20:4	11.1, 14.6,
33:6	40.9	11:9	1.3		76, 91.5
41:5	93.1	13:1	60.3, 66.1,	21:2	77
41:6-7	14.2, 33.7		73, 74	21:3	11.3, 23.2,
41:25	6.2, 47	13:3	26.4, 34.3		77
42:2	12.4	14:1	40.8, 61.2	21:15	42.6
		14:1-2	28.1, 28.5	21:31	4.5
Psalms		14:3	40.8	22:1	16.7
1:1	72.1, 72.3	14:4	22.3, 23.6	22:2	94.2
1:2	72.4, 72.5	15:2	2.6, 23.6	22:5	24.3
1:4	5.2, 19.2,	15:4	75	22:6	21.3, 22.9
	22.1	15:8	8.6		

23:3	33.1, 33.7, 33.9, 61.1	31:2	33.4, 40.4	40:9	6.3, 20.1, 85
23:3-4	33.3, 60.4	31:4	28.4	41:2	96.5
23:4	33.3, 33.4, 33.5, 70	31:5	16.2	41:3	2.8, 19.7, 28.7
		32:5	90.1, 90.2		
		32:6	24.3		
23:5	33.4, 33.6, 40.8	33:2	3.4	41:5	19.7, 25.7, 28.5
		33:6	41.11		
23:6	4.5, 33.4, 33.6	33:9	5.5, 9.4, 41.12, 97.3	41:6	110
				41:7	5.5
23:7	4.5, 22.5	33:10	42.7	43:20	12.3, 15.1, 34.2
23:8	42.7, 53.2	33:12	111.5		
23:10	1.8, 111.7	33:15	19.2	43:22	26.1, 41.13
24:4	40.1	33:19	33.4	43:24	41.13
24:9	41.11	33:20	6.1	44:2	49
24:10	87.1	33:20-21	6.1	44:8	33.8, 66.2
24:11	22.7	33:21	6.1	44:11	77
25:2	3.1	34:6	12.3	44:11-12	6.2
25:6	24.3	34:8	3.1	44:12	93.1
26:3	24.3	35:4	40.5	45:5	1.7, 18.1, 19.7
26:4	5.5, 25.5, 80.1	35:7	19.4, 34.4, 94.1	45:11	2.1, 2.8, 9.4
26:5	2.1	35:9	1.7, 2.8, 18.1, 40.3, 41.12, 42.7, 94.2	47:3	33.2
26:8	25.5, 87.1			47:9	19.7
26:10	21.2			48:7	41.9
26:13	16.1				
26:14	13.4	35:10	22.2	48:13	12.1, 12.2, 42.2
27:7	41.4	35:12	41.8		
29:6	3.4, 5.5	36:27	17.7, 33.5, 71.1, 72.4	48:15	19.1
29:7	3.2			48:18	19.1
29:8	3.2	37:3	32.3	48:19	3.4, 10.4
29:10	20.1, 33.4	37:4	32.3	49:13	91.1
29:12	34.4	37:18	2.1	49:14	40.2, 120, 123.1
29:12-13	19.7	38:3-4	40.5		
30:6	22.9	38:5	7.4	49:21	13.2
30:13	5.2, 41.13	38:7	12.2, 42.3	49:23	90.1
30:20	97.3	38:12	42.3	50:3	3.7, 13.1, 13.4, 16.4
30:21	2.1	38:13	27.5		
30:23	115	39:3	5.4	50:5	40.6, 124.1
30:25	41.8	39:13	22.7, 110	50:6	3.6, 11.3, 34.4
31:1	55.1	40:5	5.5, 6.2		

Scriptural Index 433

50:9	6.2	68:3	12.2, 22.5,	79:13	18.1
50:14	3.7		45.4, 86.2	80:3	9.4
50:19	33.4, 40.2,	68:5	29.3, 34.3,	80:17	9.1
	40.6, 87.6,		67	83:3	2.8, 33.1,
	90.1, 123.1	68:7	40.1		96.5
52:6	26.4	68:33	4.5	83:5	3.9, 33.1,
53:8	26.2, 29.2,	70:7	22.5		42.7
	41.4	70:9	3.3	83:6	9.2, 33.1,
54:9	1.4, 34.6	70:16	26.4, 34.4,		118
54:13	17.4, 27.8		34.5	83:6-7	115, 124.1
54:16	42.6	70:18	13.1	83:7	42.7, 61.1
54:20	3.1	71:3	27.3	83:8	9.2, 33.4,
54:22	97.1	72:2	24.3		103.2,
54:24	1.3, 3.1	72:2-3	13.1		111.7
56:5	17.4	72:5	2.2	83:11	1.7, 25.2
56:8	2.1, 79	72:6	2.2, 41.9	83:12	21.3
56:12	57.2	72:7	6.2, 8.3,	83:13	40.4
57:5	24.1, 111.4		12.1, 14.3,	84:9	9.1, 9.2,
57:7	93.1		41.9, 125.3		9.3, 9.4,
58:10	41.9	72:11	13.1		9.5, 23.2,
61:2	26.2, 110	72:19	30.1		23.5, 23.7,
61:10	20.4, 21.2	72:22	4.2		24.2, 31.1,
61:11	83	72:25-26	8.9		110, 123.1
61:12	5.1	72:27	62	84:13	76
61:12-13	73	72:28	4.3, 4.5	85:13	27.1
62:3	33.9, 91.1	73:12	19.5, 22.5	86:1	33.1
63:7-8	115	74:3	28.6	86:3	22.8,
64:5	1.4	74:7	2.1		41.12,
65:5	16.4	75:3	42.7, 61.2,		41.13
65:12	41.3		98	86:7	41.12
66:2	16.4, 41.11	75:11	25.4	87:4	2.8, 12.3,
67:3	28.7	76:3	18.2		20.1
67:5	22.1	76:4	3.5, 18.2,	87:6	33.3, 34.2,
67:7	42.4, 80.1		32.3		34.4
67:16	33.1, 33.7,	76:11	53.1, 90.3	87:7	20.1, 20.4
	33.8, 33.9	77:25	12.1	87:13	42.6
		77:39	3.2	88:12	42.1
67:16-17	33.7	77:49	23.2, 27.6	88:16	26.4
67:17	33.8	79:6	2.4, 18.2,	88:16-17	26.4
67:36	42.3		103.3	88:17	26.4

88:31-33	8.6, 96.2	106:16	22.3			40.1, 41.7, 124.2
88:33-34	5.4	106:20	24.3			
89:3	23.6	106:32	91.5		118:37	40.8
89:10	2.1, 2.7, 2.8, 12.3	106:40	1.3, 1.4, 111.4		118:45	78
					118:49	24.4
89:15	22.2	106:42	50.1		118:60	2.1, 41.8
90:3	5.2	108:3	17.2		118:70	33.7
90:14-15	53.2	109:3	22.5		118:71	3.3, 5.3
91:14	94.2	110:1	19.5, 22.4, 25.7		118:75	20.1, 20.3
92:1	34.4, 34.5				118:82	3.5
92:5	9.3, 111.3	110:2	41.11		118:95	70
93:10	91.6	110:3	104.1		118:97	29.4
93:17	3.8, 53.2	110:4	34.5, 41.11		118:103	97.3
93:19	1.4	110:10	12.4, 56.2, 73		118:105	24.2
93:20	97.1				118:109	9.2, 23.1
94:7-8	5.3	111:5	125.3		118:110	41.8
94:8	5.3, 23.6	111:7	5.2, 24.4		118:120	4.3
94:10	5.1	111:9	111.6		118:126	2.7
96:3	24.2	112:7	25.8, 123.1		118:140	24.2
98:3	26.2	113:9	1.8, 7.1, 7.4, 42.3, 93.2		118:155	27.7
99:3	9.3				118:163	42.6
100:7	2.6, 47				118:164	55.1
101:4	6.3	114:7	112		118:165	26.3, 26.4
101:5	2.8, 18.2	114:8	112		119:5	12.3
101:17	19.4	115:12	22.6		119:7	16.5, 90.3, 98, 112
101:27-28	8.1	115:15	64.1, 64.2			
101:28	4.2, 19.3	116:2	1.7		120:2	22.9
102:2	110	117:1	5.4		120:4	22.6
102:14	4.4, 33.5, 97.1	117:15	34.6		121:2	78
		117:18	40.8		121:3	1.8, 19.3
102:20	40.5	117:19	3.9		121:7	16.7
103:1	104.1	118:14	111.3, 111.4, 111.5, 117, 124.2		122:4	41
103:10	1.2				125:3	27.1
103:15	88.1				125:6-7	81
104:3	4.2				126:2	2.4
104:4	4.2, 4.5				126:2-3	1.7, 8.8, 28.5
105:25-26	41.5	118:28	24.3			
106:4	1.2, 1.3, 22.1, 111.4	118:29-30	21.1		126:5	28.7
		118:32	4.2, 21.1, 22.1, 24.3,		127:1	40.1
106:7	1.4, 22.1				127:2	2.4

127:3	2.6, 23.1	147:14	16.7, 18.4,	16:25	111.4,
128:7	81		19.3		111.5
129:6	3.3	147:15	41.7	16:32	2.5
129:7	13.1	147:18	24.2	18:3	14.5, 104.1
130:1	1.2, 15.3,	147:20	27.1	18:4	96.3
	27.4, 41.9	148:1-2	42.3	18:17	15.5, 21.1,
131:14	94.2	148:5	19.5		40.6
132:1	4.3, 42.4,	149:6	17.4	18:19	92.2
	80.1, 80.2,			18:21	17.7
	92.2			19:13	14.2
132:2	25.2	**Proverbs**		19:29	42.6
135:23	41.9	1:14	72.1	20:9	33.3, 33.4
136:1	2.1	1:20-21	5.1, 23.6	20:10	21.3
136:5	19.6	2:11	16.7, 32.2	22:20	15.5
136:6	19.6	2:14	3.8, 5.2,	23:1	1.6
136:8-9	23.6		14.6, 18.1	23:21	72.1
137:6	47	3:7	52.1	23:26	96.3, 103.4
138:4	97.3	3:13	15.2, 15.4,	24:16	124.1
138:8	103.1		15.5	24:32	25.3
138:14	42.7	3:17	21.1, 26.4,	25:16	15.3, 83
138:15	6.3		40.1	25:27	15.3
138:16	22.9	4:23	17.8, 31.1,	26:12	52.1
139:14	52.3		34.3, 82.1,	27:15	14.2
140:2	3.4		82.2	28:1	21.1
140:3	17.7	9:1	52.1, 52.2,	28:9	91.1
140:4	25.4, 66.3		98	28:14	56.1
140:5	5.3, 7.4,	9:2	14.7	29:11	1.7
	83, 97.1	9:9	10.1	30:15	21.2
141:4	41.10	9:10	8.6	30:15-16	21.2
141:8	70	10:9	41.5	30:32	12.2
142:2	34.3	10:19	17.3	31:10	42.1, 52.3
142:6-7	1.2	10:28	1.8	31:14	42.1
144:7	26.4, 49	10:29	41.5	31:19	41.8
144:9	42.7	12:21	103.3		
144:13	22.8	13:1	125.3	**Ecclesiastes**	
145:1	110	14:13	1.8, 5.4,	1:8	8.4
145:7-8	41		18.1	1:14	12.3
146:1	81	14:27	56.1	1:18	14.7
147:12-14	19.3, 53.2	15:3	25.8	2:17	12.3
147:13	16.7, 19.3	16:18	102.1	3:1-8	2.7

3:6	4.1	3:1	15.2, 34.2, 34.5, 41.11	2:3	33.9
4:8	42.1			5:4	19.5, 29.3, 40.5, 60.2
4:12	40.3	3:2	4.1, 15.2		
6:1	52.1	3:3	34.2	5:20	41.3, 97.3
7:5	5.4	3:6	91.1, 91.2, 91.5	5:21	47, 111.4
7:17	108			6:1	25.8, 123.1
7:19	14.1, 121	3:10	4.4, 110	6:2	123.2
7:30	116	3:11	50.1, 50.2	6:3	1.4, 2.3, 42.7, 123.1
9:1	24.4	4:2	93.1, 93.2		
10:1	17.5	4:7	8.9, 32.3	7:7	19.2
10:4	22.4, 84.1, 84.2, 106.1	4:11	4.1, 97.1	7:15	14.2, 45.2
		4:12	92.1	9:6	14.4, 53.1, 63
10:6	12.2	4:13	91.1, 92.2		
10:11	17.2	4:15	92.1	9:7	33.2
11:3	85, 111.5	4:15-16	1.7	10:3	22.6
11:9	9.2	4:16	17.7, 92.1, 92.2	11:2	14.5, 22.3, 41, 88.1
12:11	97.1				
12:13	96.3	5:1	41.12, 87.4, 92.1	11:2-3	14.7
				11:3	12.4, 14.1
Song of Songs		5:6	24.2, 41.11	11:4	5.3
1:1	40.4, 87.1, 87.2, 87.5, 89.1, 89.2	5:9	4.2	11:12	22.4
		5:17	4.2	12:3	19.3, 22.2, 96.1, 117
		6:2	91.6		
1:1-2	90.4	6:3	91.4	14:11	42.6
1:2	87.6	6:4	41.11	14:12	25.8, 42.6, 60.3
1:3	8.9, 33.9, 40.1, 41.10, 41.12, 92.1	6:9	14.1, 91.3, 91.4		
				14:13-14	60.3, 66.1
		6:12	23.6, 47	14:29	14.3
		8:1	125.1	21:12	15.2
1:7	12.1, 12.2, 40.3	8:3	1.4	26:10	27.6
		8:5	25.6, 91.5	26:17-18	3.2, 3.3, 8.6
1:10	96.2	8:6	69.2		
1:12	4.4	8:12	50.1	27:1	22.3
2:4	91.4	8:14	33.8	28:15	1.1
2:6	97.3			28:19	12.1
2:8	40.1	**Isaiah**		30:1	66.1
2:12	17.3	1:4-5	42.2	30:21	111.7, 118, 124.1
2:14	24.2	1:6	28.5, 42.2		
2:16	8.9	1:22	28.6	33:6	65.2, 88.2, 91.5
2:17	22.8	2:2	33.2		

33:15	23.6, 40.8, 42.3	53:7	34.2	17:9	7.2
		53:8	88.1	17:14	5.5, 32.3
33:17	41.10, 42.7	53:12	29.3	17:16	26.4
35:10	42.7	55:6	4.1, 15.2, 15.3	17:18	41.12
38:10	3.1, 3.2, 3.7			18:6	40.5
		55:9	22.6	18:17	5.2
38:10-11	3.9	56:8	22.4	26:3	29.2
38:11	3.2, 3.7	57:21	2.2, 19.2	29:11	76
38:12	3.3	58:2	27.5, 40.1	32:19	22.6
38:12-13	3.3	58:9	25.6	51:9	20.5
38:13	3.3	59:1	27.4		
38:14	3.4, 3.5, 22.9	59:2	3.1	**Lamentations**	
		59:11	3.4	1:12	93.2
38:15	3.5, 3.6, 22.7, 25.3, 106.1, 112	61:6	9.5	1:14	11.3
		61:7	41.12	3:1	2.7, 20.5
		61:10	40.4	3:25	4.1, 8.9
38:16	3.7, 16.7, 97.3	62:6-7	23.7	3:28	1.2
		63:1	23.6	3:44	41.11
38:17	3.7, 12.3	64:6	7.4, 28.6, 34.3	3:56	24.2
38:18	3.8			4:2	19.4, 19.6, 41
38:19	3.8, 3.9	65:1	4.1		
38:20	3.9	65:24	25.6, 107.2	4:5	2.7, 40.3
38:21	40.4	66:1	25.8		
40:1-2	103.3	66:2	3.2		
40:2	5.2	66:8	22.5	**Ezekiel**	
40:17	42.2	66:10-11	8.7	3:20	41.10
41:7	4.3	66:11	8.8	11:19	19.5
42:8	7.1	66:12	1.7	13:5	40.8
46:8	5.2, 111.6, 115, 118, 123.1			14:14	9.3, 91.7
		Jeremiah		16:42	5.4
		1:14	85	18:4	27.1, 32.3
48:22	19.2	4:19	40.5	18:23	29.2
50:2	27.4	4:22	52.1	18:24	41.10
51:3	15.5, 34.6	5:3	20.4, 20.5	18:25	55.1
51:23	40.4	6:16	118	18:30	5.2
52:5	125.2	8:4	6.3, 20.1	20:25	67
52:7	17.7	9:1	28.6, 94.2	28:13	42.6, 90.2, 94.2
53:2	123.1	9:21	28.5		
53:3	90.2	13:6-9	4.3	33:11	13.1
53:5	6.3	15:19	23.1	42:13	30.1

Daniel		Nahum		7:24	33.3
2:34	33.7	2:7	3.4	7:25	33.3
2:35	33.7			7:30	14.1, 14.7
3:21-50	96.4	**Habakkuk**		8:1	14.1, 14.7,
3:28	22.1	2:1	5.4		41.13, 60.1
3:56	28.7	3:2	5.4	9:10	5.5
5:27	29.5	3:4	29.3	9:15	2.6, 3.5,
7:10	25.7, 40.5	3:16	24.2, 28.7		41, 124.2
10:8	42.5			10:10	21.1, 21.2,
10:11	9.3	**Zechariah**			21.3
12:3	22.8, 42.7	1:9	23.2	10:17	1.7
13:22	20.2	3:3-4	34.4	11:21	86.1, 93.2
13:48	19.2, 111.2	4:14	31.1	11:24	13.1, 20.4,
14:35	22.4				25.6, 40.4
		Malachi		16:13	2.3
Hosea		1:11	42.3		
6:1-3	49	3:4	22.6	**Sirach**	
7:9	27.6	3:6	41.3	1:16	3.1, 40.3
7:11	5.2	4:2	42.1	1:27	8.7
8:4	56.1			2:1	3.2, 56.2
10:8	5.2	**Tobit**		2:14	40.6
10:11	2.8	3:24	28.5	4:25	12.2, 104.1
11:9	22.9	4:16	16.3, 18.4,	5:4	112
			61.1	7:40	1.1, 12.1,
Joel		13:21	16.7		12.4, 28.6
1:5	111.4	13:22	22.8	10:9	26.1
				10:14	27.6
Amos		**Judith**		14:22	15.4,
3:7	24.1	1:7	1.2		102.1,
6:1	19.1				102.2
6:4	19.1	**Wisdom**		15:6	1.8
6:6	19.1	1:1	41.5, 103.3	15:9	81
7:10	5.2	1:5	40.6	17:26	3.8
8:11	8.5, 71.2	1:6	28.2, 41	17:26LXX	104.1
		2:7-9	1.3	18:30	15.2
Micah		2:24	11.3	20:32	88.2
6:8	102.2	3:6	103.3	23:5	47
7:5	11.1	4:1	109	24:11	103.4
7:7	4.1	4:13	41.10	24:27	111.3
				24:29	15.3

24:30	15.1	2:14	51	6:9	25.8,
27:6	77	2:21	51		125.1,
27:12	111.7,	3:2	5.2		125.2
	125.2	3:15	105.2	6:9-10	2.3
30:24	103.1,	4:1-4	3.3	6:10	2.3, 124.2
	125.3	4:3	97.2	6:17	122
32:1	42.3	4:4	24.3, 97.2	6:21	86.2
35:21	10.1	4:16	42.4	6:25	31.2
38:25	2.6	5:1	40.1	6:28	31.2
39:20-21	52.3	5:3	66.1, 99,	6:34	1.7, 2.1
40:1	2.2, 20.4,		107.1	7:6	15.3
	42.2	5:4	41.11,	7:7	17.8
42:14	90.3		66.1, 98	7:12	16.3, 18.4,
51:4	28.6	5:5	66.1		61.2
		5:6	66.2	7:13	1.1, 1.3,
Baruch		5:7	66.2		5.1, 19.5
1:22	41.4	5:8	2.8, 16.2,	7:14	8.7, 22.1,
2:18	12.1		66.3, 82.1		41.11, 55.4
2:34	22.4	5:9	66.3, 98	7:16	23.3
3:10	82.2	5:10	29.5, 51,	8:8	24.3
3:20	1.2		66.3, 94.1	8:9	23.1
3:22-23	40.1	5:16	16.5, 40.7,	8:10	24.3, 75
3:23	42.1		125.3	8:12	12.4, 29.2,
3:24-25	33.1	5:18	93.1		111.4,
3:25	33.8	5:20	105.1		123.1
3:26	42.1	5:23	19.6	8:27	40.5
3:26-27	42.1	5:24	18.5	8:32	14.5
3:28	2.5	5:25	20.5,	9:2	25.4, 96.4
3:34-35	40.5		124.1,	9:4	25.4
3:36	33.3		124.2	9:6	25.4, 96.4
3:37	42.1	5:26	22.7	9:21	99, 107.1
3:38	34.2, 101	5:34	25.8	10:14	98
		5:37	83	10:16	17.6
		5:42	121	10:20	23.5
2 Maccabees		5:44	107.2	10:22	41.10,
15:14	4.3	6:1-18	105.2		106.1
		6:3	40.7	10:30	1.8
Matthew		6:5	17.3	10:32	24.4
1:18	51	6:5-6	93.2	10:36	27.8
1:21	53.2	6:6	111.4	10:37	97.2

10:38	97.2	15:32	111.2	23:15	42.3
11:8	47	16:16	89.1	23:24	17.1
11:12	22.8, 25.2, 99	16:17	23.6, 89.1	24:12	17.4, 121
		16:22	29.3, 29.5, 62, 101	24:13	62
11:19	125.1, 125.3			24:19	104.1
		16:24	51, 63, 94.2	24:20	111.5
11:25	42.1			24:23	4.2
11:27	89.1	17:4	33.1	24:26	22.9
11:28	22.1, 26.4, 111.2	18:6	27.5	24:33	22.9
		18:28	22.9, 34.3	24:47	123.2
11:28-30	111.2	18:32	40.5	25:1	109
11:29	19.6, 66.1	18:32-33	18.5	25:3	109
11:29-30	26.4, 97.1	18:33	25.4	25:8	109
11:30	1.8, 21.1, 97.3, 111.2, 111.3	19:6	1.7, 33.4	25:8-12	2.4
		19:8	20.5	25:10	17.8
		19:11	27.3	25:12	111.4
		19:17	96.3	25:13	17.8
12:29	8.5, 11.2	19:18	41.3	25:20	42.7
12:36	17.2	19:18-19	67	25:21	42.7
12:43	125.3	19:19	107.2	25:30	12.2
12:44-45	11.2	19:21	27.3, 41.6, 111.6	25:34	21.1, 24.4, 28.1, 111.2
12:45	27.5				
13:6	5.2	19:26	22.9	25:37	51
13:12	15.3	19:27	22.2, 27.3	25:40	51
13:16	22.2	19:28	33.4	25:41	5.2, 12.4, 42.6, 111.1, 111.2
13:22	2.1	20:1-15	15.1		
13:38	15.1, 65.1	20:6-7	4.1		
13:41	18.4	20:12	1.8		
13:43	42.7, 91.4	21:44	40.5	25:46	96.2
13:44	15.1, 65.1, 65.2	22:8	28.1	26:8-9	90.2
		22:11	91.4	26:10	90.3
13:45	65.2	22:12	28.1	26:13	87.6, 90.3
13:46	65.2	22:13	40.5	26:24	1.1, 40.3
13:47	21.1, 34.6, 65.3	22:21	34.3	26:27	4.4
		22:30	22.8	26:37	34.2
13:48	34.6, 65.3	22:39	96.5, 103.1	26:38	34.4
15:3	67	22:40	5.5, 18.4, 18.5, 50.3	26:39	3.9
15:11	28.2			26:41	55.2
15:18	28.2, 28.4	23:4	4.3	26:50	19.7
15:23	107.1	23:12	20.2, 20.3	26:69-75	4.5

Scriptural Index 441

27:29	17.5	**Luke**		7:47	40.2, 87.6
27:51	13.2	1:17	19.1	8:2	4.5
28:18	60.2	1:28	47, 49, 52.3, 87.3	8:6	1.2
Mark		1:29	17.6, 52.3	8:13	3.4, 45.5, 60.3
2:10	25.4	1:33	33.7	8:18	15.3
5:25-30	25.2	1:34	52.3	8:33	8.4
7:9	67	1:35	27.1, 52.2, 87.3	8:43-46	96.4
8:24	85			8:44	25.2
8:32	96.6	1:36	41.2	8:45	25.2
8:33	23.3, 29.5, 96.6	1:37	34.5	8:46	25.2
		1:38	52.3	8:48	96.4
8:38	24.4	1:42	87.3	9:26	111.6
9:22	1.5	1:48	47	9:33	20.2
9:28	55.2	1:52	42.7	9:35	91.6
9:42-44	29.2	1:54	45.4	10:6	90.3, 98
9:43	42.6, 72.1	1:78	22.6, 27.1, 27.3	10:16	41.3
9:48	2.4, 18.1, 41.9			10:33	33.4
		2:7	15.2, 119	10:34	5.4
9:49	2.4	2:14	7.1	10:36	33.4
10:21	65.2	2:21	41.2, 51	10:38	48
10:26	88.2	2:22	51	10:40	3.4
10:47	27.5	2:28	51	10:41	48
12:30	10.3, 29.1, 96.5, 96.6	2:49	8.8	10:42	9.4
		3:7	111.5	11:5	59
12:34	1.1	3:8	22.7, 65.1, 106.2	11:5-6	59
12:42	22.6			11:11-12	97.3
14:3	87.6, 90.1	4:14	27.1	11:13	76, 89.2
14:4-5	87.6	4:25	22.2	11:15	33.7
14:6	90.3	4:29	41	11:17	33.7
14:6-7	87.6	4:34	2.3	11:21	8.5
14:8	22.9, 90.3	5:15	25.2	11:21-22	11.2, 22.3
14:29	29.5	5:20-21	53.1	11:22	8.5, 22.4
14:33	34.2	6:12	55.2	11:23	22.4
14:36	3.9	6:38	2.6, 9.5, 15.2, 33.2	11:28	24.2, 24.4
15:17	50.1			12:2	5.2
16:1	58.1, 87.6, 90.5	6:46	91.1	12:3	91.5
		7:37-38	90.1	12:8	24.4
16:3	58.2	7:37-47	107.1	12:35	55.4
16:4-5	58.2	7:38	25.3, 87.6	12:37	42.7, 123.2

12:38	17.8	17:10	16.4, 17.1,	24:46	25.1, 33.4
12:42	56.1, 91.6		41.9	24:46-47	33.4
12:47	40.5	17:13	27.5	24:49	29.5, 41,
13:1	40.5	17:16	27.8		91.4
13:14	111.5	17:17	27.5, 27.7		
13:27	27.7	17:18	27.5, 27.8	**John**	
14:11	20.1, 20.2,	17:21	18.5	1:1	52.2
	20.3, 20.5	18:2	72.3	1:9	71.2
14:16	28.1	18:13	25.2	1:12	1.5, 11.1
14:18	22.9, 123.1	18:19	95.2, 111.6	1:14	1.5, 25.5,
14:21	8.5	19:5-6	41.7		67, 101
14:23	99	19:9	41.7	1:16	27.8
14:24	28.1	19:10	41.7	1:17	67
14:26	97.2	19:13	42.1, 42.7	1:18	52.2
14:27	28.2, 97.2	19:17	42.1	1:47	97.1
14:28	4.2	19:41	34.5	2:3	18.2, 121
14:30	4.2	19:42	22.5	2:5	56.1, 121
15:7	90.1	20:36	77	2:6	18.2, 28.5,
15:10	40.4, 91.1	21:18	1.8		55.1, 55.4,
15:11-12	8.2	21:19	2.5, 23.3,		56.1
15:12-13	40.4		98	2:6-10	18.2
15:13	8.2, 8.3,	22:15	96.5	2:7	56.1, 56.2,
	8.4	22:33	29.5		121
15:14	8.3	22:44	22.6	2:7-9	56.1
15:15	8.3, 8.4,	22:53	11.2	2:9	18.2
	8.5	22:57-62	40.2	2:10	18.2, 56.2
15:17	8.5	23:30	5.2	2:25	7.2
15:18	40.4	23:39-43	75	3:8	41.11, 75
15:19	8.5	23:40-43	41.10	3:13	28.1, 33.3,
15:19-30	27.3	23:41-42	40.2		33.4, 60.1
15:20	40.4	23:43	40.2	3:19	20.4
15:22	11.1, 40.4	23:53	58.1	3:20	62
15:23	40.4	24:5	34.2	3:29	42.3
15:25	40.4	24:6	34.2	3:34	1.4, 33.8
15:30	8.3, 8.4	24:17	90.5	4:24	23.2
16:9	99	24:18	40.5	4:34	2.4
16:19-22	19.2	24:20	13.3	5:8	25.4
16:24	8.5	24:26	33.4	5:17	92.1
16:25	21.2	24:28	97.1	5:24	24.4
16:26	110	24:29	22.8	5:25	24.2

5:27	90.2	10:10	33.2	14:26	7.4, 41	
5:28-29	24.4	10:11	92.3	14:27	26.4, 98	
5:33	111.6	10:12	3.9	14:28	29.5	
5:35	55.4	10:14	55.3	14:31	3.1	
5:44	7.1	10:17	34.2	15:3	24.3, 60.4	
6:9	2.7	10:18	33.3, 41.10	15:4	91.6	
6:15	41.10	10:27	5.3	15:5	3.2, 91.6	
6:27	15.1, 27.2	10:32	33.3	15:12	33.6, 121	
6:38	111.6	10:33	3.2	15:13	29.3, 60.2, 101, 119	
6:45	9.1	10:38	1.5			
6:52	5.1	11:6	32.3	15:15	3.9, 27.1, 29.1, 56.2	
6:54	95.2	11:14	32.3			
6:61	2.7, 5.1, 5.2, 95.2, 97.2, 97.3	11:17	104.1	15:16	27.1	
		11:33	34.2	15:26	41	
		11:35	34.2	16:13	18.3, 41	
6:64	5.1, 23.1, 24.2, 30.2	11:39	104.1, 107.1	16:20	1.8, 3.1, 5.4, 18.1, 18.2, 72.4	
6:65	90.3	11:41	25.6, 107.1			
6:67	5.1, 95.2	11:43	32.3, 104.1	16:22	33.2	
6:68-69	5.1	12:3	90.1	16:24	33.2	
7:4	10.1	12:7	87.6	17:3	82.1, 116	
7:24	90.3	12:7-8	4.4	17:4	34.6	
7:34	4.1	12:26	62	17:5	24.3	
7:37-39	96.5	12:31	8.2	17:11	10.3, 15.1	
8:11	25.3	12:32	33.7, 33.8, 33.9, 41.12	17:14	15.1	
8:12	71.2			17:17	23.6, 24.3	
8:21	24.2	12:35	17.1	17:21	10.3	
8:32	116	12:48	24.2	17:22	110	
8:34	8.2, 13.3, 14.3, 25.2	13:1	60.2	17:24	10.3	
		13:13	8.7, 40.1	18:38	15.3	
8:36	11.3	13:35	121	19:15	22.5	
8:40	41.5	14:2	33.1	19:23-24	25.2	
8:44	6.2, 19.2, 22.3	14:6	60.1, 63, 111.7, 117	19:30	34.4	
				19:34	6.3, 17.5	
8:46	28.1, 33.3	14:9	3.2	19:36	6.3, 28.2	
9:16	22.4	14:10	52.2	19:40	4.4	
9:28	7.4	14:12	2.6	20:11-15	34.2	
9:33	22.4	14:17	22.4, 25.1, 96.5	20:25	17.5	
9:39	96.2			20:26	41	
10:2	55.3	14:23	98	21:14	19.3	

21:15-17	29.1, 29.5	1:18	3.9	6:12	85
21:17	29.5	1:19	87.2	6:13	84.1
		1:20	9.1, 9.2, 49	6:14	125.1
Acts		1:21	7.1, 40.1,	6:17	25.8
1:1	60.1, 100		49, 87.2	6:19	69.1, 84.1,
1:11	34.4	1:22	87.2		85
1:13-14	41	1:24-28	1.3	6:23	116
2:27	4.4	1:25	17.8, 19.7,	7:4	16.5
2:38	42.3		27.8,	7:6	4.4
4:11	55.4		40.10,	7:14	8.5
4:12	16.4		41.13, 42.7	7:15	124.2
4:19	29.5	1:30	17.4	7:16	8.4, 124.2
5:29	29.5, 41,	2:2	96.2	7:18	8.4, 124.2
	41.3	2:4	27.1, 40.4	7:22	28.5, 115,
5:41	16.6, 18.2,	2:4-5	13.2		116
	41	2:5	8.5, 40.4	7:22-23	8.4
7:10	27.1	2:6	61.1	7:23	28.5, 124.2
7:56	5.2	2:24	125.2	7:24	2.8, 6.2,
8:20-21	42.3	2:28-29	3.7, 18.2		8.5, 20.4,
9:5	20.5	3:4	111.3		26.4
9:6	53.1	4:3	25.4	8:1	23.1,
10:2	17.6	4:15	1.3		103.1,
10:4	91.2	5:2-3	16.6, 18.2		123.1
10:34-35	107.2	5:3	58.1	8:2	76
10:42	24.4	5:3-4	3.1	8:4	23.1
13:15	33.1	5:3-5	125.1	8:5	12.2
13:22	33.4	5:4-5	18.3	8:7	23.3, 52.1
14:21	28.2	5:6	40.5	8:8	23.1
15:10	67	5:7	22.5	8:9	3.8, 93.2
15:23	18.4	5:8	29.3	8:13	1.3, 3.8,
19:8	23.7	5:12	11.3		23.1
19:15	24.1	5:19	2.5	8:13-14	23.1
22:7	10.4	5:20	13.1, 14.5	8:14	72.4, 103.1
28:25	33.5	6:3	11.1	8:15	76
		6:4-5	28.2	8:16	7.3, 25.6
Romans		6:5	28.2	8:17	22.8, 28.3,
1:11	96.5	6:6	3.1, 13.3,		42.5, 63
1:14	34.1, 91.6		26.4, 27.2	8:18	1.4, 1.7,
1:17	17.7, 21.1,	6:6-12	1.1		4.1, 22.8
	61.1, 82.1	6:9	34.5, 57.2	8:21	12.2

Ref	Loc	Ref	Loc	Ref	Loc
8:23	1.7	12:1	2.1, 67	2:7	22.8, 29.3
8:24	97.3	12:3	15.4, 108	2:8	4.3, 25.8
8:26	6.2, 25.5, 26.3, 31.3, 59, 64.2	12:10	92.3	2:9	16.7, 22.8, 29.2, 41.13, 89.1, 97.3, 105.1, 111.2
		12:11	27.5		
		12:15	34.5, 34.6, 65.3		
8:28	1.6, 26.3				
8:29	4.5, 28.3	12:17	32.2		
8:30	4.5, 21.1, 24.2, 105.1	12:18	16.3		
		12:19	20.5	2:10	5.5, 24.2, 89.1
8:32	1.5, 40.5	12:20	121		
8:35	4.4, 77	13:1	41.3	2:11	7.2, 32.1, 110
8:37	33.9	13:2	41.3		
8:38-39	11.1	13:9	67	2:12	1.5, 23.2, 24.1, 25.6
8:39	11.1, 22.3	13:9-10	56.2		
9:3	28.3	14:17	18.1, 18.3, 18.5, 19.1, 19.2, 19.6	2:13-14	67
9:5	4.5, 28.7, 33.9			2:14	19.6, 111.3
				2:15	24.2, 34.3
9:11	4.5	14:22	34.3	3:1	8.7, 87.2
9:19	2.3	15:1-3	26.4	3:1-2	8.6
9:20-21	22.9	15:19	91.6	3:11	30.1, 30.2
9:21	40.5, 42.3	16:15	34.6	3:11-12	30.1
9:22	8.5	16:20	14.1	3:12	30.1, 30.2, 33.2
9:22-23	42.5	19:20	40.5		
9:30	15.4			3:12-15	27.2, 28.7
10:2	90.3, 100			3:13	28.6
10:4	41.10, 41.13	**1 Corinthians**		3:15	28.6, 30.1, 30.2
		1:19	52.1		
10:8	10.1, 15.2	1:20	7.1, 7.2	3:16	31.1
10:10	15.5, 40.6, 82.1	1:21	29.3	3:19	7.1, 52.1
		1:23-25	57.1	4:1	32.1, 120
10:14	17.7	1:24	14.1, 52.1, 54, 57.1, 60.1, 63, 89.2, 125.1	4:3	32.1, 34.3
10:16	22.2			4:3-4	7.2, 32.1
10:17	17.7			4:4	32.1, 34.3
10:20	41.11			4:5	5.2, 7.3, 14.5
11:1	30.1	1:25	34.2		
11:13	34.3	1:30	52.1	4:7	7.3, 27.8, 41.9, 88.2
11:20	2.5	1:31	7.1, 7.2, 7.4, 23.2		
11:33	94.1			4:8	28.6
11:34	3.2	2:2	18.2, 123.1	4:9	70
11:36	8.2	2:6	102.2	5:8	8.3

6:13	19.1	12:3-11	1.1	15:52	75
6:15	90.5	12:7	88.1	15:54	60.2
6:17	4.3, 8.9,	12:8	25.5, 88.1		
	10.1, 33.8,	12:10	23.2, 24.1,	**2 Corinthians**	
	41.11,		88.2	1:3	27.6
	80.1, 81,	12:12	28.2	1:4-5	28.5
	87.4, 92.1	12:27	17.5	1:9	27.3
6:18	17.1	12:28	25.5	1:12	8.5, 40.7
6:19	27.5	13:1	88.2	1:19	22.4
6:20	125.1	13:2	77	1:23	92.3
7:25	27.3	13:4	19.6	2:11	14.4, 17.6,
7:25-26	96.3	13:4-5	3.1		22.3, 23.2,
7:29	1.4	13:5	3.9, 29.5		24.1
7:31	27.2, 96.3	13:8	2.8, 27.2,	2:16	22.7
7:32-33	26.4		110	3:5	41
7:33	2.1	13:9	123.1	3:7	41.11
7:34	26.4	13:10	1.7	3:18	8.9, 28.7,
7:40	1.1, 96.3	13:11	8.8		41.11,
9:9	29.2	13:12	1.4, 9.1,		103.2
9:18	1.8, 91.6		33.9,	4:7	18.5
9:19	34.3		41.11, 42.7	4:10	91.6
9:20-22	34.3	13:13	18.5, 45.4,	4:16	27.5
9:22	65.3		45.6	4:17	1.7, 1.8,
9:24	33.6, 33.9,	14:15	27.5		29.2, 33.2,
	41.10	15:9	91.6		104.2
9:24-25	1.8	15:10	1.7, 91.6	5:6	6.2, 41.11,
9:27	14.3, 16.5,	15:22	2.5		87.4
	23.2, 34.3,	15:23-24	22.8	5:7	87.4, 105.1
	120	15:28	1.4, 1.8,	5:10	5.2, 7.2,
10:4	5.4, 55.4		22.8, 24.2,		106.1
10:13	6.2, 13.4		33.8,	5:11	45.5
10:25	41.3		41.12, 42.7	5:13	87.2
10:27	45.5	15:32	1.3	5:15	33.5, 33.6
10:31	2.5	15:44	111.6	5:16	18.2, 101
10:32	34.3	15:45-47	28.3	5:17	34.2
11:3	90.1	15:46	8.2, 16.1	6:2	4.1, 17.3,
11:26	24.4	15:47-49	3.2		106.1,
11:31	34.3, 82.3	15:49	69.1, 86.2		111.5
11:31-32	102.2	15:50	25.2	6:4-5	22.2
12:3	22.4	15:51	53.2	6:4-6	16.1

6:14	90.4	4:30	41.2, 79	3:17	5.4, 14.2, 27.2, 69.2, 82.1
6:14-15	4.3	4:31	11.1		
6:16	90.1	5:11-12	17.7		
7:1	1.8	5:16	101, 123.1	3:18	117
9:7	2.5, 3.4, 41.6, 124.2	5:17	82.2	4:3	21.3, 33.4
		5:19	79	4:10	60.2
10:3	5.2, 28.4	5:21	17.1, 67	4:13	8.8, 33.6, 33.9, 41.12, 90.3, 110
10:17	91.6	5:24	63		
10:18	7.2, 7.4	5:25	23.1, 103.2		
11:3	11.3, 22.3, 23.2	5:26	12.3, 42.3, 56.1	4:15-16	33.6
11:14	17.6, 24.1	6:1	123.2	4:19	1.3
11:14-15	22.3	6:2	33.6, 92.3	4:22	3.1, 3.6
11:23	42.3	6:3	42.2	4:23-24	69.1
11:24-25	1.7	6:7	41.5	4:28	3.4, 17.1, 55.4, 121
11:26-27	22.5	6:8	23.1, 28.4, 82.2		
11:27	22.2, 42.3			4:29	69.1
11:29	34.3, 34.6	6:8-9	59	4:30	27.5
11:32	12.4	6:10	106.1	5:3	27.4
12:4	52.2, 97.2	6:14	4.4, 60.2	5:4	31.1, 31.3
12:7	91.7			5:6	27.3
12:9	3.3, 27.4	**Ephesians**		5:16	27.5, 106.1
12:15	34.3	1:3	19.3	5:18	29.3, 29.5
12:21	34.5, 34.6	1:4	4.5, 33.9	5:23	94.2
13:4	29.3, 57.2	1:6	33.9	5:27	28.5, 90.5, 93.1
		1:9	26.4		
Galatians		1:10	33.8	5:31-32	33.8
1:4	12.3, 15.1	1:14	1.7	5:32	33.8
2:20	78	1:18	28.7	6:5	18.5
3:21	49	1:23	33.9	6:12	8.5, 23.2, 23.3, 71.2
3:25	8.6	2:2	1.3, 8.5, 53.2		
3:27	11.1			6:15	40.4
4:3	103.3	2:3	6.2, 27.3, 76	6:17	24.3
4:4	92.1				
4:6	26.3, 89.2	2:12	8.2	**Philippians**	
4:9	77	2:12-13	27.1	1:6	3.3
4:19	51	2:14	9.4, 9.5	1:23	4.4
4:22	41.2	2:19	8.3, 12.2	2:3	41.9
4:25-26	19.4	2:20	9.5	2:6	22.5, 97.3
4:26	19.6, 22.1	3:16	115, 116	2:7	60.2

2:8	34.2, 41	3:9	3.1	5:12	33.5
2:9	41	3:13	18.5	6:8	2.1
2:10	2.3	3:16	55.1	6:16	3.6
2:12	18.5, 22.2	4:6	2.4	6:17	77
2:21	3.9, 29.5, 34.5	**1 Thessalonians**		**2 Timothy**	
3:12	33.9	1:6	5.5	1:12	27.8
3:13	6.2, 8.8, 25.4, 117, 124.2	2:19	50.1	2:4	1.2, 2.1, 90.3, 103.3
		2:19-20	1.8	2:12	28.3, 63
		3:3	27.2		
3:13-14	8.8, 16.6	4:3	125.2	2:19	4.5
3:14	40.9	4:3-4	55.4, 125.2	2:24	27.5
3:19	19.1	4:4	85	2:26	14.3
3:20	123.2	4:10-11	55.3	3:5	17.8
3:21	2.6, 34.4, 82.1, 123.1	5:3	1.3, 111.4	3:12	3.1, 53.1, 61.1
		5:17	25.5		
4:1	22.2	5:17-18	107.1	3:17	58.2
4:4	18.3	5:23	59	4:3	34.1
4:5	18.3			4:7	27.5, 41.10
4:6	27.5	**2 Thessalonians**		4:8	1.7, 50.1
4:7	16.1, 19.2, 33.2	3:7-8	55.3	**Titus**	
		3:8	12.4	2:11-12	54, 102.2
4:13	91.6	3:10	55.3	2:12	54
		3:12	55.3	2:13	8.8, 28.5, 102.2
Colossians					
1:11	11.1	**1 Timothy**		3:4	29.3
1:13	11.1, 85	1:5	45.5, 45.6	3:6	27.3
1:19	49	1:15	42.1	3:11	6.3
1:20	3.5, 66.3	2:1	25.1, 27.4, 27.5, 107.1	**Hebrews**	
1:22	32.2			1:3	22.5
1:24	90.5	2:4	30.2	1:9	33.8
2:3	33.8	2:7	55.3, 57.1, 91.6	1:14	16.4, 70, 125.1
2:9	33.8				
2:14	3.5	2:9	47	2:9	123.1
2:17	67	2:14	11.2, 66.2	2:10	91.6
2:18	23.2	2:15	23.1	2:14	11.2
3:1	116	3:13	9.5	2:16	19.5
3:1-2	8.5	4:8	97.1, 97.3, 111.2, 118	2:17	90.2
3:4	22.9, 82.1				
3:5	28.2				

4:12	24.2	1:17	13.2, 41.9, 90.2	3:14	2.5, 29.5
4:13	5.2, 7.2, 40.6	1:19	30.1, 41.7	3:15	29.4
4:15	34.2, 90.2	1:21	27.8	3:18	22.5
4:16	90.2	1:27	11.3	4:8	14.2, 93.2
5:8	41	2:17	10.1, 45.5, 58.1, 111.1	4:10	92.2
5:12	8.8			4:13	5.1
5:14	23.2	2:18	111.4	4:17	96.2
6:6	28.2	2:19	1.3, 2.2, 97.2	5:3	92.3
6:8	1.6			5:6	5.5, 27.8
6:18	4.5	2:20	45.5	5:7	121
9:3	28.1	3:2	5.5, 17.8, 18.4, 26.1, 34.2	5:8	3.3, 23.3
9:6-7	28.1			5:8-9	23.3
9:9	67			5:17	7.3
9:9-10	67	3:5	17.2, 17.5	**2 Peter**	
9:13	67	3:11	40.6	2:7	27.1
10:1	53.2, 67	3:15	52.1	2:22	8.4
10:26	28.2	3:17	24.1, 52.1	3:15	7.1, 96.3
10:27	1.3	4:3	25.5		
10:31	12.4, 17.7, 40.4, 82.2, 108	4:4	29.1	**1 John**	
		4:6	1.2	1:4	18.1
		4:17	40.5	1:8	28.6
11:6	28.3, 107.1	5:5	19.1	2:6	60.3
11:8	41	5:14	25.2	2:15-16	29.1, 45.3
11:10	78	5:16	25.2, 40.6	2:16	23.3, 29.4, 45.6, 54
11:13	25.8	5:17	16.3, 27.4		
11:13-14	2.8			3:2	1.4, 18.1, 22.8, 28.7, 41.12, 82.1, 123.1
12:3	1.8	**1 Peter**			
12:4	1.7	1:4	40.4		
12:6	5.4, 125.1	1:12	16.5, 18.1, 41.10		
12:12-13	62			3:6	4.5
12:14	41.10, 98	1:18	27.1	3:16	22.5, 34.6
12:22	91.1	2:2	8.6, 8.7	3:17	88.2
13:14	1.3, 20.2, 78	2:3	3.1	3:18	27.8, 111.6
		2:11	32.3, 32.4, 82.2, 85, 105.2	3:21	7.2
13:17	92.3			4:1	23.2
				4:12	50.3
James		2:21	60.2	4:16	117, 121
1:6	25.2, 25.6	2:22	28.1, 33.3, 34.4, 40.4	4:17	84.2, 111.7
1:14	11.1, 117			4:18	56.1, 121

5:6	8.5	3:17	5.2, 20.4	14:13	2.6, 24.4,
5:16	6.3, 7.4,	3:19	5.4, 7.4		64.1
	13.3	3:20	32.4	20:6	116
5:18	4.5	4:8	40.3	21:4	2.8, 16.5,
		5:5	41.2, 57.1,		34.6
Jude			57.2	21:5	69.2
3	2.1	6:11	41.12	21:19	16.7
		6:14	9.1	21:21	16.7, 41.12
Revelation		8:4–5	91.1	21:27	16.7
1:5	11.1, 33.1	12:9	24.1, 25.8	22:11	8.5
3:16	15.4, 24.2	12:12	1.3, 23.3	22:20	11.3

Subject Index

This selective index indicates subjects in Bernard's *Monastic Sermons*, identified in each case by sermon number and, if the sermon contains more than one paragraph, by paragraph number. God and Christ are not included in the index.

Aaron, 34.1
Abel, 66.3
Abraham, 19.5, 25.8, 41.2, 41.5
Abundance, 16.7, 33.2, 42.7
Acedia, 80.2
Adam, 2.2, 2.6, 2.7, 5.2, 11.2, 13.1, 15.1, 19.2, 20.3, 22.6, 27.7, 28.3, 28.7, 30.1, 66.1, 66.2, 69.1, 72.2, 98, 102.1
Adversary, 3.3, 20.5, 124.1
Adversity, 15.5, 41.10
Affection, 6.1, 8.1, 8.3, 13.4, 14.3, 16.5, 25.2, 32.2, 34.6, 66.2, 86.2, 96.3, 96.6, 107.1, 111.1, 115
Affliction, 2.8, 12.4, 15.1, 16.5
Agar, 42.1
Alms, 17.3, 91.2, 105.2, 109
Altar, 2.4, 34.1
Ambition, 23.3, 28.4, 45.3
Ambrose, 22.7, 40.10
Andrew, 16.6
Angels, 2.3, 9.1, 12.1, 13.1, 14.1, 14.4, 16.4, 17.6, 18.4, 19.2, 19.4, 19.5, 23.2, 23.5, 24.1, 25.8, 27.4, 27.5, 30.1, 40.4, 40.5, 41.11, 42.7, 47, 49, 52.3, 58.2, 66.1, 77, 80.1, 87.3, 124.2
Anger, 23.3, 40.3
Animals, 10.2, 11.2, 16.1, 16.3, 33.5 (*see also* Beasts)
Anxiety, 16.7, 40.3, 83
Apostasy, 26.3
Apostle(s), 1.3, 1.5, 1.6, 1.7, 1.8, 2.4, 7.1, 7.2, 7.3, 7.4, 8.4, 9.1, 11.1, 13.2, 15.4, 16.1, 16.6, 18.2, 18.3, 18.4, 19.1, 21.1, 22.2, 22.4, 23.1, 23.2, 24.3, 25.1, 25.5, 27.3, 27.4, 27.5, 29.3, 29.5, 32.1, 32.2, 33.6, 33.8, 34.3, 34.5, 34.6, 40.2, 40.6, 41.1, 41.7, 41.10, 49, 53.1, 55.3, 59, 61.1, 62, 66.2, 69.1, 80.1, 84.1, 85, 88.1, 89.1, 90.2, 91.6, 93.2, 94.1, 96.3, 96.5, 102.2, 103.2, 105.1, 106.1, 107.1, 107.2, 108, 123.1, 125.1, 125.2
Appearance, 86.2, 90.3
Appetites, 14.3, 28.5, 31.2, 33.5, 114

Archdeacon, 42.3
Ark, 41.6
Armies, 14.1, 24.3, 91.4
Arms, 25.1, 51, 117
Arrogance, 17.2, 69.1, 69.2, 83
Ascent, 33.1, 60.2, 60.4
Ascetics, 51, 91.3
Assumption, 60.1
Augustine, 2.1, 102.1, 114
Authority, 8.8, 22.4, 25.7, 34.1, 41.3, 41.5

Babylon, 2.1, 5.2, 14.6, 20.5, 23.6, 40.3
Baptism, 11.1, 11.3, 28.2, 40.4, 93.2
Beasts, 1.6, 6.1, 12.1, 12.2, 12.4, 28.7, 72.4 (*see also* Animals)
Beatitude, 8.8
Beauty, 12.2, 32.3, 34.4, 91.3, 93.1, 109, 122
Bed, 2.8, 15.2, 19.1, 31.2, 34.2, 34.5, 112
Bedroom, 8.9, 32.4, 41.10, 87.1, 91.5, 92.1
Beelzebub, 33.7
Beersheba, 94.1
Benedict, 31.1
Birds, 45.1, 72.3
Birth, 22.6, 23.4, 51, 52.4, 93.2
Bishop, 42.3, 100
Bitterness, 3.1, 3.6, 3.7, 5.4, 5.5, 8.8, 12.3, 13.4, 23.4, 30.2, 41.5, 95.1
Blame, 3.6, 34.2
Blasphemy, 25.4, 33.7, 55.1
Blessing(s), 29.1, 33.4, 33.6, 33.9, 76
Blindness, 45.6
Blood, 3.5, 6.3, 8.5, 22.6, 23.3, 23.6, 25.2, 25.3, 33.4, 40.5, 40.8, 67, 96.4, 99, 108
Bloodletting, 108

Boasting, 27.5, 47
Body, 2.6, 2.7, 2.8, 3.1, 3.5, 4.4, 5.1, 5.4, 8.2, 10.1, 10.2, 10.4, 12.1, 12.4, 13.3, 14.3, 14.4, 15.5, 16.1, 16.2, 16.5, 17.5, 19.1, 22.6, 22.8, 23.2, 23.5, 25.4, 26.4, 28.4, 30.2, 31.2, 32.1, 32.3, 33.6, 33.9, 34.3, 34.4, 34.5, 40.7, 40.9, 41.1, 41.5, 41.6, 41.11, 41.12, 47, 58.2, 59, 65.1, 67, 69.1, 74, 78, 82.1, 82.2, 84.1, 85, 86.1, 86.2, 87.4, 87.6, 90.5, 91.5, 92.1, 93.2, 96.4, 98, 106.1, 106.2, 111.1, 111.6, 114, 116, 120, 124.2
Bone(s), 6.1, 6.3, 28.2, 28.7, 32.3
Book(s), 9.1, 57.2, 96.3
Borders, 16.7, 19.3
Bosom, 15.2, 65.3
Boys, 40.9, 96.4
Bread, 1.6, 2.4, 2.7, 2.8, 8.5, 12.1, 18.2, 24.3, 27.2, 42.1, 51, 55.3, 59, 71.2, 87.4, 88.1, 97.2, 97.3, 100, 103.3
Breasts, 8.7, 87.5, 90.4
Bricks, 8.3, 71.1, 71.2
Bride, 33.4, 34.2, 40.3, 42.3, 69.2, 89.1, 89.2, 90.4, 93.1
Bridegroom, 8.1, 17.8, 28.5, 33.4, 40.3, 50.2, 87.1, 87.2, 87.4, 87.5, 89.2, 90.4
Briers, 20.4, 28.4
Brothers, 16.3, 19.5, 23.5, 27.3, 24.1, 34.6, 82.2, 82.3, 105.1
  Lay brothers, 22.2
Bulls, 16.3, 67, 91.1
Burdens, 1.7, 1.8, 2.8, 8.5, 12.3, 22.1, 25.4, 26.4, 33.6, 42.3, 42.5, 42.6, 42.7, 97.1, 111.2, 111.3
Burial, 90.3
Business, 2.1, 9.4, 42.1, 42.2, 42.7

Subject Index 453

Cain, 66.3
Calves, 2.8, 19.1, 40.4
Canaan, 40.1, 107.1
Carelessness, 27.5, 28.6
Celibates, 9.3
Centurion, 24.3
Charity, 3.1, 5.5, 7.4, 14.2, 16.1, 17.4, 17.5, 19.6, 23.5, 26.3, 27.4, 29.3, 33.8, 34.3, 56.1, 56.2, 59, 61.2, 64.2, 65.3, 80.2, 87.6, 88.2, 90.3, 91.3, 91.4, 92.2, 93.2, 95.2, 96.1, 96.5, 96.6, 101, 109, 111.3, 116, 120, 121, 125.3
Charity, fraternal, 79, 83
Chastity, 16.1, 22.3, 26.3, 27.3, 59, 61.1, 64.2, 91.3, 109, 111.3
Cheerfulness, 2.5, 41.6, 124.2
Cherubim, 41.11
Children, 2.1, 2.6, 3.9, 8.6, 8.8, 12.3, 15.1, 19.3, 21.2, 28.5, 42.5, 95.1, 98, 104.1, 115, 125.1, 125.2, 125.3
  of Adam, 42.3
Choir, 9.4
Church, 3.5, 8.7, 25.2, 27.5, 33.5, 33.8, 40.10, 41.7, 41.13, 42.3, 42.7, 58.1, 87.6, 90.5, 91.7, 93.2, 94.1, 94.2, 95.1, 96.1, 106.2
Circumcision, 17.7, 51
Citizen(s), Citizenship, 8.3, 16.3, 22.8, 40.7, 70
City, 1.3, 18.1, 18.4, 20.2, 22.1, 40.3, 41.1, 41.12, 41.13, 78, 114
  of God, 22.8
Clairvaux, 30.1
Clay, 8.3, 71.1, 71.2, 86.2
Cleanness, 21.1, 33.5
Clergy, 92.3
Cleric, 32.4
Cloister, 42.4, 70, 91.1, 91.3

Clothing, 31.2, 47
Cloud(s), 22.8, 25.8, 41.11
Columns, 16.5, 52.2, 52.4
Command, 16.4, 41.4, 41.10, 42.3, 97.1
Commandment(s), 2.5, 9.3, 17.1, 18.4, 22.9, 24.3, 33.6, 40.1, 41.3, 41.8, 45.5, 66.2, 67, 96.3, 121, 124.2
Community, 9.4, 10.2, 16.7, 17.6
Compassion, 3.7, 14.5, 16.3, 16.4, 23.4, 25.2, 42.5, 50.1, 51, 58.1, 82.3, 87.5, 104.2, 113
Complaint(s), 1.7, 2.8, 41.5
Compunction, 87.6, 88.1, 90.1, 123.1
Conception, 22.6
Concupiscence, 6.1, 11.1, 14.3, 14.4, 14.5, 14.7, 18.2, 25.4, 28.4, 28.5, 29.4, 31.2, 45.3, 50.2, 54, 63, 75, 125.3
Condemnation, 13.1, 13.2
Confession, 3.8, 15.5, 16.2, 16.5, 25.2, 40.2, 40.3, 40.6, 40.10, 55.1, 58.1, 69.2, 75, 81, 82.3, 91.1, 91.2, 94.2, 104.1, 104.2, 111.6, 113, 125.3
Confessors, 64.1
Congratulations, 16.5, 82.3, 87.5
Congregation, 22.4, 91.3, 93.2
Conscience, 1.2, 8.5, 14.1, 16.1, 16.7, 20.4, 22.6, 30.2, 34.3, 41.3, 45.5, 72.1, 96.4, 104.2, 112
Consent, 26.4, 28.5, 32.3, 45.6
Consolation, 1.4, 3.1, 5.1, 5.4, 5.5, 8.6, 8.8, 28.5, 92.1, 93.2, 103.3
Consummation, 24.2, 111.7
Contemplation, 2.1, 2.6, 3.4, 3.5, 3.7, 3.8, 5.5, 87.1, 87.2, 87.3, 87.4
Contempt, 14.6, 72.3, 94.2, 95.2
Contrition, 40.4, 40.6, 48, 87.6

Conversation, 17.3, 17.5, 17.6, 17.7, 23.2
Conversion, 3.8, 5.4, 5.5, 8.2, 8.6, 17.1, 26.2, 27.5, 27.8, 49, 91.1, 92.2
Cornelius, 91.2
Correction, 5.4, 40.8
Corruption, 4.4, 20.1, 23.1, 33.4, 41.3, 74, 82.2
Counsel, 14.4, 14.7, 24.1, 27.1, 58.1, 96.1, 96.3, 115
Country, 8.2, 8.3
Court, 7.2, 25.7
Covenant, 11.3
Creator, 3.9, 8.2, 9.1, 22.9, 23.6
Creditor, 22.8, 22.9
Crime(s), 4.5, 8.5, 25.1, 27.3, 28.7, 40.2, 42.6, 61.1
Criminals, 42.6
Cross, 3.5, 4.4, 13.1, 16.6, 17.5, 19.5, 25.1, 28.2, 29.3, 40.2, 57.2, 60.2, 63, 96.6, 111.3
Crown, 14.5, 16.6, 41.1, 42.5, 50.1, 70
Crucifixion, 60.2
Cruelty, 41.2, 74
Cunning, 22.3, 24.1, 72.3
Cupidity, 15.1, 75
Curiosity, 6.2, 14.2, 14.7, 16.7, 54, 74, 80.2, 125.3
Curse, 28.2, 65.1

Dancing, 40.4, 41.6
Danger, 22.5, 26.2, 41.1, 42.3, 88.2
Daniel, 9.3, 91.7
Darkness, 1.8, 5.2, 7.3, 11.1, 12.2, 20.4, 23.2, 29.2, 40.3, 42.6, 71.2, 85
Daughter(s), 3.4, 13.4, 21.2, 22.7, 41.10, 107.1

David, 3.3, 4.5, 5.3, 6.1, 6.3, 32.3, 40.2, 41.6, 53.2, 96.2, 124.2
Dawn, 22.8, 91.3
Day, 49, 72.5
Deacon, 42.3
Death, 1.1, 1.3, 1.6, 2.3, 2.4, 2.5, 2.8, 3.8, 6.2, 6.3, 11.3, 12.4, 13.1, 13.3, 16.2, 17.5, 17.7, 19.1, 19.2, 19.5, 20.1, 20.2, 20.4, 21.3, 22.3, 22.9, 25.5, 27.3, 28.2, 28.5, 29.3, 34.3, 40.3, 42.3, 42.4, 57.2, 60.2, 64.1, 72.5, 75, 85, 106.2, 107.2, 111.5, 112, 116, 119
Debauchery, 1.3, 69.1, 69.2
Debt, Debtors, 18.5, 22.5, 22.7, 22.8, 22.9, 33.5, 34.1, 34.3, 42.2
Deceit, 3.1, 80.2
Deception, 1.1, 1.3
Decree, 40.3, 40.5
Degradation, 12.2, 41.1
Delight(s), 25.6, 33.2, 34.5, 40.3, 41.13, 91.5
Demon(s), 2.2, 4.5, 33.2, 42.7, 55.2, 72.1, 91.4
Descent, 42.2, 60.2, 60.4
Desert, 12.3, 91.1, 91.5, 94.2
Desire, 7.1, 8.4, 8.5, 8.6, 8.9, 9.3, 14.3, 14.4, 16.7, 23.3, 25.6, 28.4, 28.5, 29.3, 32.4, 33.1, 41.11, 42.7, 65.1, 69.1, 69.2, 70, 72.2, 72.4, 75, 77, 82.2, 85, 87.1, 94.2, 96.1, 96.5, 96.6, 101, 111.1, 115, 123.1
Desires, carnal, 32.3, 32.4, 105.2
Despair, 3.8, 6.3, 87.1, 104.1, 104.2, 112
Destruction, 23.4, 111.4
Devil, 3.3, 6.2, 8.5, 11.1, 11.3, 12.4, 14.3, 23.2, 23.3, 33.7, 42.6, 60.3, 60.4, 71.2, 72.1, 72.3, 84.2, 94.1, 97.2, 111.1, 111.3, 121

Subject Index

Devotion, 2.5, 3.7, 8.6, 17.1, 23.6, 24.2, 25.6, 41.6, 48, 60.4, 87.6, 88.1, 90.1, 90.3
Diadem, 50.1, 50.2
Dignity, 19.5, 40.2, 41.10, 120
Dinah, 14.3
Dirt, Dirtiness, 17.1, 17.2, 31.3, 45.6, 81, 93.2, 121 (*see also* Filth)
Disciple(s), 5.1, 8.7, 23.1, 23.2, 40.1, 40.2, 55.2, 89.2, 90.5, 91.6, 92.2, 96.4, 96.5, 98, 100, 121
Discipline, 5.4, 8.6, 42.4, 55.4, 80.2, 82.3, 92.2, 97.2, 100, 103.3, 104.2
Discretion, 40.7, 82.3, 91.4, 100
Discussion, 17.6, 22.5
Disease, 32.3, 96.4, 108
Disobedience, 1.3, 2.5, 17.1, 63, 66.1, 103.3
Divinity, 16.5, 19.3, 33.8, 34.2, 45.1, 49, 60.1, 87.4, 90.1, 90.2, 119
Doctrine, 34.1, 49, 91.5, 91.7, 94.2, 121
Dogs, 2.3, 15.3, 100
Donkey, 12.4, 29.2, 41.2
Door, 17.7, 28.5, 28.6, 32.4, 42.3
Dove, 3.4, 3.5, 5.2, 17.6, 89.1
Dragons, 87.5
Drink, 19.1, 23.3, 31.2, 41.12, 45.1, 51, 87.4, 121
Dung, 2.7, 5.4, 25.1, 25.8, 40.3, 82.2, 123.1
Duty, 9.5, 11.2

Ears, 7.4, 8.4, 10.4, 15.3, 16.7, 17.6, 23.6, 24.1, 24.2, 28.4, 41.5, 41.7, 42.3, 58.2, 77, 95.2, 97.3, 111.2, 116
Earth, 1.6, 2.3, 12.2, 21.3, 22.9, 31.2, 34.2, 40.5, 74, 92.1, 124.2

Eating, 45.1, 92.1
Ecclesiastes, 50.1
Egypt, 8.3, 22.1, 51, 71.1, 71.2
Elect, 4.4, 8.1, 27.3, 33.8, 41.13, 42.7, 72.4, 87.2, 87.4
Elijah, 84.2, 94.1
Elisha, 2.4, 95.1
Embarrassment, 104.1, 104.2
Emotions, 50.1, 50.3
Enemies, 10.2, 10.3, 16.7, 17.4, 22.5, 23.3, 23.4, 25.5, 27.8, 28.7, 29.1, 31.3, 32.4, 40.7, 70, 82.2, 97.2, 107.2, 121, 123.2
Enticement, 28.4, 55.4
 Carnal, 9.3, 40.3
Envy, 11.3, 28.4, 40.3, 42.3, 48, 82.3, 83
Ephraim, 2.8
Equality, Equals, 92.2, 92.3, 116
Eternity, 3.9, 21.2, 21.3, 27.2, 33.9, 64.2, 111.7, 116
Ethics, 45.2
Evangelist(s), 16.1, 96.5
Eve, 2.7, 11.2, 22.3, 23.2, 66.1, 66.2, 66.3, 72.1, 98
Evil, 3.8, 5.2, 11.2, 12.1, 14.1, 14.2, 14.3, 14.6, 14.7, 17.1, 17.5, 22.7, 25.4, 28.5, 28.7, 33.5, 66.3, 71.1, 72.2, 72.3, 72.5, 85, 124.2, 125.3
Evil one, 2.3, 8.5, 14.4
Evils, 2.1, 12.3, 28.5, 41.3
Exaltation, 20.2, 20.3
Excommunication, 100
Excuses, 27.3, 41.5, 66.3
Exile, 12.2, 12.3, 22.5, 47, 50.1, 102.1
Eye(s), 2.8, 3.1, 3.5, 4.4, 5.5, 7.2, 8.4, 8.8, 10.1, 10.4, 16.1, 16.2, 16.7, 19.3, 22.2, 22.9, 25.2, 26.4, 28.4, 28.6, 28.7, 40.3, 40.6, 40.9, 41.7,

41.9, 41.11, 42.7, 45.3, 47, 54, 70, 74, 104.2, 116, 123.1
Ezekiel, 91.7

Face, 6.2, 8.9, 22.6, 26.4, 40.3, 41.6, 41.11, 41.12, 86.2, 121, 122
Faith, 15.3, 15.4, 17.7, 23.2, 25.2, 25.6, 28.2, 28.3, 33.5, 34.1, 41.2, 45.4, 45.5, 45.6, 49, 52.2, 52.4, 58.1, 64.2, 75, 78, 87.4, 96.4, 105.1, 105.2, 111.1, 111.4, 125.3
Fall, 2.6, 45.3, 45.4, 102.1
Falsehood, 40.8, 90.4
Family, 10.2, 41.2, 42.3, 50.1
Famine, 8.3, 8.5, 71.1, 95.1
Farm, Farmer, 1.8, 8.3, 17.3, 81, 85
Fasting, Fasts, 14.3, 24.1, 55.2, 65.2, 67, 95.2, 105.2, 122
Fat, 16.7, 22.9, 33.7
Father, 3.1, 3.9, 7.3, 8.1, 8.2, 8.8, 21.2, 27.3, 28.1, 31.2, 41.2, 125.2, 125.3
Fear, 3.1, 3.2, 3.3, 3.7, 4.3, 4.4, 5.5, 7.3, 8.6, 8.7, 12.1, 12.4, 14.1, 14.3, 14.7, 16.7, 17.7, 29.3, 40.4, 40.6, 50.2, 50.3, 56.2, 61.1, 66.2, 72.3, 72.4, 73, 96.1, 104.1, 104.2, 111.1, 117, 121, 123.2, 125.3
of God, 26.4, 56.1
Feebleness, 32.3, 90.3
Feelings, 29.1, 86.2
Feet, 13.1, 24.2, 24.3, 25.3, 25.6, 28.5, 40.4, 40.8, 41.7, 41.10, 42.2, 72.3, 78, 87.1, 87.6, 90.1, 90.2, 90.5, 98, 107.1
Fellowship, 64.2, 92.2
Field, 15.1, 65.1
Filth, 6.2, 8.4, 17.2, 33.3 (see also *Dirt, Dirtiness*)

Fingers, 10.1, 19.5, 21.2
Fire, 1.6, 1.8, 2.4, 6.3, 12.3, 12.4, 19.1, 24.2, 28.6, 28.7, 29.2, 30.1, 30.2, 40.4, 40.5, 41.2, 42.6, 71.2, 72.1, 74, 87.6, 95.1, 96.4, 99, 109, 111.2, 121
Firewood, 28.5
Fish, 34.6, 65.3, 97.3
Flame, 1.8, 28.6, 40.3, 41.2, 96.4
Flattery, 17.2, 96.1, 97.1
Flavor, 2.4, 73
Flesh, 1.3, 2.6, 3.7, 3.8, 5.2, 6.1, 6.2, 6.3, 8.4, 8.9, 10.2, 12.2, 12.4, 19.1, 21.2, 23.1, 23.2, 23.3, 23.6, 24.1, 28.4, 29.2, 29.3, 29.4, 30.2, 32.3, 33.2, 33.8, 34.2, 34.4, 34.5, 40.3, 40.7, 41.11, 45.3, 49, 50.2, 52.4, 54, 55.4, 57.1, 57.2, 60.2, 63, 66.1, 69.1, 71.2, 72.1, 78, 79, 82.2, 82.3, 84.1, 87.4, 90.2, 91.1, 91.5, 93.2, 96.4, 98, 101, 103.1, 111.3, 112, 123.1, 124.2
Flock, 12.1, 17.8, 29.5, 55.3, 100
Food, 2.4, 2.7, 2.8, 8.8, 12.1, 12.3, 14.7, 15.1, 18.1, 19.1, 23.3, 24.2, 24.3, 31.2, 87.4, 93.2, 94.2
Fool(s), Foolishness, 5.4, 7.1, 7.2, 73, 125.2
Force, 14.4, 22.3
Foreigner, 8.3, 27.5, 27.8
Forgetfulness, 41.10, 42.6, 55.2
Forgiveness, 3.8, 25.4, 33.4, 53.1, 87.1, 87.6, 107.2
Fornication, 14.4, 17.1, 26.3, 27.3, 55.4, 125.2
Fortitude, 14.3, 14.7, 41.8, 50.2, 50.3, 52.3, 72.2, 76, 113
Foundation, 30.1, 30.2, 33.1, 78, 91.3
Fountain, 19.3, 22.2, 56.1, 96.1
Fragility, 40.9, 123.2

Subject Index

Fragrance, 2.8, 90.1
Frailty, 14.3, 33.5, 34.5
Frankincense, 91.1
Freedom, 11.1, 34.3, 41.1, 41.2, 116
Friend(s), Friendship, 10.3, 16.7, 22.5, 27.1, 27.8, 29.1, 99, 101, 103.1, 103.4, 121
Fruit, 1.7, 16.2, 16.5, 22.7, 22.9, 27.1, 28.7, 41.10, 50.2, 59, 65.1, 76, 91.2, 91.6, 92.1, 94.2, 105.1, 125.3
Furnace, 40.3, 96.4, 103.3
Future, 7.2, 16.7, 50.3, 56.1, 61.2, 92.1, 97.1, 97.3, 99, 106.1, 106.2, 111.2, 111.6

Galilee, 58.2
Garden, 2.6, 92.1, 92.3, 94.2
Garments, 17.1, 25.2, 28.2, 34.4, 40.4, 47, 91.4, 96.4, 99, 107.1
Gates, 16.7, 19.3, 22.3, 28.7, 32.4
Gehenna, 4.3, 12.4, 32.4, 40.3, 40.7, 42.6, 70
Generation, 3.3, 4.5, 27.5, 33.4, 33.6, 41.4
Genitals, 74
Gentiles, 55.3, 125.2
Giants, 15.2, 40.1, 42.1
Gift, divine, 87.3
Gifts, 1.6, 8.6, 13.2, 14.1, 17.1, 27.4, 27.8, 33.8, 41.9, 42.3, 61.2, 87.1, 88.1, 88.2, 90.1, 91.7, 103.2, 107.2, 123.1
Glass, 9.1, 16.7, 41.11
Glorification, 7.3, 21.1, 34.4, 42.5, 103.4, 105.1, 105.2
Glory, 1.4, 1.5, 1.7, 1.8, 2.5, 2.6, 4.1, 7.1, 7.2, 7.3, 8.9, 11.1, 12.2, 12.3, 12.4, 15.3, 16.7, 19.1, 21.1, 21.3, 22.5, 22.8, 25.5, 25.7, 28.5, 33.2, 33.4, 41.1, 42.3, 45.5, 50.1, 60.2, 76, 91.6
Glue, 4.3, 4.5, 15.1
Gluttony, 55.2
Goad, 20.5, 72.4
Goal, 22.1, 25.4, 41.10
Goats, 67, 91.1
Gold, 15.1, 19.4, 28.6, 28.7, 29.2, 30.2, 33.2, 42.1, 96.2, 103.3
Gomorrah, 18.2
Good works, 23.1, 33.5, 40.2, 40.7, 87.1, 106.1, 106.2
Goodness, 13.2, 16.4, 23.6, 107.2
Goods, 8.4, 23.6, 41.3, 42.1
  Eternal, 16.5, 16.6, 16.7
  Spiritual, 16.5
Gospel, 5.1, 5.3, 17.8, 25.4, 27.7, 40.4, 51, 58.2, 67, 87.3, 90.5, 91.6, 95.2, 96.5, 97.1, 99, 104.1, 105.1, 107.1, 124.1, 125.3
Gossip, 17.4
Grace, 1.2, 2.6, 3.1, 3.3, 3.4, 8.6, 10.1, 13.1, 14.5, 16.1, 16.6, 17.1, 17.8, 21.1, 21.3, 22.2, 25.3, 25.4, 25.5, 25.6, 27.4, 27.5, 27.8, 28.2, 33.8, 45.5, 55.4, 76, 87.2, 87.3, 92.2, 94.1
Grain, 16.7, 56.1, 81
Gratitude, 23.6, 27.8
Greeks, 91.6
Gregory, 9.1, 25.5, 29.1, 58.1, 72.4, 95.2, 96.1
Grief, 3.1
Groans, 16.3, 42.5
Grumbling, 26.3, 41.5
Guilt, 4.2, 34.6, 40.6, 45.4, 84.1, 99

Habakkuk, 5.4, 29.3
Habit, 8.5, 25.7, 27.6, 71.2
Hair, 25.3, 107.1

Hand(s), 2.8, 5.5, 9.2, 10.4, 17.1, 17.2, 22.2, 23.1, 24.3, 25.1, 27.8, 33.3, 33.5, 33.7, 40.4, 40.7, 41.13, 41.7, 41.8, 41.13, 58.1, 74, 87.1, 90.3

Happiness, 1.8, 3.9, 16.7, 18.4, 19.6, 20.1, 21.1, 22.1, 33.2, 41.10, 77, 111.1

Harlot(s), 8.3, 8.4, 111.3

Harp, 3.1, 9.4

Head, 27.6, 28.2, 28.3, 28.5, 28.6, 33.6, 34.3, 34.4, 41.12, 42.2, 58.2, 90.2, 90.3, 90.4, 90.5, 100
of the Household, 8.1, 8.6, 23.1

Health, 6.1, 16.2, 16.4, 32.3, 42.2, 45.4, 96.4, 114

Hearing, 10.2, 10.4, 17.7, 22.2

Heart, 1.2, 2.8, 3.1, 4.2, 5.2, 5.3, 5.4, 5.5, 6.1, 7.2, 7.4, 8.9, 9.2, 9.4, 10.1, 12.1, 13.2, 14.2, 14.3, 14.5, 15.2, 15.4, 16.1, 16.2, 16.7, 17.1, 17.2, 17.6, 17.8, 19.1, 19.5, 19.6, 23.5, 23.6, 24.2, 25.3, 25.4, 26.3, 26.4, 28.2, 28.4, 28.5, 28.7, 29.1, 29.2, 29.4, 30.2, 31.1, 31.2, 33.2, 33.3, 33.4, 33.5, 33.7, 34.3, 34.4, 34.5, 40.5, 40.6, 40.7, 41.2, 41.4, 41.9, 45.5, 52.2, 58.2, 60.4, 65.3, 69.1, 69.2, 72.2, 72.5, 82.1, 86.2, 87.6, 90.3, 90.5, 94.2, 95.2, 96.2, 96.3, 96.4, 96.6, 110, 111.1, 111.6, 115, 123.1, 124.1

Heaven, 3.5, 3.9, 4.5, 9.1, 13.1, 14.1, 16.3, 16.5, 20.1, 22.5, 22.7, 22.8, 25.2, 25.8, 28.1, 30.1, 34.2, 40.4, 42.5, 60.1, 60.2, 60.3, 65.1, 87.4, 92.1, 99, 103.1, 124.2

Hell, 2.3, 2.6, 2.8, 3.1, 3.2, 3.7, 3.8, 3.9, 4.3, 12.3, 14.1, 16.1, 19.1, 19.2, 20.1, 20.2, 25.1, 34.2, 42.5, 42.6, 103.1, 104.2, 111.1, 111.4, 111.5

Help, 16.4, 54, 91.6

Hem, 25.2, 96.4, 99, 107.1

Hemor, 14.3

Hezekiah, 3.2, 3.3, 3.5, 3.6, 3.7

Hippocrates, 55.2

Holiness, 9.3, 27.3, 90.3

Homeland, 16.7, 41.2, 42.3

Honey, 1.8, 4.1, 9.1, 15.3, 18.1, 29.4, 72.3, 83, 96.2, 97.1, 97.2, 111.3

Honor, 22.5, 42.3, 56.2

Hope, 3.2, 4.4, 5.5, 16.5, 16.6, 18.2, 45.4, 45.5, 45.6, 73, 97.3, 104.1, 104.2, 112, 123.2, 125.1

House, 8.5, 11.2, 23.1, 33.2, 41.1, 42.4, 114

Human, 2.6, 3.2, 6.2, 23.5
 Beings, 2.1, 2.2, 7.2, 10.2, 13.1, 20.3, 22.9, 27.4, 74
 Condition, 15.1
 Nature, 9.1, 22.3
 Spirit, 17.8

Humanity, 2.1, 2.5, 33.8, 42.5, 90.2

Humiliation, 3.3, 20.5

Humility, 2.5, 5.5, 7.4, 16.1, 17.1, 19.6, 24.2, 25.4, 26.1, 26.2, 26.3, 27.4, 40.1, 40.6, 41.9, 45.5, 47, 57.2, 59, 60.3, 62, 64.2, 80.2, 88.2, 91.3, 100, 104.2, 111.3, 119, 123.2

Hunger, 2.2, 8.3, 8.5, 12.3, 15.4, 51, 71.1, 71.2

Husband, 22.7, 59, 66.1, 80.1

Hypocrisy, 72.2, 123.1

Hyssop, 6.2

Ignorance, 11.1, 11.2, 12.1, 24.2, 26.2, 49, 64.2, 66.2, 71.2

Illyricum, 91.6

Subject Index

Image, 3.2, 24.1, 40.3, 116
Imitation, 16.1, 16.3, 16.4, 60.3, 60.4, 61.2, 62, 63, 92.2
Impatience, 2.5, 26.3, 122
Imperfections, 7.4, 25.4
Impurity, 7.4, 18.2, 28.6, 40.6
Incarnation, 29.2, 29.3, 60.2, 60.3, 87.3, 119
Indignation, 23.2, 27.6
Infants, 22.5, 28.2, 104.1, 119
Infirmity, 16.7, 25.2, 31.3, 34.5, 41.1, 90.2
Ingratitude, 27.5, 27.6, 27.7, 27.8, 40.5
Inheritance, 8.2, 8.3, 8.8, 28.5, 40.4, 41.2, 125.1
Iniquity, 12.4, 13.4, 15.5, 16.4, 22.7, 27.7, 34.2, 40.6, 41.10, 42.6, 45.3, 64.2, 84.1, 90.3, 103.2
Injury, 98, 107.2
Innocence, 8.1, 8.5, 22.6, 22.7, 33.4, 33.5, 40.4, 60.4, 61.1, 69.2
Insensitivity, 27.5, 58.2
Instruction, 8.7, 26.3
Insult(s), 14.4, 17.2, 40.5, 61.2
Intellect, 11.1, 15.3, 91.5, 105.1
Intelligence, 9.5, 50.2
Intention, 32.2, 40.7, 107.2
Intercession(s), 25.4, 25.5, 25.6, 27.5
Intoxication, 54, 87.4
Isaac, 41.2, 79
Isaiah, 4.3, 7.4, 9.5, 15.2, 33.2, 103.3, 107.2, 123.1
Ishmael, 41.2
Israel, 8.3, 22.6, 41.7, 42.1, 71.1

Jacob, 14.3, 31.2, 42.1
James, 24.1, 25.5, 52.1
Jealousy, 5.4, 31.3, 70, 74, 80.2, 82.3

Jerome, 14.4, 19.1
Jerusalem, 1.8, 16.7, 19.6, 22.1, 34.5, 91.1, 91.6
Jesus, 2.3, 5.1, 8.7, 9.5, 16.6, 17.5, 19.7, 22.4, 25.4, 34.2, 40.4, 41.1, 48, 50.1, 51, 53.2, 60.1, 87.6, 90.1, 90.3
Jews, 1.7, 4.4, 13.1, 15.3, 17.5, 18.2, 33.3, 33.7, 34.3, 53.1, 55.1, 67
Jezebel, 94.1
Job, 2.1, 6.3, 7.4, 9.3, 91.7, 104.1, 124.1
John, 7.2, 16.7, 20.4, 84.2, 95.2
Jokes, dirty, 27.5
Joseph, 51, 53.2
Journey, 41.8, 41.9, 62
Joy, 1.8, 2.5, 2.6, 3.1, 3.7, 3.8, 5.2, 5.4, 16.7, 18.1, 18.2, 18.3, 18.5, 19.2, 19.3, 19.6, 19.7, 22.2, 33.2, 34.2, 40.3, 40.4, 41.10, 41.11, 41.12, 41.13, 42.5, 42.7, 50.2, 50.3, 72.4, 87.1, 87.2
Judah, 98
Judas, 30.1
Judea, 8.5, 18.2
Judges, 20.5, 23.1, 25.6, 29.5, 33.4, 40.4, 60.2, 61.1, 99
Judgment, 1.3, 5.2, 6.3, 7.2, 8.3, 8.5, 12.4, 20.4, 24.4, 32.1, 34.3, 41.7, 60.2, 82.3, 90.1, 90.2, 96.1, 96.2, 102.1, 111.1, 115
   Day of, 17.2, 27.7, 51, 104.2
   Divine, 32.1
   Human, 32.1
Justice, 2.5, 6.3, 12.3, 15.5, 17.1, 18.4, 18.5, 19.2, 19.4, 19.7, 21.3, 22.2, 23.6, 26.4, 27.6, 29.5, 32.4, 34.2, 34.4, 41.9, 41.10, 50.1, 50.2, 50.3, 52.3, 52.4, 54, 58.1, 66.2, 69.2, 72.2, 91.7, 94.1, 102.1,

103.2, 103.3, 105.1, 108, 111.6,
    113, 116
Justification, 21.1, 105.1, 105.2

Kindness, 23.6, 25.2, 25.4, 27.8, 28.1,
    29.3, 40.2, 40.4, 87.6
King, 2.7, 8.9, 22.5, 25.7, 40.2, 41.9,
    41.10, 50.1
Kingdom, 16.1, 18.1, 21.1, 22.8, 28.1,
    28.2, 29.2, 33.7, 40.2, 42.5, 65.1,
    111.2
  of God, 18.4
  of Heaven, 99
Kiss(es), 87.1, 87.2, 89.1, 89.2
Knowledge, 14.2, 14.7, 16.7, 21.2,
    22.3, 26.2, 29.1, 33.8, 49, 60.4,
    88.1, 89.2, 100, 114, 116
  Moral, 92.2
  Worldly, 87.5

Laban, 3.4
Labor(s), 2.1, 2.4, 9.4, 12.4, 21.2, 21.3,
    22.6, 24.4, 27.2, 30.1, 34.3, 55.3,
    67, 72.5
Ladder, 28.5, 61.1, 61.2
Lamb, 28.1, 41.7, 57.2, 94.2
Lamp(s), 1.8, 24.2, 55.4, 109
Laughter, 93.2
Law, 1.3, 8.2, 8.4, 8.6, 14.3, 16.3, 16.7,
    25.1, 26.3, 27.3, 28.1, 28.5, 29.1,
    29.4, 33.6, 34.1, 34.3, 40.5, 41.7,
    42.6, 67, 72.4, 72.5, 124.2
Lazarus, 25.6, 107.1
Laziness, 58.2
Leaders, religious, 9.5
Lent, 22.9
Leper(s), Leprosy, 2.3, 27.5, 27.7
Levity, 30.1, 80.2
Life, 1.1, 1.3, 1.4, 2.2, 2.3, 2.8, 3.1,
    3.3, 3.4, 3.6, 3.7, 4.4, 5.5, 6.3,
    10.1, 17.4, 17.7, 20.1, 21.1, 22.1,
    22.2, 22.5, 22.6, 22.7, 22.8, 29.2,
    33.2, 33.3
  Apostolic, 27.3
  Eternal, 5.1, 24.4, 26.4, 29.2, 96.1,
    116
  Monastic, 95.2
  Religious, 8.6
  Spiritual, 23.2
  Worldly, 70
Light, 2.8, 3.1, 3.6, 5.2, 12.3, 14.5,
    17.1, 17.6, 20.4, 22.8, 24.2, 26.4,
    30.2, 40.7, 41.11, 45.2, 71.2,
    91.3, 107.1, 125.3
Linen, 19.2, 33.2
Lion, 11.2, 23.3, 57.2
Lip(s), 17.2, 25.7, 28.2, 47, 89.2, 93.2,
    124.2
Love, 4.3, 4.4, 7.4, 8.9, 10.1, 10.2,
    11.1, 16.4, 17.4, 19.5, 22.5, 23.6,
    29.1, 29.2, 29.3, 29.4, 29.5, 34.5,
    40.2, 45.4, 45.5, 45.6, 50.2, 50.3,
    56.1, 56.2, 66.2, 69.1, 69.2, 72.4,
    73, 77, 78, 88.1, 89.2, 101, 103.1,
    115, 116, 117, 119, 121
  Carnal, 29.1, 101
  Divine, 4.4, 4.5, 10.1, 10.3, 15.4,
    87.3
  Spiritual, 101
Loving-kindness, 1.2, 14.2, 14.7, 16.4,
    17.3, 20.5, 27.3, 29.3 87.6
Lucifer, 42.6, 60.3, 66.1
Luke, 96.4
Lust, 15.5, 17.2, 28.4, 31.3

Madness, 7.2, 22.9, 23.6, 42.3
Majesty, 15.3, 17.7, 23.6, 28.7, 41.1
Malice, 8.3, 22.3
Man, Men, 11.2, 29.4, 90.3
Manna, 95.2, 111.3

Subject Index

Mara, 2.4
Marketplace, 42.4, 42.6, 42.7
Markets, 17.3, 42.3
Marriage, 3.4, 9.3, 41.10, 91.1
Martha of Bethany, 3.4, 9.4, 9.5, 48
Martyrs, Martyrdom, 6.1, 27.4, 40.7, 40.9, 61.2, 64.1, 96.4
Mary Magdalene, 4.5, 25.3, 34.2, 90.5
Mary of Bethany, 9.4, 9.5, 48
Mary, the Blessed Virgin, 17.6, 22.6, 28.1, 47, 49, 51, 52.2, 52.3, 52.4, 56.1, 87.3
Mary, the mother of James, 90.5
Mary, the penitent, 40.2, 90.1, 90.5
Master, 8.1, 41.3, 100
Measure, 21.3, 86.1, 86.2
Medicine, 24.2, 34.5
Meditation, 2.6, 8.6, 8.8, 16.1, 27.1
Members, 8.4, 28.2, 28.3, 28.5, 90.5
Memory, 8.2, 18.2, 31.2, 32.2, 32.3, 32.4, 42.7, 45.1, 45.6, 72.1, 100, 113, 124.1
Mercenaries, 72.4, 115
Merchants, 17.3, 42.1, 42.2, 65.2, 99
Mercy, 3.7, 4.1, 4.4, 5.3, 5.4, 7.4, 13.1, 13.2, 13.3, 13.4, 14.2, 14.5, 16.4, 22.5, 22.6, 25.1, 25.6, 26.4, 27.1, 27.3, 27.4, 27.6, 33.4, 33.6, 40.4, 41.7, 42.1, 42.5, 45.4, 76, 87.1, 90.1, 90.2, 105.2, 107.2, 125.3
Merit, Merits, 41.10, 87.2, 105.1, 107.2
Micah, 102.2
Milk, 4.1, 8.6, 8.7, 8.8, 33.7, 93.1, 97.1
Mind, 6.3, 8.4, 16.6, 17.5, 17.8, 22.3, 23.5, 25.7, 31.2, 32.4, 34.4, 50.2, 58.1, 72.4, 87.1, 91.5, 106.2
Minister(s), 9.5, 32.1, 62, 121
Ministry, 34.3, 120

Miracle(s), 9.1, 22.6, 41.12, 49
Misery, 41.1, 42.2
Misfortune, 110, 111.1
Mite(s), 22.6, 22.8, 22.9
Monastery, 2.1
Money, 42.3
Monk(s), 14.4, 17.1, 22.2, 22.4, 26.2, 27.4, 27.5, 27.6, 27.7, 30.2, 32.4, 42.4, 93.2
Moon, 91.3, 111.7, 125.2
Morals, 28.2, 28.3, 52.2, 52.4, 67, 71.1, 92.2, 92.3
Morning, 3.3, 3.4
Mortification (of the flesh), 40.7, 91.1
Moses, 2.4, 8.5, 10.1, 67, 95.2
Mother, 2.1, 12.3, 21.2, 28.1, 41.2, 50.1, 50.2
Mountain(s), 6.2, 19.4, 22.1, 28.5, 33.1, 33.2, 33.3, 33.7, 33.8, 33.9, 34.4, 61.1, 61.2, 94.2
Mourning, 5.4, 34.1
Mouth, 2.8, 10.1, 10.4, 15.2, 15.5, 17.1, 17.6, 17.7, 22.2, 22.4, 24.3, 25.3, 28.2, 28.4, 40.7, 69.1, 72.5, 81, 87.1, 87.2, 89.1, 107.1, 111.6
Mud, 8.4, 22.5, 25.1, 31.2, 40.9, 42.3, 45.4, 86.2
Murderer, 22.3, 40.4
Music, 40.4
Myrrh, 91.1
Mysteries, 22.6, 29.4, 41.7, 94.1

Nail(s), 4.3, 4.4, 14.6, 17.5, 22.5
Name, 2.3, 7.1, 26.2, 26.4, 41.1, 53.1, 53.2
Nation(s), 27.1, 41.2
Nature, 3.5, 3.6, 4.3, 8.1, 10.1, 16.1, 16.4, 16.6, 31.2, 40.9, 92.2
Nature, human, 9.1, 22.3

Negligence, 14.1, 14.7, 27.3, 125.3
Neighbor, 10.3, 15.5, 17.7, 18.4, 19.4, 27.5, 33.2, 33.4, 33.5, 33.6, 34.3, 40.8, 45.5, 50.3, 54, 55.4, 61.1, 64.2, 69.2, 80.1, 80.2, 88.1, 88.2, 96.5, 96.6, 102.2, 103.1, 107.2, 113, 122, 123.2, 125.3
Net, 21.1, 34.6
Night, 49, 91.3, 109
Noah, 9.3, 91.7
Novice(s), 8.6, 8.7, 22.2, 40.7

Obedience, 2.4, 2.5, 10.2, 15.5, 26.3, 27.2, 40.2, 40.10, 41.1, 41.2, 41.3, 41.4, 41.5, 41.6, 41.9, 45.5, 58.1, 63, 64.2, 79, 80.2, 103.3, 114
Odor, 33.9, 91.1, 91.2, 92.2
Offense, 23.6, 28.3, 34.3, 40.2, 40.4, 96.4
Offerings, blood, 75
Oil, 2.4, 5.3, 5.4, 9.1, 25.2, 33.8, 72.3, 83, 97.1, 109, 124.2
Ointment, 4.4, 17.5, 19.1, 25.3, 33.9, 40.1, 58.2, 87.6, 90.1, 90.2, 90.3, 90.4, 90.5
Oldness, 13.1, 40.9, 69.1
Omnipotence, 26.1, 111.6
Opinion(s), 26.3, 40.7, 62
Order, 30.1, 30.2, 93.2, 95.2, 114
Orders, 40.5, 41.4, 41.7
Origen, 34.1, 34.5
Ovid, 41.6, 100

Pain, 2.1, 12.4, 34.2, 40.5, 41.2, 42.3, 42.5, 61.2, 72.3, 93.2
Parable, 65.1, 93.1, 109
Paradise, 2.6, 12.2, 13.1, 15.1, 20.1, 26.2, 30.1, 32.3, 40.2, 42.4, 42.6, 42.7, 60.3, 66.1, 66.3, 72.1, 90.2, 94.2, 96.1, 102.1, 103.1, 117

Paralytic, 25.4, 96.4
Pardon, 25.3, 45.5, 67
Parent(s), 10.2, 10.4, 11.2, 42.3
Passion, 6.3, 25.5, 29.2, 29.3, 29.4, 29.5, 41.10, 49, 61.2, 75, 101
Passions, 16.1, 28.4, 29.1
Pastor, 8.7, 40.7, 41.3, 95.2, 100
Path, 4.2, 9.4, 20.4, 24.2, 40.1, 40.3, 40.10, 41.8, 118
Patience, 2.4, 13.1, 13.2, 15.5, 16.1, 23.3, 27.4, 40.4, 58.1, 61.2, 80.2, 82.3, 125.1
Patriarch, 41.2
Paul, 7.1, 19.1, 23.1, 23.2, 27.4, 34.3, 34.5, 41.1, 51, 53.1, 55.3, 87.2, 89.2, 90.2, 91.6, 96.2, 96.3, 118
Peace, 3.7, 9.2, 9.3, 9.4, 9.5, 12.3, 16.3, 16.4, 16.5, 16.7, 18.4, 18.5, 19.2, 19.3, 19.4, 19.6, 19.7, 23.7, 26.3, 26.4, 32.3, 33.2, 40.4, 42.7, 53.2, 61.2, 66.3, 76, 98, 114
Peacemakers, 90.3, 98
Pearls, 15.3, 41.12, 65.2
Penance, 1.3, 5.2, 15.1, 22.7, 33.4, 34.5, 40.4, 65.1, 75, 104.1, 106.1, 106.2, 108
Penitence, 34.3, 45.5, 87.1
Penitent(s), 81, 91.1, 91.5
Perdition, 23.3, 111.5
Perfection, 3.3, 27.5, 110
Perfume, 90.3, 91.2, 92.2
Persecution, 3.1, 29.5, 40.9, 41.8, 51, 94.1
Perseverance, 40.9, 41.8, 41.10, 58.1, 91.4, 111.7
Peter, 25.1, 27.3, 29.1, 29.3, 29.5, 40.2, 41.1, 62, 89.1, 96.3, 96.6, 101, 107.2
Pharaoh, 71.1, 71.2
Pharisees, 41.1, 67

Subject Index

Philistine, 41.9
Philosophers, Philosophy, 7.1, 7.2, 40.1
Physician(s), 40.1, 45.4, 54, 96.4, 107.1, 108
Piety, 4.1, 33.5, 48, 54, 72.1, 91.1, 97.1, 109, 125.3
Pigs, 8.3, 8.4
Pilate, 15.3
Pilgrims, Pilgrimage, 96.3, 105.2
Pleasure, 1.3, 1.4, 1.6, 1.7, 4.2, 5.5, 6.2, 8.4, 10.2, 12.3, 12.4, 14.3, 15.1, 16.2, 18.1, 21.2, 23.3, 23.4, 24.1, 25.4, 26.2, 28.4, 28.5, 31.2, 32.3, 33.5, 40.3, 40.7, 40.8, 42.7, 45.6, 54, 59, 72.1, 74, 79, 80.2, 82.2, 83, 94.2, 97.3, 103.3
Poison, 17.4, 29.4, 56.1, 72.3
Pontiff, 42.3
Poor, 2.4, 111.6
Position, 84.1, 84.2
Possessions, 22.1, 111.6
Pot, Pottery, 2.4, 22.9, 95.1
Poverty, 2.7, 8.4, 20.5, 21.3, 27.5, 48, 93.2, 99, 111.3
Power, 1.5, 3.3, 3.9, 8.5, 11.1, 11.2, 21.1, 22.4, 25.2, 25.4, 29.3, 29.5, 34.5, 40.5, 41.1, 41.3, 41.10, 56.2, 57.2, 60.1, 60.4, 72.3, 84.2
Divine, 13.3
Praise, 3.4, 3.8, 5.4, 7.1, 7.3, 15.5, 19.3, 21.1, 40.2, 81, 83, 99
Prayer, 3.5, 16.2, 16.3, 16.4, 22.5, 25.1, 25.3, 25.5, 25.6, 25.7, 25.8, 27.5, 41.11, 42.5, 55.2, 65.2, 82.3, 89.2, 91.1, 95.2, 101, 105.2, 107.1, 107.2, 113, 125.2
Preacher(s), 50.1, 51, 91.5, 91.6, 95.1, 95.2, 98
Preaching, 47, 56.1

Predestination, 4.5, 21.1, 33.9
Prelate(s), 9.3, 9.5, 91.1, 91.7, 92.2, 92.3, 93.2, 95.1, 123.2
Preparation, 2.1, 2.5, 28.1, 42.5
Present, 50.3, 92.1, 106.1
Pretense, 17.8, 28.6, 40.6, 91.7, 97.1, 97.2
Pride, 2.2, 6.2, 7.4, 14.1, 20.5, 21.2, 40.3, 40.4, 40.6, 40.7, 41.9, 47, 54, 59, 60.3, 60.4, 66.1, 66.3, 72.3, 74, 102.1, 123.2
Priest, high, 28.1
Priests, 32.4, 40.6, 41.1, 59
Prince, 8.2, 8.7, 21.3, 33.7, 40.2, 42.3
Prince of darkness, 8.5, 23.3
Prince of devils, 33.7
Prison, 8.6, 12.3, 14.7, 16.3, 22.2, 22.5, 41.1, 41.11
Prize, 1.8, 16.6, 33.6
Prodigal, 8.2, 8.4, 8.5, 27.3, 40.4
Profession, 27.3, 32.4, 33.6
Promise(s), 4.3, 15.4, 25.6, 33.4, 40.4, 41.10, 45.5, 72.4, 111.3
Property, 8.3, 27.3, 72.3, 72.5
Prophet, 1.2, 2.1, 2.4, 2.7, 2.8, 5.2, 5.3, 5.4, 5.5, 6.2, 7.3, 8.1, 8.5, 8.6, 8.8, 9.2, 9.3, 12.3, 13.1, 14.3, 16.1, 16.7, 17.7, 19.4, 23.2, 25.5, 25.7, 26.2, 26.4, 27.6, 28.1, 29.4, 33.1, 33.4, 33.5, 34.4, 40.2, 40.5, 41.10, 42.2, 49, 60.4, 62, 67, 73, 80.1, 83, 92.2, 93.2, 94.2, 95.1, 96.2, 96.5, 97.1, 102.2, 104.1, 110, 111.2, 111.3, 115, 123.1, 124.1, 124.2
Protection, 11.1, 96.1, 96.4
Proud, 1.2, 8.1
Proverb, 14.4, 17.3, 27.5
Prudence, 15.2, 15.5, 29.4, 50.2, 50.3, 52.4, 72.2, 113

Psalm, 3.5, 5.1, 5.3, 6.1, 6.3, 8.1, 8.9, 9.3, 9.5, 23.2, 27.7, 27.8, 34.4, 41.13, 72.3, 77, 94.1, 94.2, 124.1

Psalmist, 2.2, 4.2, 41.7, 47, 53.2, 66.2, 71.1, 71.2, 80.1, 103.2, 125.3

Psalmody, 8.6, 55.1

Psaltery, 9.4

Punishment, 1.3, 1.7, 4.2, 8.6, 32.3, 34.2, 34.6, 40.3, 40.5, 42.5, 60.3, 96.2, 103.3, 111.1, 116, 121

Purgatory, 16.1, 16.5, 42.5

Purification, 18.2, 28.4, 42.5, 51, 55.4

Purity, 16.2, 16.4, 17.1, 33.4, 45.5, 55.4, 60.4, 80.2, 107.2

Purple, 19.2, 33.2

Pusillanimity, 34.6, 111.2

Ram, 67, 79

Ramparts, 22.6, 41.8

Rapture, 115

Reading, 82.3, 113

Reason, 2.6, 5.4, 8.4, 14.5, 16.3, 17.3, 32.2, 32.3, 32.4, 33.5, 42.7, 45.1, 45.2, 45.6, 72.2, 74, 86.2, 89.2, 91.5, 104.2, 115, 124.1

Reasoning, 11.1, 25.3, 110

Rebuke, 5.4, 7.4, 27.5

Redeemer, 4.3, 19.5, 22.3

Redemption, 13.1, 22.6, 42.5, 119

Religion, 11.3

Remedy, 11.2, 12.3, 14.4, 14.6, 66.1, 103.3, 104.2

Remorse, 3.4, 3.7, 25.1, 53.1, 55.1, 81, 87.6

Repentance, 3.7, 8.7, 13.2, 13.3, 15.4, 22.7, 22.8, 25.4, 28.3, 30.2, 40.4, 41.10, 51, 87.1, 91.1, 91.7, 104.2

Reproach, 7.2, 29.3, 40.8, 41.1

Reputation, 16.5

Resistance, 8.7, 25.1

Resurrection, 24.2, 33.3, 41.12, 49, 57.2, 58.2, 60.2, 72.5, 78, 90.5, 96.6, 111.6, 116
  of the Body, 87.4

Retribution, divine, 8.3

Reuben, 31.2

Revelation, 20.4, 89.1

Revenge, 61.1, 66.2

Reward(s), 1.7, 8.8, 15.4, 40.3, 41.1, 41.7, 42.3, 61.2, 71.2, 105.1, 106.2

Riches, 42.3, 42.7, 77, 90.4, 91.5, 111.3, 111.4

Righteousness, 7.4, 28.6, 40.8, 41.10

River(s), 1.7, 18.1, 19.7, 61.1, 93.1, 96.1

Road(s), 1.3, 40.8, 79

Robbery, 25.1, 27.3, 33.4, 85, 97.3

Robe(s), 11.1, 40.4, 41.12

Rock(s), 9.1, 13.2, 23.6, 45.1

Romans, 96.5

Roof, 14.2, 25.8, 78, 91.5

Root, 8.4, 21.2, 27.2

Ropes, 4.3, 4.4

Rule, 22.4, 25.7, 25.8, 26.1, 41.3, 95.2

Rumor, 17.4, 17.5

Sabaoth, 2.3, 12.2

Sackcloth, 19.7, 34.4

Sacrament(s), 8.5, 16.7, 22.6, 22.9, 27.5, 33.6, 33.8, 40.6, 67, 91.6

Sacrifice, 2.4, 2.5, 26.2, 28.2, 40.2, 40.7, 41.2, 42.5, 67, 79, 123.1

Sadness, 1.8, 2.5, 3.8, 18.1, 34.2, 41.6, 50.2, 50.3, 58.2, 72.4, 80.2

Saint(s), 2.1, 3.4, 4.3, 9.2, 9.5, 16.3, 16.7, 25.7, 26.3, 27.4, 34.6, 41.12, 42.7, 50.1, 64.1, 74, 87.4, 103.2, 105.1, 125.2

Subject Index

Salome, 90.5
Salomon, 12.2
Salt, 2.4, 18.1, 41.9, 48
Salvation, 1.6, 2.1, 2.5, 3.1, 3.2, 3.7, 3.9, 6.1, 8.6, 8.7, 13.2, 13.3, 15.1, 16.4, 22.4, 22.5, 25.5, 27.7, 29.2, 40.3, 40.6, 40.7, 53.1, 55.4, 65.1, 65.2, 76, 91.5, 105.1, 111.5
Samaritan, 27.8, 33.4
Samuel, 23.7
Satan, 11.3, 14.1, 14.4, 22.3, 22.4, 23.3, 47, 97.2
Satisfaction, 22.7, 40.6
Saul, 41.9
Savior, 22.2, 22.4, 22.5, 27.5, 27.7, 96.1
Scales, 14.2, 33.7
Scandal(s), 17.4, 18.4, 19.6, 24.1, 26.3, 61.1, 98
Scapulars, 21.3
School, 22.2, 22.5, 40.1, 121
Scourging, 2.2, 2.5, 125.1, 125.2, 125.3
Scripture, 3.1, 3.2, 8.4, 8.7, 12.4, 13.4, 14.5, 15.2, 17.1, 17.4, 17.7, 18.2, 18.4, 19.3, 20.1, 22.3, 22.8, 23.1, 23.2, 23.3, 24.2, 26.3, 26.4, 27.4, 27.5, 31.2, 40.6, 41.5, 50.1, 52.2, 57.2, 69.1, 75, 77, 84.1, 85, 87.2, 87.5, 87.6, 92.1, 92.3, 94.1, 96.2, 102.2, 106.1, 116, 125.1
Seals, 57.1, 57.2
Seas, 42.3, 94.2
Seasoning, 2.4, 48, 95.2
Secrets, 24.2, 32.1, 40.4, 40.7, 88.2, 113
Security, 30.1, 116
Seed, 1.2, 10.1, 33.2, 103.4
Self-control, 13.3, 15.5, 45.5, 52.3, 55.2, 58.1, 59, 61.1, 63, 64.2, 69.2, 80.2, 103.3, 109, 113, 125.2, 125.3
Self-glorification, 7.4, 91.7
Self-will, 15.5, 21.2, 22.1, 40.7, 41.4, 45.1, 58.1, 63, 72.3, 72.5, 111.6
Senses, 8.4, 10.1, 10.2, 10.3, 10.4, 27.7, 28.4, 28.5, 47, 61.1, 64.2, 84.1, 94.2, 116
Seraphim, 123.2
Sermon on the Mount, 105.2
Sermons, 95.1, 95.2
Serpent, 11.2, 14.3, 17.6, 22.3, 23.2, 24.1, 49, 52.3, 66.3, 97.3
Servant(s), 2.7, 8.5, 8.6, 8.8, 11.1, 13.3, 14.3, 16.4, 17.1, 17.8, 18.5, 22.9, 23.1, 23.7, 24.1, 24.3, 25.2, 25.4, 27.1, 27.5, 29.1, 32.4, 34.3, 40.1, 40.5, 41.9, 42.1, 56.1, 56.2, 59, 60.2, 79, 94.2, 115, 125.1
Service, 77, 121
Servitude, 8.3, 8.5, 16.5, 23.2, 23.4, 41.2, 63, 120
Severity, 40.7, 63
Shackles, 12.3, 15.1
Shame, 4.3, 4.4, 12.1, 12.4, 14.3, 19.2, 25.6, 28.5, 28.7, 61.2, 72.3, 91.7, 104.1, 104.2
Sheep, 5.3, 9.3, 19.1, 33.2, 92.3, 93.1, 93.2, 100
Shepherd, 33.2, 55.3, 92.3, 100
Sichem, 14.3
Sicknesses, 20.5, 108, 117
Sighs, 3.5, 16.4, 31.3, 42.5, 87.1
Sight, 8.6, 10.3, 34.3, 87.4
Sign(s), 41.6, 45.4, 45.5
Silence, 23.7, 40.8, 55.1
Silver, 28.7, 29.2, 30.2, 33.2, 96.2
Simeon, 51
Simon, 42.3
Simon Bar-Jonah, 89.1

Sin, 1.1, 1.3, 1.6, 3.1, 3.5, 3.6, 3.7, 3.8, 4.2, 4.3, 4.5, 5.4, 6.1, 6.3, 7.4, 8.2, 8.3, 8.4, 8.5, 8.7, 11.1, 11.3, 12.4, 13.1, 13.3, 14.1, 14.2, 14.4, 14.5, 15.4, 16.1, 16.2, 16.5, 17.3, 20.4, 22.7, 22.8, 24.1, 24.2, 24.3, 25.1, 25.3, 25.4, 25.6, 26.4, 27.2, 27.5, 27.7, 28.1, 28.2, 28.5, 29.3, 32.3, 33.4, 33.5, 34.1, 34.2, 34.3, 34.4, 34.5, 40.2, 40.3, 40.4, 40.6, 40.8, 41.1, 41.3, 42.4, 45.5, 53.1, 61.1, 62, 65.2, 66.1, 66.2, 66.3, 67, 72.2, 80.2, 82.2, 84.1, 88.1, 91.1, 91.2, 91.7, 93.2, 94.1, 96.4, 102.1, 103.3, 104.1, 104.2, 107.1, 108, 113, 116, 125.2
  Original, 8.5
  Venial, 13.1, 13.3
Singing, 3.1, 3.5
Sinner(s), 1.3, 3.4, 5.2, 5.3, 8.5, 13.1, 13.4, 14.5, 22.2, 24.2, 25.2, 27.4, 27.6, 27.7, 28.2, 28.7, 30.2, 32.3, 34.5, 34.6, 40.2, 40.4, 40.8, 42.2, 42.6, 50.1, 55.1, 59, 72.3, 81, 87.1, 90.1, 90.2, 91.3, 107.1, 107.2, 123.1
Sion, 9.2, 19.4, 50.1
Skin, 6.1, 6.3, 22.9, 86.1, 93.2, 124.2
Slave(s), Slavery, 3.1, 3.9, 8.3, 8.6, 22.5, 23.4, 26.4, 41.2, 42.1, 71.1, 72.4
Sleep, 22.5, 23.3, 24.4, 28.5
Smell, 10.2, 10.4, 28.4
Smoke, 14.2, 30.2, 91.1
Snakes, 17.4, 111.4
Sobriety, 15.4, 54, 111.3
Softness, 28.4, 30.1
Soldiers, 40.6, 41.9, 42.3
Solitaries, 1.2
Solomon, 15.3, 41.5, 50.1, 50.2, 52.1, 52.3, 56.1, 102.2, 104.1

Son, 3.1, 3.2, 8.3, 8.8, 21.2, 41.2, 42.3, 52.2, 57.1, 79
  of Charity, 34.5
  of Man, 28.1
Song, 40.3, 55.1, 103.4
Song of Songs, 41.11, 47, 69.2, 87.3
Sorrow, 1.4, 2.2, 2.4, 2.5, 2.7, 2.8, 12.1, 12.3, 18.2, 20.5, 40.5
Soul, 1.4, 2.5, 2.6, 2.8, 3.2, 3.3, 3.5, 3.6, 3.7, 3.8, 4.1, 4.5, 5.2, 5.5, 6.1, 6.2, 6.3, 7.1, 8.1, 8.2, 8.5, 8.6, 8.7, 8.9, 9.1, 9.2, 9.5, 10.1, 10.4, 12.1, 12.4, 14.1, 14.7, 15.4, 16.1, 16.3, 18.2, 18.4, 19.1, 20.5, 22.2, 22.6, 23.1, 23.3, 23.4, 23.6, 23.7, 24.2, 25.4, 25.7, 25.8, 26.4, 27.8, 28.4, 28.7, 29.1, 29.3, 29.4, 31.1, 31.3, 32.1, 32.2, 32.3, 33.4, 33.5, 33.8, 34.3, 34.4, 34.5, 34.6, 40.2, 40.4, 40.9, 41.1, 41.3, 41.10, 41.12, 42.1, 42.7, 45.1, 63, 70, 74, 75, 78, 84.1, 85, 86.2, 87.2, 90.1, 90.3, 91.6, 98, 103.1, 106.1, 110, 144, 116, 117
  Carnal, 24.2
  Rational, 45.1, 89.2
Spear, 6.3, 17.5
Speech, 5.1, 15.5, 17.2, 24.2, 32.2, 97.3
Spices, 4.4, 33.8, 58.1, 87.6, 90.5, 92.2
Spirit, 3.7, 3.8, 4.3, 5.1, 5.5, 7.2, 7.4, 8.3, 8.4, 10.1, 12.3, 14.1, 14.4, 22.4, 23.1, 23.2, 23.3, 23.4, 23.5, 24.1, 24.3, 24.4, 25.1, 25.6, 25.8, 26.3, 27.5, 28.4, 28.6, 30.2, 31.2, 31.3, 32.1, 33.4, 33.5, 33.8, 40.2, 40.4, 40.6, 41.1, 41.11, 52.4, 59, 67, 72.1, 85, 86.2, 91.5, 92.1, 94.1, 101, 112, 123.1

Carnal, 23.2
Evil, 8.5
Holy, 3.2, 5.5, 6.2, 7.3, 18.1, 18.3, 18.5, 19.6, 19.7, 22.4, 22.6, 23.1, 42.3, 52.2, 88.1, 88.2, 89.1, 91.5, 92.1, 93.1, 95.1, 103.1
Human, 17.8
of the Lord, 8.9
Spouse, 8.9, 12.1, 33.8, 41.11, 42.3, 42.7, 56.2, 92.1, 115
Spring, 17.8, 96.1, 96.2, 96.3, 96.4, 96.5, 117
Stain, 17.1, 28.2, 28.4, 28.5, 32.3
Stars, 22.9, 33.4, 40.5
Stench, 31.3, 42.6
Steps, 24.3, 60.2, 65.1, 103.2, 103.3, 103.4, 123.1, 124.2
Stew, 2.4, 95.1
Steward, 56.2, 91.6, 95.2
Sticks, 6.3, 100
Stones, 9.1, 16.7, 18.2, 33.2, 33.7, 42.6, 55.4, 58.2, 97.2, 97.3, 98
Storeroom(s), 92.1, 92.2, 92.3
Stranger(s), 8.3, 25.8, 27.8, 40.5, 41.2
Strength, 3.3, 13.4, 24.3, 29.1, 29.3, 34.4, 34.5, 41.5, 41.9, 96.1, 96.4, 96.6
Struggle, 23.2, 24.4
Stubbornness, 18.4, 28.4, 79, 80.2
Subordinate(s), 41.10, 92.2, 92.3, 93.2, 95.1, 123.2
Suffering, 1.7, 2.1, 2.6, 2.7, 2.8, 12.3, 13.2, 14.7, 15.1, 16.2, 22.8, 25.1, 34.2, 34.4, 40.9, 41.2, 50.1, 61.2
Suggestion, 23.3, 45.6
Sulamite, 23.6, 47
Sun, 5.2, 9.1, 22.8, 28.7, 42.3, 91.3, 91.4, 111.7, 125.2
Superiors, 24.1, 26.3, 41.3, 41.5, 60.4, 92.3, 93.2

Supplicant, Supplication, 25.1, 25.2, 25.6
Suspicion, 16.7, 23.3, 33.7, 80.2
Swallow, 3.4, 3.5
Swamp, 22.8, 25.7
Sweetness, 3.1, 3.6, 5.4, 14.6, 16.4, 18.3, 21.1, 22.5, 29.2, 29.4, 42.1, 42.7, 56.1, 91.5, 96.4, 97.1, 97.3, 125.1
Swine, 8.3, 15.3
Sword, 17.4, 24.2, 24.3, 41.2, 41.9, 111.1
Synagogue, 50.1

Tabernacle, 28.5, 41.5, 78
Table, 2.6, 14.7, 24.3, 94.2
Talkativeness, 55.1, 74
Taste, 3.1, 10.2, 10.4, 15.4, 41.12, 73, 93.2, 95.2, 96.4
Teacher, 8.6, 8.7, 40.1, 40.7, 40.10, 55.3, 60.4, 91.5, 95.1, 95.2, 121
Teaching, 40.5, 45.4, 45.5, 72.3
Tears, 1.2, 2.4, 3.4, 8.4, 8.6, 14.2, 16.4, 16.5, 18.2, 19.6, 22.5, 25.3, 25.4, 28.2, 28.6, 29.4, 30.2, 31.3, 42.7, 61.1, 94.2, 103.3, 107.1, 112
Valley of, 42.7, 115
Teeth, 93.1, 93.2
Temperance, 50.2, 50.3, 72.2
Temple, 5.5, 31.1, 91.5, 98, 123.1
Temptation, 1.1, 3.1, 3.2, 3.3, 3.4, 3.7, 3.8, 4.3, 6.2, 13.4, 14.4, 22.5, 23.6, 24.3, 24.4, 25.5, 28.4, 45.5, 47, 60.3, 61.2, 82.2, 84.1, 94.1, 96.1
Tepidity, 15.4, 28.6
Testaments, New and Old, 92.1
Testimony, 7.2, 7.3, 7.4, 111.4
Thanks, 3.4, 27.5, 27.6, 27.8, 87.2, 123.1

Thanksgiving, 15.5, 25.6, 27.8, 34.6
Theman, 40.1, 42.1
Thessalonians, 55.3, 125.2
Thief, 40.2, 75
Thistles, 28.4, 125.3
Thorns, 17.5, 20.5, 28.4, 41.10, 50.1, 61.2, 65.1, 91.5, 97.3, 125.3
Thought(s), 2.2, 2.8, 6.2, 8.6, 10.1, 16.1, 16.7, 23.2, 23.5, 24.1, 24.2, 25.4, 31.1, 31.2, 31.3, 32.2, 32.3, 32.4, 33.5, 45.6, 61.1
Threat, 29.2, 72.4
Throne, 22.2, 25.8, 40.4, 90.2, 91.5, 123.1
Time, 1.3, 1.4, 1.7, 7.3, 17.3, 17.4, 48
Toil, 2.1, 2.2, 2.5, 2.7, 4.2, 16.5, 21.2, 22.1, 27.2, 42.3, 51, 97.1, 97.2, 105.1
Tomb, 34.2, 34.5, 58.2, 104.1, 107.1
Tongue, 2.8, 17.2, 17.4, 17.5, 17.6, 17.7, 22.6, 30.2, 41.7, 47, 58.1, 74, 95.2, 96.3, 97.1, 97.2, 97.3
Tonsure, 27.6
Torment, 8.5, 40.3, 40.9, 41.1, 96.4
Torture, Torturer, 12.4, 16.6, 22.5, 28.6, 42.6, 96.4
Touch, 10.2, 10.4, 28.4, 74
Transgressions, 26.2, 41.4, 115
Traps, 20.4, 41.10, 91.7
Treasures, 13.2, 15.1, 16.4, 33.8, 65.2, 86.2, 91.5, 111.6
Tree, 2.4, 10.1, 11.2, 22.3, 26.2, 85, 102.1
Tribulation(s), 16.6, 18.2, 26.3, 28.2, 28.3, 28.4, 28.5, 34.3, 41.8, 41.13, 77, 93.2, 125.1
  Day of, 28.7
Trinity, 40.8, 42.7, 45.1, 45.4, 45.6, 52.2, 57.1, 80.1, 92.1
Trivium, 45.2

Truth, 3.8, 3.9, 7.2, 7.4, 10.1, 15.1, 15.3, 17.1, 17.8, 18.2, 18.3, 19.1, 19.2, 20.3, 20.4, 20.5, 21.1, 22.4, 23.2, 23.6, 24.3, 25.1, 28.6, 33.8, 40.6, 41.1, 41.3, 51, 69.2, 87.1, 90.4, 96.1, 96.2, 96.3, 97.1, 111.6, 116, 125.3

Understanding, 14.5, 42.7, 88.1
Union, 4.3
  Carnal, 33.8
Unity, 21.3, 23.5, 33.4, 33.5, 33.8, 42.4, 65.2, 65.3, 80.1, 108

Vainglory, 31.3, 40.1, 41.9, 56.1, 72.3, 74, 122, 123.2
Vanities, 16.1, 23.3, 24.1
Vanity, 6.2, 19.1, 19.4, 20.4, 21.2, 23.3, 23.4, 26.1, 40.7, 40.8, 80.2, 83, 111.3
Verse, 34.4, 72.4
Vessels, 34.6, 40.5, 40.6, 42.3, 85, 94.2, 109, 125.2
  of Wrath, 8.5, 42.5
  Earthen, 19.4, 19.6, 40.5, 41.1
Vicars, 9.5
Vice, 1.3, 8.2, 8.5, 14.6, 14.7, 26.3, 27.8, 28.4, 31.2, 31.3, 41.9, 42.6, 51, 55.1, 61.1, 71.1, 91.7, 95.2, 108, 117, 122, 124.1
Victory, 14.5, 41.1
Vigilance, 17.7, 17.8, 25.8
Vigils, 17.7, 22.9, 40.7, 41.3, 55.2, 65.2, 95.2
Vigor, 22.4, 41.8, 104.2
Vincent, 96.4
Vine, 2.6, 23.1, 91.6
Vineyard, 15.1, 17.3
Violence, 3.5, 11.1, 11.2, 14.4, 22.9, 25.2, 99

Subject Index

Virgin(s), 2.4, 109; *see also* Mary, the Blessed Virgin,
Virginity, 47, 49, 52.3, 96.3
Virtues, 3.1, 9.2, 14.7, 16.1, 19.4, 23.5, 24.1, 25.1, 25.3, 26.3, 27.5, 33.4, 33.5, 40.2, 40.4, 41.8, 41.9, 41.10, 42.7, 45.5, 50.3, 52.2, 52.3, 59, 61.1, 64.2, 71.1, 72.2, 87.1, 87.6, 89.2, 91.3, 91.7, 92.2, 95.2, 111.1, 111.7, 116, 117, 123.1
Vision, 9.1, 10.3, 16.1, 16.5, 22.2, 24.4, 25.8, 41.12, 42.7, 94.2
Voice(s), 5.2, 5.3, 5.4, 11.2, 16.5, 16.6, 22.2, 23.7, 24.2, 27.5, 41.2, 41.3, 74, 87.4, 88.2, 91.1, 91.3, 91.5, 96.2, 96.5, 102.1, 103.4, 104.1, 111.6
Vomit, 15.3, 83
Vows, 20.4

Wages, 1.8, 8.6, 15.1
Wall(s), 9.4, 9.5, 19.3, 93.2
Washing, 93.2, 122
Water, 1.2, 1.6, 2.4, 8.4, 8.5, 12.3, 18.2, 19.3, 22.2, 28.6, 56.1, 56.2, 71.2, 74, 91.1, 94.1, 94.2, 96.1, 96.2, 96.4, 96.5, 117, 121
  Jars, Pots, 18.2, 28.5, 55.1, 55.2, 55.3, 55.4, 56.1, 56.2
Way, 21.1, 22.1, 22.2, 40.2
Weakness, 3.3, 13.4, 16.1, 17.7, 22.1, 26.4, 28.5, 29.3, 34.2, 34.4, 34.6, 66.2, 124.2
Wealth, 19.1, 19.2, 72.2, 77
Wedding, 2.4, 17.8, 18.2, 28.5
Weeping, 3.1, 3.4, 12.4, 111.4
Weight, 21.3, 22.1, 86.1, 86.2
Wicked, 1.3, 13.1, 19.2, 27.6

Wickedness, 8.3, 14.6, 21.2, 23.3, 24.1, 28.4, 28.5, 31.2, 49, 72.3, 94.1
Widow, 23.1, 96.3
Wife, 2.1, 2.6, 11.2, 14.2, 23.1, 41.6, 42.3, 59, 66.2, 80.1, 102.1
Will, 1.6, 2.3, 3.1, 5.5, 8.2, 8.5, 11.1, 11.2, 11.3, 14.2, 14.3, 15.2, 22.6, 26.2, 26.3, 26.4, 27.4, 29.2, 31.2, 32.2, 32.3, 34.2, 40.5, 41.4, 41.5, 41.6, 41.7, 45.1, 45.3, 45.6, 60.3, 72.2, 89.2, 92.2, 94.1, 98, 103.4, 108, 124.1, 124.2
  Divine, 26.4, 66.2
Wind, 3.2, 5.2, 17.7
Wine, 5.4, 18.2, 19.1, 29.3, 29.5, 34.1, 56.1, 56.2, 87.5, 88.1, 92.2, 121
Wings, 42.7, 123.2
Wisdom, 2.4, 2.5, 2.6, 3.1, 3.2, 5.1, 8.6, 9.1, 10.1, 12.4, 14.1, 14.2, 14.6, 14.7, 15.1, 15.2, 15.3, 15.4, 15.5, 16.7, 18.1, 18.3, 23.3, 23.6, 24.1, 25.5, 28.2, 29.1, 29.3, 33.3, 33.8, 40.1, 41.1, 41.13, 42.3, 42.7, 45.2, 47, 49, 52.1, 52.2, 52.4, 54, 57.1, 60.1, 64.2, 69.2, 73, 88.1, 89.2, 96.1, 96.3, 98, 102.2, 103.1, 103.3, 103.4, 108, 111.7, 125.1, 125.3
Wise, 5.4, 7.1, 7.2
Witness, 33.1, 58.2
Woman, 7.4, 11.2, 22.3, 23.1, 25.2, 25.3, 28.6, 29.4, 34.3, 40.3, 49, 52.3, 58.1, 58.2, 66.1, 66.2, 87.6, 90.2, 90.3, 96.4, 102.1, 107.1, 111.4 (*see also* Sulamite)
Womb, 49, 50.2, 51, 87.3
Word, 10.1, 24.2, 24.3, 29.3, 40.1, 49, 73, 87.2, 87.3, 89.2, 92.1
  Divine, 8.5, 71.2

Word(s), 5.1, 17.2, 17.3, 17.4, 17.6, 17.7, 17.8, 18.2, 19.1, 23.3, 25.1, 34.1, 40.10, 110
Work, 2.6, 8.2, 15.5, 28.7, 34.6
Works, 2.6, 3.3, 7.4, 17.1, 40.8, 41.11, 45.5
  Immoral, 105.2
World, 4.4, 4.5, 9.1, 11.1, 11.3, 15.1, 20.1, 23.3
Worms, 22.5, 23.6, 27.6, 29.2, 42.6, 72.1
Worship, 72.1, 105.2
Wounds, 6.2, 16.1, 20.5, 32.3, 34.5, 40.4, 40.6, 42.3, 88.1

Wrath, 5.4, 13.2, 22.7, 23.2, 23.3, 27.6, 32.3, 40.4, 76

Yoke, 1.8, 2.8, 11.3, 13.3, 20.4, 21.1, 26.4, 42.2, 71.2, 97.1, 97.3, 111.2, 111.3

Zachaeus, 41.7
Zeal, 90.3, 100, 111.5, 123.2
Zechariah, 34.4
Zion, 22.8, 103.2, 111.7

www.ingramcontent.com/pod-product-compliance
Lightning Source LLC
Chambersburg PA
CBHW031227290426
44109CB00012B/187